Principles for Dealing with

THE CHANGING WORLD ORDER

ALSO BY RAY DALIO

Principles: Life and Work

Principles for Navigating Big Debt Crises

Principles for Success

Principles for Dealing with

THE CHANGING WORLD ORDER

RAY DALIO

AVID READER PRESS

NEW YORK LONDON TORONTO SYDNEY NEW DELHI

Avid Reader Press
An Imprint of Simon & Schuster, Inc.
1230 Avenue of the Americas
New York, NY 10020

First Avid Reader Press hardcover edition November 2021

Interior design by Creative Kong

Manufactured in the United States of America

1 3 5 7 9 10 8 6 4 2

Library of Congress Cataloging-in-Publication Data has been applied for.

ISBN 978-1-9821-6027-2
ISBN 978-1-9821-6479-9 (ebook)

To my grandchildren and those of their generation who will be participants in the continuation of this story: may the Force of Evolution be with you.

WITH APPRECIATION

To all who helped me learn, you each have my deep gratitude for giving me valuable bits and pieces that I could put together to make this book. If it wasn't for the conversations we had, the thoughts you shared in your writings, and the histories and statistics that you dug out from archives, this book would have not been possible. In some cases you are still with us and in some cases you are not, but you are all in my thoughts. I am especially grateful to Henry Kissinger, Wang Qishan, Graham Allison, Lee Kuan Yew, Liu He, Paul Volcker, Mario Draghi, Paul Kennedy, Richard N. Haass, Kevin Rudd, Steven Kryger, Bill Longfield, Neil Hannan, H. R. McMaster, Jiaming Zhu, Larry Summers, Niall Ferguson, Tom Friedman, Heng Swee Keat, George Yeo, Ian Bremmer, and Zhiwu Chen.

I also want to thank Peer Vries, Benjamin A. Elman, Pamela Kyle Crossley, Sybil Lai, James Zheng Gao, Yuen Yuen Ang, Macabe Keliher, David Porter, Victor Cunrui Xiong, David Cannadine, Patricia Clavin, Duncan Needham, Catherine Schenk, and Steven Pincus, among others for their valuable perspectives.

I am also very grateful to those who helped convert these concepts and writings into a book, which was nearly as much of an undertaking as coming up with them. I am grateful to Mark Kirby above all others for his unwavering devotion, talent, and patience. I am also grateful to Michael Kubin, Arthur Goldwag, and Phil Revzin, who all provided helpful comments on the manuscript, and to Jim Levine, my literary agent, and Jofie Ferrari-Adler, my editor, who helped create this book and get it out there.

Beyond these people were many others, including Gardner Davis, Udai Baisiwala, Jordan Nick, Michael Savarese, Jonathan Bost, Stephen McDonald, Elena Gonzalez Malloy, Khia Kurtenbach, Alasdair Donovan, Floris Holstege, Anser Kazi, Chris Edmonds, Julie Farnie, and Brian De Los Santos, who contributed significantly behind the scenes—as did all the people at Bridgewater, who together created the most amazing learning platform imaginable.

PART I
HOW THE WORLD WORKS
21

PART II
HOW THE WORLD HAS WORKED OVER THE LAST 500 YEARS
241

PART III
THE FUTURE
461

HOW TO READ THIS BOOK

- In writing this book I wrestled with whether to make it complete or concise and decided to try to make it both by bolding passages to create a quick-read version. **If you want to read the concise version, read what is in bold, and if you want more, it's all available to you.**

- I also wanted to convey some principles that are timeless and universal truths for dealing with reality well, which I denoted by ● ***putting a red dot in front of them and italicizing.***

- For some subjects, I had embellishments that I thought would be interesting to some but not all readers, so I chose to present them as an addendum to the respective chapter. Feel free to read or skip as you like.

- At the back of this book, you can find a glossary that explains the abbreviations you see in some of the charts.

- Finally, to keep this book from becoming much too long, there is also a lot of supplemental material available at economicprinciples.org, including reference material, citations, more data on the indices, etc.

INTRODUCTION

The times ahead will be radically different from those we've experienced in our lifetimes, though similar to many times in history.

How do I know that? Because they always have been.

Over the last 50 or so years, in order to handle my responsibilities well, I have needed to understand the most important factors that go into making countries and their markets succeed and fail. I learned that to anticipate and handle situations that I had never faced before I needed to study as many analogous historical cases as possible to understand the mechanics of how they transpired. That gave me principles for dealing with them well.

A few years ago, I observed the emergence of a number of big developments that hadn't happened before in my lifetime but had occurred numerous times in history. Most importantly, I was seeing the confluence of huge debts and zero or near-zero interest rates that led to massive printing of money in the world's three major reserve currencies; big political and social conflicts within countries, especially the US, due to the largest wealth, political, and values gaps in roughly a century; and the rising of a new world power (China) to challenge the existing world power (the US) and the existing world order. The most recent analogous time was the period from 1930 to 1945. This was very concerning to me.

I knew that I couldn't really understand what was happening and deal with what would be coming at me unless I studied past analogous periods, which led to this study of the rises and declines of empires, their reserve currencies, and their markets. In other words, to develop an understanding of what is happening now and might happen over the next few years, I needed to study the mechanics behind similar cases in history—e.g., the 1930–45 period, the rise and fall of the Dutch and British empires, the rise and fall of Chinese dynasties, and others.[1] I was in the midst of doing those studies when the COVID-19 pandemic struck, which was another one of those big events that never happened in my lifetime but had happened many times before. Past pandemics became a part of this study and showed me that surprising acts of nature—e.g., diseases, famines, and floods—need to be considered as possibilities because those surprising big acts of nature that rarely come along were by any measure even more impactful than the biggest depressions and wars.

As I studied history, I saw that it typically transpires via relatively well-defined life cycles, like those of organisms, that evolve as each generation transitions to the next. In fact, the history and the future of humanity can be seen as just the aggregate of all the individual life stories evolving through time. I saw these stories flow together as one all-encompassing story from the beginning of recorded history up to this moment, with the same things happening over and over again for basically the same reasons, while still evolving. **By seeing many interlinking cases evolve together, I could see the patterns and cause/effect relationships that govern them and could imagine the future based on what I learned. These events happened many**

[1] To be clear, while I am describing these cycles of the past, I'm not one of those people who believes that what happened in the past will necessarily continue into the future without understanding the cause/effect mechanics that drive changes. My objective above all else is to have you join with me in looking at the cause/effect relationships and then to use that understanding to explore what might be coming at us and agree on principles to handle it in the best possible way.

times throughout history and were parts of a cycle of rises and declines of empires and most aspects of empires—e.g., of their education levels, their levels of productivity, their levels of trade with other countries, their militaries, their currencies and other markets, etc.

Each of these aspects or powers transpired in cycles, and they were all interrelated. For example, nations' levels of education affected their levels of productivity, which affected their levels of trade with other countries, which affected the levels of military strength required to protect trade routes, which together affected their currencies and other markets, which affected many other things. Their movements together made up the economic and political cycles that occurred over many years—e.g., a very successful empire or dynasty could have its cycle last 200 or 300 years. **All the empires and dynasties I studied rose and declined in a classic Big Cycle that has clear markers that allow us to see where we are in it.**

This Big Cycle produces swings between 1) peaceful and prosperous periods of great creativity and productivity that raise living standards a lot and 2) depression, revolution, and war periods when there is a lot of fighting over wealth and power and a lot of destruction of wealth, life, and other things we cherish. I saw that the peaceful/creative periods lasted much longer than the depression/revolution/war periods, typically by a ratio of about 5:1, so one could say that the depression/revolution/war periods were transition periods between the normally peaceful/creative periods.

While the peaceful/creative periods are certainly more enjoyable for most people, all these realities have their purposes for advancing evolution, so in the broader sense they are neither good nor bad. The depression/revolution/war periods produce a lot of destruction, but like cleansing storms, they also get rid of weaknesses and excesses (such as too much debt) and produce a new beginning in the form of a return to fundamentals on a sounder footing (albeit painfully). After the conflict is resolved, it is clear who has what power, and because most people desperately want peace, there is a resolution that produces new monetary, economic, and political systems—together, a new world order—and fosters the next peaceful/creative period. Within this Big Cycle are other cycles. For example, there are long-term debt cycles that last about 100 years and short-term debt cycles that last about eight years. This short-term cycle also has within it longer, prosperous expansion periods that are interrupted by shorter recession periods, and within these cycles are shorter cycles, and so on.

Before I get your head spinning with all this cycle stuff, the main thing I want to convey is that when the cycles align, the tectonic plates of history shift, and the lives of all people change in big ways. These shifts will sometimes be terrible and sometimes terrific. They certainly will happen in the future, and most people will fail to anticipate them. In other words, ● ***the swinging of conditions from one extreme to another in a cycle is the norm, not the exception.*** It was a very rare country in a very rare century that didn't have at least one boom/harmonious/prosperous period and one depression/civil war/revolution period, so we should expect both. Yet, most people throughout history have thought (and still think today) that the future will look like a slightly modified version of the recent past. That is because ● ***the really big boom periods and the really big bust periods, like many things, come along about once in a lifetime and so they are surprising unless one has studied the patterns of history over many generations.*** Because the swings between great and terrible times tend to be far apart ● ***the future we encounter is likely to be very different from what most people expect.***

For example, my dad and most of his peers who went through the Great Depression and World War II never imagined the post-war economic boom because it was more different from than similar to what they had experienced. I understand why, given those experiences, they wouldn't think of borrowing and putting their hard-earned savings into the stock market, so it's understandable that they missed out on profiting from the boom. Similarly, I understand why, decades later, those who only experienced debt-financed booms and never experienced depression and war would borrow a lot in order to speculate and would consider depression and war implausible. The same is true with money:

money used to be "hard" (i.e., linked to gold) after World War II until governments made money "soft" (i.e., fiat) to accommodate borrowing and prevent entities from going broke in the 1970s. As a result, most people at the moment of my writing this book believe that they should borrow more, even though borrowing and debt-financed booms have historically led to depressions and internal and external conflicts.

Understanding history in this way also raises questions whose answers provide us with valuable clues on what the future will be like. For example, throughout my life, the dollar has been the world's reserve currency, monetary policy has been an effective tool for stimulating economies, and democracy and capitalism have been widely regarded as the superior political and economic systems. Anyone who studies history can see that ● ***no system of government, no economic system, no currency, and no empire lasts forever, yet almost everyone is surprised and ruined when they fail.*** Naturally I asked myself how would I and the people I care about know when we are entering one of these depression/revolution/war periods and how would we know how to navigate them well. Because my professional responsibility is to preserve wealth regardless of the environment, I needed to develop an understanding and strategy that would have worked throughout history, including through these sorts of devastating times.

The purpose of this book is to pass along what I learned that has helped me and that I believe might help you. I present it for your consideration.

HOW I LEARNED TO ANTICIPATE THE FUTURE BY STUDYING THE PAST

While it might seem odd that an investment manager who is required to make investment decisions on short time frames would pay so much attention to long-term history, through my experiences I have learned that I need this perspective. My approach isn't an academic one created for scholarly purposes; it is a very practical one that I follow in order to do my job well. The game I play requires me to understand what is likely to happen to economies better than the competition does, so I have spent roughly 50 years closely observing most major economies and their markets—as well as their political conditions, since those affect both—trying to understand what is happening well enough to bet on it. From my years of wrestling with the markets and trying to come up with principles for doing it well, I've learned that ● ***one's ability to anticipate and deal well with the future depends on one's understanding of the cause/effect relationships that make things change, and one's ability to understand these cause/effect relationships comes from studying how they have changed in the past.***

I arrived at this approach after the painful learning that the biggest mistakes in my career came from missing big market moves that hadn't happened in my lifetime but had happened many times before. The first of these big surprises for me came in 1971 when I was 22 years old and clerking on the floor of the New York Stock Exchange as a summer job. I loved it because it was a fast-pasted game of making and losing money played on a trading floor with people who liked to have a blast with each other—so much so that traders used to have water pistol fights right on the trading floor. I was engrossed in this game of watching the big developments in the world and betting on how they would drive the markets. Sometimes it could be dramatic.

On a Sunday night—August 15, 1971—President Richard Nixon announced that the US would renege on its promise to allow paper dollars to be turned in for gold. As I listened to Nixon speak, I realized that the US government had defaulted on a promise and that money as we knew it had ceased to exist. That couldn't be good, I thought. So on Monday morning I walked onto the floor of the exchange expecting pandemonium as stocks took a dive. There was pandemonium all right, but not the sort I expected. Instead of falling, the stock market jumped about 4 percent as the dollar plummeted. I was shocked. That's because I hadn't experienced a currency devaluation before. In the days that followed, I dug into history and saw that there were many cases of currency devaluations that had had similar effects on stock markets. By studying further, I figured out why, and I learned something valuable that would help me many times in my future. It took a few more of those painful surprises to beat the realization into my head that I needed to understand all the big economic and market moves that had happened in the last 100-plus years and in all major countries.

In other words, if some big and important event had happened in the past (like the Great Depression), I couldn't say for sure that it wouldn't happen to me, so I had to figure out how it worked and be prepared to deal with it. Through my research I saw that there were many cases of the same types of things happening (e.g., depressions) and that by studying them just like a doctor studies many cases of a particular type of disease, I could gain a deeper understanding of how they work. I studied these qualitatively and quantitatively through my experiences, by speaking with preeminent experts, reading great books, and digging into statistics and archives with my great research team.

From that learning came a visualization of an archetypical sequence of how rises and declines in wealth and power typically happen. The archetype helps me see the cause/effect relationships that drive how these cases typically progress. With that archetypical template specified, I can study deviations from it to try to explain them. Then I put these mental models into algorithms both to monitor conditions relative to my archetypes and to help me make decisions based on them. This process helps me refine my understanding of the cause/effect relationships to the point where I can create decision-making rules—i.e., principles for dealing with my realities—in the form of "if/then" statements—i.e., if X happens, then make Y bet. Then I watch actual events transpire relative to that template and what we are expecting. I do these things in a very systematic way with my partners at Bridgewater Associates. If events are on track, we continue to bet on what typically comes next; if events start to deviate from our template, we try to understand why and course correct. This process has helped me both understand the big cause/effect sequences that typically drive their progressions and gain a lot of humility. I do this continuously and will continue to do it until I die, so what you are reading is a work in progress.[2]

THIS APPROACH AFFECTS HOW I SEE EVERYTHING

Seeing events in this way helped shift my perspective from being caught in the blizzard of things coming at me to stepping above them to see their patterns through time.[3] The more related things I could understand in this way, the more I could see how they influence each other—e.g., how the economic cycle works with the political one—and how they interact over longer periods of time.

I believe that the reason people typically miss the big moments of evolution coming at them in life is because they experience only tiny pieces of what's happening. We are like ants preoccupied with our jobs of carrying crumbs in our very brief lifetimes instead of having a broader perspective of the big-picture patterns and cycles, the important interrelated things driving them, where we are within the cycles, and what's likely to transpire. From gaining this perspective, I've come to believe that throughout history there are only

[2] For example, I have followed this approach for debt cycles because I've had to navigate many of them over the last 50 years and they are the most important force driving big shifts in economies and markets. If you are interested in my template for understanding big debt crises and seeing all the cases that make it up, you can get *Principles for Navigating Big Debt Crises* in free digital form at economicprinciples.org or in print form for sale in bookstores or online. I've studied many big, important things (e.g., depressions, hyperinflation, wars, balance of payments crises, etc.) by following this approach, usually because I was compelled to understand unusual things that appeared to be germinating around me. It was that perspective that allowed Bridgewater to navigate the 2008 financial crisis well when others struggled.

[3] I approach just about everything this way. For example, in building and running my business, I had to understand the realities of how people think and learn principles for dealing with these realities well, which I did using this same approach. If you are interested in what I learned about such non-economic and non-market things, I conveyed it in my book *Principles: Life and Work*, which is free in an iOS/Android app called Principles in Action or is for sale in the usual bookstores.

a limited number of personality types[4] going down a limited number of paths, which lead them to encounter a limited number of situations to produce a limited number of stories that repeat over time. The only things that change are the clothes the characters are wearing, the languages they are speaking, and the technologies they're using.

THIS STUDY AND HOW I CAME TO DO IT

One study led to another, which led me to do this study. More specifically:

- **Studying money and credit cycles throughout history made me aware of the long-term debt and capital markets cycle (which typically lasts about 50 to 100 years), which has led me to view what is happening now in a very different way than if I hadn't gained that perspective.** For example, interest rates hit 0 percent and central banks printed money and bought financial assets in response to the 2008 financial crisis. I had studied that happening in the 1930s, which helped me see how and why central bank actions of creating a lot of money and credit/debt 90 years ago pushed financial asset prices up, which widened the wealth gap and led to an era of populism and conflict. We are now seeing the same forces at play in the post-2008 period.
- In 2014, I wanted to forecast economic growth rates in a number of countries because they were relevant to our investment decisions. I used the same approach of studying many cases to find the drivers of growth and come up with timeless and universal indicators for anticipating countries' growth rates over 10-year periods. Through this process, I developed a deeper understanding of why some countries did well and others did

[4] In my book *Principles: Life and Work*, I share my perspective on these different ways of thinking. I won't describe them here but will direct you there should you be interested.

poorly. I combined these indicators into gauges and equations that we used (and continue to use) to produce 10-year growth estimates across the 20 largest economies. Besides being helpful to us, I saw that this study could help economic policy makers because, by seeing these timeless and universal cause/effect relationships, they could know that if they changed X, it would have Y effect in the future. I also saw how these 10-year leading economic indicators (such as the quality of education and the level of indebtedness) were worsening for the US relative to big emerging countries such as China and India. This study is called "Productivity and Structural Reform: Why Countries Succeed and Fail, and What Should Be Done So Failing Countries Succeed." (This study, and every other study mentioned here, is available for free at economicprinciples.org.)

- Soon after the Trump election in 2016 and with increases in populism in developed countries becoming more apparent, I began a study called "Populism: The Phenomenon." That highlighted for me how gaps in wealth and values led to deep social and political conflicts in the 1930s that are similar to those that exist now. It also showed me how and why populists of the left and populists of the right are more nationalistic, militaristic, protectionist, and confrontational—and what such approaches led to. I saw how powerful the conflict between the economic/political left and right could become and the significant impact this conflict has on economies, markets, wealth, and power, which gave me a better understanding of events that were and still are transpiring.
- From doing these studies, and from observing numerous things that were happening around me, I saw that America was experiencing very large gaps in people's economic conditions, which were obscured by looking only at economic averages. So I divided the economy into quintiles, looking at the top 20 percent of income earners, the next 20 percent, and so on down to the bottom 20 percent, and examined the

conditions of these populations individually. This resulted in two studies. In "Our Biggest Economic, Social, and Political Issue: The Two Economies—The Top 40% and the Bottom 60%," I saw the dramatic differences in conditions between the "haves" and the "have-nots," which helped me understand the greater polarity and populism I saw emerging. Those findings, as well as the close contact my wife and I were having through her philanthropic work with the reality of wealth and opportunity gaps in Connecticut communities and their schools, led to the research that became my study called "Why and How Capitalism Needs to Be Reformed."

- At the same time, through my many years of international dealings in and research on other countries, I saw huge global economic and geopolitical shifts taking place, especially in China. **I have been going to China for 37 years and am lucky enough to have become well-acquainted with the thinking of top economic policy makers and a broad range of others. Having this direct contact has helped me see up close the reasoning behind their actions, which have produced remarkable advances.** It is a fact that these people have led China to become an effective competitor with the US in production, trade, technology, geopolitics, and world capital markets, so how they've done this must be examined and understood without bias.

My most recent study, on which this book is based, came about because of my need to understand three big forces that hadn't happened before in my lifetime and the questions they prompt:

1. **The Long-Term Debt and Capital Markets Cycle: At no point in our lifetimes have interest rates been so low or negative on so much debt as they are as of this writing. The value of money and debt assets is being called into question by the supply-and-demand picture for them. In 2021, more than $16 trillion of debt was at negative interest rates and**

an unusually large amount of additional new debt will soon need to be sold to finance deficits. This is happening at the same time as huge pension and healthcare obligations loom large on the horizon. These circumstances raised some interesting questions for me. Naturally I wondered why anyone would want to hold debt yielding a negative interest rate and how much lower interest rates could be pushed. I also wondered what will happen to economies and markets when they can't be pushed lower and how central banks could be stimulative when the next downturn inevitably comes. Would central banks print a lot more currency, causing its value to go down? What would happen if the currency that the debt is denominated in goes down while interest rates are so low? These questions in turn led me to ask what central banks would do if investors flee debt denominated in the world's major reserve currencies (i.e., the dollar, the euro, and the yen), which would be expected if the money that they are being paid back in is both depreciating in value and paying interest rates that are so low.

A reserve currency is a currency that is accepted around the world for transactions and savings. The country that gets to print the world's primary currency (now the US, but as we'll see this has changed through history) is in a very powerful position, and debt that is denominated in the world's reserve currency (i.e., US dollar-denominated debt now) is the most fundamental building block for the world's capital markets and the world's economies. It is also the case that all reserve currencies in the past have ceased to be reserve currencies, often coming to traumatic ends for the countries that enjoyed this special power. So I also began to wonder whether, when, and why the dollar will decline as the world's leading reserve currency, what might replace it, and how that would change the world as we know it.

2. **The Internal Order and Disorder Cycle: Wealth, values, and political gaps are now larger than at any other point during**

my lifetime. By studying the 1930s and other prior eras when polarization was also high, I learned that which side wins out (i.e., left or right) will have very big impacts on economies and markets. So naturally I wondered what today's gaps will lead to. My examinations of history have taught me that ● ***when wealth and values gaps are large and there is an economic downturn, it is likely that there will be a lot of conflict about how to divide the pie.*** How will people and policy makers interact with each other when the next economic downturn arrives? I was especially concerned because of the limitations on central banks' abilities to cut interest rates adequately to stimulate the economy. In addition to these traditional tools being ineffective, printing money and buying financial assets (now called "quantitative easing") also widens the wealth gap because buying financial assets pushes up their prices, which benefits the wealthy who hold more financial assets than the poor do. How would that play out in the future?

3. **The External Order and Disorder Cycle: For the first time in my life, the United States is encountering a true rival power. (The Soviet Union was only a military rival, never a significant economic one.) China has become a rival power to the United States in most ways and is becoming strong in most ways at a faster rate.** If trends continue, China will be stronger than the United States in the most important ways that an empire becomes dominant. Or at the very least, it will be a worthy competitor. I have seen both countries up close for most of my life, and I now see how conflict is increasing fast, especially in the areas of trade, technology, geopolitics, capital, and economic/political/social ideologies. I can't help but wonder how these conflicts, and the changes in the world order that will result from them, will transpire in the years ahead and what effects that will have on us all.

To gain the perspective I needed about these factors and what their confluence might mean, I looked at the rises and declines of all the major empires and their currencies over the last 500 years, focusing most closely on the three biggest ones: the US Empire and the US dollar, which are most important now; the British Empire and the British pound, which were most important before that; and the Dutch Empire and the Dutch guilder before that. I also focused less closely on the six other significant, though less financially dominant, empires of Germany, France, Russia, Japan, China, and India. Of those six, I gave China the most attention and looked at its history back to the year 600 because 1) China was so important throughout history, 2) it's so important now and will likely be even more important in the future, and 3) it provides many cases to look at of dynasties rising and declining, which helped me better understand the patterns and the forces behind them. In these cases, a clearer picture emerged of how other influences, most importantly technology and acts of nature, played significant roles.

From examining all these cases across empires and across time, I saw that the great empires typically lasted roughly 250 years, give or take 150 years, with big economic, debt, and political cycles within them lasting about 50 to 100 years. By studying how these rises and declines worked individually, I could see how they worked on average in an archetypical way, and then I could examine how they worked differently and why. Doing that taught me a lot. My challenge now is trying to convey it to you.

You can miss seeing these cycles if you watch events too close up or if you are looking at the averages rather than the individual cases. Almost everyone talks about what is happening now and nobody talks about these big cycles, even though they are the biggest drivers of what is happening now. When looking at the whole or at averages, you don't see the individual cases of rises and declines, which are far greater. For example, looking at a stock market average (e.g., the S&P 500) and not looking at individual companies will lead you to miss the important fact that almost all the individual cases that make up the average have periods of birth, growth, and death. If you experienced any one of these, you would have had a hell of a ride up followed by a hell of a ride down into ruin unless you diversified and rebalanced your bets (e.g., the way it is done by S&P to create the index) or were able to discern the rising periods from the declining periods ahead of the crowd so as to be able to move well. By "move" I don't just mean move your position in markets—in the case of rising and falling empires, I mean "move" in nearly everything, including where you live.

This leads me to my next point: ● ***to see the big picture, you can't focus on the details.*** While I will attempt to paint this big, sweeping picture accurately, I can't paint it in a precise way. Also, in order for you to see it and understand it, you can't try to do so in a precise way. That is because we are looking at mega-macro cycles and evolution over very long time frames. To see them, you will have to let go of the details. Of course, when the details are important, which they often are, we will need to go from the very big imprecise picture to a more detailed one.

Looking at what happened in the past from this mega-macro perspective will radically alter how you see things. For example, because the span of time covered is so large, many of the most fundamental things that we take for granted and many of the terms we use to describe them do not exist over the full period of time. As a result, I will be imprecise in my wording so that I can convey the big picture without getting tripped up on what might seem to be big things but, in the scope of what we are looking at, are relative details.

For example, I wrestled with how much I should worry about the differences between countries, kingdoms, nations, states, tribes, empires, and dynasties. Nowadays we think mostly in terms of countries. However, countries as we know them didn't come into existence until the 17th century, after the Thirty Years' War in Europe. In other words, before then there were no countries—generally speaking, though not always, there were states and kingdoms instead. In some places, kingdoms still exist and can be confused with being countries, and in some places they are both. Generally speaking, though not always, kingdoms are small, countries are bigger, and empires are biggest (spreading beyond the kingdom or the country). The relationships between them are often not all that clear. The British Empire was mostly a kingdom that gradually evolved into a country and then into an empire that extended way beyond England's borders, so that its leaders controlled broad areas and many non-English peoples.

It's also the case that each of these types of singularly controlled entities—states, countries, kingdoms, tribes, empires, etc.—controls its population in different ways, which further confuses things for those who seek precision. For example, in some cases empires are areas that are occupied by a dominant power, while in other cases empires are areas influenced by a dominant power through threats and rewards. The British Empire generally occupied the countries in its empire while the American Empire has controlled more via rewards and threats—though that is not entirely true, as at the time of this writing the US has military bases in at least 70 countries. Though it is clear that there is an American Empire, it is less clear exactly what is in it. Anyway, you get my point—that trying to be precise can stand in the way of conveying the biggest, most important things. So you are going to have to bear with my sweeping imprecisions. You will also understand why I will henceforth imprecisely call these entities countries, even though not all of them were countries, technically speaking.

Along these lines, some will argue that my comparing different countries with different systems in different times is impossible. While I can understand that perspective, I want to assure you that I will seek to explain whatever major differences exist and that the timeless and universal similarities are much greater than the differences. It would be tragic to let the differences stand in the way of seeing the similarities that provide us with the lessons of history we need.

REMEMBER THAT WHAT I DON'T KNOW IS MUCH GREATER THAN WHAT I KNOW

In asking these questions, from the outset I felt like an ant trying to understand the universe. I had many more questions than answers, and I knew that I was delving into numerous areas that others have devoted their lives to studying. One of the benefits of my circumstances is that I can speak with the world's best scholars who have studied history in depth as well as with the people who are in, or have been in, the positions of making history. This allowed me to triangulate with the best of them. While each had in-depth perspectives on some pieces of the puzzle, none had the holistic understanding that I needed to adequately answer all my questions. But by speaking with all of them and triangulating what I learned with the research I did myself, the pieces started to fall into place.

The people and tools at Bridgewater were also invaluable to this research. Because the world is a complicated place, playing the highly competitive game of making sense of the past, processing what's going on in the present, and using that information to bet on the future requires hundreds of people and great computer power. For example, we actively consume about a hundred million data series that are run through our logic frameworks that systematically convert this information into trades in every market we can trade within every major country in the world. I believe that our ability to see and process information about all major countries and all major markets is unparalleled. It was through this machine that I could see and attempt to understand how the world I'm living in works and I relied on it in doing this study.

Still, I can't be sure that I'm right about anything.

While I have learned an enormous amount that I will put to good use, I know that what I know is still only a tiny portion of what I need to know to be confident in my outlook for the future. I also know from experience that if I wait to learn enough to be satisfied with what I know before acting or sharing, I'd never be able to use or convey what I have learned. So please understand that while this study will provide you with my very top-down, big-picture perspective on what I've learned and my very low-confidence outlook for the future, you should approach my conclusions as theories rather than facts. Keep in mind that even with all of this, I have been wrong more times than I can remember, which is why I value diversification of my bets above all else. So please realize that I'm just doing the best I can to openly convey my thinking to you.

You might be wondering why I wrote this book. In the past, I would have been silent about what I've learned. However, I am now in the phase of my life that silently achieving more isn't as important to me as passing along what I have learned in the hope that it can be of use to others. My main objectives are to convey to you my model for how the world works—to share with you a single digestible story of the last 500 years that shows how and why history "rhymes" with what is happening today—and to help you and others make better decisions so we all might have a better future.

HOW THIS STUDY IS ORGANIZED

As with all my studies, I will attempt to convey what I learned in both shorter, simpler ways (such as videos you can find online), longer, more comprehensive ways (like this book), and even more comprehensive ways for those who want additional charts and historical examples (available along with everything else not printed in the book at economicprinciples.org). In order to make the most important concepts easy to understand, this book is written in the vernacular, favoring clarity over precision. As a result, some of my wording will be by and large accurate but not always precisely so.

In Part I, I will summarize all that I learned in a simplified archetype of the rises and declines of empires, drawing from all my research of specific cases. I will first distill my findings into an index of the total power of empires, which provides an overview of the ebbs and flows of different powers and which is constituted from eight indices of different types of power. I will then go into more detail on a list of 18 determinants that I believe to be the key forces behind the rises and falls of empires and then I will cover in more detail the three big cycles mentioned previously. **In Part II, I will show the individual cases in greater depth, walking through the story of the**

major reserve currency empires over the last 500 years, including a chapter focused on the present day conflicts between the US and China. Finally, in the concluding Part III, I will discuss what all of this means for the future.

PART I

HOW THE WORLD WORKS

CHAPTER 1

THE BIG CYCLE IN A TINY NUTSHELL

As explained in the introduction, the world order is now rapidly shifting in important ways that have never happened in our lifetimes but have happened many times before. My objective is to show you those cases and the mechanics that drove them and, with that perspective, attempt to imagine the future.

What follows here is an ultra-distilled description of the dynamics that I saw in studying the rises and declines of the last three reserve currency empires (the Dutch, the British, and the American) and the six other significant empires over the last 500 years (Germany, France, Russia, India, Japan, and China), as well as all of the major Chinese dynasties back to the Tang Dynasty in around the year 600. The purpose of this chapter is simply to provide an archetype to use when looking at all the cycles, most importantly the one that we are now in.

In studying these past cases, I saw clear patterns that occurred for logical reasons that I briefly summarize here and cover more completely in subsequent chapters. While the focus of this chapter and this book are on those forces that affected the big cyclical swings in wealth and power, I also saw ripple-effect patterns in all dimensions of life, including culture and the arts, social mores, and more, which

I will touch on later. Between this simple archetype and the cases shown in Part II, we will see how the individual cases fit the archetype (which is essentially just the average of those cases) and how well the archetype describes the individual cases. Doing this, I hope, will help us better understand what is happening now.

I'm on a mission to figure out how the world works and to gain timeless and universal principles for dealing with it well. It's both a passion and a necessity for me. While the curiosities and concerns that I described earlier pulled me into doing this study, the process of conducting it gave me a much greater understanding of the really big picture on how the world works than I expected to get, and I want to share it with you. It made much clearer to me how peoples and countries succeed and fail over long swaths of time, it revealed giant cycles behind these ups and downs that I never knew existed, and, most importantly, it helped me put into perspective where we now are.

For example, through my research, **I learned that the biggest thing affecting most people in most countries through time is the struggle to make, take, and distribute wealth and power, though they also have struggled over other things too, most importantly ideology and religion**. These struggles happened in timeless and universal ways and had huge implications for all aspects of people's lives, unfolding in cycles like the tide coming in and out.

I also saw how, throughout time and in all countries, the people who have the wealth are the people who own the means of wealth production. In order to maintain or increase their wealth, they work with the people who have the political power, who are in a symbiotic relationship with them, to set and enforce the rules. I saw how this happened similarly across countries and across time. While the exact form of it has evolved and will continue to evolve, the most important dynamics have remained pretty much the same. The classes of those who were wealthy and powerful evolved over time (e.g., from monarchs and nobles who were landowners when agricultural land was the most important source of wealth, to capitalists and elected or autocratic political officials now that capitalism produces capital assets and that wealth and political power are generally not passed along in families) but they still cooperated and competed in basically the same ways.

I saw how, over time, this dynamic leads to a very small percentage of the population gaining and controlling exceptionally large percentages of the total wealth and power, then becoming overextended, and then encountering bad times, which hurt those least wealthy and least powerful the hardest, which then leads to conflicts that produce revolutions and/or civil wars. When these conflicts are over, a new world order is created, and the cycle begins again.

In this chapter, I will share more of this big-picture synthesis and some of the details that go along with it. While what you're reading here are my own views, you should know that the ideas I express in this book have been well-triangulated with other experts. About two years ago, when I felt that I needed to answer the questions I described in the introduction, I decided to immerse myself in studying with my research team, digging through archives, speaking with the world's best scholars and practitioners who each had in-depth understandings of bits and pieces of the puzzle, reading relevant great books by insightful authors, and reflecting on the prior research I've done and the experiences that I've had from investing globally for nearly 50 years.

Because I view this as an audacious, humbling, necessary, and fascinating undertaking, I am worried about missing important things and being wrong, so my process is iterative. I do my research, write it up, show it to the world's best scholars and practitioners to stress test it, explore potential improvements, write it up again, stress test it again, and so on, until I get to the point of diminishing returns. This study is the product of that exercise. While I can't be sure that I have the formula for what makes the world's greatest empires and their markets rise and fall exactly right, I'm pretty confident that I got it by and large right. I also know that what I learned is essential for my putting what is happening now into perspective and for imagining how to deal with important events that have never happened in my lifetime but have happened repeatedly throughout history.

UNDERSTANDING THE BIG CYCLE

For reasons that are explained in this book, I believe that we are now seeing an archetypical big shift in relative wealth and power and the world order that will affect everyone in all countries in profound ways. This big wealth and power shift is not obvious because most people don't have the patterns of history in their minds to see this one as "another one of those." So in this first chapter, I will describe in a very brief way how I see the archetypical mechanics behind rises and declines of empires and their markets working. I have identified 18 important determinants that have explained almost all of the basic ebbs and flows through time that have caused ups and downs in empires. We will look at them in a moment. Most of them transpire in classic cycles that are mutually reinforcing in ways that tend to create a single very big cycle of ups and downs. This archetypical Big Cycle governs the rising and declining of empires and influences everything about them, including their currencies and markets (which I'm especially interested in). **The most important three cycles are the ones I mentioned in the introduction: the long-term debt and capital markets cycle, the internal order and disorder cycle, and the external order and disorder cycle.**

Because these three cycles are typically the most important, we will be looking at them in some depth in later chapters. Then we will apply them to history and the present day so that you can see how they play out in real examples.

These cycles drive swings back and forth between opposites—swings between peace and war, economic boom and bust, the political left and political right being in power, the coalescing and disintegrating of empires, etc.—that typically occur because people push things to extremes that surpass their equilibrium levels, which leads to swings that get overdone in the opposite direction. **Embedded in the swings in one direction are the ingredients that lead to the swings in the opposite direction.**

These cycles have remained essentially the same through the ages for essentially the same reason that the fundamentals of the human life cycle have remained the same over the ages: because human nature doesn't change much over time. For example, fear, greed, jealousy, and other basic emotions have remained constants and are big influences that drive cycles.

While it is true that no two people's life cycles are exactly the same and the typical life cycle has changed over the millennia, the archetype of the human life cycle—of children being raised by parents until they are independent, at which point they raise their own children and work, which they do until they get old, retire, and die—remains essentially the same. Similarly the big money/credit/capital markets cycle, which builds up too much debt and debt assets (e.g., bonds) until the debts can't be serviced with hard money, remains essentially the same. As always, this leads to people trying to sell their debt assets to make purchases and finding out they can't because there are far too many debt assets relative to the amount of money and the value of stuff there is to buy. Once this happens, defaults prompt those who manufacture money to make more. That cycle has been essentially the same for thousands of years. So have the cycles of internal order and disorder and external order and disorder. We will explore how human nature and other dynamics drive these cycles in the coming chapters.

EVOLUTION, CYCLES, AND THE BUMPS ALONG THE WAY

Evolution is the biggest and only permanent force in the universe, yet we struggle to notice it. While we see what exists and what happens, we don't see evolution and the evolutionary forces that make things exist and happen. Look around you. Do you see evolutionary change? Of course not. Yet you know that what you are looking at is changing—albeit slowly from your perspective—and you know that in time it won't exist and other things will exist in its place. To see this change, we have to devise ways to measure things and watch the measurements change. Then, once we can see the change, we can study why it happens. This is what we must do if we are going to successfully think about the changes ahead and how to deal with them.

Evolution is the upward movement toward improvement that

occurs because of adaptation and learning. Around it are cycles. To me, most everything transpires as an ascending trajectory of improvement with cycles around it, like an upward-pointing corkscrew:

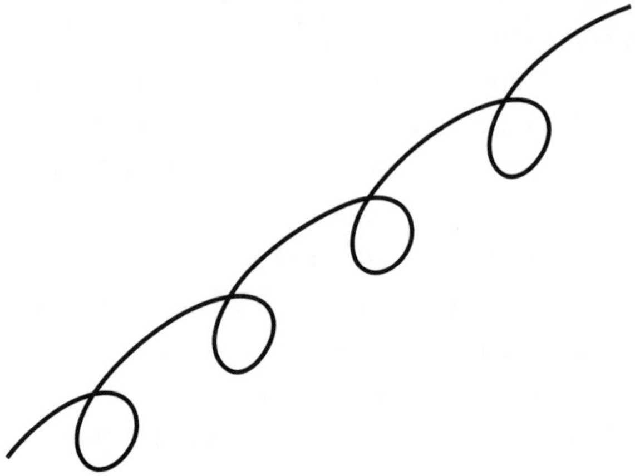

Evolution is a relatively smooth and steady improvement because the gaining of knowledge is greater than the losing of knowledge. Cycles on the other hand move back and forth, producing excesses in one direction that lead to reversals and excesses in the other, like the swinging of a pendulum. For example, over time our living standards rise because we learn more, which leads to higher productivity, but we have ups and downs in the economy because we have debt cycles that drive actual economic activity up and down around that uptrend. These evolutionary and sometimes revolutionary changes around the trend are not always smooth and painless. Sometimes they are very abrupt and painful as mistakes are made, learning occurs, and better adaptations result.

Together evolution and cycles make the upward corkscrew-type movements that we see in everything—wealth, politics, biology, technology, sociology, philosophy, etc.

Human productivity is the most important force in causing the world's total wealth, power, and living standards to rise over time. Productivity—i.e., the output per person, driven by learning, building, and inventiveness—has steadily improved over time. However, it has risen at different rates for different people, though always for the same reasons—because of the quality of people's education, inventiveness, work ethic, and economic systems to turn ideas into output. These reasons are important for policy makers to understand in order to achieve the best possible outcomes for their countries, and for investors and companies to understand in order to determine where the best long-term investments are.

This constantly increasing trend is the product of humanity's capacity to evolve, which is greater than any other species' because our brain gives us a unique capacity to learn and think abstractly. As a result, our inventions of technologies and ways of doing things have advanced uniquely. That evolution has led to the continuous evolutions that make up the changing world order. Technological advances in communications and transportation have brought everyone in the world closer together, which has changed the nature of relationships of people and empires in profound ways. We see such evolutionary improvements apparent in just about everything—greater life expectancy, better products, better ways of doing things, etc. Even our way of evolving has evolved in the form of coming up with better ways to create and innovate. This has been true for as long as human history has been written. As a result of this, charts of most everything show more upward slopes toward improvement than up and down movements.

This is shown in the following charts: estimated output (i.e., estimated real GDP) per person and life expectancy over the last 500 years. These are probably the two most widely agreed-upon measures of well-being, though they are imperfect. You can see the magnitudes of their evolutionary uptrends relative to the magnitudes of the swings around them.

The fact that the trends are so pronounced relative to the swings around the trends shows how much more forceful the power of human inventiveness is relative to everything else. As shown from this top-down, big-picture perspective, output per person appears to be steadily improving, though very slowly in the early years and faster starting in the 19th century, when the slope up becomes much

steeper, reflecting the faster productivity gains. This shift from slower productivity gains to faster productivity gains was primarily due to the improvements in broad learning and the conversion of that learning into productivity. That was brought about by a number of factors going as far back as Gutenberg's printing press in Europe in the mid-15th century (printing had already been in use in China for centuries), which increased the knowledge and education available to many more people, contributing to the Renaissance, the Scientific Revolution, the Enlightenment, the invention of capitalism, and the First Industrial Revolution in Britain. We will delve into these shortly.

GLOBAL REAL GDP PER CAPITA (LOG)

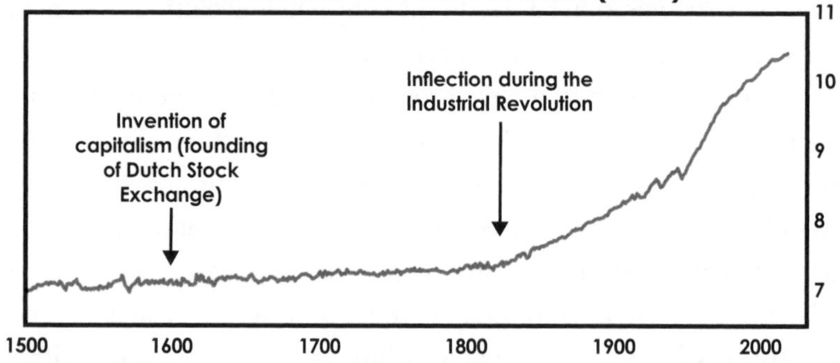

Global real GDP is primarily a mix of European countries before 1870 due to limited reliable data coverage across other countries before that point

GLOBAL LIFE EXPECTANCY AT BIRTH

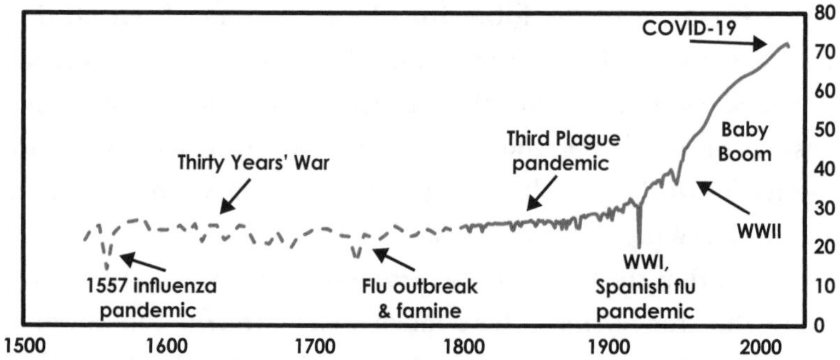

Dashed line based on experience of Great Britain only

The broader-based improvements in productivity that came from the invention of capitalism, entrepreneurship, and the Industrial Revolution also shifted wealth and power away from an agriculture-based economy in which landownership was the principal source of power, and monarchs, nobles, and the clergy worked together to maintain their grip on it. The shift moved toward an industry-based economy in which inventive capitalists created and owned the means of production of industrial goods and worked together with those in government to maintain the system that allowed them to have the wealth and power. In other words, since the Industrial Revolution, which brought about that change, we have been operating in a system in which wealth and power have primarily come more from the combination of education, inventiveness, and capitalism, with those who run governments working with those who control most of the wealth and education.

How this evolution with big cycles around it happens also continues to evolve. For example, while ages ago agricultural land and agricultural production were worth the most and that evolved into machines and what they produced being worth the most, digital things that have no apparent physical existence (data and information processing) are now evolving to become worth the most.[5] This is creating a fight over who obtains the data and how they use it to gain wealth and power.

THE CYCLES AROUND THE UPTREND

While significant, because these learnings and productivity improvements are evolutionary, they don't cause big abrupt shifts in

[5] At this time, humanity is evolving its ways of thinking and increasing productivity in more dramatic ways than ever before—even more dramatically than the discovery and usage of the scientific method. We are doing this through the development of artificial intelligence, which is an alternative way of thinking via an alternative brain that can make discoveries and process them into instructions of what should be done. Humanity is essentially creating an alternative species that has enormous capacity to see past patterns and process many different ideas very quickly, has little or no common sense, has trouble understanding the logic behind relationships, and doesn't have emotions. This species is simultaneously smart and stupid, helpful and dangerous. It offers great potential and needs to be well-controlled and not blindly followed.

who has what wealth and power. The big abrupt shifts come from booms, busts, revolutions, and wars, which are primarily driven by cycles, and these cycles are driven by logical cause/effect relationships. For example, the forces of increased productivity, entrepreneurship, and capitalism that marked the end of the 19th century also produced big wealth gaps and overindebtedness that led to economic downturns that, in the first half of the 20th century, led to anti-capitalism, communism, and big conflicts over wealth and power within and between countries. What you can see is evolution marching on with big cycles around it. ● ***Throughout time, the formula for success has been a system in which well-educated people, operating civilly with each other, come up with innovations, receive funding through capital markets, and own the means by which their innovations are turned into the production and allocation of resources, allowing them to be rewarded by profit making.*** **However, over the long run capitalism has created wealth and opportunity gaps and overindebtedness that have led to economic downturns and revolutions and wars that have caused changes in the domestic and world orders.**

As you can see in the following charts, history shows us that almost all of these turbulent times were due to fighting over wealth and power (i.e., conflicts in the form of revolutions and wars, often driven by money and credit collapses and big wealth gaps), and severe acts of nature (like droughts, floods, and epidemics). It also shows that how bad these periods get depends almost exclusively on how strong countries are and their ability to endure them.

● ***Countries with large savings, low debts, and a strong reserve currency can withstand economic and credit collapses better than countries that don't have much savings, have a lot of debt, and don't have a strong reserve currency.*** Likewise those that have strong and capable leadership and civil populations can be managed better than those that don't have these, and those that are more inventive will adapt better than those that are less inventive. As you will see later, these factors are measurable timeless and universal truths.

GLOBAL DEATHS BY CATEGORY (RATE PER 100K PEOPLE, 15YMA)

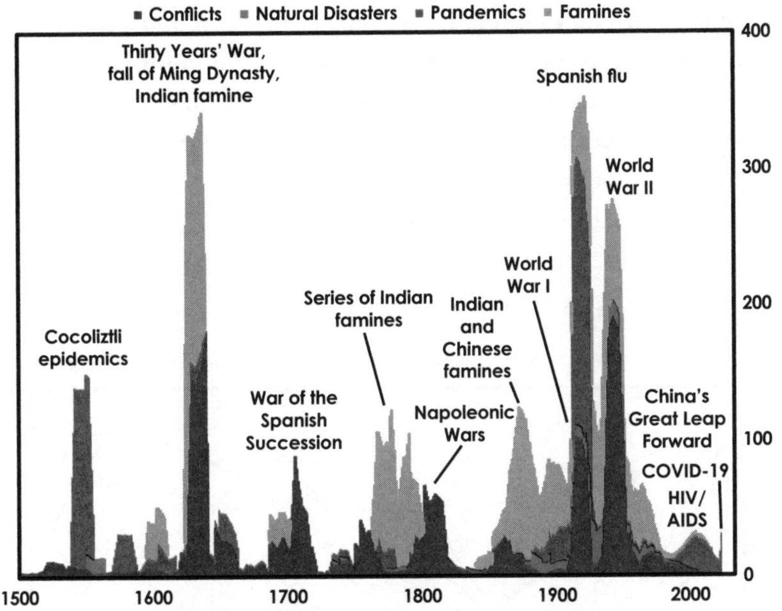

ESTIMATED DEATHS FROM CONFLICT (MAJOR POWERS, %POPULATION, 15YMA)

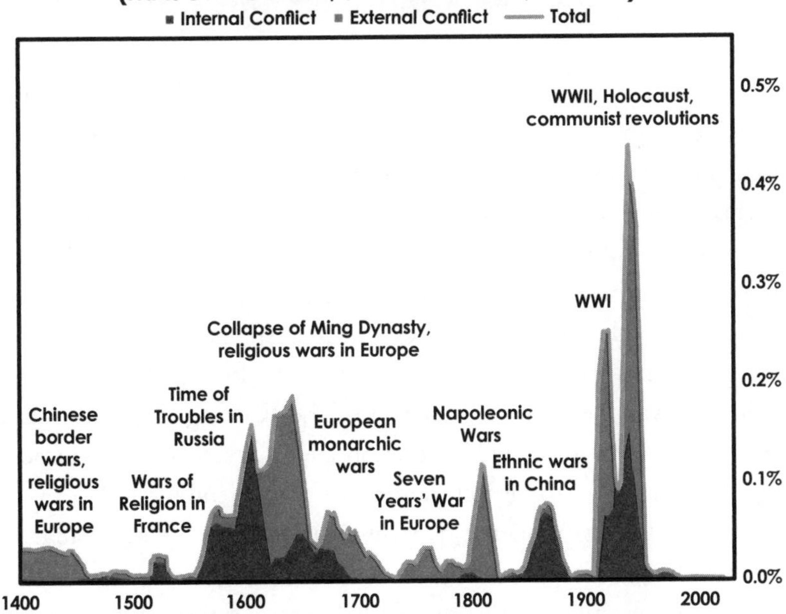

Based on deaths as a share of the population for the major powers and thus will differ from the estimate of global conflict deaths shown in the prior chart

Because these turbulent times are small in relation to the evolutionary uptrend of humanity's capacity to adapt and invent, they barely show up in the previous charts of GDP and life expectancy, appearing only as relatively minor wiggles. Yet these wiggles seem very big to us because we are so small and short-lived. Take the 1930–45 depression and war period, for example. The levels of the US stock market and global economic activity are shown in the next chart. As you can see, the economy fell by about 10 percent, and the stock market fell by about 85 percent and then began to recover.

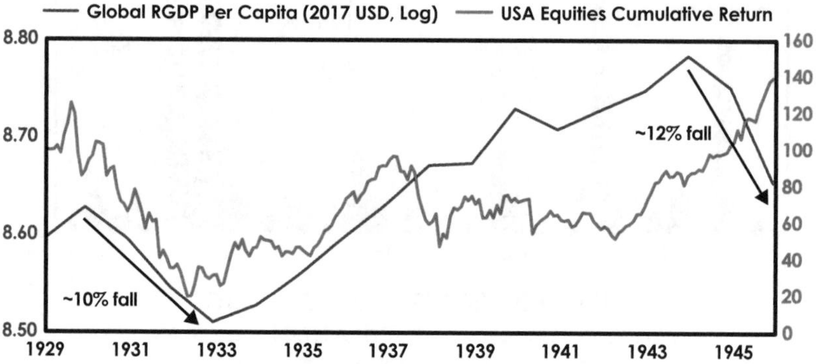

This is part of the classic money and credit cycle that has happened for as long as there has been recorded history and that I will explain more completely in Chapter 3. Briefly, a credit collapse happens because there is too much debt. Typically, the central government has to spend a lot of money it doesn't have and make it easier for debtors to pay their debts and the central bank always has to print money and liberally provide credit—like they did in response to the economic plunge driven by the COVID pandemic and a lot of debt. The 1930s debt bust was the natural extension of the Roaring '20s boom that became a debt-financed bubble that popped in 1929. That produced a depression that led to big central government spending and borrowing financed by big money and credit creation by the central bank.

Back then, the popping of the bubble and the resulting economic bust were the biggest influences on the 1930–45 period's internal and external fights for wealth and power. Then, like now and like in most other cases, there were large wealth gaps and conflict, which when heightened by debt/economic collapses, led to revolutionary changes in social and economic programs and big wealth transfers that were manifest in different systems in different countries. Clashes and wars developed over which of these systems—e.g., capitalism or communism, democracy or autocracy—were best. **There are always arguments or fights between those who want to make big redistributions of wealth and those who don't.** In the 1930s, Mother Nature also gave the US a painful drought.

Looking over the whole of the cases I examined, past economic and market declines lasted about three years, give or take a few years, depending on how long it took to do the debt restructuring and/or debt monetization process. The quicker the printing of money to fill the debt holes, the quicker the closing of the deflationary depression and the sooner the worrying about the value of money began. In the 1930s US case, the stock market and the economy bottomed the day that the newly elected president, Franklin D. Roosevelt, announced that he would default on the government's promise to let people turn in their money for gold, and that the government would create enough money and credit so that people could get their money out of the banks and others could get money and credit to buy things and invest. That took three-and-a-half years from the initial stock market crash in October 1929.[6]

Still there was fighting over wealth and power within and between countries. The emerging powers of Germany and Japan challenged the existing leading world powers of Great Britain, France, and eventually the US (which was dragged into World War II). The war period raised the economic output of things that were used in the war, but it would be a misnomer to call the war years a "productive" period—even though when measured in output per person, it was—because there was so much destruction. At the end of the war, global GDP per capita had fallen by about 12 percent, much of which was driven by declines in the economies of countries that lost the war. The stress

[6] In 2008, it took two months from the crash to the printing of money; in 2020, it took just weeks.

test that these years represented wiped out a lot, made clear who the winners and losers were, and led to a new beginning and a new world order in 1945. Classically that was followed by a lengthy period of peace and prosperity that became overextended so that all countries are now, 75 years later, being stress tested again.

Most cycles in history happen for basically the same reasons. For example, the 1907–19 period began with the Panic of 1907 in the US, which, like the 1929–32 money and credit crisis following the Roaring '20s, was the result of a boom period (the Gilded Age in the US, which was the same time as the Belle Époque in continental Europe and the Victorian Era in Great Britain) becoming a debt-financed bubble that led to economic and market declines. These declines also happened when there were large wealth gaps that led to big wealth redistributions and contributed to a world war. The wealth redistributions, like those in the 1930–45 period, came about through large increases in taxes and government spending, big deficits, and big changes in monetary policies that monetized the deficits. Then the Spanish flu intensified the stress test and the resulting restructuring process. This stress test and global economic and geopolitical restructuring led to a new world order in 1919, which was expressed in the Treaty of Versailles. That ushered in the 1920s debt-financed boom, which led to the 1930–45 period and the same things happening again.

These periods of destruction/reconstruction devastated the weak, made clear who the powerful were, and established revolutionary new approaches to doing things (i.e., new orders) that set the stage for periods of prosperity that eventually became overextended as debt bubbles with large wealth gaps and led to debt busts that produced new stress tests and destruction/reconstruction periods (i.e., wars), which led to new orders and eventually the strong again gaining relative to the weak, and so on.

What are these destruction/reconstruction periods like for the people who experience them? Since you likely haven't been through one of these and the stories about them are very scary, the prospect of being in one is worrisome to most people. It is true that these destruction/

reconstruction periods have produced tremendous human suffering both financially and, more importantly, in lost or damaged human lives. While the consequences are worse for some people, virtually no one escapes the damage. Still, without minimizing them, history has shown us that typically the majority of people stay employed in depressions, are unharmed in shooting wars, and survive natural disasters.

Some people who struggled through them have even described these very difficult times as bringing about important, good things like drawing people closer together, building strength of character, learning to appreciate the basics, etc. For example, Tom Brokaw called the people who went through the 1930–45 period "the Greatest Generation" because of the strength of character it gave them. My parents and aunts and uncles who went through the Great Depression and World War II, as well as others of their era whom I've spoken to in other countries who went through their own versions of this destruction period, saw it that way too. Keep in mind that economic destruction periods and war periods typically don't last very long—roughly two or three years. And the lengths and severities of natural disasters (like droughts, floods, and epidemics) vary, though they typically lessen in painfulness as adaptations are made. One rarely gets all three of these types of big crises—economic, revolution/war, and natural disaster—at the same time.

My point is that **while these revolution/war periods typically lead to a lot of human suffering, we should never, especially in the worst of times, lose sight of the fact that one can navigate them well—and that humanity's power to adapt and quickly get to new and higher levels of well-being is much greater than all the bad stuff that can be thrown at us**. For that reason, I believe that it is smart to trust and invest in humanity's adaptability and inventiveness. So, while I am pretty sure that in the coming years both you and I and the world order will experience big challenges and changes, I believe that humanity will become smarter and stronger in very practical ways that will lead us to overcome these challenging times and go on to new and higher levels of prosperity.

Now let's look at the cycles of rises and declines in the wealth and power of the major countries over the last 500 years.

PAST BIG CYCLE SHIFTS IN WEALTH AND POWER

The chart of rising productivity shown earlier was for the whole world (to the best of our ability to measure it). It doesn't show the shifts in wealth and power that occurred between countries. To understand how those happen, let's start with the big-picture basics. Throughout recorded history various forms of groups of people (e.g., tribes, kingdoms, countries, etc.) have gained wealth and power by building it themselves, taking it from others, or finding it in the ground. When they gathered more wealth and power than any other group, they became the world's leading power, which allowed them to determine the world order. When they lost that wealth and power, which they all did, the world order—and all aspects of life—changed in profound ways.

The next chart shows the relative wealth and power of the 11 leading empires over the last 500 years.

RELATIVE STANDING OF GREAT EMPIRES

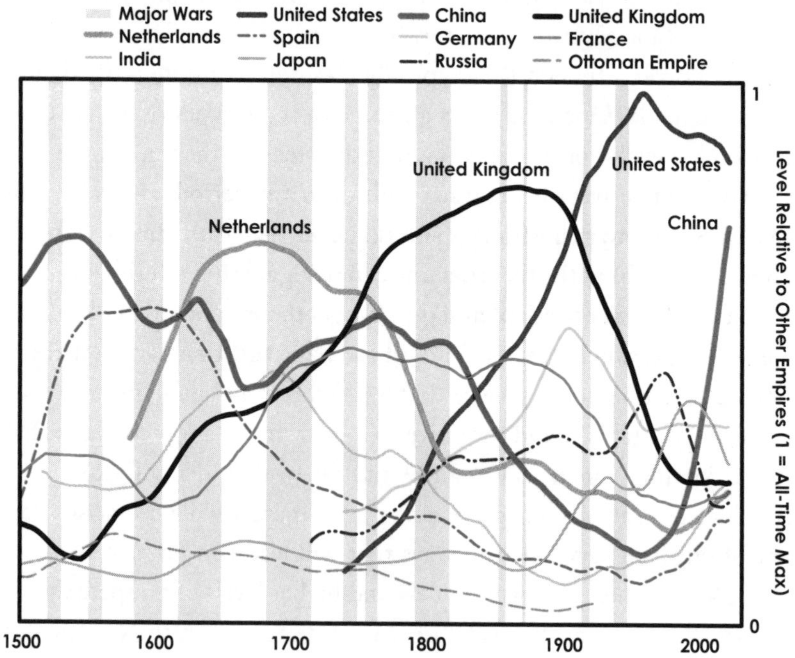

Each one of these indices[7] of wealth and power is a composite of eight different determinants that I will explain shortly. Though these indices aren't perfect because all data through time isn't perfect, they do an excellent job of painting the big picture. As you can see, nearly all of these empires saw periods of ascendancy followed by periods of decline.

Take a moment to study the thicker lines on the chart, which represent the four most important empires: the Dutch, British, American, and Chinese. These empires held the last three reserve currencies—the US dollar now, the British pound before it, and the Dutch guilder before that. China is included because it has risen to be the second most powerful empire/country and because it was so consistently powerful in most years prior to around 1850. To very briefly summarize the story this chart shows:

- **China was dominant for centuries (consistently out-competing Europe economically and otherwise), though it entered a steep decline starting in the 1800s.**
- **The Netherlands, a relatively small country, became the world's reserve currency empire in the 1600s.**
- **The UK followed a very similar path, peaking in the 1800s.**
- **Finally, the US rose to become the world's superpower over the last 150 years, though particularly during and after World War II.**
- **The US is now in relative decline while China is rising again.**

[7] These indices are made up of a number of different statistics, some of which are directly comparable and some of which are broadly analogous or broadly indicative. In some cases, a data series that stopped at a certain point had to be spliced with a series that continued back in time. Additionally, the lines shown on the chart are 30-year moving averages of these indices, shifted so that there is no lag. I chose to use the smoothed series because the volatility of the unsmoothed series was too great to allow one to see the big movements. Going forward, I will use these very smoothed versions when looking at the very long term and much less smoothed or unsmoothed versions when looking at these developments up close because the most important developments are best captured this way.

Now let's look at the same chart that extends the data all the way back to the year 600. I focused on the first chart (which covers just the last 500 years) rather than the second (which covers the last 1,400 years) because it highlights the empires I studied most intently and is simpler—though with 11 countries, 12 major wars, and over 500 years, it can hardly be called simple. Still, the second is more extensive and worth glancing at. I left out the shading of the war periods to lessen the complexity. As shown, **in the pre-1500 period, China was almost always the most powerful, though the Middle Eastern caliphates, the French, the Mongols, the Spanish, and the Ottomans were also in the picture.**

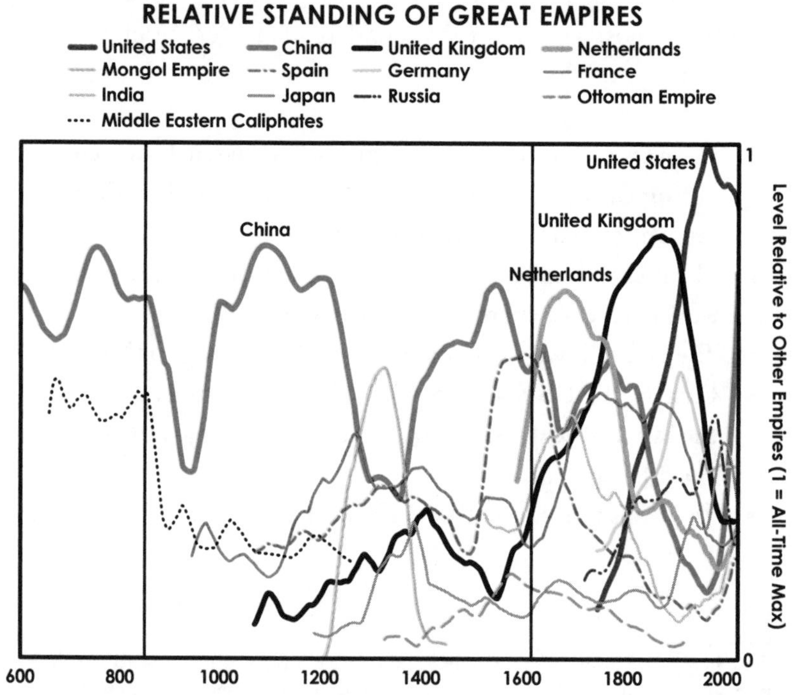

An important thing to remember: while the leading powers covered in this study were the richest and most powerful, they weren't necessarily the best-off countries for two reasons. First, while wealth and power are what most people want and will fight over

most, some people and their countries don't think that these things are the most important and wouldn't think of fighting over them. Some believe that having peace and savoring life are more important than having a lot of wealth and power and wouldn't consider fighting hard enough to gain enough of the wealth and power to make it into this study, though some of them enjoyed greater amounts of peace than those who fought for wealth and power. (By the way, I think there is a lot to be said for putting peace and savoring life ahead of gaining wealth and power—interestingly, there was little correlation between the wealth and power of a nation and the happiness of its people, which is a subject for another time.) Second, this group of countries excludes what I will call the "boutique countries" (like Switzerland and Singapore) that score very high in wealth and living standards but aren't large enough to become one of the biggest empires.

EIGHT DETERMINANTS OF WEALTH AND POWER

The single measure of wealth and power that I showed you for each country in the prior charts is a roughly equal average of 18 measures of strength. While we will explore the full list of determinants later, let's begin by focusing on the key eight shown in the next chart: **1) education, 2) competitiveness, 3) innovation and technology, 4) economic output, 5) share of world trade, 6) military strength, 7) financial center strength, and 8) reserve currency status.**

This chart shows the average of each of these measures of strength across all the empires I studied, with most of the weight on the most recent three reserve countries (i.e., the US, the UK, and the Netherlands).[8]

[8] We show where key indicators were relative to their history by averaging them across the cases. The chart is shown such that a value of 1 represents the peak in that indicator relative to history and 0 represents the trough. The timeline is shown in years with 0 representing roughly when the country was at its peak (i.e., when the average across the gauges was at its peak). In the rest of this chapter, we walk through each of the stages of the archetype in more detail.

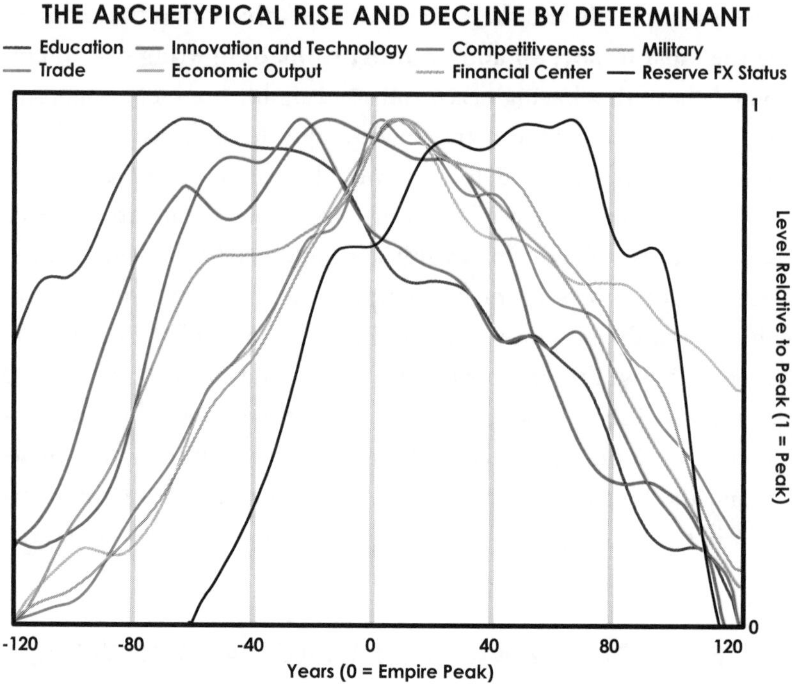

The lines in the chart do a pretty good job of telling the story of why and how the rises and declines took place. You can see how rising education leads to increased innovation and technology, which leads to an increased share of world trade and military strength, stronger economic output, the building of the world's leading financial center, and, with a lag, the establishment of the currency as a reserve currency. And you can see how for an extended period most of these factors stayed strong together and then declined in a similar order. The common reserve currency, just like the world's common language, tends to stick around after an empire has begun its decline because the habit of usage lasts longer than the strengths that made it so commonly used.

I call this cyclical, interrelated move up and down the Big Cycle. Using these determinants and some additional dynamics, I will next describe the Big Cycle in more detail. But before I start, it's worth reiterating that all of these measures of strength rose and declined over the arc of the empire. That's because these **strengths and weaknesses are mutually reinforcing**—i.e., strengths and weaknesses in education, competitiveness, economic output, share of world trade, etc., contribute to the others being strong or weak, for logical reasons.

THE ARCHETYPICAL BIG CYCLE

Broadly speaking, we can look at these rises and declines as happening in three phases:

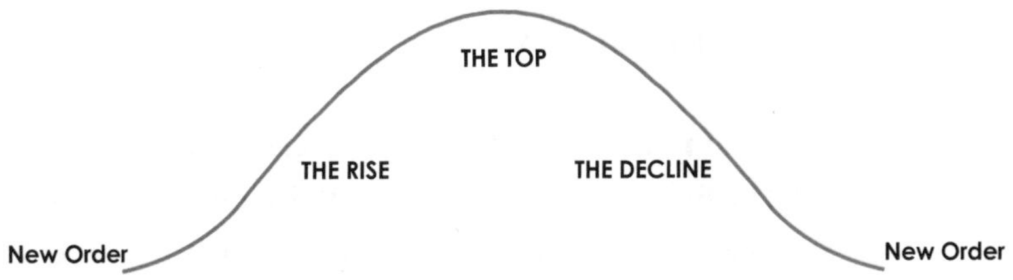

The Rise:
The rise is the prosperous period of building that comes after a new order. It is when the country is fundamentally strong because there are a) relatively low levels of indebtedness, b) relatively small wealth, values, and political gaps between people, c) people working effectively together to produce prosperity, d) good education and infrastructure, e) strong and capable leadership, and f) a peaceful world order that is guided by one or more dominant world powers, which leads to . . .

The Top:
This period is characterized by excesses in the form of a) high levels of indebtedness, b) large wealth, values, and political gaps, c) declining education and infrastructure, d) conflicts between different classes of people within countries, and e) struggles between countries as overextended empires are challenged by emerging rivals, which leads to . . .

The Decline:
This is the painful period of fighting and restructuring that leads to great conflicts and great changes and the establishment of new internal and external orders. It sets the stage for the next new order and a new period of prosperous building.

Let's look at each of these in more detail.

THE RISE

The rise phase begins when there is . . .

- . . . **strong enough and capable enough leadership to gain power and design an excellent system to increase the country's wealth and power**. Looking at the historically great empires, this system typically involves . . .
- . . . **strong education**, which is not just teaching knowledge and skills; it also includes teaching . . .
- . . . **strong character, civility, and work ethic development**. These are typically taught in families, schools, and/or religious institutions. If done well, this provides a healthy respect for rules and laws and order within society, leads to low corruption rates, and is effective in encouraging people to work together to improve productivity. The better the country does this, the more there will be a shift from producing basic products to . . .
- . . . **innovating and inventing new technologies**. For example, the Dutch were superbly inventive—at their peak they came up with a quarter of all major inventions in the world. One of these were ships that could travel around the globe to collect great riches. They also invented capitalism as we know it. Innovation is generally enhanced by being . . .
- . . . **open to the best thinking in the world** to be able to learn the best ways of doing things and by . . .

- . . . **the workers, the government, and the military all working well together.**

As a result of all of these things, the country . . .

- . . . becomes more **productive** and . . .
- . . . more **competitive in world markets**, which shows up in its . . .
- . . . **share of world trade rising.** You can see this happening today as the US and China are now roughly comparable in both their economic outputs and their shares of world trade.
- As a country trades more globally, it must protect its trade routes and foreign interests and it must be prepared to defend itself from attack so it develops **great military strength.**

If done well, this virtuous cycle leads to . . .

- . . . **strong income growth**, which can be used to finance . . .
- . . . **investments in infrastructure, education, and research and development.**
- **The country must develop systems to incentivize and empower those who have the ability to make or get wealth.** In all of these past cases, the most successful empires used a capitalist approach to incentivize and develop productive entrepreneurs. Even China, which is run by the Chinese Communist Party, uses a state-capitalism approach to incentivize and enable people. To do that incentivizing and financial enabling well, the country . . .
- . . . has to have **developing capital markets**—most importantly its lending, bond, and stock markets. That allows people to **convert their savings into investments to fund innovation and development** and share in the successes of those who are making great things happen. The inventive Dutch created the first publicly listed company (the Dutch East India Company)

and the first stock market to fund it. These were integral parts of their machine that produced a lot of wealth and power.

- As a natural consequence, all of the greatest empires developed **the world's leading financial center** for attracting and distributing the capital of their times. Amsterdam was the world's financial center when the Dutch were preeminent, London was when the British were on top, New York is now, and China is quickly developing its own financial center in Shanghai.
- As the country expands its international dealings to become the largest trading empire, its transactions can be paid in its currency, and people around the world want to save in it, so it becomes **the world's leading reserve currency**, which enables the country to borrow more, and at lower rates, than other countries because others want to lend in it.

This series of cause/effect relationships leading to mutually supportive financial, political, and military powers has gone together for as long as there has been recorded history. **All of the empires that became the most powerful in the world followed this path to the top.**

THE TOP

In the top phase, the country sustains the successes that fueled its rise, but embedded in the rewards of the successes are the seeds of decline. Over time, obligations pile up, breaking down the self-reinforcing circumstances that fueled the rise.

- **As people in the country, which is now rich and powerful, earn more, that makes them more expensive and less competitive** relative to people in other countries who are willing to work for less.
- At the same time people from **other countries naturally copy the methods and technologies of the leading power, which**

further reduces the leading country's competitiveness. For example, British shipbuilders hired Dutch designers to design better ships that were built by less expensive British workers, making them more competitive, which led the British to rise and the Dutch to decline.

- Also, **as people in the leading country become richer, they tend to not work as hard. They enjoy more leisure, pursue the finer and less productive things in life, and at the extreme become decadent.** Values change from generation to generation during the rise to the top—from those who had to fight to achieve wealth and power to those who inherited it. The new generation is less battle-hardened, steeped in luxuries, and accustomed to the easy life, which makes them **more vulnerable to challenges.**
- Additionally, **as people get used to doing well, they increasingly bet on the good times continuing—and borrow money to do that—which leads to financial bubbles.**
- Within capitalist systems, **financial gains come unevenly so the wealth gap grows.** Wealth gaps are self-reinforcing because rich people use their greater resources to expand their powers. **They also influence the political system to their advantage and give greater privileges to their children—like better education—causing the gaps in values, politics, and opportunity to develop between the rich "haves" and the poor "have-nots." Those who are less well-off feel the system is unfair so resentments grow.**
- **As long as the living standards of most people are still rising, these gaps and resentments don't boil over into conflict.**

During the top, the leading country's financial picture begins to change. Having a **reserve currency** gives it the "exorbitant privilege"[9]

[9] "Exorbitant privilege" is a way of describing a reserve currency that was coined by French Finance Minister Valéry Giscard d'Estaing as a description of the position of the US.

of being able to borrow more money, which gets it deeper into debt. This boosts the leading empire's spending power over the short term and weakens it over the longer run.

- **Inevitably, the country begins borrowing excessively, which contributes to the country building up large debts with foreign lenders.**
- While this boosts spending power over the short term, **it weakens the country's financial health—and weakens the currency—over the longer term. In other words, when borrowing and spending are strong, the empire appears very strong, but its finances are in fact being weakened because the borrowing sustains the country's power beyond its fundamentals by financing both domestic overconsumption and international military conflicts** required to maintain the empire.
- Also the costs of maintaining and defending the empire become greater than the revenue it brings in, so **having an empire becomes unprofitable**. For example, the British Empire became massive, bureaucratic, and lost its competitive advantages as rival powers—particularly Germany—soared, leading to an increasingly expensive arms race and world war.
- The **richer countries get into debt by borrowing from poorer countries that save more**—that is one of the earliest signs of a wealth and power shift. This started in the United States in the 1980s when it had a per capita income 40 times that of China's and started borrowing from the Chinese who wanted to save in dollars because the dollar was the world's reserve currency.
- **If the empire begins to run out of new lenders, those holding their currency begin to look to sell and get out rather than buy, save, lend, and get in—and the strength of the empire begins to fall.**

THE DECLINE

The decline phase typically comes from internal economic weakness together with internal fighting, or from costly external fighting, or both. Typically, the country's decline comes gradually and then suddenly.

Internally . . .

- When debts become very large, and **there is an economic downturn** and the empire can no longer borrow the money necessary to repay its debts, this creates great domestic hardships and forces the country to choose between **defaulting on its debts and printing a lot of new money.**
- **The country nearly always chooses to print a lot of new money**, at first gradually and eventually massively. This **devalues the currency and raises inflation.**
- Typically at those times when the government has problems funding itself—at the same time as there are bad financial and economic conditions, and large wealth, values, and political gaps—there are great **increases in internal conflict between the rich and poor and different ethnic, religious, and racial groups.**
- **This leads to political extremism that shows up as populism of the left or of the right.** Those of the left seek to redistribute the wealth while those of the right seek to maintain the wealth in the hands of the rich. **This is the "anti-capitalist phase," when capitalism, capitalists, and the elites in general are blamed for the problems.**
- Typically during such times **taxes on the rich rise, and when the rich fear their wealth and well-being will be taken away, they move to places, assets, and currencies they feel safer in. These outflows reduce the country's tax revenue, which leads to a classic self-reinforcing, hollowing-out process.**

- **When the flight of wealth gets bad enough, the country outlaws it. Those seeking to get out begin to panic.**
- **These turbulent conditions undermine productivity**, which **shrinks the economic pie** and causes **more conflict about how to divide the shrinking resources**. Populist leaders emerge from both sides and pledge to take control and bring about order. **That's when democracy is most challenged because it fails to control the anarchy and because the move to a strong populist leader who will bring order to the chaos is most likely.**
- As conflict within the country escalates, it leads to some form of **revolution or civil war to redistribute wealth and force the big changes**. This can be peaceful and maintain the existing internal order, but it's more often **violent and changes the order**. For example, the Roosevelt revolution to redistribute wealth was relatively peaceful, while the revolutions that changed the domestic orders in Germany, Japan, Spain, Russia, and China, which also happened in the 1930s for the same reasons, were much more violent.

These civil wars and revolutions create what I call new internal orders. I'll explore how internal orders change in a cyclical way in Chapter 5. But the important thing to note for now is that internal orders can change without leading to a change in the world order. **It's only when the forces that produce internal disorder and instability align with an external challenge that the entire world order can change.**

Externally . . .

- **When there is a rising great power that is capable of challenging the existing great power and existing world order, there is a rising risk of great international conflict,**

especially if there is internal conflict going on within the existing great power. Typically the rising international opponent will seek to exploit this domestic weakness. This is especially risky if the rising international power has built up a comparable military.

- **Defending oneself against foreign rivals requires great military spending, which has to occur even as domestic economic conditions are deteriorating** and the leading great power country can least afford it.
- Since there is no viable system for peacefully adjudicating international disputes, these **conflicts are typically resolved through tests of power**.
- As bolder challenges are made, **the leading empire is faced with the difficult choice of fighting or retreating**. Fighting and losing are the worst, but retreating is bad too because it allows the opposition to progress and it shows that one is weak to those other countries that are considering what side to be on.
- **Poor economic conditions cause more fighting for wealth and power, which inevitably leads to some kind of war.**
- **Wars are terribly costly. At the same time, they produce the necessary tectonic shifts that realign the world order to the new reality of wealth and power.**
- **When those holding the reserve currency and debt of the declining empire lose faith and sell them, that marks the end of its Big Cycle.**

When all of these forces line up—indebtedness, civil war/revolution at home, war abroad, and a loss of faith in the currency—a change in the world order is typically at hand.

You can see these forces summarized in their typical progression in the following chart.

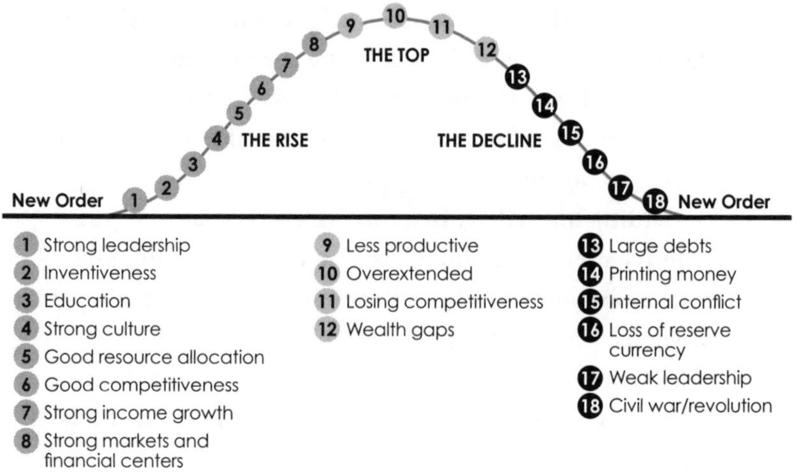

I threw a lot at you in the last few pages. You might want to read them again slowly so you can see if the sequence makes sense to you. Later, we will get into a number of specific cases in greater depth and you will see the patterns of these cycles emerge, albeit not in a precise way. The fact that they occur and the reasons for them occurring are less disputable than the exact timing of their occurrences.

To summarize, around the upward trend of productivity gains that produce rising wealth and better living standards, there are cycles that produce prosperous periods of building in which the country is fundamentally strong because there are relatively low levels of indebtedness, relatively small wealth, values, and political gaps, people working effectively together to produce prosperity, good education and infrastructure, strong and capable leadership, and a peaceful world order that is guided by one or more dominant world powers. These are the prosperous and enjoyable periods. When

they are taken to excess, which they always are, the excesses lead to depressing periods of destruction and restructuring in which the country's fundamental weaknesses of high levels of indebtedness, large wealth, values, and political gaps, different factions of people unable to work well together, poor education and infrastructure, and the struggle to maintain an overextended empire under the challenge of emerging rivals lead to a painful period of fighting, destruction, and then a restructuring that establishes a new order, setting the stage for a new period of building.

Because these steps unfold in a logical sequence of timeless and universal cause/effect relationships, it is possible to create a health index of where a country stands by looking at these measures. When the measures are strong/good, the condition of the country is strong/good and the period ahead is much more likely to be strong/good; when the ratings of these items are weak/bad, the condition of the country is weak/bad and the period ahead is much more likely to be weak/bad.

In the following table, to help paint the picture, I converted most of our measures into colors, with dark green being a very favorable reading and dark red being a very unfavorable reading. It is the average of these readings that defines which stage of the cycle a country is in, in much the same way as it is the average of the eight readings of power that I use as my measure of total power. Like those power readings, while one could reconfigure them to produce marginally different readings, they are broadly indicative in a by-and-large way. Here, I am showing this to exemplify the typical process, not to look at any specific case. I will however show specific quantitative readings for all the major countries later in this book.

ROUGH QUANTITATIVE SCORING OF MEASURES BY STAGE IN CYCLE

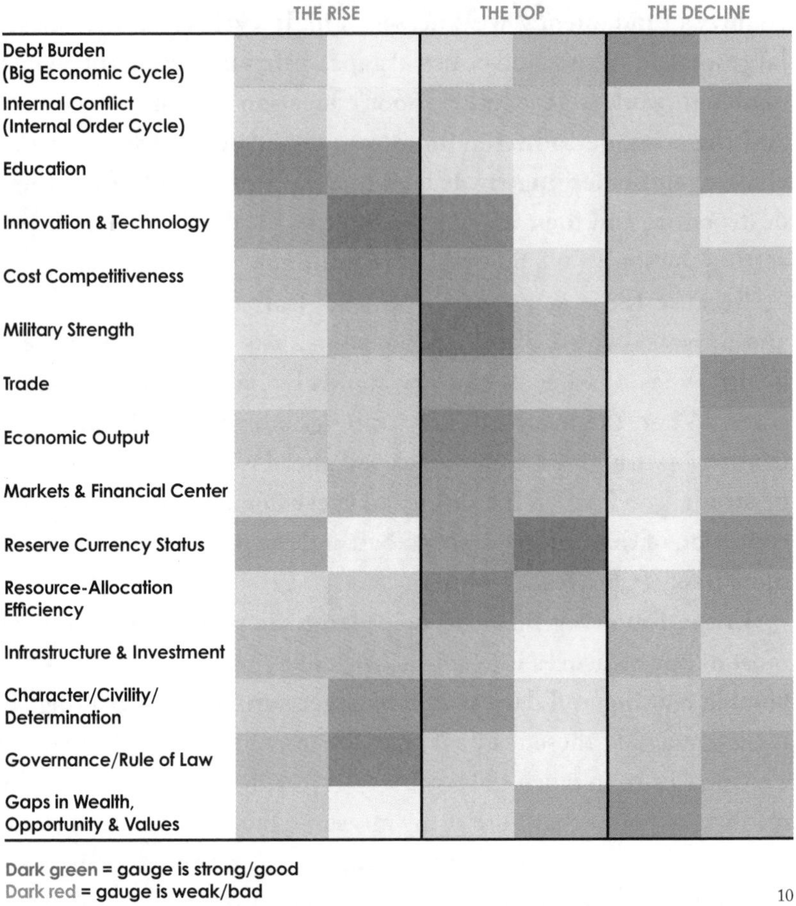

[10]

Since all of these factors, both ascending and descending, tend to be mutually reinforcing, it is not a coincidence that large wealth gaps, debt crises, revolutions, wars, and changes in the world order have tended to come as a perfect storm. The Big Cycle of an empire's rise and decline looks like the following chart. The bad periods of destruction and restructuring via depression, revolution, and war, which largely tear down

[10] Acts of nature, external order, and geology are not included in cycle analysis. Readings use proxies for determinants with limited history.

the old system and set the stage for the emergence of a new system, typically take about 10 to 20 years, though variations in the range can be much larger. They are depicted by the shaded areas. They are followed by more extended periods of peace and prosperity in which smart people work harmoniously together and no country wants to fight the world power because it's too strong. These peaceful periods last for about 40 to 80 years, though variations in the range can be much larger.

CHANGES TO THE WORLD ORDER (CONCEPTUAL EXAMPLE)

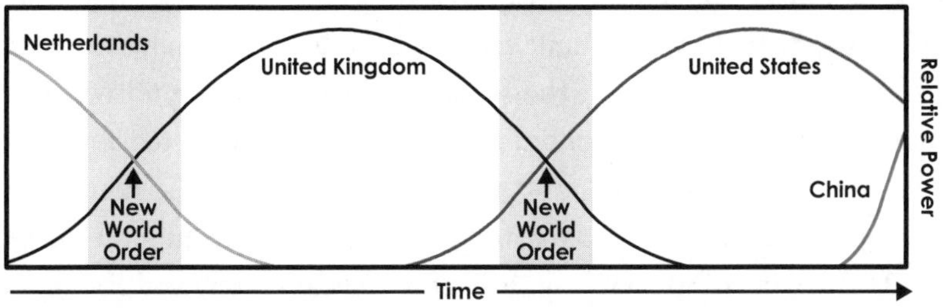

For example, when the Dutch Empire gave way to the British Empire and when the British Empire gave way to the US Empire, most or all of the following things happened:

End of the Old, Beginning of the New (e.g., Dutch to British)

- Debt restructuring and debt crisis
- Internal revolution (peaceful or violent) that leads to large transfers of wealth from the "haves" to the "have-nots"
- External war
- Big currency breakdown
- New domestic and world order

End of the Old, Beginning of the New (e.g., British to US)

- Debt restructuring and debt crisis
- Internal revolution (peaceful or violent) that leads to large transfers of wealth from the "haves" to the "have-nots"
- External war
- Big currency breakdown
- New domestic and world order

A PREVIEW OF WHERE WE ARE NOW

As previously explained, the last major period of destroying and restructuring happened in 1930–45, which led to the period of building and the new world order that began in 1945 with the creation a new global monetary system (built in 1944 in Bretton Woods, New Hampshire) and a US-dominated system of world governance (locating the United Nations in New York and the World Bank and the International Monetary Fund in Washington, DC). The new world order was the natural consequence of the US being the richest country (it then had two-thirds of the world's gold stock and gold was then money), the dominant economic power (it then accounted for about half of world production), and the strongest military (it then had a monopoly on nuclear weapons and the strongest conventional forces).

At the time of my writing, it is now 75 years later, and the major old empires, which are also the major reserve currency empires, are classically approaching the end of a long-term debt cycle when there are large debts and typical monetary policies don't work well. Politically fragmented central governments have recently tried to fill in their financial holes by giving out a lot of money that they are borrowing, while central banks have tried to help by printing a lot of money (i.e., monetizing government debt). All this is happening when there are big wealth and values gaps and a rising world power that is competing with the leading world power in trade, technology development, capital markets, and geopolitics. And on top of all this, as of this writing we have a pandemic to contend with.

Simultaneously, great human thinking, working with computer intelligence, is creating great ways of addressing these challenges. If we can all deal with each other well, we will certainly get past this difficult time and move on to a new prosperous period that will be quite different. At the same time, I am equally confident that there will be radical changes that will be traumatic for many people.

That is how the world works in a nutshell. Now I will give a more expanded description.

CHAPTER 2

THE DETERMINANTS

In the last chapter I described the Big Cycle in a tiny nutshell. In this and the other chapters that follow in Part I, I will flesh out how I see the perpetual-motion machine working. In this chapter, I will review the most important determinants and summarize how I put them into my "model."

As the saying goes, and most people agree, "history rhymes." It "rhymes" because its most important events repeat, though never in exactly the same way. That is because, while the cause/effect relationships behind those events are timeless and universal, all things evolve and influence each other in different ways. By studying many analogous events in different times and places, their underlying causes and effects become clearer. I have learned that history's continuously evolving story transpires like a perpetual-motion machine that is driven by cause/effect relationships that both evolve and repeat over time.

To deal with the realities that are coming at me, my process is to . . .

- **Interact with this machine and try to understand how it works**
- **Write down my observations of its workings, along with the principles I have learned for dealing with them**

- **Backtest those principles through time**
- **Convert the principles into equations and program them into a computer that helps me with my decision making**
- **Learn from my experiences and my reflections on my experiences, so I can refine my principles**
- **Do that over and over again**

Imagine a chess player who records their criteria for making different moves in different situations, which they then encode into a computer that plays alongside them like a partner. Each player brings what they are best at to the game. The human player is more inventive, more lateral in thinking, and better able to reason, while the computer can calculate more data faster, is better able to identify patterns, and is much less emotional. This never-ending process of learning, building, using, and refining in partnership with computers describes what I do, except my game is global macro investing, not chess.

In this chapter, I will share my description of the workings of the perpetual-motion machine that drives the rises and declines of empires and their reserve currencies as I have come to understand it thus far, giving you a glimpse into how I play my game. While I'm sure my mental model is wrong and incomplete in any number of ways, it is the best one that I have now and it has proven invaluable to me. I am passing it along for you to probe and explore, take or leave, and build on as you like. My hope is that I will prompt you and others to think about the timeless and universal cause/effect relationships that drive the realities that are coming at us, and the best principles for dealing with them. By stress testing and improving this model through full-throated debate, we will get to the point where we have a largely agreed-upon template of the processes and their causes. By using that template, we can then strive to agree on which stage each country is in and what the best practices are for interacting with it, whether we are individuals taking care of our own interests or we are leaders taking care of our country's.

In the last chapter, I conveyed a very simplified description of the determinants of the evolution and cyclical rises and declines of empires—most importantly, what I believe to be the primary drivers of the Big Cycles. In this chapter, I will explain the model in much greater detail. It is based on what I saw happen repeatedly through time in the 11 leading empires of the last 500 years, the 20 most important countries of the last 100 years, and the major dynasties of China over the last 1,400 years. To be clear, I do not consider myself to be an expert historian in these cases, and these cases represent only a small percentage of all cases. I only glanced at some of the most important empires in early history, such as the Roman, Greek, Egyptian, Byzantine, Mongol, Han, Sui, Arab, and Persian empires, and I completely neglected many of the other empires that have risen and declined throughout the world in Africa, South Asia, the Pacific Islands, and precolonial North and South America. In other words, what I didn't examine was much greater than what I did examine. Still, I believe I have seen enough to develop a good mental model that applies to most countries, which has been very helpful to my efforts to understand what is going on today and which helps me to form a valuable, though hazy, picture of the future.

THE CONSTRUCTION OF MY MENTAL MODEL OF THE PERPETUAL-MOTION MACHINE

Just as we can see the arc of the human life cycle from birth to death and how one generation impacts the next, we can do the same with countries and empires. We can see how values, assets, liabilities, and experiences are handed down and how their evolutionary effects ripple out across the generations. We can tell when an empire is approaching its peak and when it is in decline.

● ***All peoples throughout history have had systems or orders for governing how they deal with each other. I call the systems within countries "internal orders," those between countries "external orders," and those that apply to the whole world "world orders." These orders affect each other and are always changing.*** Such orders have always existed at every level—within families, companies, cities, states, and countries, as well as internationally. They determine who has what powers and how decisions are made, including how wealth and political control are divided. What they are and how they run is a function of human nature, culture, and circumstances. The US now has a certain set of existing political conditions within its democratic system, but both the conditions and the system are ever-changing because of the pressure of timeless and universal forces.

The way I see it, at any moment in time there are both 1) the existing set of conditions that include the existing domestic and world orders and 2) timeless and universal forces that cause changes in these conditions. Most people tend to pay too much attention to what exists relative to the timeless and universal forces that produce the changes. I do the opposite in my attempt to anticipate change. **Everything that has happened and everything that will happen has had and will have determinants that make it happen. If we can understand those determinants, we can understand how the machine works and anticipate what will likely be coming at us next.**

Since everything that happened and will happen was and is due to the interactions of the parts of this perpetual-motion machine, one can say that everything is predestined. I believe that, if we had a perfect model that took every cause/effect relationship into consideration, we could perfectly forecast the future—that the only thing that stands in the way is our inability to model all those cause/effect dynamics. While that might or might not be right, it tells you where I'm coming from and what I'm striving for.

Most people don't see things that way. Most people believe the future is unknowable and that destiny doesn't exist. To be clear, while having a perfect model that gives a nearly perfect picture of that predestined future would be great, I don't expect my model to come close to that. My goal is simply to have a crude yet evolving model that gives me a leg up relative to the competition and relative to the position I would be in if I didn't have the model.

To build this model, I looked at history quantitatively as well as qualitatively because 1) by measuring conditions and their changes, I can more objectively determine the cause/effect relationships behind them, develop a likely range of expectations, and systemize my decision making accordingly but 2) I can't measure everything quantitatively.

My process is to look at many cases to observe how their determinants created the effects that define them. To give a simple example, a lot of debt (a determinant) together with tight money (another determinant) will typically produce a debt crisis (the effect). Similarly, when the three big cycles that I described in the last chapter come together in a bad way (heavy indebtedness with the central bank printing a lot of money; internal conflict stemming from gaps in wealth, values, and politics; and the rise of one or more competing powers), that typically leads to the decline of an incumbent empire.

In my mental model, the relationship between the determinants and their effects in the various cases looks like this:

How the Machine Works = (f)...

	Case 1	Case 2	Case 3	Case 4	Case 5	Case 6	Case 7	Case 8	Case 9	Case 10, Etc
Determinant 1	Effect	Effect	Effect	Effect	Effect	Effect	Effect	Effect	Effect	Effect
Determinant 2	Effect	Effect	Effect	Effect	Effect	Effect	Effect	Effect	Effect	Effect
Determinant 3	Effect	Effect	Effect	Effect	Effect	Effect	Effect	Effect	Effect	Effect
Determinant 4	Effect	Effect	Effect	Effect	Effect	Effect	Effect	Effect	Effect	Effect
Determinant 5	Effect	Effect	Effect	Effect	Effect	Effect	Effect	Effect	Effect	Effect
Determinant 6	Effect	Effect	Effect	Effect	Effect	Effect	Effect	Effect	Effect	Effect
Determinant 7	Effect	Effect	Effect	Effect	Effect	Effect	Effect	Effect	Effect	Effect
Determinant 8	Effect	Effect	Effect	Effect	Effect	Effect	Effect	Effect	Effect	Effect
Determinant 9	Effect	Effect	Effect	Effect	Effect	Effect	Effect	Effect	Effect	Effect
Determinant 10	Effect	Effect	Effect	Effect	Effect	Effect	Effect	Effect	Effect	Effect
Etc										

Determinants lead to effects that become subsequent determinants that produce subsequent effects that become linked together

in many cases. So we can look at each case and see what happened (the effect) and what made it happen (its determinants). Or we can look at the determinants to see the effects they had to make up the various cases. The determinants are both what exists and the energy that produces changes; like energy and matter, at the end of the day they're the same. They create new circumstances and new determinants that create the next changes.

That is how I quite literally try to model the perpetual-motion machine.

THE 3, THE 5, THE 8, AND THE 18 DETERMINANTS

In the last chapter, I introduced you to what I believe are the three big cycles and the eight most important determinants of the rises and declines of empires and their currencies. **Because thinking about all of these determinants and their interactions is complex, I suggest that you keep the three big cycles in mind as the most important things to watch: 1) the cycle of good and bad finances (e.g., the capital markets cycle), 2) the cycle of internal order and disorder (due to degrees of cooperation and fighting over wealth and power largely caused by wealth and values gaps), and 3) the cycle of external order and disorder (due to the degrees of the competitiveness of existing powers in fighting for wealth and power).** I hope you will join me in trying to understand these three cycles and know where countries are in them. History and logic show that when a country simultaneously has all three in their good phases it is strong and rising, and when all three are in their bad phases it is weak and declining.

If I were to add two more determinants to keep in mind, they would be 4) the pace of innovation and technological development to solve problems and make improvements and 5) acts of nature, most importantly droughts, floods, and diseases. That is because innovation and technological advances can solve most problems and further evolution, and acts of nature such as droughts, floods,

and diseases have had enormous impacts throughout history. These are the five most important forces, which I call the "Big Five," so when they are moving in the same direction—toward improving or toward worsening—most everything else follows.

I also introduced the eight powers that I could measure that seemed to be the most important. You can review them along with the big cycles in the following list. These indicators both reflect and drive the upswings and downswings. The chart of the archetypical rise and decline by factor in Chapter 1 showed the average readings of these along the path of the archetypical cycle. Each of these types of power rising and declining in cycles comes together with the other cycles to make the one Big Cycle of the empire's rise and decline.

And then there are the other determinants such as geology/geography, rule of law, and infrastructure that matter too. The whole list of 18 factors[1] included in my model is shown on the next page. You can also read a detailed description of all 18 at the end of Chapter 14.

[1] I want to clarify the difference between a determinant and a cycle because sometimes I will use these terms in ways that might not be clear. A determinant is a factor (e.g., the supply of money) while a cycle is a series of self-reinforcing determinants that lead to events transpiring in a certain way—e.g., central banks making lots of money and credit available eventually leads to strong economic growth, inflation, and bubbles, which then prompt central banks to reduce the money supply, which produces market and economic downturns, which then lead the central banks to increase the supply of money to . . . etc. So, cycles themselves are determinants that are a collection of complementary forces that interact in a process to produce the same results again and again through time.

THE THREE BIG CYCLES

Healthy	Big Debt/Money/Capital Markets/Economic Cycle	Unhealthy
Order	Big Cycle of Internal Order and Disorder	Disorder
Peace	Big Cycle of External Order and Disorder	War

OTHER KEY DETERMINANTS (EIGHT KEY MEASURES OF POWER)

High	Education	Low
High	Innovation & Technology	Low
Strong	Cost Competitiveness	Weak
Strong	Military Strength	Weak
Favorable	Trade	Unfavorable
High	Economic Output	Low
Strong	Markets and Financial Center	Weak
Strong	Reserve Currency Status	Weak

ADDITIONAL DETERMINANTS

Favorable	Geology	Unfavorable
Efficient	Resource-Allocation Efficiency	Poor
Beneficial	Acts of Nature	Disruptive
High	Infrastructure and Investment	Low
Strong	Character/Civility/Determination	Weak
Strong	Governance/Rule of Law	Weak
Small	Gaps in Wealth, Opportunity & Values	Large

I find measuring and weighing all these things in my head, plus all of the other important dynamics at play, to be impossible. That is why I analyze them with the aid of a computer. I will share my analysis for the top 11 countries in the appendix after Chapter 14: The Future. I also provide detail on some components for the top 20 countries at economicprinciples.org.

Though none of these determinants is determinative on its own, I think you will find that when considered together they paint a pretty clear picture of which part of its life cycle a country is in and the direction it is headed in. For the fun of it you might want to go through a little exercise of ticking off where each of those measures is for each country you're interested in. Rank each country on a 1–10 scale for each attribute, beginning with 10 on the far left and 1 on the far right. If you add all these rankings up, the higher the number, the greater the probability of the country rising on a relative basis. The lower the number, the more likely it will fall. Take a moment to calculate where the United States is, where China is, where Italy is, where Brazil is, and so on.

Because I systematize as much as I can, I push to quantify whatever possible into a decision-making system. So, with the help of my team, I have developed gauges that look at things like internal and external conflict, political gaps, etc., to help me better understand where countries are in their cycles. Some of the less key determinants are aggregated as subcomponents of the key determinants.

While I measure and describe the determinants discretely, they are not separate. They interact with each other and blend together, typically reinforcing each other and the whole cycle's rise and fall. For example, stronger education leads to stronger technological innovation, which leads to increased productivity and increased shares of trade, greater wealth, more military power, and eventually the establishment of a reserve currency. Further, having strong leaders, a population that is well-educated and civil with each other, a system that efficiently allocates capital and other resources, access to natural resources, and favorable geography all help a lot, and when they decline, they tend to decline together.

Of course, not all of the indicators can be expressed in numbers and equations; things like human nature and the power dynamics that affect behaviors and outcomes are better described in words. I call these things dynamics. The following table shows a list of other main dynamics that I keep in my head while trying to evaluate where nations are and what is likely to come next.

DYNAMICS TO PAY ATTENTION TO

Country	Self-Interest	**Individual**
Important	Desire to Gain Wealth and Power	**Not important**
Extensive	Learning from History	**Limited**
Strong	Multigenerational Psychological Cycle	**Decadent**
Long-Term	Time Frame of Decision Making	**Short-Term**
Competent	Leadership	**Weak**
Open	Openness to Global Thinking	**Closed**
Productive	Culture	**Unproductive**
Cooperative	Class Relationships	**Divisive**
Moderate	Political Left/Right	**Partisan**
Cooperative	Prisoner's Dilemma	**At War**
Win-Win	Relationships	**Lose-Lose**
Favorable	Balance of Power	**Unfavorable**
Peace	Peace/War Cycle	**War**

That's a lot. It is both too little and too much—too little to do full justice to the subjects (which have all been the focus of whole books and doctoral theses) and too much to process and digest. I have tried to cram a small portion of what I've learned about them into the summaries that follow. Fuller accounts of a number of these dynamics are contained in an addendum immediately following this chapter if you're interested in diving more deeply into any of them. **While I'm sure that what follows doesn't include all the most important determinants, I also know that the ones I'm highlighting here and in the following chapters represent the most important influences that have repeatedly driven the most important events throughout history.** Of course, I look forward to being corrected and guided by others to make my descriptions more complete.

EXPLORING THE DETERMINANTS AND DYNAMICS

I find that knowing the different circumstances countries face, as well as the strategies and group dynamics they bring to facing these circumstances, helps me understand what moves are likely to come next and how these moves will impact the key determinants. I will explain a bit more about how these look to me, which I will do by examining the machine from the top down.

As I see it, the determinants and dynamics that drive events fall into two types:

1. **Inherited Determinants:** They include a country's geography, geology, and acts of nature such as weather and diseases.
2. **Human Capital Determinants:** They are the ways people are with themselves and each other. They are driven by human nature and different cultures (which differentiate their approaches).

These two big categories contain within them many important factors, ranging from qualities that are highly specific to countries (like their geography) to those that are universal (like the human tendency to favor short-term gratification over long-term goals), and they can be discerned at every level, whether in individuals, cities, countries, or empires.

INHERITED DETERMINANTS

By inherited determinants of a country's well-being I mean its geography, geology, genealogy, and acts of nature. These are big drivers of each country's and each people's stories. For example, you can't understand the success of the United States without recognizing that it is separated from European and Asian powers by two oceans and blessed with most of the minerals, metals, and other natural resources it needs to be prosperous and self-sufficient, including the topsoil, water, and temperate climate that allows it to produce most of its own food. These factors enabled it to be largely isolationist until a little more than a century ago while investing in education, infrastructure, and innovation in ways that made it strong. Let's briefly review those.

1. Geography. Where a country is, what's around it, and what its terrain is like are all important determinants. For example, the geographies of the United States and China—both with large expanses of land bounded by large natural barriers of water and mountains—created the inclination for them to be one big whole, increasing the commonalities of their people (e.g., shared language, government, culture, etc.). In contrast, the geography of Europe (i.e., having many more natural boundaries within it) reinforced its divisions into different states/countries, leading to fewer commonalities among its people (e.g., different languages, governments, cultures, etc.).

2. Geology. The natural resources on and under a country's surface are critically important, but geology should not be overvalued relative to human capital. History shows us that every commodity has declined in value (in inflation-adjusted terms) with big up and down cycles around that downtrend. That is because inventiveness changes what is in demand—e.g., new energy sources replacing old ones, fiber-optic cable replacing copper wiring, etc.—and natural resources are depleted over time. Many Middle Eastern countries' wealth, power, and relevance to the rest of the world rose with the importance of petroleum and may fall as the world turns away from fossil fuels. The most vulnerable position to be in is having a high reliance on one or a few commodities because they are highly cyclical and sometimes lose value altogether.

3. Acts of Nature. Acts of nature come in many forms, such as epidemic diseases, floods, and droughts. Throughout history they have affected the well-being of countries and the course of their evolution even more than wars and depressions. The Black Death killed an estimated 75–200 million people in the years around 1350, and smallpox killed more than 300 million people in the 20th century, which is more than double the number that died in its wars. Droughts and floods have caused massive famines and loss of life. Such catastrophes tend to come along unexpectedly and act as stress tests, revealing the underlying strengths and weaknesses of societies.

4. Genealogy. Regarding genealogy, I'm no expert on genetics, so I have little to offer other than to say that all people come into this world with inherited genes that affect how they behave to some extent, so it is logical that the genetic makeup of a country's population should have some effect on its outcomes. Having said that, I should point out that most of the evidence I have seen indicates that only a small percentage (15 percent or less) of the variations in the behaviors of people between populations could potentially be explained by genetic differences, so genetics seems to be a relatively minor determinant in relation to the other influences I am mentioning.

HUMAN CAPITAL DETERMINANTS

● ***While the inherited assets and liabilities of a country are very important, history has shown that the way people are with themselves and others is the most important determinant.*** By that I mean whether they hold themselves to high standards of behavior, whether they are self-disciplined, and whether they are civil with others in order to be productive members of their societies is most important. These qualities plus flexibility and resilience (i.e., the capacity to adapt to both "bad" and "good" things) allows people to minimize setbacks and maximize opportunities. Character, common sense, creativity, and consideration in most people make for a productive society.

Because capital is an income-producing asset, human capital can be defined as a human who generates income. ● ***When humans have the capacity to produce more revenue than they expend, there is good human capital and self-sufficiency.*** I call this "self-sufficient plus," which is what all people, companies, and countries should strive for in order for them individually and collectively to be strong financially. The likelihood of having good human capital and being "self-sufficient plus" is improved through quality education, a culture of hard work and cooperation, training, etc. Societies that don't have good human capital are either drawing down their resources or getting deeper into debt they won't be able to pay back (i.e., they're headed for trouble).

● ***While many countries have natural resources that they are able to draw upon, human capital is the most sustainable capital because inherited assets that are drawn down eventually disappear, whereas human capital can exist forever.***

Human capital is why people who come up with new ideas and build them out (e.g., entrepreneurs) beat giants with vast resources (just look at Elon Musk and his startup Tesla, which rivals resource-rich General Motors, Ford, and Chrysler; or Steve Jobs and Bill Gates, whose computer startups surpassed giants like IBM; and so on). Great human capital allows people to overcome their weaknesses and identify and capitalize on their opportunities. It is the attribute that has allowed small countries like the Netherlands, England, Switzerland, and Singapore to achieve great wealth and (in some cases) power.

THE MOST IMPORTANT HUMAN NATURE DETERMINANTS

Across societies and throughout time, people share the same human nature, which makes them much more alike than different. People behave similarly when faced with similar circumstances, driving the Big Cycles.

5. Self-Interest. Self-interest, especially self-survival, is the most powerful motivator for most people, organizations, and governments. However, which self-interest—e.g., the individual's, the family's, the country's, etc.—matters most is a critical determinant of the society's success. See the addendum that follows this chapter to learn more.

6. The Drive to Gain and Keep Wealth and Power. The quest for wealth and power is a powerful motivator of individuals, families, companies, states, and countries, though that's not totally true because different individuals, families, companies, states, and countries value wealth and power differently relative to other things. For some, wealth and power are not nearly as important as other things that life has to offer. But for most, especially those who become the most wealthy and powerful, the pursuit of wealth and power is all-consuming. **To be successful over the long run, a country must earn an amount that is at least equal to what it spends. Those that earn and spend modestly and have a surplus are more sustainably successful than those that earn and spend a lot more and have deficits. History shows that when an individual, organization, country, or empire spends more than what it earns, misery and turbulence are ahead.** For more, see the addendum.

7. Capital Markets. The ability to save and obtain buying power through one's capital markets is essential to a country's well-being.

For that reason, how well they are developed is an important determinant of a country's success.

8. The Ability to Learn from History. Most people don't have this, which is an impediment, though it varies by society. For example, the Chinese are excellent at this. Learning from one's own experiences is not adequate because, as explained earlier, many of the most important lessons don't come in one's lifetime. In fact, many encounters in the future will be more opposite than similar to what one encountered before in life. Since the peace/boom period at the beginning of the cycle is opposite to the war/bust period at its end, the periods people face later in their lives are more likely to be more opposite than similar to the ones they encountered earlier in their lives. More specifically, in my opinion, if you don't understand what happened since at least 1900 and how that rhymes with what is happening now, there is a high likelihood that you will find yourself in trouble.

9. The Big Multigenerational Psychological Cycle. Different generations think differently because of their different experiences, which leads them to make their decisions differently, which affects what happens to them and to subsequent generations. This is reflected in the adage "from shirtsleeves to shirtsleeves in three generations." Three generations is also roughly the length of time of a typical long-term debt cycle. However, history shows that when these cycles are handled well—i.e., strong human capital is maintained over many generations—they can go on for many generations. This multigenerational cycle takes place over several stages that are described in the addendum to this chapter.

10. Favoring Short-Term Gratification over Long-Term Well-Being. This is another differentiator of people's and society's successes. Those who favor long-term well-being over short-term well-being tend to do better. The human propensity to choose short-term enjoyment over long-term well-being naturally exaggerates the highs and lows of the cycle because it pulls the good times forward at the expense of the future. That happens in many harmful ways, most classically by creating the debt boom and bust cycle. Governments are especially vulnerable to this because of how the political dynamic works. More specifically, a) politicians are motivated to prioritize the near term over the long term, b) they don't like to face limitations and difficult financial trade-offs (e.g., choosing whether to spend on the military for defense or to spend on social programs), and c) it is politically threatening to take money away from people by taxing them. This leads to a host of political and other problems.

11. Humanity's Inventiveness. Humanity's greatest power is what drives human evolution, which is manifest in increased productivity and higher living standards. Unlike other species, humans have a unique capacity to learn and evolve their intellectual understanding; plus, they invent things that materially change their circumstances, producing advances in everything. These advances produce the upward trending corkscrew I described in Chapter 1. To imagine what it would be like if humankind didn't have this ability, look at other species. Without humanity's unique ability to invent, our lives would be pretty much the same generation after generation. Because there would be far fewer new things, there would be fewer surprises and advances. In fact, some periods of human history were very much like that. However, it varies greatly from one society to another. For more, see the addendum to this chapter.

DETERMINANTS SHAPED BY CULTURE

12. Culture. As the saying goes, "culture is destiny." Cultural differences—differences in how people believe they should be with each other—matter enormously. All societies create cultures based on how they think reality works, and they all provide principles for guiding how people should deal with reality, and most importantly how they should deal with each other. Culture drives the formal and informal ways each society works. Individuals known and unknown, such as Jesus, Confucius, Mohammed, Buddha, Mahavira, Guru Nanak, Plato, Socrates, Marx, and many others, have conveyed approaches to life that were captured in books such as the Hebrew Bible and the New Testament, the Talmud, the Quran, the I Ching, the Five Books and Four Classics, the Analects, the Upanishads, the Bhagavad Gita, the Brama Sutras, *Meditations*, *Republic*, *Metaphysics*, *The Wealth of Nations*, and *Das Kapital*. These, together with the discoveries of scientists, artists, politicians, diplomats, investors, psychologists, etc., all encountering their realities and adapting to them in their own ways, are what determines a people's culture.

13. Openness to Global Thinking. This is a good leading indicator of strength because isolated entities tend to miss out on the world's best practices, which weakens them, while learning about the best the world has to offer helps people be their best. Isolation also prevents them from benefiting from the challenge of facing off against the world's best competitors. History is littered with cases in which countries were isolated, sometimes because they chose to cut themselves off to protect their cultures (e.g., the late Tang, late Ming, and early PRC periods in China, and the Edo period in Japan) and sometimes because of circumstances like natural disasters and internal fighting. Both reasons lead them to fall behind in their technology, with terrible consequences. In fact, it is one of the most common reasons for empires and dynasties failing.

14. Leadership. Everything I've mentioned so far is influenced by the people in leadership positions. Life is like a game of chess or the Chinese board game Go, in which every move helps determine the outcome and some players know how to make better moves than others. In the future, more and more of those moves will be made with the aid of computers, but for now they are still made by people. In reading history you see over and over how its course has been changed by the uniqueness—sometimes excellence, sometimes terribleness—of a relatively few people in key areas such as the government, the sciences, finance and commerce, the arts, and so on. In each generation, roughly a few hundred people made all the difference. Studying what these key people in these key roles were like, what they did in different situations, and the consequences of what they did helps us understand how this perpetual-motion machine works.

DETERMINANTS SHAPED BY HOW INDIVIDUALS AND GROUPS INTERACT WITH EACH OTHER

15. Wealth Gaps. Large and widening wealth gaps tend to lead to periods of greater conflict, especially when economic conditions become bad and people are fighting over a shrinking pie.

16. Values Gaps. While wealth matters, it is not the only thing that people fight over. Values (e.g., in religions and ideologies) matter a lot too. History shows us that widening values gaps, especially during periods of economic stress, have tended to lead to periods of greater conflict, while shrinking values gaps tend to lead to periods of greater harmony. This dynamic is driven by the fact that people tend to coalesce into tribes that are bound together (often informally) by the magnetism of their members' commonalities. Naturally, such tribes operate with each other in ways that are consistent with their shared values. When under stress, people with greater values gaps also prove to have greater conflict. They frequently demonize members of other tribes rather than recognizing that those other tribes, like themselves, are simply doing what is in their self-interest in the best ways they know how.

17. Class Struggles. ● ***In all countries throughout time, though to varying degrees, people are sorted into "classes," either because they choose to be with people like themselves or because others assign them to a class.*** Power is usually shared among three or four classes who in aggregate make up only a small percentage of the population. The classes people are in typically determine who their friends and allies are and who their enemies are. They are sorted into these classes whether they like it or not because people stereotype. While rich and poor are the most common class distinctions, there are many other important ones, such as race, ethnicity, religion, gender, lifestyle, location (e.g., urban versus rural), and politics (right versus left). Early in the Big Cycle, when times are good, there is generally more harmony among the classes, and when things are bad toward the end, there is more fighting. **Class warfare has profound effects on the internal order**, which I will explore in Chapter 5. For more on this determinant, see the addendum to this chapter.

18. The Political Left/Right Cycle. In all societies there are swings between the political left and the political right that determine how wealth and power are distributed. The swings are sometimes peaceful and sometimes violent and are always important to understand. Typically, the big cycle in the capital markets, along with cycles in wealth, values, and class divisions, drive the political left/right cycle because these create the motivations for political change. When capital markets and economies are booming, wealth gaps typically increase. While some societies succeed at striking a relatively sensible and steady balance between left and right, more frequently we see cyclical swings between norms. These swings typically occur throughout empires' rises and declines, in roughly 10-year cycles. The big economic crises that mark the end of the Big Cycle often herald revolutions. For more, see the addendum to this chapter.

19. The Prisoner's Dilemma Must Be Solved for Peace to Exist. The prisoner's dilemma is a concept from game theory that explains why, even when the best thing for two parties to do is to cooperate, the logical thing for each to do is to kill the other first. That is because survival is of paramount importance, and while you don't know for certain if your opponent will attack you, you do know that it is in their interest to defeat you before you defeat them. It's for this reason that deadly wars are best avoided by both sides establishing mutually assured protections against existential harms. Exchanging benefits and creating interdependencies that would be intolerable to lose further reduces the risk of conflict.

20. Whether There Are Win-Win Relationships or Lose-Lose Relationships. It is up to both parties to choose what kind of relationship they have. That is true at all levels of relationships, from individuals up to countries. Most fundamentally, parties can choose whether to have a cooperative win-win relationship or a threatening lose-lose relationship—i.e., to be allies or enemies—though actions by both determine what type of relationship they will have and whether it will work well. To be clear, win-win relationships can exist between competitors as long as each side does not pose an existential risk to the other (see the prisoner's dilemma). All that's required is that they know and respect each other's existential red lines. Parties in win-win relationships can have tough negotiations, competing like two friendly merchants in a bazaar or two teams at the Olympics. Having win-win relationships is obviously better than having lose-lose relationships, but sometimes there are irreconcilable differences that must be fought over because they can't be negotiated away.

21. The Big Balance of Power Cycle That Drives the Big Peace/War Cycle Both Within Countries and Between Countries. The balance of power dynamic is the timeless and universal dynamic of allies and enemies working to gain wealth and power. It drives virtually all struggles for power, from office politics to local politics, and from national politics to geopolitics. In some cultures this game is played a bit differently than in other cultures—e.g., in Western society it is played more like chess while in Asian societies it is played more like Go—though the objective is the same: to dominate the other side. It has always existed and still exists everywhere and appears to transpire along a consistent series of steps, which I describe in more detail when discussing the internal order in Chapter 5 (even though these same forces apply equally to internal and external power struggles). For a more complete explanation of how the balance of power cycle works, see the addendum to this chapter.

22. Military Strength and the Peace/War Cycle. History shows us that military strength—whether one's own or another's via alliances—is a critical determinant of outcomes, sometimes because the mere threat of force is power and sometimes because the use of force is required. Military strength is readily observable and measurable, but it can also be qualitatively assessed. Internationally, military strength is especially important because there is no effective international judicial and enforcement system. This leads to countries needing to fight to test their relative powers and a cycle of war and peace that I will explain when discussing the external order cycle in Chapter 6.

ALL THESE THINGS COME TOGETHER TO DETERMINE INTERNAL ORDERS, EXTERNAL ORDERS, AND HOW THEY CHANGE

I have repeatedly seen all of these determine the levels and the rises and declines in wealth and power of all peoples. I have seen them together create the circumstances the people of a country and/or its leaders face and how they face them. They drive the internal and world orders and changes in them.

● ***Like everything else, internal orders and world orders are constantly evolving and moving circumstances forward through time, as existing circumstances interact with each other and the forces that act on them to produce new circumstances.***

Evolution occurs because of logical cause/effect relationships in which existing conditions and determinants propel changes that create a new set of conditions and determinants that propel the next changes and so on, like matter and energy interacting in a perpetual-motion machine. Because a given set of circumstances creates a limited set of possibilities, by properly identifying the circumstances and understanding the cause/effect relationships, one can improve one's understanding of the possibilities of what will come next and how to make wise decisions.

For example, all countries now have their existing way of choosing new leaders. In the US, the president is chosen both by the voters in accordance with the democratic system laid out in the Constitution and by how people choose to operate within the system. How well this works depends on how effective both are, which is a result of prior determinants, such as how effectively those in previous generations dealt with and modified the system. The people now interacting with the system are different from those of previous generations, who were shaped by different circumstances, so we should expect different outcomes based on how people today are different.

Not having the historical perspective to recognize those differences is a handicap. Once we see them and understand how the perpetual-motion machine works, we can see how different systems such as communism, fascism, autocracies, democracies, and evolutionary descendants and hybrids of these, such as state capitalism in China, evolve through time. Seeing this, we can imagine how new forms of internal orders to divide wealth and allocate government political power may evolve and affect our lives, based on how people choose to be with each other and how human nature enters into their choices.

Now that I have described my mental model of how the world works rather superficially, in the rest of Part I, I will focus on the most important determinants—namely the three big cycles of debt and capital markets, internal order, and external order—in more detail. I will also describe what I believe all this means for investing. Before you go on to that, you might want to look over the addendum to this chapter, which fleshes out some of the determinants that I only briefly covered in this chapter. On the other hand, if you're feeling bogged down, you can skip it. That's why I made it an addendum.

CHAPTER 2

DETERMINANTS ADDENDUM

In Chapter 2 I introduced some concepts that I thought might be worth explaining in greater depth but didn't want to include in the body of the chapter because these explorations could be too much, so I decided to include them here as an addendum in case you are interested in exploring them further. To help you make the connection I refer to each determinant or dynamic by title and number from Chapter 2.

5. Self-Interest. While self-interest is the primary motivator for most people, organizations, and governments, the question of which "self" is most important—is it the individual, the family, the tribe (i.e., community), the state, the country, the empire, humankind, all living things, the universe? The following diagram shows the possible units. The ones on the top are more encompassing and the ones on the bottom are the less consolidated. **What are most people in your society, and what are you, willing to die for?**

THE UNIVERSE
↕
ALL LIVING THINGS
↕
HUMANKIND
↕
EMPIRE
↕
COUNTRY
↕
STATE
↕
TRIBE
(i.e., community)
↕
FAMILY
↕
INDIVIDUAL

The "self" that people are most attached to is the one they will do the most to protect and this will drive their behaviors. For example, when people are willing to die for their country, their country will be more likely to be protected than if the individual self is more important, in which case individuals will run from deadly combat. Within countries one might see tribes be much more important than countries, which would lead to an entirely different dynamic than if the opposite were true. That is why **I find this dynamic worth keeping an eye on**, especially in conflicts.

In looking at history across countries **I saw changes in the primary unit that most people and societies optimized for**. For example, before around 1650[1] tribes and states were more important than countries. History shows that the groupings that people collect in and that are the

[1] The Peace of Westphalia in 1648 created countries—i.e., sovereign states—as we now know them.

most important to them evolve. Gatherings of individuals and families make up a tribe (i.e., a community); gatherings of tribes (or communities) make up a state (e.g., the state of Georgia); gatherings of states make up a country (e.g., the United States); gatherings of states or countries that are under unified control make up an empire (e.g., the British Empire). Sometimes smaller groupings coalesce into bigger ones, changing boundaries in the process. For example, over the last 150 years in Europe, states coalesced into nations, many of which have coalesced into the European Union. And sometimes they break up into smaller units. For example, the Soviet Union broke up into its constituent countries, and some Middle Eastern countries have broken up into warring tribes.

Over the last few years, the world has been moving from being more globalist to being more nationalist. At the same time, the United States appears to be losing its cohesion as people's views about how they should be with each other are becoming more divergent. These divergences are leading people to migrate to the states that align with their preferences, causing those states to be more relevant individually than as parts of a unified whole. History and logic show us that these changes in domestic and international orders are typically accompanied by conflicts because there is a lot of disagreement about how they should work—e.g., what states' rights are relative to national rights. Because most people haven't seen such changes before, they fail to recognize them for what they are. They are important to stay on top of because they show the changing locus of control, which typically signals a change in one's rights and obligations.

Think about it. What are you seeing happen? Are you seeing coalescing or dissolving? From what level to what other level? What implications do these changes have for you and where you want to be?

6. The Drive to Gain and Keep Wealth and Power. For the purposes of discussing the big cycles in later chapters, it's worth defining wealth a bit more specifically and looking at its impact on countries that have it or lack it. I believe the following to be by and large true:

Wealth = Buying Power. Without getting too nuanced, let's call wealth buying power to distinguish it from money and credit. That distinction is important because the value of money and credit changes. For example, when a lot of money and credit are created, they go down in value, so having more money won't necessarily give one more wealth or buying power.

Real Wealth ≠ Financial Wealth. Real wealth is what people buy because they want to have and use it, such as a house, car, streaming video service, etc. Real wealth has intrinsic value. Financial wealth consists of financial assets that are held to a) receive an ongoing income in the future and/or b) be sold in the future to get money to buy the real assets people will want. Financial wealth has no intrinsic value.

Making Wealth = Being Productive. Over the long run the wealth and buying power you have will be a function of how much you produce. That is because real wealth doesn't last long and neither do inheritances. That is why being continuously productive is so important. If you look at societies that expropriated the wealth of the rich and tried to live off it and weren't productive (e.g., Russia after the revolutions of 1917), you will see that it didn't take them long to become poor. The less productive a society, the less wealthy and hence the less powerful. By the way, spending money on investment and infrastructure rather than on consumption tends to lead to greater productivity, so investment is a good leading indicator of prosperity.

Wealth = Power. That is because if one has enough wealth one can buy most anything—physical property, the work and loyalty of others, education, healthcare, influential powers of all sorts (political, military, etc.), and so on. Through time and across countries, history has shown that there is a symbiotic relationship between those who have wealth and those who have political power, and that the type of deal they have between them determines the ruling order. That ruling order continues until the rulers are overthrown by others who grab the wealth and power for themselves.

Wealth and power are mutually supportive. For example, in 1717 the British East India Company effectively brought together financial capital, people with commercial capabilities, and people with military capabilities to force India's Mughal emperor to trade with them, which was the first step toward the British colonization of India, the fall of the Mughal Empire in the 18th century, and then its complete failure in the 19th century, when the British exiled the emperor and executed his children after the 1857 Indian Rebellion. The British did these things because they had the wealth and power to do them in pursuit of more wealth and power.

Wealth Decline = Power Decline. There isn't an individual, organization, country, or empire that hasn't failed when it lost its buying power. ● ***To be successful one must earn an amount that is at least equal to the amount one spends.*** Those who spend modestly and have a surplus are more sustainably successful than those who earn a lot more and have deficits. History shows that when an individual, organization, country, or empire spends more than what they earn, misery and turbulence are ahead. History also shows that countries that have higher percentages of people who are self-sufficient tend to be more socially, politically, and economically stable.

9. The Big Multigenerational Psychological Cycle. The rises and declines of countries correspond to these psychological and economic cycles in the following ways and stages. Because these stages are so useful in understanding the behavior of a country's people and leaders, I am always trying to assess what stages different countries are in.

Stage 1: People and Their Countries Are Poor and They Think of Themselves as Poor. In this stage, most people have very low incomes and subsistence lifestyles. As a result they don't waste money because they value it a lot, and they don't have much debt because nobody wants to lend to them. Some people have potential and some do not, but in most cases their poverty and lack of resources prevent them from gaining the education and other capabilities that would allow them to pull themselves up. One's inherited circumstances and approach to life are the biggest determinants of who emerges richer from this stage and who does not.

How fast countries evolve through this stage depends on their cultures and their abilities. **I call countries in this stage "early-stage emerging countries."** Those that advance typically work hard and gradually accumulate more money than they need to survive, which they save because they worry about not having enough in the future. The evolution through this stage to the next typically takes about a generation. Starting about 40 years ago until about 10 to 15 years ago the "Asian Tigers" of Hong Kong, Singapore, Taiwan, and South Korea and then China were examples of economies in this stage.

Stage 2: People and Their Countries Are Rich but Still Think of Themselves as Poor. Because people who grew up with financial insecurity typically don't lose their financial cautiousness, people in this stage still work hard, sell a lot to foreigners, have pegged exchange rates, save a lot, and invest efficiently in real assets like real estate, gold, and local bank deposits, and in bonds of the reserve currency countries. Because they have a lot more money, they can and do invest in the things that make them more productive—e.g., human capital development, infrastructure, research and development, etc. This generation of parents wants to educate their children well and get them to work hard to be successful. They also improve their resource-allocation systems, including their capital markets and their legal systems. This is the most productive phase of the cycle.

Countries in this stage experience rapidly rising income growth and rapidly rising productivity growth at the same time. The productivity growth means two things: 1) inflation is not a problem and 2) the country can become more competitive. During this stage, debts typically do not rise significantly relative to incomes and sometimes they decline. This is a very healthy period and a terrific time to invest in a country if it has adequate property rights protections.

You can tell countries in this stage from those in the first stage because they have gleaming new cities next to old ones, high savings rates, rapidly rising incomes, and, typically, rising foreign exchange reserves. **I call countries in this stage "late-stage emerging countries."** While countries of all sizes can go through this stage, when big countries go through it, they are typically emerging into great world powers.

Stage 3: People and Their Countries Are Rich and Think of Themselves as Rich. At this stage, people's incomes are high, so labor becomes more expensive. But their prior investments in infrastructure, capital goods, and research and development are still paying off by producing productivity gains that sustain their high living standards. Priorities shift from an emphasis on working and saving in order to protect oneself from bad times, to savoring the finer things in life. People become more comfortable spending more. Arts and sciences typically flourish. This change in the prevailing psychology is reinforced as a new generation of people who did not experience the bad times become an increasingly large percentage of the population. Signs of this change in mindset are reflected in statistics that show reduced work hours (e.g., typically there is a reduction in the workweek from six days to five) and big increases in expenditures on leisure and luxury goods relative to necessities. At their best, these periods are early- and mid-stage "Renaissance periods."

Large countries in this stage almost always become world economic and military powers.[2] Typically, they develop their militaries in order to project and protect their global interests. Prior to the mid-20th century, large countries at this stage literally controlled foreign governments and created empires from them to provide the cheap labor and cheap natural resources they needed to remain competitive. Starting in the early to mid-20th century, when the US Empire began ruling by "speaking softly and carrying a big stick," American "influence" and international

[2] Japan from 1971 to 1990 is an exception with regards to the military.

agreements have allowed developed countries to have access to emerging countries' cheap labor and investment opportunities without directly controlling their governments. In this stage countries are on top of the world and are enjoying it. **I call countries in this stage "peak health countries." The United States was in this stage from 1950 to 1965. China is now moving into it.** The key is to maintain the determinants leading to strength for as long as possible.

Stage 4: People and Their Countries Are Poorer and Still Think of Themselves as Rich. In this stage, debts rise relative to income. The psychological shift behind this leveraging up occurs because the people who lived through the first two stages have died off or become irrelevant and those whose behavior matters most are used to living well and not worrying about the pain of not having enough money. Because the workers in these countries earn and spend a lot, they become expensive, and because they are expensive, they experience slower real income growth rates. Since they are reluctant to constrain their spending in line with their reduced income growth rates, they lower their savings rates, increase their debts, and cut corners. Because their spending continues to be strong, they continue to appear rich, even though their balance sheets are deteriorating. The reduced level of efficient investments in infrastructure, capital goods, and research and development slows their productivity gains. Their cities and infrastructure become older and less efficient than in the two previous stages. They increasingly rely on their reputation rather than on their competitiveness to fund their deficits. Countries typically spend a lot of money on the military at this stage to protect their global interests, sometimes in very large amounts because of wars. Often, though not always, countries run "twin deficits"—i.e., both balance of payments and government deficits. In the last few years of this stage, bubbles frequently occur.

Whether because of wars[3] or bursting financial bubbles or both,

[3] Germany in World War I and the UK in World War II are classic examples.

what typifies this stage is an accumulation of debt that can't be paid back in non-depreciated money. **I call countries in this stage "early declining countries."** While countries of all sizes can go through this stage, when big countries go through it, they are typically approaching their decline as great empires.

Stage 5: People and Their Countries Are Poor and They Think of Themselves as Poor. This is when the gaps described in Stage 4 cease to exist and the reality of the country's situation is hitting home. After bubbles burst and deleveragings occur, private debts grow, while private sector spending, asset values, and net worths decline in a self-reinforcing negative cycle. To compensate, government debt and government deficits grow, and central bank "printing" of money typically increases. Central banks and governments cut real interest rates and increase nominal GDP growth so that it is comfortably above nominal interest rates in order to ease debt burdens. As a result of these low real interest rates, weak currencies, and poor economic conditions, their debt and equity assets perform poorly. Increasingly, these countries have to compete with less expensive countries that are in earlier stages of development. Their currencies depreciate and they like it because it makes the deleveraging less painful. As an extension of these economic and financial trends, countries in this stage see their power in the world decline further. **I call countries in this stage "clearly declined countries."** It typically takes a long time—if it ever happens—for clearly declined empires' psychologies and attributes to go through the full cycle that brings them to their old peaks again. The Romans and the Greeks never have, though the Chinese have a few times.

11. Humanity's Inventiveness. ● ***Humanity's capacity to invent solutions to its problems and to identify how to make things better has proven to be far more powerful than all of its problems combined.*** Because knowledge is gained more than it is lost, it advances more in spurts and sputters than in cycles that have downs as well as ups. The spurts come when societies are in the upward swings of the Big Cycle and the sputters come when they are in the downward swings. The Renaissance periods of great creativity that produce advances in just about all areas—the sciences, the arts, philosophies about how people should be with each other and govern, etc.—come more during the peaceful and prosperous parts of the Big Cycle, when the systems for creating innovations are good rather than bad.

While specific inventions and the ways they come about have evolved through time, they have unwaveringly evolved toward doing and making things better, replacing manual labor with machines and automation, and making people around the world more interconnected. There are always new inventions and improvements. The most important and undeniable trend of technological advancement has been toward higher living standards. That trend is likely to accelerate in unimaginable ways. Beyond that, computerization is changing the character of decision making, making it faster and less emotional. As helpful as that is, it also poses certain dangers.

● ***The degree of inventiveness and innovation in a society is the main driver of its productivity.*** An innovative and commercial spirit is the lifeblood of a thriving economy. Without innovation, productivity growth would grind to a halt. Innovations that allow a country's workers to produce more relative to the rest of the world feed into their cost competitiveness, making them more attractive places to do business.

The drive to tinker and invent, to discover, to improve from prior failures—this is how people learn and find new and better ways of creating things of value. In a market-based system, the most powerful way to drive innovation is to bring new ideas to market and to commercialize and profit from them. The marketplace is incredibly efficient at weeding out bad ideas and pricing good ones. In this way the concepts of innovation and commercialism go hand in hand. They capture whether people in a society value new knowledge and the creation of new things, and whether incentives are aligned to encourage them to seek a profit by commercializing them.

In other words:

● ***Innovation + Commercial Spirit + Thriving Capital Markets***

=

Great Productivity Gains

=

Increases in Wealth and Power

Because there are big differences in the strengths of these determinants, I try to measure them and take them into consideration in my model.

17. Class Struggles. For as long as there has been recorded history, in almost all societies a very small percentage of the population (the "ruling classes" or "the elites") have controlled most of the wealth and power (though those percentages have varied).[4] Naturally those who benefit from and control the system by and large like the system and seek to maintain it. Because those with wealth can influence those with power and because those with power can influence those with wealth, these ruling classes or elites have alliances among themselves and want to maintain the existing order with everyone following its dictums and laws, even as the system increases the gaps between those with power and wealth and those without them. As a result, all internal orders are run by certain classes of people who have wealth and power and who operate in symbiotic relationships with each other to maintain the order. Though aligned not to disrupt the order that benefits them, throughout time these elites have struggled with each other over wealth and power and have also struggled with non-elites who want wealth and power. When times are good and most people prosper, the struggles are smaller; when times are bad, the struggles are worse. And when things are very bad for a large percentage of the people—e.g., there is an unresolvable debt crisis, a very

[4] For example, in the last century, the wealth share of the top 1 percent in the US ranged from close to 50 percent in the 1920s to a bit over 20 percent in the late 1970s; in the UK, it ranged from over 70 percent in 1900 to around 15 percent in the 1980s and is currently around 35 percent (figures from World Inequality Database). These shifts in inequality can be seen at least as far back as the Roman Republic, as Walter Scheidel describes in *The Great Leveler*.

bad economy, a very bad act of nature—the resulting suffering, stress, and struggles typically lead to revolutions and/or civil wars.

As Aristotle said a long time ago: "The poor and the rich quarrel with one another, and whichever side gets the better, instead of establishing a just or popular government, regards political supremacy as the prize of victory."

Classically, the Big Cycle transpires with periods of peace and productivity that increase wealth in a disproportionate way, which leads to a very small percentage of the population gaining and controlling exceptionally large percentages of the wealth and power, then becoming overextended, which leads to encountering bad times that hurt those who are the least wealthy and powerful the hardest, which then leads to conflicts that produce revolutions and/or civil wars, which then lead to the creation of a new order and the cycle beginning again.

● ***Throughout time and in all countries the people who have the wealth are the people who own the means of wealth production and, in order to maintain it, they work with the people who have the power to set and enforce the rules.*** While that has always been the case, the exact form of it has evolved and will continue to evolve.

For example, as explained in Chapter 1, for most of the 13th through 19th centuries, the prominent internal order all around the world consisted of the ruling classes or elites being 1) the monarchy, which ruled in conjunction with 2) the nobility, which controlled the means of production (at the time that capital was agricultural land), and/or 3) the military. Workers were viewed as part of the means of production and had essentially no say in how the order was run.

Even societies that had little or no contact with each other developed in similar ways because they had similar situations to deal with and because the nature of their decision making was similar.[5] Across

[5] For example, for much of history Europe, China, and most countries had monarchs and nobles as the ruling classes, yet they were a bit different. In Europe, the church was also part of the ruling mix. In Japan, the monarchy (the emperor and his ministers), the military, and the business community (the merchants and artisans) were the ruling elites.

countries there always were, and still are, different levels of governance at the country level, the state/province level, the municipality level, etc., and there are timeless and universal ways that they operate and interact with each other that have been pretty consistent across the world. The monarchs needed people to manage the day-to-day operations for them. The top people were ministers, who oversaw the bureaucracies of people who did the various jobs that needed to be done for government to work. What exists today is simply the result of the natural evolutions of these timeless and universal ways of interacting, with different countries' own cultural flavors thrown in. For example, the roles of the ministers who helped the monarchs evolved into the roles of prime ministers and other ministers that now exist in almost all countries (though in the United States they are called "secretaries").

Over time, these systems have evolved in varied but logical ways as a result of struggles for wealth and power. For example, in England around 1200 there was a wealth and power struggle that evolved gradually at first and then abruptly into a civil war, which is how these shifts tend to evolve, between the nobility and the monarchy. Like most of these struggles, the fight was over money and the power to determine who got how much money. The monarchy under King John wanted to get more tax money and the nobles wanted to give less tax money. They disagreed over how much say the nobles should have on the matter, so they had a civil war. The nobles won and gained more power to set the rules, which led to what they first called a "council," which soon became the first Parliament, which evolved into what exists in England today. The peace treaty that formalized this deal into law in 1215 is called the Magna Carta. Like most laws, this one didn't matter much relative to power so another civil war broke out in which the nobles and the monarchy again fought over wealth and power. In 1225 they wrote up a new Magna Carta under Henry III (King John's son), which those with power got to interpret and enforce. A few decades later, the fighting picked up again. In that war, the nobles cut off tax payments to the monarchy, which forced Henry III to give in to the nobles' demands. These struggles went on constantly, leading the orders to evolve.

Fast forward to the 15th, 16th, and 17th centuries and one can see that there were big changes in the sources of wealth, at first because of global exploration and colonialism (starting with the Portuguese and the Spanish) and later because of the invention of capitalism (stocks and bonds) and labor-saving machines that fueled the Industrial Revolutions (particularly helping the Dutch and then the British), which made those who profited from these sources of wealth more powerful—i.e., the shifts in wealth and power over these centuries were from a) landowning nobles (who then had the wealth) and monarchies (who then had the political power) to b) capitalists (who in the later period had the wealth) and elected representatives or autocratic government leaders (who in the later period had the political power). Almost all countries made these shifts—some peacefully but most painfully.

For example, in France for most of the 17th and 18th centuries, the king ruled in a balance of power arrangement with three other classes: 1) the clergy, 2) the nobility, and 3) the commoners. There were representatives of these groups who voted. The first two classes, who accounted for only 2 percent of the population, had more votes than—or eventually the same number of votes as—the commoners, who made up 98 percent of the population. They called this internal order based on three classes the ancien régime (which means "old order"). Then practically overnight it changed in a revolutionary way via the French Revolution, which began on May 5, 1789, when the third class—the commoners—had enough of that system, overthrew the others, and took the power for itself. In most countries around the world at the time, the same basic ruling order prevailed—i.e., the monarchy and nobles, who accounted for a very small percentage of the population and had most of the wealth, ruled until all of a sudden there was a civil war/revolution that led the old order to be replaced with a very different new ruling order.

Though the internal orders for managing these class struggles were and are different in different countries, they evolved similarly across countries. For example, they evolved both gradually (through reforms) and abruptly (through civil wars/revolutions) and they evolved into those orders that now exist in all countries. I expect they will continue to evolve gradually and abruptly to produce new domestic orders. While the classes who have the wealth and political power change, the processes that produce these changes have remained pretty much the same through time right up to today. These changes have occurred through struggles that have led to both a) peaceful reforms through negotiations and b) violent reforms via civil wars and revolutions. The peaceful reforms tend to come earlier in the cycle and the violent civil wars and revolutionary reforms tend to come later in the cycle for logical reasons that we will delve into later.

I cannot overstate the importance of class struggles relative to individual struggles. We, especially those of us in the United States, which is thought of as a "melting pot," tend to focus more on individual struggles and not give adequate attention to class struggles. I didn't fully realize the importance of class struggles until I did my extensive study of history, which led me to this principle:

● ***In all countries throughout time (though in varying degrees) people find themselves within "classes" either because they choose to be with people like them or because others stereotype them as part of certain groups.*** Power is usually shared among three or four classes. Who and what people feel most connected with, are around most, and are most like will determine which class or classes they are in; how people are classed determines who their friends or allies are and who their enemies are. While rich and poor and right (i.e., capitalist) and left (i.e., socialist) are the most common big class distinctions, there are many other important distinctions, such as race, ethnicity, religion, gender, lifestyle (e.g., liberal or conservative), and location (e.g., urban versus suburban versus rural). Generally speaking, people tend to cluster in these classes, and when times are good early in the cycle there is more harmony among these classes and when things are bad there is more fighting among them.

While I love that the United States is the country where these class distinctions matter least, people's classes still matter in the US and they matter a lot more during stressful times when class conflicts intensify.

To help you get the picture in a more intimate way, let's do a simple exercise. Assume that most people who don't know you well look at you as being in a member of one or several classes, because that's a good assumption. Now, to imagine how you are perceived, look at the following list and ask yourself which classes you fall into. After you answer that, ask yourself which classes you feel an affinity for and expect to be your allies. Which classes do you not like or view as your enemies? Which ones are the ruling classes, and which ones are the revolutionary classes who want to topple them? Which ones are on the ascent, and which ones are on the decline? You might consider writing these down and thinking about them because during periods of greater conflict the classes you are in or are assumed to be in will become more important in determining who you will be with and against, what you will do, and where you will end up.

1. **Rich or poor?**
2. **Right, left, or moderate?**
3. **Race?**
4. **Ethnicity?**
5. **Religion?**
6. **Gender?**
7. **Lifestyle (e.g., liberal or conservative)?**
8. **Location (e.g., urban, suburban, or rural)?**

Still today only a small percentage of the population, which comes from only a few of these classes, has most of the wealth and power and rules as "the elites." To me it is clear that the capitalist class now has the most financial power in most countries and political power in democracies lies in the hands of all the people who choose to vote, while in autocracies it lies in the hands of the limited number of people selected by whatever process they have to make selections.[6] So, for

[6] That doesn't mean that those who run autocracies don't ultimately report to the people because the people could overthrow the government.

the most part today, those are the "ruling classes" and "the elites" who oversee the current domestic orders, though they are now under attack, so this is probably shifting. For example, there is now a big movement in the United States to be much more inclusive of members of different classes in both the capitalist money-making world and in the political world. These shifts can be good or bad depending on whether they are handled peacefully or violently and smartly or stupidly. **One timeless and universal truth that I saw go back as far as I studied history, since before Confucius who lived around 500 BCE, is that** ● ***those societies that draw on the widest range of people and give them responsibilities based on their merits rather than privileges are the most sustainably successful because 1) they find the best talent to do their jobs well, 2) they have diversity of perspectives, and 3) they are perceived as the fairest, which fosters social stability.***

I presume that the current internal orders of countries, like those of the past, will continue evolving to become something different through the struggles of different classes with each other over how to divide wealth and political power. Because this wealth and power dynamic is very important, it is worth watching closely to discern which classes are gaining and which ones are losing wealth and power (e.g., AI and information technology developers are now evolving to gain it at the expense of those who are being replaced by such technologies) and also to discern the reactions to these shifts that lead the cycles to change.

So, as I see it, everything is changing in classic ways driven by a tried-and-true perpetual-motion machine. This machine has produced, and is producing, different systems, such as communism, fascism, autocracies, democracies, and evolutionary descendants and hybrids of these, such as "state capitalism" in China. It will produce new forms of internal orders to divide wealth and allocate political power that will affect our lives greatly, all based on how people choose to be with each other and how human nature enters into how they make their choices.

18. The Political Left/Right Cycle. Capitalists (i.e., those of the right) and socialists (i.e., those of the left) don't just have different self-interests—they have different deep-seated ideological beliefs that they are willing to fight for. The typical perspective of the rightist/capitalist is that self-sufficiency, hard work, productivity, limited government interference, allowing people to keep what they make, and individual choice are morally good and good for society. They also believe that the private sector works better than the public sector, that capitalism works best for most people, and that self-made billionaires are the biggest contributors to society. Capitalists are typically driven crazy by financial supports for people who lack productivity and profitability. To them, making money = being productive = getting what one deserves. They don't pay much attention to whether the economic machine is producing opportunity and prosperity for most people. They can also overlook the fact that their form of profit making is suboptimal when it comes to achieving the goals of most people. For example, in a purely capitalist system, the provision of excellent public education—which is clearly a leading cause of higher productivity and greater wealth across a society—is not a high priority.

The typical perspective of the leftist/socialist is that helping each other, having the government support people, and sharing wealth and opportunity are morally good and good for society. They believe that the private sector is by and large run by capitalists who are greedy, while common workers, such as teachers, firefighters, and laborers, contribute more to society. Socialists and communists tend to focus on dividing the pie well and typically aren't very good at increasing its size. They favor more government intervention, believing those in government will be fairer than capitalists, who are simply trying to exploit people to make more money.

I've had exposure to all kinds of economic systems all over the world and have seen why ● ***the ability to make money, save it, and put it into capital (i.e., capitalism) is an effective motivator of people and allocator of resources that raises people's living standards. But capitalism is also a source of wealth and opportunity gaps that are unfair, can be counterproductive, are highly cyclical, and can be destabilizing. In my opinion, the greatest challenge for policy makers is***

to engineer a capitalist economic system that raises productivity and living standards without worsening inequities and instabilities.

21. The Big Balance of Power Cycle That Drives the Big Peace/War Cycle Both Within Countries and Between Countries. In studying a lot of history and experiencing a tiny sliver of it myself I have seen how the balance of power dynamic drives virtually all struggles for power—e.g., office politics within organizations, local and national politics in shaping the domestic order, and international politics in shaping the world order. It applies equally well to determining the formations and changes in world orders as in domestic orders. The dynamic transpires in a series of steps explained here, though how exactly it unfolds depends on the order and people at the time these stages unfold:

Step 1: The formation of alliances. When there isn't roughly equal power (e.g., if in the US the Democrats have much more power than the Republicans or vice versa), the more powerful party will take advantage of and control the less powerful party. To neutralize the stronger party, the weaker party naturally finds other parties to join it in opposing the stronger party so collectively they can have the same or more power as the opposition. The weaker party does this by giving the other parties what they want in return for their support. If the formerly weaker party collectively gains more power than the formerly stronger party from doing this, the formerly stronger party cuts deals with other parties to ally with them to eliminate the superiority of the opposition. As a result, allies who have very different vested interests unite in opposing the common enemy—as the saying goes, "the enemy of my enemy is my friend." This dynamic naturally leads to the different sides having roughly equal amounts of power and splits within themselves. Sometimes the differences within the parties are so great that some segments want to destroy the other segments in order to gain control of their party. This alliance- and enemy-forming dynamic happens at all different levels of relationships, from the most important international alliances that define the most important elements of the world order down to the most important alliances within countries that define the internal orders, down to those within states, within cities, within organizations, and among individuals. The most important evolutionary shift to affect these has been the shrinking of the world to make allies and enemies more global. In the old days they were less global (e.g., European countries formed alliances to fight other European countries, Asian countries did the same in Asia, etc.), but as the world has shrunk because of improved transportation and communications it has become more interconnected and bigger and more global alliances have developed. That is why there were two big sides in World Wars I and II and likely will be going forward.

Step 2: War to determine the winners and losers. Big fights typically happen when both sides have roughly equal powers and existential differences exist between them. Big fights typically don't occur when there are big asymmetries in power because it would be stupid for obviously weaker entities to fight obviously stronger ones, and if they did fight, the fights would be small in scale. However, sometimes when there are roughly equal levels of power on both sides, stalemates and gridlocks rather than big fights can occur when the existential threat of harming oneself in the process of trying to beat the other side is greater than the gains that would come from having a fight to the death. For example, when there is mutually assured destruction—e.g., as the US and the Soviet Union faced—there is more likely to be a stand-off than a fight.

While these big fights are typically violent, they can be nonviolent if the entities have nonviolent rules of engagement that they adhere to that allow the resolution of disputes, most importantly the existential ones. For example, in the 2020 US election, the two political parties had roughly equal amounts of power and irreconcilable differences so that they had a big fight for political control. That led to the storming of the US Capitol on January 6, 2021, but eventually the peaceful transfer of political power as set out in the Constitution prevailed. History has shown that, when there are not clear rules and/or when the parties don't abide by them, the fighting will be far more brutal, often to the death.

Step 3: Fighting among the winners. History shows us that after the fight for power in which the common enemy is defeated, those who united against the common enemy typically fight among themselves for power and those in the losing party do the same as they plan their next attack. I call this the "purge" state of the balance of power dynamic. It has happened in all cases, with the Reign of Terror in France and the Red Terror in the Soviet Union being the most well-known. This same sort of fighting has happened between countries, as with the US and the Soviet Union, who were allies in World War II. Similarly, the united front of Chinese communists and nationalists that fought the Japanese in the war immediately battled each other for power when the war was over. Understanding this typical dynamic, one should look out for internal fighting among the winners right after the big war is over. We should always watch whether the factions within the same parties are inclined to fight each other for control of their parties. When new regimes (i.e., the winning parties) come to power watch what they do with the enemies they defeated. What happens next depends on the system and the leaders in the system. In the US and generally in democracies, the rules allow the losers to remain unharmed and unconstrained, which allows them to try to regain power and fight again. In harsh autocracies, the losers are eliminated one way or another.

Step 4: Peace and prosperity occur but eventually lead to excesses reflected in large wealth and opportunity gaps and overindebtedness. History shows us that because of this dynamic the best of times—i.e., when there is peace and prosperity—typically happens after a war, when the leadership and power structure are clearly established so there isn't big fighting for power within the country or with other countries—because there is an obviously more powerful entity that enables the less powerful entities to have a good life.

Step 5: Increasing conflict leads to revolutionary changes in domestic and world orders. For as long as there is peace and prosperity for the majority of the people, which will only be the case if the system is fair and the majority of the people remain self-disciplined and productive, peace and prosperity are likely to continue. However, as previously discussed, periods of peace and prosperity also tend to encourage big wealth gaps and debt bubbles that lead to conflicts when prosperity fades and there are other things to fight over.

This cycle tracks the internal and external order and disorder cycles that we will explore in Chapters 5 and 6.

CHAPTER 3

THE BIG CYCLE OF MONEY, CREDIT, DEBT, AND ECONOMIC ACTIVITY

What most people and their countries want most is wealth and power, and money and credit are the biggest influences on how wealth and power rise and decline. If you don't understand how money and credit work, you can't understand how the system works, and if you don't understand how the system works, you can't understand what's coming at you.

For example, if you don't understand how the Roaring '20s led to a debt bubble and a big wealth gap, how the bursting of that debt bubble led to the 1930–33 Great Depression, and how the depression led to conflicts over wealth all over the world, you won't understand why Franklin D. Roosevelt was elected president in 1932. You also won't understand why, soon after his inauguration, he announced a new plan in which the central government and the Federal Reserve would together provide a lot of money and credit, a change that was similar to what was happening in other countries at the time and that is similar to what is happening today in response to the pandemic-caused crisis. Unless you understand how money and credit work, you can't understand why the world changed as it did in 1933 or what happened next (World War II), how the war was won and lost, and why the new world order was created as it was in 1945. But when you can recognize the underlying mechanics that drove all of those things in the past, you can also understand what is happening now and have a much better sense about what is likely to happen in the future.

In speaking with several of the world's most renowned historians and political practitioners, including current and former heads of state, foreign ministers, finance ministers, and central bankers, we recognized that we each held different pieces of the puzzle to explain how the world works. I had been lacking an adequate practical understanding of the workings of politics and geopolitics, and they lacked an adequate practical understanding of the way that money and credit work. Several told me that understanding money and credit in this way has been the biggest missing piece in their quest to understand the lessons of history, and I explained to them that their perspectives helped me understand the political dynamics that affect policy choices. This chapter is focused on the money, credit, and economic piece.

Let's start with money and credit.

THE TIMELESS AND UNIVERSAL FUNDAMENTALS OF MONEY AND CREDIT

● ***All entities—people, companies, nonprofit organizations, and governments—deal with the same basic financial realities, and always have.* They have money that comes in (i.e., revenue) and money that goes out (i.e., expenses) that, when netted, make up their net income. These flows are measured in numbers that appear in income statements. If an entity brings in more than it spends, it has a profit that causes its savings to go up. If it spends more than it earns, its savings go down, or it makes up the difference by borrowing or taking money from someone else. If an entity has many more assets than liabilities (i.e., a large net worth), it can spend above its income by selling assets until the money runs out, at which point it has to slash its expenses. If it doesn't have much more in assets than it has in liabilities and its income falls beneath the amount it**

needs to pay out to cover the total of its operating expenses and its debt-service expenses, it will have to cut its expenses or will default or restructure its debts.

All of an entity's assets and liabilities (i.e., debts) can be shown in its balance sheet. Whether it writes those numbers down or not, every country, company, nonprofit organization, and individual has them. When economists, for example, combine each entity's income, expenses, and savings, they get all entities' incomes, expenses, and savings. ● ***The way entities collectively handle their finances as reflected in their income statements and balance sheets is the biggest driver of changes in internal and world orders.*** **If you can take your understanding of your own income, expenses, and savings, imagine how that applies to others, and put them together, you will see how the whole thing works.**

Take a moment to think about your own financial situation. How much income do you have now relative to your expenses and how much will you have in the future? How much savings do you have and what are those savings invested in? Now play things out. If your income fell or disappeared, how long would your savings last? How much risk do you have in the value of your investments and savings? If that value fell by half, how would you be financially? Can you easily sell your assets to get cash to pay your expenses or service your debts? What are your other sources of money, from the government or from elsewhere? These are the most important calculations you can make to ensure your economic well-being. Now look at others—other people, businesses, nonprofit organizations, and governments—realizing that the same is true for them. See how we are interconnected and what changes in conditions might mean for you and others who might affect you. Since the economy is the sum of these entities operating in this way, it will help you understand what is happening and what is likely to happen.

For example, since one entity's spending is another's income, when one entity cuts its expenses, that will hurt not just that entity, but it will also hurt others who depend on that spending to earn income. Similarly, since one entity's debts are another's assets, an

entity that defaults reduces other entities' assets, which requires them to cut their spending. This dynamic produces a self-reinforcing downward debt and economic contraction that becomes a political issue as people argue over how to divide the shrunken pie.

As a principle, ● ***debt eats equity.*** **What I mean by that is that debts have to be paid above all else. For example, if you own a house (i.e., you have "equity" ownership) and you can't make the mortgage payments, the house will be sold or taken away. In other words, the creditor will get paid ahead of the owner of the house. As a result, when your income is less than your expenses and your assets are less than your liabilities (i.e., debts), you are on the way to having to sell your assets.**

Unlike what most people intuitively think, **there isn't a fixed amount of money and credit in existence. Money and credit can easily be created by central banks. People, companies, nonprofit organizations, and governments like it when central banks make a lot of money and credit because it gives them more spending power. When the money and credit are spent, it makes most goods, services, and investment assets go up in price. It also creates debt that has to be repaid, which requires people, companies, nonprofit organizations, and governments to eventually spend less than they earn, which is difficult and painful. That is why money, credit, debt, and economic activity are inherently cyclical. In the credit-creation phase, demand for goods, services, and investment assets and the production of them are both strong, and in the debt-repayment phase, both are weak.**

But what if the debts never had to be paid back? Then there would be no debt squeeze and no painful paying back period. But that would be terrible for those who lent because they'd lose their money, right? Let's think for a moment to see if we can find a way of resolving debt issues without harming either borrowers or lenders.

Since governments have the ability to both make and borrow money, why couldn't the central bank lend money at an interest rate of about 0 percent to the central government to distribute as it likes to support the economy? Couldn't it also lend to others at low rates and allow those debtors to never pay it back? Normally debtors have to pay back the original amount borrowed (principal) plus interest in installments over a period of time. But the central bank has the power to set the interest rate at 0 percent and keep rolling over the debt so that the debtor never has to pay it back. That would be the equivalent of giving the debtors the money, but it wouldn't look that way because the debt would still be accounted for as an asset that the central bank owns, so the central bank could still say it is performing its normal lending functions. **This is the exact thing that happened in the wake of the economic crisis caused by the COVID-19 pandemic. Many versions of this have happened many times in history. Who pays? It is bad for those outside the central bank who still hold the debts as assets—cash and bonds—who won't get returns that would preserve their purchasing power.**

The biggest problem that we now collectively face is that for many people, companies, nonprofit organizations, and governments, their incomes are low in relation to their expenses, and their debts and other liabilities (such as those for pensions, healthcare, and insurance) are very large relative to the value of their assets. It may not seem that way—in fact, it often seems the opposite—because there are many people, companies, nonprofit organizations, and governments that look rich even while they are in the process of going broke. They look rich because they spend a lot, have plenty of assets, and even have plenty of cash. However, if you look carefully, you will be able to identify those that look rich but are in financial trouble because they have incomes that are below their expenses and/or liabilities that are greater than their assets, so if you project what will likely happen to their finances in the future, you will see that they will have to cut their expenses and sell their assets in painful ways that will leave them broke. We each need to do those projections of what the future will look like for our own finances, for others who are relevant to us, and for the world economy. In a nutshell, for some people, companies, nonprofit organizations, and countries, **the liabilities are enormous relative to the net incomes and the asset values that are required to meet those obligations, so they are financially weak, but they don't**

look that way because they spend a lot financed by borrowing.

If anything I've written here is confusing to you, I urge you to take a moment to try to apply it to your own circumstances. Pencil out what your financial safety margin looks like (how long will you be financially OK if the worst-case scenario happens—e.g., you lose your job and your investment assets fall to be only half as much to account for possible price falls, taxes, and inflation). Then do that calculation for others, add them up, and then you will have a good picture of the state of your world. I've done that with the help of my partners at Bridgewater and find it invaluable in imagining what is likely to happen.[1]

In summary, these basic financial realities work for all people, companies, nonprofit organizations, and governments in the same way they work for you and me, with the one big, important exception I mentioned earlier. All countries can create money and credit out of the air to give to people to spend or lend out. By producing money and giving it to debtors in need, central banks can prevent the debt crisis dynamic that I just explained. For that reason I will modify the prior principle to say: ● ***debt eats equity but central banks can feed debt by printing money instead.*** It should be no surprise that governments print money when debt crises cause politically unacceptable amounts of equity-eating debt and corresponding economic pain.

However, not all money that governments print is of equal value.

The monies (i.e., currencies) that are widely accepted around the world are called reserve currencies. At the time of my writing this, the world's dominant reserve currency is the US dollar, which is created by the US central bank, the Federal Reserve. A much less important reserve currency is the euro, which is produced by the Eurozone countries' central bank, the European Central Bank. The Japanese yen, the Chinese renminbi, and the British pound are relatively small reserve currencies now, though the renminbi is quickly growing in importance.

● ***Having a reserve currency is great while it lasts because it gives***

[1] You can find more of my perspective on this in several papers at economicprinciples.org.

a country exceptional borrowing and spending power and significant power over who else in the world gets the money and credit needed to buy and sell internationally. However, having a reserve currency typically sows the seeds of a country ceasing to be a reserve currency country. That is because it allows the country to borrow more than it could otherwise afford to borrow, and the creation of lots of money and credit to service the debt debases the value of the currency and causes the loss of its status as a reserve currency. The loss of its reserve currency status is a terrible thing because ● ***having a reserve currency is one of the greatest powers a country can have because it gives the country enormous buying power and geopolitical power.***

In contrast, non-reserve currency countries often find themselves in need of money in a reserve currency (e.g., dollars) when they have a lot of debt denominated in that currency, which they can't print, or they don't have much savings in that currency and their ability to earn the currency they need falls off. **When countries desperately need reserve currencies to service their reserve currency-denominated debts, and to buy things from sellers who only accept reserve currencies, they can go bankrupt.** This has happened often in the past and it is where things now stand for a number of countries. It is also where things stand for local governments and states and for many of us. This configuration of circumstances has been handled in the same way, so it's easy to see how this machine works—and that is what I will show you in this chapter.

Let's start with the basics and build from there.

WHAT IS MONEY?

Money is a medium of exchange that can also be used as a storehold of wealth.

By "medium of exchange," I mean something that can be given to others to buy things. Basically, people produce things in order to exchange them with people who have other things they want. Because carrying around non-money objects in the hope of exchanging them for what one wants (i.e., bartering) is inefficient, virtually every society that has ever existed has created a form of money (i.e., currency), which is something portable that everyone agrees is of value so it can be exchanged for what they want.

By a "storehold of wealth," I mean a vehicle for storing buying power between acquiring it and spending it. While one of the most logical things to store wealth in is a claim on money that can be used later, people also store their wealth in assets that they expect will retain their value or appreciate (such as gold, silver, gems, paintings, real estate, stocks, and bonds). By holding on to something that appreciates, they figure that they can do a bit better than just holding on to the currency—and, when needed, can always exchange the thing they're holding to get the currency to buy the things they want to buy. This is where credit and debt come into the picture. It is important to understand the difference between money and debt. Money is what settles claims—you pay your bills and are done. Debt is a promise to deliver money.

When lenders lend, for example, they assume the money plus the interest they receive back will buy more goods and services than if they had simply held on to the money. When all goes well, the borrowers use the money productively and earn a profit with it themselves, so they can pay the lenders back and still have money left over. While the loan is outstanding, it is an asset for the lender (e.g., a bond) and a liability (i.e., debt) for the borrower. When the money is paid back, the assets and liabilities disappear, and both the borrower and lender are better off, having essentially split the profits that came from the productive lending. Such lending is also good for society, which benefits from the resulting productivity gains.[2]

It's important to realize that **most money and credit (especially**

[2] While borrowers are typically willing to pay interest, which is what gives lenders the incentive to lend, nowadays there are some debt assets that have negative interest rates, which is a weird story that we will explore later.

the government-issued money that now exists) have no intrinsic value. They are just journal entries in an accounting system that can easily be changed. The purpose of that system is to help allocate resources efficiently so that productivity can grow, rewarding both lenders and borrowers, but the system periodically breaks down. When that happens (as it always has, since the beginning of time), the currency supply is "monetized"[3] and currency values fall or are destroyed, and wealth shifts in a big way, sending shockwaves through the economy and markets.

What all this means is that the debt and credit machine doesn't work perfectly. Supplies, demands, and values of money cycle up and down. The upswings produce joyful abundance. The downswings produce painful restructurings.

Let's now get into how these cycles work, building from the fundamentals up to where we are now.

MONEY, CREDIT, AND WEALTH

While money and credit are associated with wealth, they aren't the same thing as wealth. Because money and credit can buy wealth (i.e., goods and services), the amount of money and credit you have and the amount of wealth you have look pretty much the same. But you cannot create more wealth simply by creating more money and credit. To create more wealth, you have to be more productive. The relationship between the creation of money and credit and the creation of wealth is often confused, yet it is the biggest driver of economic cycles. Let's look at it more closely.

There is typically a mutually reinforcing relationship between the creation of money and credit and the creation of goods, services, and investment assets that are produced, which is why they're often confused as being the same thing. **Think of it this way: there is both**

[3] Monetized means the central bank's creation of money to buy debt.

a financial economy and a real economy. Though they are related, they are different. Each has its own supply-and-demand factors that drive it. In the real economy, supply and demand are driven by the amount of goods and services produced and the number of buyers who want them. When the level of goods and services demanded is strong and rising and there is not enough capacity to produce the things demanded, the real economy's capacity to grow is limited. If demand keeps rising faster than the capacity to produce, prices go up and inflation rises. That's where the financial economy comes in. Facing inflation, central banks normally tighten money and credit to slow demand in the real economy; when there is too little demand, they do the opposite by providing money and credit to stimulate demand. **By raising and lowering supplies of money and credit, central banks are able to raise and lower the demand and production of financial assets, goods, and services.** But they're unable to do this perfectly, so we have the short-term debt cycle, which we experience as alternating periods of growth and recession.

Then of course there is the value of money and credit to consider, which is based on its own supply and demand. When a lot of a currency is created relative to the demand for it, it declines in value. Where the money and credit flow is important to determining what happens. For example, when they no longer go into lending that fuels increases in economic demand and instead go into other currencies and inflation-hedge assets, they fail to stimulate economic activity and instead cause the value of the currency to decline and the value of inflation-hedge assets to rise. At such times high inflation can occur because the supply of money and credit has increased relative to the demand for it, which we call "monetary inflation." That can happen at the same time as there is weak demand for goods and services and the selling of assets so that the real economy is experiencing deflation. That is how inflationary depressions come about. For these reasons **we have to watch movements in the supplies and demands of both the real economy and the financial economy to understand what is likely to happen financially and economically.**

For example, how financial assets are produced by the government through fiscal and monetary policy has a huge effect on who gets the buying power that goes along with them, which also determines what the buying power is spent on. Normally money and credit are created by central banks and flow into financial assets, which the private credit system uses to finance people's borrowing and spending. But in moments of crisis, governments can choose where to direct money, credit, and buying power rather than it being allocated by the marketplace, and capitalism as we know it is suspended. This is what happened worldwide in response to the COVID-19 pandemic.

Related to this confusion between the financial economy and the real economy is the relationship between the prices of things and the value of things. Because they tend to go together, they can be confused as being the same thing. They tend to go together because when people have more money and credit, they are more inclined to spend more and can spend more. To the extent that spending increases economic production and raises the prices of goods, services, and financial assets, it can be said to increase wealth because the people who already own those assets become "richer" when measured by the way we account for wealth. However, that increase in wealth is more an illusion than a reality for two reasons: 1) the increased credit that pushes prices and production up has to be paid back, which, all things being equal, will have the opposite effect when the bill comes due and 2) the intrinsic value of a thing doesn't increase just because its price goes up.

Think about it this way: if you own a house and the government creates a lot of money and credit, there might be many eager buyers who would push the price of your house up. But it's still the same house; your actual wealth hasn't increased, just your calculated wealth. It's the same with any other investment asset you own that goes up in price when the government creates money—stocks, bonds, etc. The amount of calculated wealth goes up but the amount of actual wealth hasn't gone up because you own the exact same thing you did before it was considered to be worth more. In other words, using the market values of what one owns to measure one's wealth gives an illusion of changes in wealth that don't really exist. As far as understanding how the economic machine works, the important thing to understand is that **money and credit are stimulative when they're given out and depressing when they have to be paid back. That's what normally makes money, credit, and economic growth so cyclical.**

The central bankers who control money and credit (i.e., central banks) vary the costs and availability of money and credit to control markets and the economy. When the economy is growing too quickly and they want to slow it down, central bankers make less money and credit available, causing both to become more expensive. This encourages people to lend rather than borrow and spend. When there is too little growth and central bankers want to stimulate the economy, they make money and credit cheap and plentiful, which encourages people to borrow and invest and/or spend. These variations in the cost and availability of money and credit also cause the prices and quantities of goods, services, and investment assets to rise and fall. But banks can only control the economy within their capacities to produce money and credit growth, and their capacities to do that are limited.

Think of the central bank as having a bottle of stimulant it can inject into the economy as needed. When the markets and the economy sag, it delivers shots of the money and credit stimulant to pick them up. When the markets and economy are too strong, it gives them less or no stimulant. These moves lead to cyclical rises and declines in the amounts and prices of money and credit, and of goods, services, and financial assets. These moves typically come in the form of short-term debt cycles and long-term debt cycles. The short-term debt cycles of ups and downs typically last about eight years, give or take a few. The timing is determined by how long it takes the stimulant to raise demand to the point that it reaches the limits of the real economy's capacity to produce. Most people have seen enough of these short-term debt cycles—popularly known as "the business cycle"—to know what they are like, to such an extent that they mistakenly think they will go on working this way forever.

I distinguish them from the long-term debt cycle, which typically plays out over 50 to 75 years (and so contains about six to 10 short-term debt cycles).[4] Because the crises that occur as these long-term debt cycles play out happen only once in a lifetime, most people don't expect them. As a result they typically take people by surprise and do a lot of harm. **The long-term debt cycle that is now in the late-cycle phase was designed in 1944 in Bretton Woods, New Hampshire, and began in 1945, when World War II ended and the dollar/US-dominated world order began.**

These long-term debt cycles are driven by the amount of stimulant left in the central bank's bottle. They start after previously existing excess debts have been restructured and central banks have a full bottle of stimulant. They end when debts are high and the bottle of stimulant is nearly empty or, more specifically, **when the central bank loses its ability to produce money and credit growth that passes through the economic system to produce real economic growth. Throughout history, central governments and central banks have created money and credit, which weakened their own currencies and raised their levels of monetary inflation to offset the deflation that comes from deflationary credit and economic contractions. This typically happens when debt levels are high, interest rates can't be adequately lowered, and the creation of money and credit increases financial asset prices more than it increases actual economic activity. At such times those who are holding the debt (which is someone else's promise to give them currency) typically want to exchange the debt they are holding for other storeholds of wealth. Once it is widely perceived that money and debt assets are no longer good storeholds of wealth, the long-term debt cycle is at its end, and a restructuring of the monetary system has to occur.**

Since these cycles are big deals and have happened virtually

---

[4] By the way, please understand that these rough estimates of cycle times are just rough estimates, and to know where we are in these cycles we need to look more at the conditions than the amount of time.

everywhere for all of recorded history, we need to understand them and have timeless and universal principles for dealing with them well. But most people, including many economists, don't even acknowledge their existence. That's because to get a sample size of observations that is large and diverse enough to give one a good understanding, one has to have studied them over many hundreds of years in many different countries. In Part II we will do just that, examining the most important of these cycles across history and around the world, with reference to the timeless and universal mechanics of why money and credit work and fail to work as mediums of exchange and storeholds of wealth. In this chapter, I will synthesize all those cases so I can show you how they work archetypically.

I will begin with the basics of the long-term debt cycle from way back when and bring you up to the present, giving you the classic template. To be clear, I'm not saying that all cases transpire exactly like this one, but I am saying that they almost all follow this pattern closely.

THE LONG-TERM DEBT CYCLE

The long-term debt cycle transpires in six stages:

Stage 1: It begins with a) little or no debt and b) money being "hard."

The debt burdens from the last cycle were largely wiped out by restructuring and debt monetization, and because of the consequences of these, particularly inflation, there is a return to hard money like gold and silver (and sometimes copper and other metals like nickel) or sometimes a link to a hard currency. For example, after the destruction of debt and money in Germany's Weimar Republic money became backed by gold-denominated assets and land and pegged to the dollar, and after its destruction in Argentina in the late 1980s money became linked to the dollar.

At this stage, money being "hard" is important because no trust—or credit—is required to carry out an exchange. Any transaction can be settled on the spot, even if the buyer and seller are strangers or enemies. There is an old saying that "gold is the only financial asset that isn't someone else's liability." When you receive gold coins from a buyer, you can melt them down and exchange the metal and still receive almost the same value as if you had spent them, unlike a debt asset like paper money, which is a promise to deliver value (which isn't much of a promise, given how easy it is to print). When countries are at war and there is no trust in their intentions or abilities to pay, they can still pay in gold. So gold (and, to a lesser extent, silver) can be used as both a safe medium of exchange and a safe storehold of wealth.

Stage 2: Then come claims on hard money (i.e., notes or paper money).

Because carrying a lot of metal money around is risky and inconvenient and creating credit is attractive to both lenders and borrowers, credible parties arise that put the hard money in a safe place and issue paper claims on it. These parties came to be known as "banks," though they initially included all sorts of institutions that people trusted, such as temples in China. **Soon people treat these paper "claims on money" as if they are money itself.** After all, they can be redeemed for tangible money or used to buy things directly. This type of currency system is called a "linked currency system" because the value of the currency is linked to the value of something, typically "hard money," such as gold and silver.

Stage 3: Then comes increased debt.

At first there are the same number of claims on the "hard money" as there is hard money in the bank. Then the holders of paper claims and the banks discover the wonders of credit and debt. Holders of paper claims loan them to banks in exchange for interest payments. The banks like to do that because they can lend the money to others who can pay a higher interest rate, allowing the banks to make a profit. Those who borrow from the bank like it because it gives them buying power they didn't previously have. And the whole society likes it because it leads asset prices and production to rise. Since everyone is happy with how things are going, they do a lot of it. More lending and borrowing happens over and over again many times, there is a boom, and the quantity of the claims on the money (i.e., debt assets) rises relative to the amount of actual goods and services there are to buy. Eventually the claims become much larger than the actual hard money in the bank.

Trouble approaches when there isn't enough income to service one's debts, or when the amount of claims people are holding in the expectation that they can sell them to get money to buy goods and services increases faster than the amount of goods and services by an amount that makes the conversion from that debt asset (e.g., a bond) impossible. These two problems tend to come together.

Concerning the first of these problems, think of debt as negative earnings and a negative asset that eats up earnings (because earnings have to go to pay it) and eats up other assets (because other assets have to be sold to get the money to pay the debt). It is senior—meaning it gets paid before any other type of asset—so when incomes and the values of assets fall, there is a need to cut expenditures and sell off assets to raise the needed cash. When that's not enough, there needs to be a) debt restructurings (in which debts and debt burdens are reduced, which is problematic for both the debtor and the creditor because one person's debts are another's assets) and/or b) the central bank printing money paired with the central government handing out money and credit to fill in the holes in incomes and balance sheets (which is what is happening now).

Stage 4: Then debt crises, defaults, and devaluations come, which leads to the printing of money and the breaking of the link to hard money.

As for the second problem, this happens when holders of debt don't believe they are going to get adequate returns from it relative to other storeholds of wealth and the costs of goods and services. Debt assets (e.g., bonds) are held by investors who believe they are storeholds of wealth that can be sold to get money, which can be used to buy things. When holders of debt assets try to make the conversion to real money and real goods and services and find out that they can't, a "run" occurs, by which I mean that lots of holders of that debt try to make the conversion to money, goods, services, and other financial assets. The bank, regardless of whether it is a private bank or a central bank, is then faced with the choice of allowing that flow of money out of the debt asset, which will raise interest rates and cause the debt and economic problems to worsen, or of printing money, in the form of issuing bonds and buying enough of the bonds to prevent interest rates from rising and hopefully reverse the run out of them. Inevitably the central bank breaks the link, prints the money, and devalues it because not doing that causes an intolerable deflationary depression. The key at this stage is to create enough money and devaluation to offset the deflationary depression but not so much as to produce an inflationary spiral. When this is done well, I call it a "beautiful deleveraging," which I describe more completely in my book *Principles for Navigating Big Debt Crises.* Sometimes that buying works temporarily; however, if the ratio of claims on money (debt assets) to the amount of "hard" money there is and the quantity of goods and services there is to buy are too high, the bank is in a bind that it can't get out of. It simply doesn't have enough "hard" money to meet the claims. When that happens to a central bank it has the choice either to default or to break the link to the hard money, print the money, and devalue it. Inevitably the central bank devalues. When these debt restructurings and currency devaluations are too big, they lead to the breakdown and possible destruction of the monetary system. The more debt (i.e., claims on money and claims on goods and services) there is, the more it will be necessary to devalue the money.

Remember, there is always a limited amount of goods and services because the amount is constrained by the economy's ability to produce. Also remember that, as shown in our example of paper money being claims on hard money, there is a limited amount of that hard money (e.g., gold on deposit), while the amount of paper money (the claims on that hard money) and debt (the claims on that paper money) is constantly growing. As the amount of paper money claims grows relative to the amount of hard money in the bank and goods and services in the economy, the risk increases that the holders of those debt assets may not be able to redeem them for the amounts of hard money or goods and services that they expect to receive for them.

A bank that can't deliver enough hard money to meet the claims being made on it is in trouble whether it is a private bank or a central bank, though central banks have more options than private banks. That's because a private bank can't print the money or change the laws to make it easier to pay their debts, while some central banks can. **Private banks must either default or get bailed out by the government when they get into trouble, while central banks can devalue their claims (e.g., pay back 50–70 percent) if their debts are denominated in their national currency. If the debt is denominated in a currency that they can't print, then they too must ultimately default.**

Stage 5: Then comes fiat money, which eventually leads to the debasement of money.

Central banks want to stretch the money and credit cycle to make it last for as long as it can because that is so much better than the alternative. So when the system of hard money and claims on hard money becomes too painfully constrictive, governments typically abandon it in favor of what is called "fiat money." No hard money is involved in fiat systems; there is just paper money that the central bank can print without restriction. As a result, there is no risk that the central bank will have its stash of hard money drawn down and have to default on its promises to deliver it. Rather, the risk is that, freed from the constraints on the supply of tangible gold, silver, or some other hard asset, the people who control the printing presses (i.e., the central bankers working with the commercial bankers) will create ever more money and debt assets and liabilities in relation to the amount of goods and services being produced until the time comes when those holding the enormous amount of debt will try to turn it in for goods and services, which will have the same effect as a run on a bank and result in either debt defaults or the devaluation of money.

The shift from a system in which the debt notes are convertible to a tangible asset (e.g., gold and silver) at a fixed rate to a fiat monetary system in which there is no such convertibility last happened in the US on the evening of August 15, 1971. As I mentioned earlier, I was watching on TV when President Nixon told the world that the dollar would no longer be tied to gold. I thought there would be pandemonium with stocks falling. Instead, they rose. Because I had never seen a devaluation before, I didn't understand how it works.

In the years leading up to 1971 the US government had spent a lot of money on military and social programs, then referred to as "guns and butter" policy, that it paid for by borrowing money, which created debt. The debt was a claim on money that could be exchanged for gold. Investors treated this debt as an asset because they got paid interest on it and because the US government promised that it would allow the holders of those notes to exchange them for the gold that was held in US vaults. As the spending and budget deficits grew, the US had to issue much more debt—i.e., create many more claims on gold—even though the amount of gold in the bank didn't increase. Investors who were astute enough to notice could see that the amount of outstanding claims on gold was much larger than the amount of gold in the bank. They realized that if this continued the US would have to default, so they turned in their claims. Of course, the idea that the US government, the richest and most powerful government in the world, would default on its promise to give gold to those who had claims on it seemed implausible at the time. So, while most people were surprised by Nixon's announcement and the effects on the markets, those who understood the mechanics of how money and credit work were not.

When credit cycles reach their limit, it is the logical and classic response for central governments and their central banks to create a lot of debt and print money that will be spent on goods, services, and investment assets in order to keep the economy moving. That was done during the 2008 debt crisis, when interest rates could no longer be lowered because they had already hit 0 percent. It also happened in a big way in 2020 in response to the plunge triggered by the COVID pandemic. That was also done in response to the 1929–32 debt crisis, when interest rates had similarly been driven to 0 percent. At the time I am writing this, the creation of debt and money has been happening in amounts greater than at any time since World War II.

To be clear, printing money and giving it out for spending rather than supporting spending with debt growth is not without its benefits—money spends like credit, but in practice (rather than in theory) it doesn't have to be paid back. There is nothing wrong with having an increase in money growth instead of an increase in credit/debt growth, if the money is put to productive use. The risk is that it will not be. If money is printed too aggressively and it is not used productively, people will stop using it as a storehold of wealth and shift their wealth into other things.

History has shown that ● ***we shouldn't rely on governments to protect us financially.*** On the contrary, we should expect most governments to abuse their privileged positions as the creators and users of money and credit for the same reasons that you might commit those abuses if you were in their shoes. That is because no one policy maker owns the whole cycle. Each comes in at one or another part of it and does what is in their interest to do given their circumstances at the time and what they believe is best (including breaking promises, even though the way they collectively handle the whole cycle is bad).

Since early in the debt cycle governments are considered trustworthy and they need and want money as much as or more than anyone else does, they are typically the biggest borrowers. Later in the cycle, new government leaders and new central bankers have to face the challenge of paying back debts with less stimulant in the bottle. To make matters worse, governments also have to bail out debtors whose failures would hurt the system—the "too big to fail" syndrome. As a result, they tend to get themselves into cash flow jams that are much larger than those of individuals, companies, and most other entities.

In virtually every case, the government contributes to the accumulation of debt with its actions and by becoming a large debtor itself. When the debt bubble bursts, the government bails itself and others out by buying assets and/or printing money and devaluing it. The larger the debt crisis, the more that is true. While undesirable, it is understandable why this happens. ● ***When one can manufacture money and credit and pass them out to everyone to make them happy, it is very hard to resist the temptation to do so.***[5] It is a classic financial move. **Throughout history, rulers have run up debts that won't come due until long after their own reigns are over, leaving it to their successors to pay the bill.**

Printing money and buying financial assets (mostly bonds) holds interest rates down, which stimulates borrowing and buying. Those investors holding bonds are encouraged to sell them. The low interest rates also encourage investors, businesses, and individuals to borrow and invest in higher-returning assets, getting what they want through monthly payments they can afford.

This leads central banks to print more money and buy more bonds and sometimes other financial assets. That typically does a good job of pushing up financial asset prices but is relatively inefficient at getting money, credit, and buying power into the hands of those who need them most. That is what happened in 2008 and what happened for most of the time until the 2020 coronavirus-induced crisis. When money printing and purchasing of financial assets fail to get money and credit to where they need to go, the central government borrows money from the central bank (which prints it) so the government can spend it on what it needs to be spent on. The Fed announced that plan on April 9, 2020. That approach of printing money to buy debt (called "debt monetization") is vastly more politically palatable as a way of shifting wealth from those who have it to those who need it than

[5] Some central banks have made acting on this temptation harder by separating themselves from the direct control of politicians, but virtually every central bank has to bail out their government at some point, so devaluations always happen.

imposing taxes because those who are taxed get angry. **That is why central banks always end up printing money and devaluing.**

When governments print a lot of money and buy a lot of debt, they cheapen both, which essentially taxes those who own it, making it easier for debtors and borrowers. When this happens to the point that the holders of money and debt assets realize what is going on, they seek to sell their debt assets and/or borrow money to get into debt they can pay back with cheap money. They also often move their wealth into better storeholds, such as gold and certain types of stocks, or to another country not having these problems. At such times central banks have typically continued to print money and buy debt directly or indirectly (e.g., by having banks do the buying for them) while outlawing the flow of money into inflation-hedge assets, alternative currencies, and alternative places.

Such periods of "reflation" either stimulate a new money and credit expansion that finances another economic expansion (which is good for stocks) or devalue the money so that it produces monetary inflation (which is good for inflation-hedge assets, such as gold, commodities, and inflation-linked bonds). Earlier in the long-term debt cycle, when the amount of outstanding debt isn't large and there is a lot of room to stimulate by lowering interest rates (and failing that, printing money and buying financial assets), there is a strong likelihood that credit growth and economic growth will be good. Later in the long-term debt cycle, when the amount of debt is large and there isn't much room to stimulate, there is a much greater likelihood of monetary inflation accompanied by economic weakness.

While people tend to believe that a currency is pretty much a permanent thing and that "cash" is the safest asset to hold, that's not true. ● ***All currencies devalue or die, and when they do, cash and bonds (which are promises to receive currency) are devalued or wiped out.*** **That is because printing a lot of currency and devaluing debt is the most expedient way of reducing or wiping out debt burdens.** When debt burdens are sufficiently reduced or eliminated, the credit/debt expansion cycles can begin again, as described in the next chapter.

As I explained comprehensively in my book *Principles for Navigating Big Debt Crises*, **there are four levers that policy makers can pull to bring debt and debt-service levels down relative to the income and cash flow levels required to service debts:**

1. **Austerity (spending less)**
2. **Debt defaults and restructurings**
3. **Transfers of money and credit from those who have more than they need to those who have less than they need (e.g., raising taxes)**
4. **Printing money and devaluing it**

These levers typically progress from one to another for logical reasons:

- Austerity is deflationary and doesn't last long because it's too painful.
- Debt defaults and restructurings are also deflationary and painful because the debts that are wiped out or reduced in value are someone's assets; as a result, defaults and restructurings are painful for both the debtor who goes broke and has their assets taken away and for the creditor who loses wealth when the debt is written down.
- Transfers of money and credit from those who have more than they need to those who have less than they need (e.g., raising taxes to redistribute wealth) is politically challenging but more tolerable than the first two ways and is typically part of the resolution.
- Compared to the others, ● ***printing money is the most expedient, least well-understood, and most common big way of restructuring debts.*** In fact, it seems good rather than bad to most people because:
  - It helps to relieve debt squeezes.
  - It's tough to identify any harmed parties that the wealth was taken away from to provide this financial wealth

(though they are the holders of money and debt assets).

- In most cases it causes assets to go up in the depreciating currency that people measure their wealth in, so it appears that people are getting richer.

This is what has been happening during the coronavirus crisis as central governments and banks send out large amounts of money and credit. Note that you don't hear anyone complaining about the money and credit creation; in fact, people say that governments would be cheap and cruel if they didn't provide a lot more of it. Hardly anyone acknowledges that governments don't actually have this money to give out. Governments aren't rich entities with piles of money lying around. They are just their people collectively, who will ultimately have to pay for the creation and giving out of money. Now imagine what those same citizens would say if government officials cut expenses to balance their budgets and asked them to do the same, making lots of them go broke, and/or if they sought to redistribute wealth from those who have more to those who have less by raising taxes. The money and credit producing path is much more acceptable politically than either of those options. It's as if you changed the rules of Monopoly to allow the banker to make more money and redistribute it whenever too many players are going broke and getting angry.

Stage 6: Then the flight back into hard money.

When taken too far, the overprinting of fiat currency leads to the selling of debt assets and the earlier-described "bank run" dynamic, which ultimately reduces the value of money and credit, which prompts people to flee out of both the currency and the debt. History teaches us that people typically turn to gold, silver, stocks that maintain their real value, and currencies and assets in other countries not having these problems. Some people think that there has to be an alternative reserve currency to go to for this flight to happen, but that's not true as the same dynamic of the breakdown of the monetary system and the running to other assets has happened in cases in which there was no alternative currency (e.g., in dynastic China and during the Roman Empire). There are a lot of things people run to when money is devalued, including rocks (used for construction) in Germany's Weimar Republic. The debasement of the currency leads people to run from it and from debt denominated in it and into something else.

At this stage of the debt cycle there is typically economic stress caused by large wealth and values gaps. These gaps lead to higher taxes and fighting between the rich and the poor. This also makes those with wealth want to move to hard assets, other currencies, and other countries. Naturally those who are governing the countries that are suffering from this flight from their debt, their currency, and their country want to stop it. So governments make it harder to invest in assets like gold (by outlawing gold transactions and ownership, for example), foreign currencies (via eliminating the ability to transact in them), and foreign countries (by establishing foreign exchange controls to prevent money from leaving the country). Eventually the debt is largely wiped out, usually by making the money to pay it back plentiful and cheap, which devalues both the money and the debt.

When the devaluations and defaults become so extreme that the money and credit system breaks down, necessity generally compels governments to go back to some form of hard currency to rebuild people's faith in the value of money as a storehold of wealth. Quite often, though not always, the government links its money to gold or a hard reserve currency with a promise to allow holders of that new money to convert it to the hard money. Sometimes that hard money is another country's. For example, over the past decades many weak-currency countries have linked their money to the US dollar or simply dollarized their economy (i.e., used the dollar as their own medium of exchange and storehold of wealth).

To review, holding debt as an asset that provides interest is typically rewarding early in the long-term debt cycle when there isn't a lot of debt outstanding, but holding debt late in the cycle, when

there is a lot of debt outstanding and it is closer to being defaulted on or devalued, is risky relative to the interest rate being given. So, holding debt is a bit like holding a ticking time bomb that rewards you while it is still ticking and blows you up when it stops. And as we've seen, that big blowup (i.e., big default or big devaluation) happens something like once every 50 to 75 years.

These cycles of building debts and writing off debts have existed for thousands of years and in some cases have been institutionalized. For example, the Old Testament describes a year of Jubilee every 50 years, in which debts were forgiven. Knowing that the debt cycle would happen on that schedule allowed everyone to act in a rational way to prepare for it.

Helping you understand this debt cycle so that you are prepared for it, rather than surprised by it, is my main objective in writing this book.

Ironically, **the closer most people are to the blowup, which is also when the claims outstanding are largest relative to the amount of hard money and tangible wealth there is, the riskier the situation is but the safer people tend to feel. That is because they have held the debt and enjoyed the rewards of doing so. The longer it has been since the last blowup, the more people's memories of it have faded**—even as the risks of holding the debt rise and the rewards for holding it decline. To properly assess the risk/reward of holding the time bomb, one must remain constantly aware of the amount of debt that needs to be paid relative to the amount of hard money there is to pay it, the amount of debt payments that have to be made relative to the amount of cash flow the debtors have, and the amount of interest they bring in.

THE LONG-TERM DEBT CYCLE IN SUMMARY

For thousands of years, there have always been three types of monetary systems:

Type 1: Hard money (e.g., metal coins)
Type 2: Paper money (claims on hard money)
Type 3: Fiat money

Hard money is the most restrictive system because money can't be created unless the supply of the metal or other intrinsically valuable commodity that is the money is increased. Money and credit are more easily created in the second type of system, so the ratio of the claims on hard money to the actual hard money held rises, which eventually leads to a run on the banks. The result is a) defaults, when the bank closes its doors and depositors lose their hard assets, and/or b) devaluations of the claims on money, which mean depositors get back less. In the third type of system, governments can create money and credit freely, which works for as long as people continue to have confidence in the currency and fails when they no longer do.

Throughout history, countries have transitioned across these different types of systems for logical reasons. When a country needs more money and credit than it currently has, whether to deal with debts, wars, or other problems, it naturally moves from Type 1 to Type 2, or Type 2 to Type 3, so that it has more flexibility to print money. Then creating too much money and debt depreciates their value, causing people to get out of holding debt and money as a storehold of wealth and move back into hard assets (like gold and silver) and other currencies. Since this typically takes place when there is wealth conflict and sometimes war, there is also typically a desire to get out of the country. Such countries need to re-establish confidence in their currency as a storehold of wealth before they can restore their credit markets.

The following diagram conveys these different transitions. There are many historical examples, from the Song Dynasty in China to Weimar Germany, of countries making the full transition from constrained types of monetary systems (Type 1 and Type 2) to fiat money (Type 3), then back to a constrained currency as the fiat currency hyperinflates.

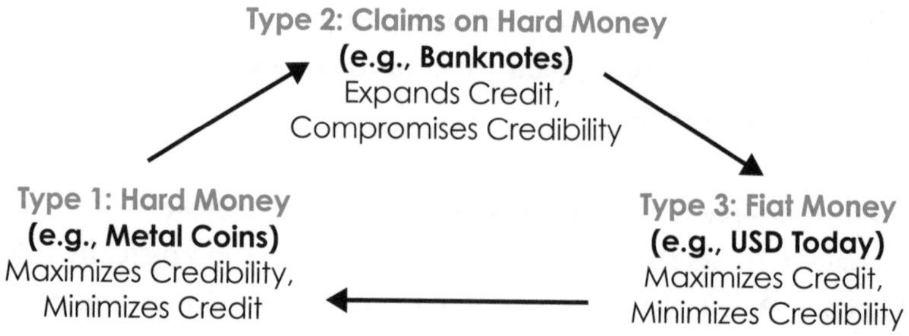

This big cycle typically plays out over something like 50 to 75 years; its ending is characterized by a restructuring of debts and the monetary system itself. The abrupt parts of these restructurings—i.e., the periods of debt and currency crisis—typically happen quickly, lasting only a few months to up to three years, depending on how long it takes the government to act. However, their ripple effects can be long-lasting, for example, when a currency ceases to be a reserve currency. Within each of these currency regimes there are typically two to four big debt crises—i.e., big enough to cause banking crises and debt write-downs or devaluations of 30 percent or more—but not big enough to break the currency system. Because I have invested in many countries for nearly half a century, I have experienced dozens of them. They all run the same way, which I explain in greater depth in my book *Principles for Navigating Big Debt Crises.*

In the next chapter, I will go into more detail on the causes of and risks associated with money changing its value, showing what has happened in the past, which is pretty shocking.

CHAPTER 4

THE CHANGING VALUE OF MONEY

This chapter examines the concepts introduced in the prior chapter in a more granular way to show you how consistent they are with the actual cases they are derived from. While we will get a bit more into the mechanics here than we did in Chapter 3, I have written this chapter in a way that should be accessible to the general reader and, at the same time, precise enough to satisfy the needs of skilled economists and investors.

As previously explained, there is a real economy and there is a financial economy, and the two are closely entwined but different. Each has its own supply-and-demand dynamics. In this chapter we will focus on the supply-and-demand dynamics of the financial economy to explore what determines the value of money.

Most people worry about whether their assets are going up or down; they rarely pay much attention to the value of their currency. Think about it. How worried are you about your currency declining? And how worried are you about how your stocks or your other assets are doing? If you are like most people, you are not nearly as aware of your currency risk as you need to be.

So, let's explore currency risks.

ALL CURRENCIES ARE DEVALUED OR DIE

Of the roughly 750 currencies that have existed since 1700, only about 20 percent remain, and all of them have been devalued. If you went back to 1850, as an example, the world's major currencies wouldn't look anything like the ones today. While the dollar, pound, and Swiss franc existed in 1850, the most important currencies of that era have died. In what is now Germany, you would have used the gulden or the thaler. There was no yen, so in Japan you might have used the koban or the ryo instead. In Italy you would have used one or more of six currencies. You would have used different currencies in Spain, China, and most other countries as well. Some were completely wiped out (in most cases they were in countries that had hyperinflation and/or lost wars and had large war debts) and replaced by entirely new currencies. Some were merged into currencies that replaced them (e.g., the individual European currencies were merged into the euro). And some remain in existence but were devalued, like the British pound and the US dollar.

WHAT DO THEY DEVALUE AGAINST?

The goal of printing money is to reduce debt burdens, so the most important thing for currencies to devalue against is debt (i.e., increase the amount of money relative to the amount of debt, to make it easier for debtors to repay). Debt is a promise to deliver money, so giving more money to those who need it lessens their debt burden. Where this newly created money and credit then flow determines what happens next. **In cases in which debt relief facilitates the flow of this money and credit into productivity and profits for companies, real stock prices (i.e., the value of stocks after adjusting for inflation) rise.**

When the creation of money sufficiently hurts the actual and prospective returns of cash and debt assets, it drives flows out of

those assets and into inflation-hedge assets like gold, commodities, inflation-indexed bonds, and other currencies (including digital). This leads to a self-reinforcing decline in the value of money. At times when the central bank faces the choice between allowing real interest rates (i.e., the rate of interest minus the rate of inflation) to rise to the detriment of the economy (and the anger of most of the public) or preventing real interest rates from rising by printing money and buying those cash and debt assets, they will choose the second path. This reinforces the bad returns of holding cash and those debt assets.

The later in the long-term debt cycle this happens, the greater the likelihood there will be a breakdown in the currency and monetary system. This breakdown is most likely to occur when the amounts of debt and money are already too large to be turned into real value for the amounts of goods and services they are claims on, the level of real interest rates that is low enough to save debtors from bankruptcy is below the level required for creditors to hold the debt as a viable storehold of wealth, and the normal central bank levers of allocating capital via interest rate changes (which I call Monetary Policy 1, or MP1) and/or printing money and buying high-quality debt (Monetary Policy 2, or MP2) don't work. This turns monetary policy into a facilitator of a political system that allocates resources in an uneconomic way.

There are systemically beneficial devaluations (though they are always costly to holders of money and debt), and there are systemically destructive ones that damage the credit/capital allocation system but are needed to wipe out debt in order to create a new monetary order. It's important to be able to tell the difference.

To do that I will start by showing how the values of currencies have changed in relation to both gold and consumer-price-index-weighted baskets of goods and services. These are relevant comparisons because gold is the timeless and universal alternative currency, while money is meant to buy goods and services so its buying power is of paramount importance. I will also touch on how a currency's value changes in relation to other currencies/

debt and in relation to stocks because they too can be storeholds of wealth. The picture that all these measures convey is broadly similar when a devaluation is big enough. Many other things (real estate, art, etc.) are also alternative storeholds of wealth, but gold will make my point nicely.

IN RELATION TO GOLD

This chart shows spot exchange rates of the three major reserve currencies in relation to gold since 1600. We will examine all of this in depth later. For now I would like to focus on both the spot currency returns and the total returns of interest-earning cash in all the major currencies since 1850.

RESERVE CURRENCIES VS GOLD (SPOT FX)

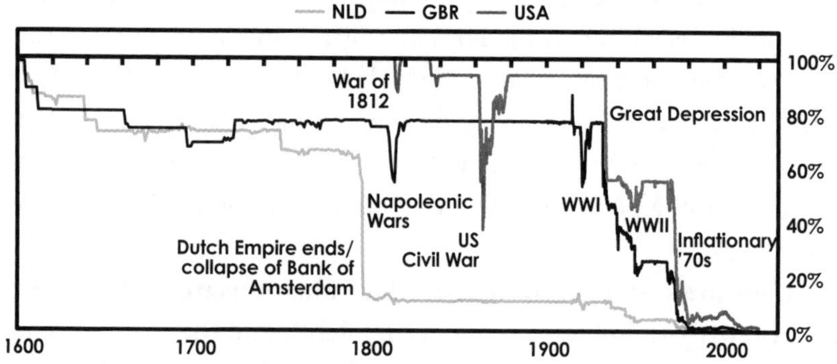

As the next two charts show, devaluations typically occur fairly abruptly during debt crises that are separated by longer periods of prosperity and stability. I noted six devaluations, but of course there were many more of minor currencies.

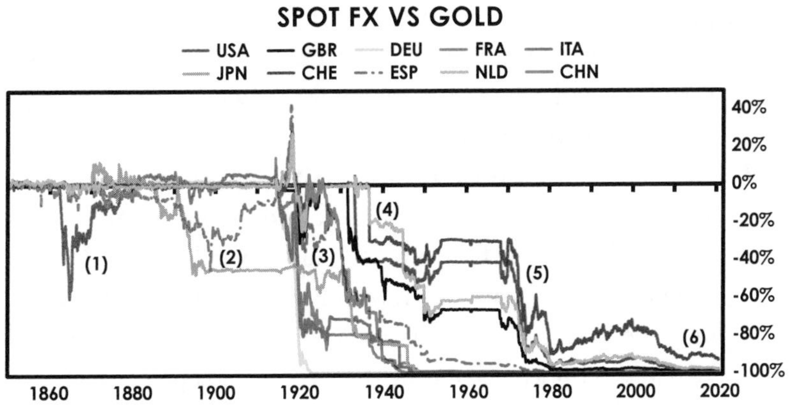

To properly compare the returns of holding cash in a currency to gold, we have to take into account the interest one would earn on cash. This chart shows the total return (i.e., price changes plus interest earned) on cash in each major currency versus gold.

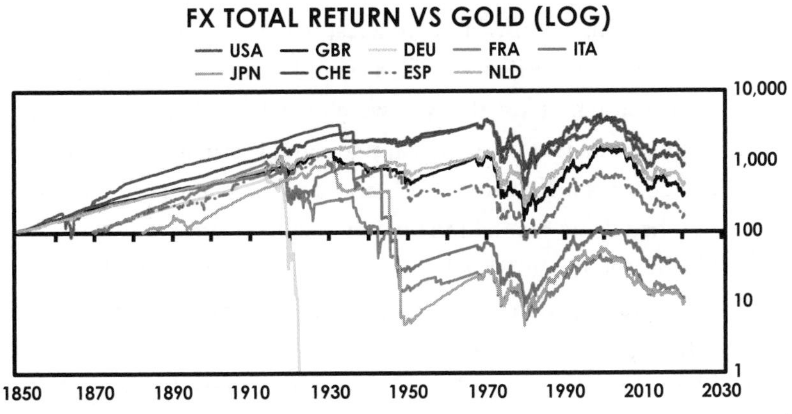

[1]

Here are the most notable takeaways:

- **Big devaluations are abrupt and episodic rather than evolutionary.** Over the last 170 years, there were six time frames when really big devaluations of major currencies occurred (and

[1] Due to a lack of data, several charts in this chapter do not show China.

plenty more of minor currencies).

- In the 1860s, during its civil war, the US suspended gold convertibility and printed paper money (known as "greenbacks") to help monetize war debts.
- Around the time the US returned to its gold peg in the mid-1870s, a number of other countries joined the gold standard; most currencies remained fixed against it until World War I. Major exceptions were Japan (which was on a silver-linked standard until the 1890s, which led its exchange rate to devalue against gold as silver prices fell during this period) and Spain, which frequently suspended convertibility to support large fiscal deficits.
- During World War I, warring countries ran enormous deficits that were funded by central banks' printing and lending of money. Gold served as money in foreign transactions, as international trust (and hence credit) was lacking. When the war ended, a new monetary order was created with gold and the winning countries' currencies, which were tied to gold.
- Still, between 1919 and 1922 several European countries, especially those that lost the war, were forced to print and devalue their currencies. The German mark and German mark debt sank between 1920 and 1923. Some of the winners of the war also had debts that had to be devalued to create a new start.
- With debt, domestic political, and international geopolitical restructurings done, the 1920s boomed, particularly in the US, inflating a debt bubble.
- The debt bubble burst in 1929, requiring central banks to print money and devalue it throughout the 1930s. More money printing and more money devaluations were required during World War II to fund military spending.
- In 1944–45, as the war ended, a new monetary system that linked the dollar to gold and other currencies to the dollar was created. The currencies and debts of Germany, Japan, and Italy, as well as those of China and a number of other countries, were quickly and totally destroyed, while those of most winners of

the war were slowly but still substantially depreciated. This monetary system stayed in place until the late 1960s.

- In 1968–73 (most importantly in 1971), excessive spending and debt creation (especially by the US) required breaking the dollar's link to gold because the claims on gold that were being turned in were far greater than the amount of gold available to redeem them.
- That led to a dollar-based fiat monetary system, which allowed the big increase in dollar-denominated money and credit that fueled the inflation of the 1970s and led to the debt crisis of the 1980s.
- Since 2000, the value of money has fallen in relation to the value of gold due to money and credit creation and because interest rates have been low in relation to inflation rates. Because the monetary system has been free-floating, it hasn't experienced the abrupt breaks it did in the past; the devaluation has been more gradual and continuous. Low, and in some cases negative, interest rates have not provided compensation for the increasing amount of money and credit and the resulting (albeit low) inflation.

Now let's take a closer look at these events:

The returns from holding currencies (in short-term debt that collects interest) were generally profitable between 1850 and 1913 relative to the returns from holding gold. Most currencies were able to remain fixed against gold or silver, and lending and borrowing worked well for those who did it. That prosperous period is called the Second Industrial Revolution, when borrowers turned the money they borrowed into earnings that allowed their debts to be paid back at high interest rates. Times were turbulent nevertheless. For example, in the early 1900s in the US, a debt-financed speculative boom in stocks grew overextended, causing a banking and brokerage crisis. That led to the Panic of 1907, at the same time that the large wealth gap and other social issues (e.g., women's suffrage and trade unionization) were causing political tensions. **Capitalism was challenged, and taxes started to rise to fund the wealth redistribution process.** Both the Federal Reserve and the US federal income tax were instituted in 1913.

Though a world away, China was impacted by the same dynamic. A stock market bubble led by rubber production stocks (China's equivalent of the railroad stock bubbles that contributed to panics in the US throughout the 19th century) burst in 1910, causing the crash that some have described as a factor in the debt/money/economic downswing that brought about the end of Imperial China.

But throughout most of that period, Type 2 monetary systems (i.e., those with notes convertible into metal money) remained in place in most countries, and the holders of those notes got paid good interest rates without having their currencies devalued. The big exceptions were the US devaluation to finance its civil war debts in the 1860s, the frequent devaluations of Spain's currency due to its weakness as a global power, and the sharp devaluations in Japan's currency due to its remaining on a silver-linked standard until the 1890s, while silver prices were falling relative to gold.

SPOT FX VS GOLD (1850–1913)

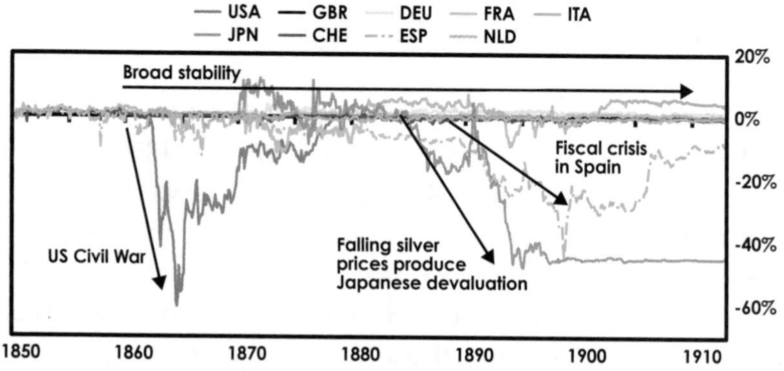

When World War I began in 1914, countries borrowed a lot to fund it. This led to the late-debt-cycle breakdowns and devaluations that came when war debts had to be wiped out, effectively

destroying the monetary systems of the war's losers. The Paris Peace Conference that ended the war in 1918 attempted to institute a new international order around the League of Nations, but those efforts at cooperation could not forestall the debt crises and monetary instability caused by the huge war indemnities that were placed on the defeated powers, as well as the large war debts that the victorious Allied powers owed each other (particularly the US).

Germany suffered a complete wipeout of the value of money and credit, which led to the most iconic hyperinflation in history during the Weimar Republic (which I describe in great detail in *Principles for Navigating Big Debt Crises*). The Spanish flu pandemic also occurred during the period, beginning in 1918 and ending in 1920. **With the exception of the US, virtually every country devalued its currency because they had to monetize some of their war debts.** Had they not done so, they wouldn't have been able to compete in world markets with the countries that did. China's silver-based currency rallied sharply relative to gold (and gold-linked currencies) near the end of the war as silver prices rose, and then mechanically devalued as silver prices fell sharply amid the post-war deflation in the US. **That period of war and devaluation that established the new world order in 1918 was followed by an extended and productive period of economic prosperity, particularly in the US, known as the Roaring '20s. Like all such periods, it led to big debt and asset bubbles and large wealth gaps.**

SPOT FX VS GOLD (1913–1930)

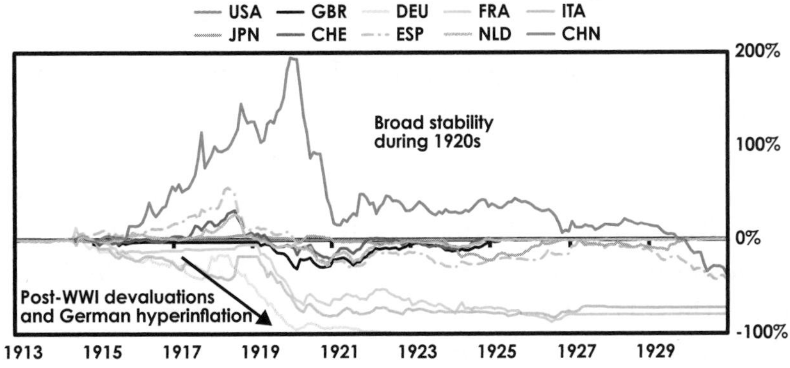

Different versions of the same thing happened during the 1930s. Between 1930 and 1933, a global debt crisis caused economic contractions that led to money printing and competitive devaluations in virtually every country, eroding the value of money moving into World War II. Conflicts over wealth within countries led to greater conflicts between them. All the warring countries built up war debts while the US gained a lot of wealth in the form of gold during the war. **Then, after the war, the value of money and debt was completely wiped out for the losers (Germany, Japan, and Italy) as well as for China, and was severely devalued for the UK and France, even though they were among the winners. A new world order and a period of prosperity followed the war.** We won't examine it, other than to mention that the excessive borrowing that took place set in motion the next big devaluation, which happened between 1968 and 1973.

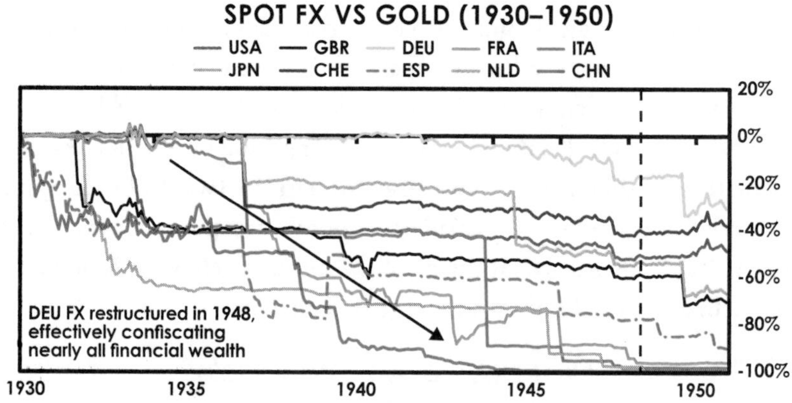

By the mid-1950s, the dollar and the Swiss franc were the only currencies worth even half of their 1850s exchange rate. As shown in the following chart, the downward pressure on currencies and upward pressure on gold started in 1968. **On August 15, 1971, President Nixon ended the Bretton Woods monetary system, devaluing the dollar and leaving the monetary system in which the dollar was backed by gold and instituting a fiat monetary system. (I will cover this episode in more detail in Chapter 11.)**

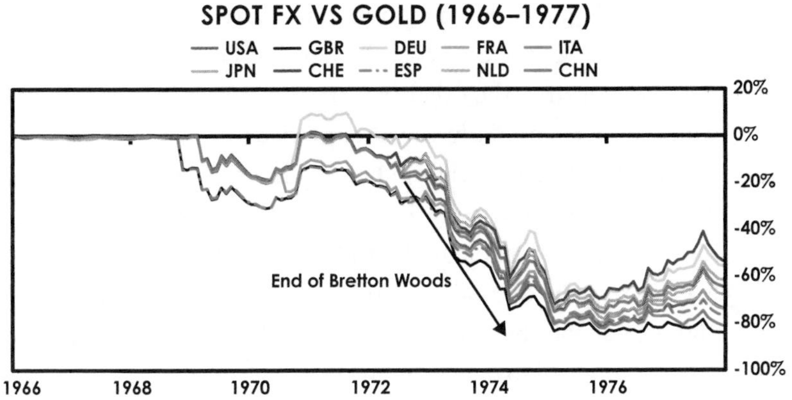

Since 2000, we have seen a more gradual and orderly loss of total return in currencies when measured in gold, consistent with the broad fall in real rates across countries.

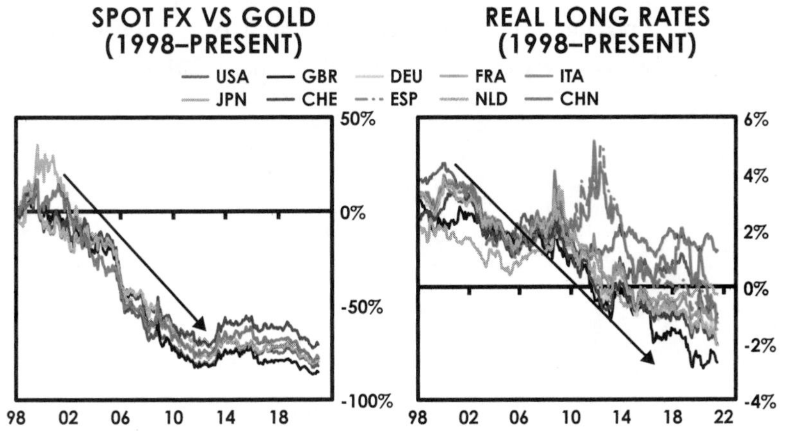

In summary:

- The average annual return of interest-earning cash currency between 1850 and the present was 1.2 percent, which was a bit higher than the average real return of holding gold, which was 0.9 percent, though there were huge differences in returns at various periods of time and in various countries.

- You would have received a positive real return for holding bills in about half of the countries during that period and a negative real return in the other half. In the case of Germany, you would have been totally wiped out twice.
- Most of the real returns from holding interest-earning cash currency would have come in the periods of prosperity, when most countries were on gold standards that they adhered to (e.g., during the Second Industrial Revolution, when debt levels and debt-service burdens were relatively low and income growth was nearly equal to debt growth).
- The real return for bills since 1912 (the modern fiat era) has been -0.1 percent. The real return of gold during this era has been 1.6 percent. You would only have made a positive real return holding interest-earning cash currency in about half of the countries during this era, and you would have lost meaningfully in the rest (over 2 percent a year in France, Italy, and Japan, and over 18 percent a year in Germany, due to the hyperinflation).

CURRENCY AND GOLD REAL RETURNS OF MAJOR COUNTRIES SINCE 1850 (VS CPI, ANN)

	Real Returns (vs CPI), Ann					
	1850–Present		1850–1912		1912–Present	
Country	Continuous Govt Bill Investment	Gold	Continuous Govt Bill Investment	Gold	Continuous Govt Bill Investment	Gold
United Kingdom	1.4%	0.7%	3.1%	-0.1%	0.5%	1.1%
United States	1.6%	0.3%	3.6%	-1.0%	0.4%	1.0%
Germany	-12.9%	2.0%	3.0%	-0.9%	-18.2%	3.1%
France	-0.7%	0.6%	2.6%	-0.3%	-2.6%	1.1%
Italy	-0.6%	0.3%	4.7%	-0.5%	-2.6%	0.5%
Japan	-0.7%	1.0%	5.0%	0.4%	-2.2%	1.2%
Switzerland	1.5%	0.0%	3.4%	-0.5%	0.5%	0.3%
Spain	1.4%	1.1%	4.5%	0.1%	0.3%	1.5%
Netherlands	1.4%	0.5%	3.3%	0.0%	0.4%	0.7%
China	—	3.3%	—	—	—	3.3%
Average	1.2%	0.9%	3.6%	-0.3%	-0.1%	1.6%

Data for Switzerland is since 1851; data for Germany, Spain, and Italy is since 1870; data for Japan is since 1882; data for China is since 1926 (excluding 1948–50). Average return is un-rebalanced and doesn't include China.

The next chart shows the real returns from holding gold between 1850 and the present. From 1850 to 1971, gold returned (through its appreciation) an amount that roughly equaled the amount of money lost to inflation on average, though there were big variations around that average both across countries (e.g., Germany seeing large gold outperformance, while countries with only limited devaluations, like the US, saw gold prices not keep up with inflation) and across time (e.g., the 1930s currency devaluations and the World War II-era devaluations of money that were part of the formation of the Bretton Woods monetary system in 1944). After the war, gold stayed steady in price across most countries, while money and credit expanded until 1971. Then, in 1971, there was a shift from a Type 2 monetary system (notes backed by gold) to a Type 3 fiat monetary system. That delinking of currencies from gold gave central banks the unconstrained ability to create money and credit. That led to high inflation and low real interest rates, which led to the big appreciation in the real gold price until 1980–81, when interest rates were raised significantly above the inflation rate, leading currencies to strengthen and gold to fall until 2000. That is when central banks pushed interest rates down relative to inflation rates and, when they couldn't push rates any lower by normal means, printed money and bought financial assets, which supported gold prices.

REAL RETURN OF GOLD (VS CPI, LOG)

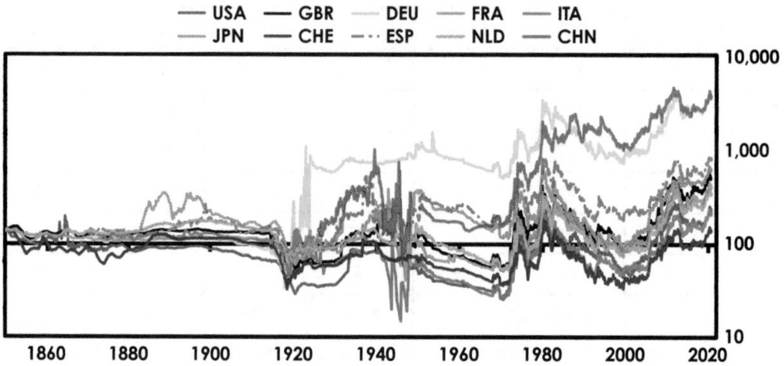

THE VALUE OF CURRENCIES IN RELATION TO GOODS AND SERVICES

Thus far we have looked at the market values of currencies in relation to the market value of gold. That raises the question as to whether gold is an appropriate gauge of value. **The next chart shows the value of interest-earning currency in terms of the consumer price index (CPI) baskets of goods and services in those currencies, reflecting their changes in buying power.** As can be clearly seen, the two World Wars were very bad and there have been ups and downs in the years since. For about half of the currencies, interest-earning cash provided a return above the rate of inflation. For the other half it provided negative real returns. In all cases, there were big and roughly 10-year-long swings around those averages. In other words, **history has shown that**

there are very large risks in holding interest-earning cash currency as a storehold of wealth, especially late in debt cycles.

REAL RETURN OF BILLS (VS CPI)

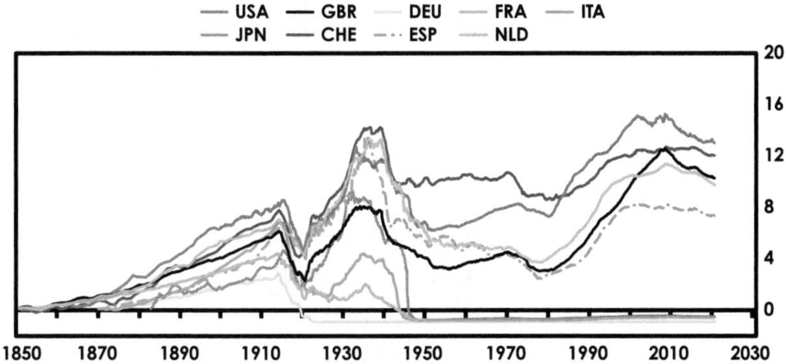

THE PATTERNS OF COUNTRIES DEVALUING AND LOSING THEIR RESERVE CURRENCY STATUS

A currency devaluing and a currency losing its reserve currency status aren't necessarily the same, though both are caused by debt crises. The loss of reserve currency status is a product of chronic large devaluations. As previously explained, increasing the supply of money and credit reduces the value of money and credit. This is bad for holders of money and credit but a relief to debtors. When this debt relief allows money and credit to flow into productivity and profits for companies, real stock prices rise. But it can also damage the actual and prospective returns of cash and debt assets enough to drive people out of them and into inflation-hedge assets and other currencies. The central bank then prints money and buys cash and debt assets, which reinforces the bad returns of holding them. The later in the long-term debt cycle this happens, the greater the likelihood that there will be a breakdown in the currency and monetary system. Policy makers and investors must be able to tell the difference between systemically beneficial devaluations and systemically destructive ones.

What do these devaluations have in common?

- **All the economies in the major cases that we examine in depth in Part II experienced a classic "run" dynamic, in which there were more claims on the central bank than there was hard currency available to satisfy them.** That hard currency was typically gold, though it was US dollars for the UK reserve currency decline because at that time the pound was linked to the dollar.
- **Net central bank reserves start falling prior to the actual devaluation, in some cases years ahead.** It's also worth noting that in several cases countries suspended convertibility before the actual devaluation of the exchange rate. The UK did this in 1947 and ahead of the 1949 devaluation, and the US did it in 1971.
- **The run on the currency and the devaluations typically occur alongside significant debt problems**, often related to wartime spending (e.g., the Fourth Anglo-Dutch War for the Netherlands, the World Wars for the UK, and the Vietnam War for the US), which put pressure on the central bank to print. The worst situations are when countries lose wars; that typically leads to the total collapse and restructuring of their currencies and their economies. However, winners of wars that end up with debts much larger than their assets and reduced competitiveness (e.g., the UK after the World Wars) also lose their reserve currency status, though more gradually.
- **Typically, central banks initially respond by letting short-term rates rise, but that is too economically painful, so they quickly capitulate and increase the supply of money.** After the money devalues, they typically cut rates.
- **Outcomes diverge significantly across the cases, with a key variable being how much economic and military power the country retains at the time of the devaluation.** The more it has, the more willing savers are to continue holding their money there. More specifically for the major reserve currencies:

- For the Dutch, the collapse of the guilder was massive and relatively quick; it took place over less than a decade, with the actual circulation of guilders falling swiftly by the end of the Fourth Anglo-Dutch War in 1784. The collapse came as the Netherlands entered a steep decline as a world power, first losing to the British and subsequently facing invasion from France.
- For the UK, the decline was more gradual: it took two devaluations before it fully lost its reserve currency status after Bretton Woods, though it experienced periodic balance of payments strains over the intervening period. Many who held reserves in pounds continued to do so because of political pressures, and their assets significantly underperformed US assets during the same time.
- In the case of the US, there were two big abrupt devaluations (in 1933 and 1971) and more gradual devaluations against gold since 2000, but they haven't cost the US its reserve currency status.
- Typically, a country loses its reserve currency status when there is an already established loss of economic and political primacy to a rising rival, which creates a vulnerability (e.g., the Netherlands falling behind the UK, or the UK falling behind the US), and there are large and growing debts monetized by the central bank printing money and buying government debt. This leads to a weakening of the currency in a self-reinforcing run that can't be stopped because the fiscal and balance of payments deficits are too great for any cutbacks to close.

In Part II, we will see the last 500 years of history as one continuous story of rises and declines of empires and the reasons for them, and you will see the same cause/effect relationships driving the rises and declines. But first we need to explore the big cycles of internal and external order/disorder, which we will do in the next two chapters.

CHAPTER 5

THE BIG CYCLE OF INTERNAL ORDER AND DISORDER

How people are with each other is the primary driver of the outcomes they get. Within countries there are systems or "orders" for governing how people are supposed to behave with each other. These systems and the actual behaviors of people operating within them produce consequences. In this chapter, we will explore the timeless and universal cause/effect relationships that shape the internal orders and the behaviors that drive the shifts between periods of order and periods of disorder.

Through my research, I saw how changes in internal orders (i.e., countries' systems for governing internally) and changes in the world order (i.e., the systems determining power between countries) happen continuously and everywhere in similar and increasingly interconnected ways that flow together as one all-encompassing story from the beginning of recorded time up to this moment. Seeing many interlinking cases evolve together helped me to discover the patterns that govern them and to imagine the future based on what I've learned. Most importantly I saw how the constant struggle for wealth and power produced continuously evolving internal systems/orders and external systems/orders and saw how these internal and external orders affect each other—with the whole thing (i.e., the world order) working like a perpetual-motion machine that evolves while doing the same things over and over again for basically the same reasons.

● ***The biggest thing affecting most people in most countries through time is how people struggle to make, take, and distribute wealth and power, though they also struggle over other things, most importantly ideology and religion.*** **I saw how these struggles happened in timeless and universal ways, and how these struggles had huge implications for all aspects of people's lives, starting with what happened with taxes, the economy, and how people were with each other through periods of boom and bust and peace and war, and how they unfolded in cyclical ways, like the tide coming in and out.**

I saw that when these struggles took the form of healthy competition that encouraged human energy to be put into productive activities, they produced productive internal orders and prosperous times, and when those energies took the form of destructive internal fighting, they produced internal disorder and painfully difficult times. I saw why the swings between productive order and destructive disorder typically evolved in cycles driven by logical cause/effect relationships and how they happened in all countries for mostly the same reasons. I saw that those that rose to achieve greatness did so because of a confluence of key forces coming together to produce that greatness and those that declined did so because these forces dissipated.

At the time of this writing, there is growing disorder in a number of leading countries around the world, most importantly in the United States. I wanted to put that disorder into perspective so I built indices of it and conducted the research I am sharing in this chapter. Because how the US handles its disorder will have profound implications for Americans, others around the world, and most economies and markets, in this chapter I am focusing more on the US than on other countries.

This simplified chart shows approximately where the US and China are within the archetypical Big Cycle, as measured by the previously described determinants. The US is in the stage—which I call Stage 5—when there are bad financial conditions and intensifying conflict at the same time the leading empire still has other great strengths (e.g., technology and military) that are declining on a relative basis. Classically this stage comes after periods of great excesses in spending and debt and the widening of wealth and political gaps and before there are revolutions and civil wars.

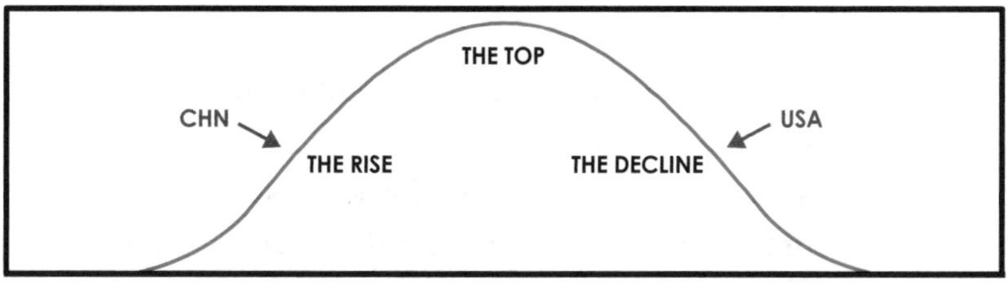

To be clear, I am not saying that the United States or other countries are inevitably headed into a period of greater decline or more internal and external conflict. However, I am saying that it is important to watch the markers in order to understand both what is happening and the full range of possibilities for the period ahead. In this chapter, I explore those markers by drawing on the lessons from analogous historical cases.

THE SIX STAGES OF THE INTERNAL CYCLE

Internal orders typically (though not always) change through a relatively standard sequence of stages, like the progression of a disease. By looking at their symptoms we can tell which stages countries are in. For example, just as Stage 3 cancer is different from Stage 4 cancer in ways defined by different conditions that exist and have come about as a result of things that happened in prior stages, the same is true for the different stages of the big internal cycle. Like diseases, different conditions warrant different actions to address them and they produce a different range of probabilities that those actions will lead to. For example, an old, unhealthy set of circumstances produces a range of possibilities and warrants different actions than a young, healthy set. **As with cancer, it is best to stop the progress before getting into the later stages.**

From studying history it appears to me that the stages of the archetypical cycle from internal order to internal disorder and back are as follows:

- **Stage 1, when the new order begins and the new leadership consolidates power**, which leads to . . .
- . . . **Stage 2, when the resource-allocation systems and government bureaucracies are built and refined**, which if done well leads to . . .
- . . . **Stage 3, when there is peace and prosperity**, which leads to . . .
- . . . **Stage 4, when there are great excesses in spending and debt and the widening of wealth and political gaps**, which leads to . . .
- . . . **Stage 5, when there are very bad financial conditions and intense conflict**, which leads to . . .
- . . . **Stage 6, when there are civil wars/revolutions**, which leads to . . .
- . . . Stage 1, which leads to Stage 2, etc., with the whole cycle happening over again.

Each stage presents a different set of conditions that the people facing them have to deal with. Some of these circumstances are much more difficult than others to resolve. For example, early in the long-term debt cycle, when there is plenty of capacity for governments to create debt to finance spending, it is easier to deal with the circumstances at hand than late in the long-term debt cycle when there is little or no capacity to create money and credit to finance spending. For these reasons the range of possible paths forward and the challenges that leaders face depend on where in the cycle a country is. These different stages present different challenges that require different qualities, understandings, and skills from leaders in order to effectively deal with them.[1] How well those facing these circumstances—e.g., you facing your circumstances and our leaders facing our collective circumstances—understand and adapt to them affects how good or bad the outcomes will be within the range of possibilities that exist given the circumstances. Different cultures have established different ways of approaching these circumstances. Those leaders and cultures who understand them and can adapt to their circumstances will produce much better outcomes than those who don't. That is where timeless and universal principles come in.

While the length of time spent in each of these stages can vary a lot, the evolution through them generally takes 100 years, give or take a lot and with big undulations within the cycle. Like evolution in general, the evolution of internal orders occurs in a cyclical way in which one stage typically leads to the next through a progression of stages that repeat and, in the process, evolve to higher levels of development. For example, Stage 1 (when the new internal order is created by new leaders who came to power via a civil war/revolution) normally comes after Stage 6 (when there is a civil war/revolution, which is the low point in the cycle), which leads to the next stage and so on up to Stage 3 (which is the high point in the cycle because there is a lot of peace and prosperity in that stage), which gets overdone in Stages 4 and 5 and so on, leading to the next new order (Stage 1). That happens over and over again in an upward-evolving way. Again, that archetypical cycle typically takes 100 years, give or take a lot. Within each cycle there are similar, smaller cycles. For example, there is a short-term debt cycle that leads to bubbles and recessions that come along roughly every eight years, there are political cycles that move political control between the right and the left that come along with roughly equal frequency, etc. **Every country is now going through them, and many of them are in different stages. For example, China and India are in very different stages than the United States and most**

[1] To get a rich picture of what makes great leaders great in different types of circumstances, I recommend Henry Kissinger's forthcoming book on leadership.

European countries. Which stages countries are in versus other countries affects the relations between countries and is the primary determinant of the world order. We will explore all of this in the last chapter of this book. The cycle's archetypical evolution transpires as shown in the following diagram.

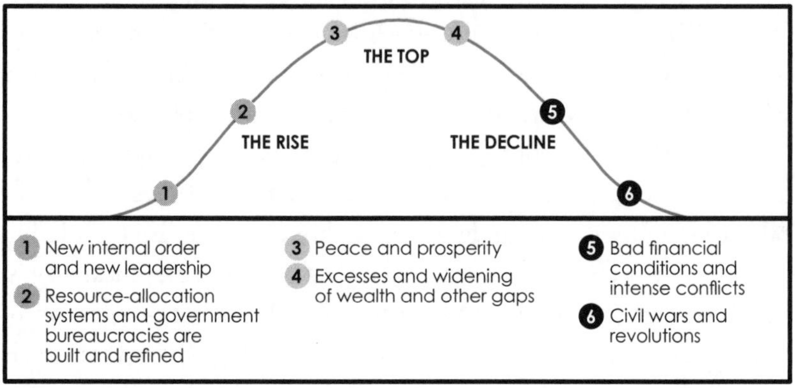

That is the complete internal order cycle. But of course the cycle repeats, with new leaders replacing the old ones and the whole cycle beginning again. How quickly a nation is able to rebuild and achieve new heights of prosperity depends on 1) how severe the civil war/revolution that ended the prior cycle was and 2) how competent the leaders of the new cycle are at establishing the things required for success.

These cycles have taken place for as long as there has been recorded history (and probably before), so many cycles are linked together, and they are upward-sloping because of evolutionary gains that are made over time.

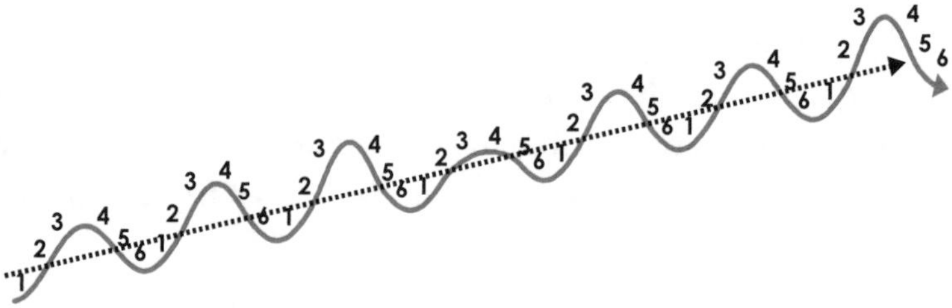

To see this at the country level, let's look at China. **The following chart shows my estimates of China's *absolute* powers and its figurative Big Cycles going back to around the year 600.** This is an ultra-simplified chart (i.e., there were many more dynasties and complexities). I am presenting it in this way so you can see how this evolution transpired from the 30,000-foot level.

MAJOR CHINESE DYNASTIES AND THEIR STAGES (WITH INDICATIVE UPWARD EVOLUTION)

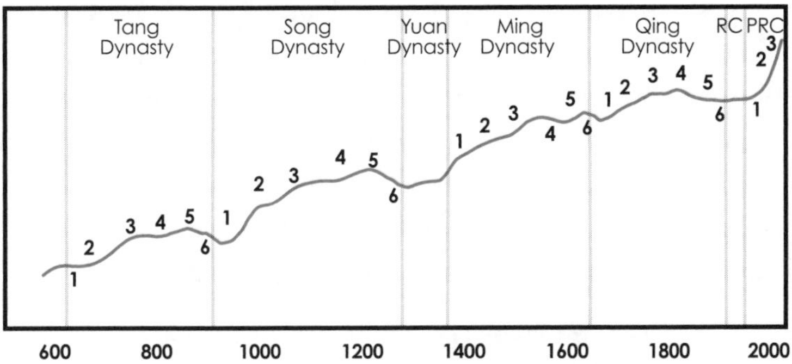

The next chart shows China's *relative* powers. The differences between the charts are due to the fact that the first one shows the absolute level of power while the second one shows the level of power relative to other empires.

MAJOR CHINESE DYNASTIES AND THEIR STAGES

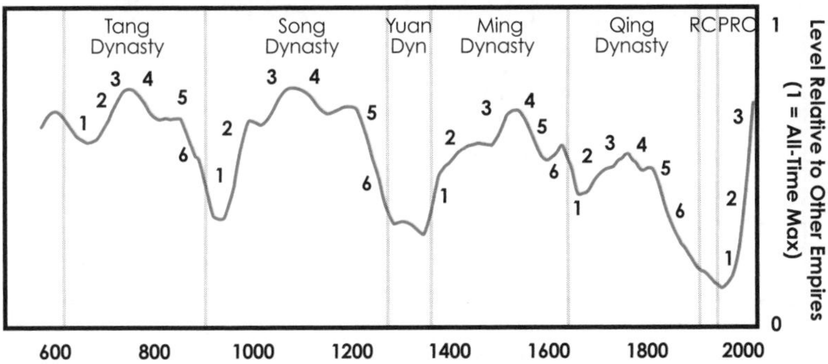

Since different countries are typically in different stages of the cycle and since they take wealth and global political power from each other, some countries are rising while others are declining, so the whole is less volatile than any one country. In other words, the differences have had a diversifying effect that has made the whole world's evolution smoother than that of any individual country. That is shown in the next chart, which is an update to the global real GDP chart I showed you in Chapter 1. This chart is not a figurative representation. It is literally the best estimate we have of real GDP per capita. Embedded in this chart are the rises and falls of major empires (particularly the Dutch and the British empires and the Ming and Qing dynasties), numerous wars, and numerous booms and busts, all of which are called out. These events don't show up at the global level because they diversify each other and because they are small relative to the big trends, even though they are huge from the perspective of the people living through them.

GLOBAL RGDP PER CAPITA (2017 USD, LOG)

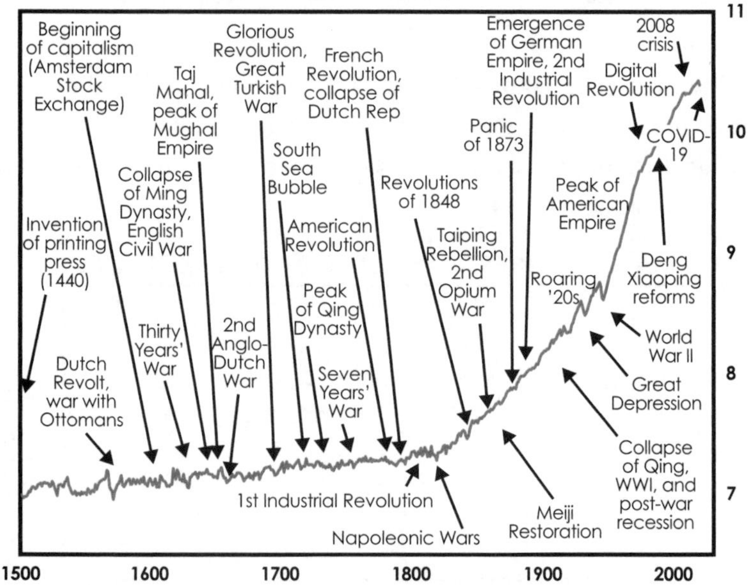

Global RGDP is primarily a mix of European countries before 1870 due to limited reliable data coverage across other countries before that point.

To reiterate, the figurative pictures of the archetypical six-stage cycle I just painted are simplified versions of what really happens. I wanted to show you a simplified version that conveys the essence of the stages and then descend into the details. While the cycle by and large progresses as I described, it doesn't always progress exactly as I described. For example, like the stages of a disease (let's say Stage 3 cancer), being in one stage doesn't mean that the progression to the next stage is inevitable. But it does tell us a lot that is very valuable. As with a disease, certain symptoms are clearly exhibited that allow one to identify which stage in the cycle one is in, and being in that stage signifies the risks and ways of treating the situation that are essential to know and are different from those that exist in different stages. For example, being in Stage 5 means that certain conditions exist that make it more likely that the cycle will progress to Stage 6 than if it were in Stage 4 with Stage 4 conditions. By having clear and objective markers to identify which stage each country (or state or city) is in, and by having an understanding of the cause/effect relationships that produce changes, one can better know the range of possibilities and position oneself accordingly, though one can never get them exactly right.

As an example, we made an index of the number of economic red flags that have existed at different times in history, including measures of high inequality, high debt and deficits, inflation, and bad growth, to show how indicative they are of subsequent civil wars and revolutions. The following chart shows the estimated likelihood of a civil-war-type conflict based on the number of red flags. Based on what we have seen in the past, we estimate that when there are 60–80 percent of the red flags present, there is around a 1-in-6 chance of severe internal conflict. When lots of these conditions are in place (greater than 80 percent) there is around a 1-in-3 chance of a civil war or revolution—so not very probable but still too probable for comfort. The US is in the 60–80 percent bucket today.

HISTORICAL LIKELIHOOD OF INTERNAL CONFLICT BASED ON SHARE OF ECONOMIC MEASURES WORSE THAN THRESHOLD (>1Z)

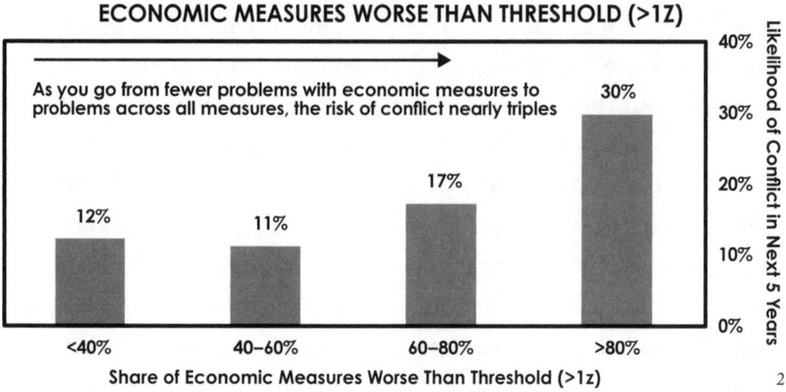

[2]

While I won't take you through all of the factors in each stage and their various configurations, I will outline the forces and milestones to pay most attention to in each stage, with a special emphasis on the current state of disorder in the United States and how things are progressing.

Delving into the Six Stages of the Cycle

We will now delve into what the archetypical six stages look like in greater detail so we can identify them easily when we see them and so we can better imagine what might come next.

Stage 1: When the New Order Begins and the New Leadership Consolidates Power

To fight a civil war or to have a revolution—even a peaceful one—is to have a great conflict in which one side wins and the other side

[2] This chart is based on historical analysis of nine great powers (covering about 2,200 years of history in total). The likelihood of conflict is based on major cases of civil war, rebellion, and revolution but excludes peaceful revolutions that did not change the existing system. The analysis does not count the probability of conflict arising in a period when a country is already in the midst of internal conflict (and the five years following) to avoid counting periods in which economic conditions were bad because of the conflict itself.

loses and the country suffers damages. Stage 1 is what follows the war; it is a time when the winners gain control and the losers must submit. While the winners were strong enough to win, at this first stage of the new order, they must also be wise enough to consolidate power and rebuild the country.

After winning power, the new leaders typically mop up the remaining opposition and fight among themselves for power. In fact, one might say that revolutions typically come in two parts—the first part is the fight to bring down the established leaders and systems, and the second part is the fight to remove those who were loyal to the former leaders and the fight for power among those who won. I will call the second part "purges" and touch on them in this section.

These consolidation of power/purge periods range widely in form and severity, depending on the degrees of conflict between the new leaders and their opposition, the amount of conflict between the new leaders themselves, and the levels of development of the various government departments and bureaucracies that they are inheriting.

This is the stage when, in some cases, the remaining opposition is killed or imprisoned so that the new leaders are assured that their enemies won't come back fighting. It is also when those revolutionaries who were on the winning side of the revolution fight against each other for power.

This stage has happened after virtually all civil wars/revolutions. Its intensity varies, usually in proportion to the intensity of the civil war/revolution that preceded this stage. At its worst, this post-revolution fighting to consolidate power produced some of the most brutal periods in a given country's history—e.g., the post-1789 French Revolution period called the Reign of Terror, the post-1917 Russian Revolution period called the Red Terror, the post-1949 Chinese Civil War period called the Anti-Rightist Campaign, etc. In some cases these purges happened a single time right after the revolution (e.g., the Reign of Terror), while in other cases they came and went episodically over decades (e.g., China's Cultural Revolution happened 17 years after the Chinese Communist Party came to power). These purges are done to consolidate power and persecute perceived ideological enemies or enemies of the state, and they are sometimes more brutal than the revolution itself. At their best, and if conditions allow because the basic system and respect for it is maintained, they're like the period after the US Civil War or during the peaceful Roosevelt revolution of the 1930s.

During this stage the leaders who do best are "consolidators of power." They typically have qualities similar to those who did best in the revolution in the prior stage—as they are strong, smart fighters who are willing and able to win at all costs. But in this stage they have to be much more politically astute because the enemies are much less apparent. Tang Emperor Taizong and Rome's Caesar Augustus excelled at this stage. More recently, leaders such as the US Founding Fathers, France's Napoleon, and Germany's Otto von Bismarck also exemplify how to effectively move from the war period to the rebuilding period.

This stage is over when the new authorities are clear and everyone is sick of the fighting and is well into the rebuilding.

Stage 2: When Resource-Allocation Systems and Government Bureaucracies Are Built and Refined

I call this phase "early prosperity" because it is typically the beginning of a peaceful and prosperous period.

After the new leaders have torn down the old order and consolidated power, or overlapping with that time, the new leaders have to start building a new system to better allocate resources. This is the stage when system and institution building are of paramount importance. What is required is designing and creating a system (order) that leads to people rowing in the same direction in pursuit of similar goals, with respect for rules and laws, and putting together an effective resource-allocation system that leads to rapidly improving productivity that benefits most people. This redesigning and rebuilding period has to be done even after lost wars because rebuilding still must occur. Examples of countries being in this stage include the United States in the 15 years after it declared independence in 1776; the early Napoleonic era immediately after Napoleon grabbed power in a coup at the end of the French Revolution in 1799; the early Japanese Meiji Restoration period immediately after the political revolution in 1868; the post-war periods in Japan, Germany, and most countries in the late 1940s through most of the 1950s; the post-civil war period in China; and Russia after the breakup of the Soviet Union.

A timeless and universal principle to keep in mind during this stage is that ● ***to be successful the system has to produce prosperity for most people, especially the large middle class.*** As Aristotle conveyed in *Politics*: "Those states are likely to be well-administered in which the middle class is large, and stronger if possible than both the other classes . . . where the middle class is large, there are least likely to be factions and dissensions . . . For when there is no middle class, and the poor are excessive in number, troubles arise, and the state soon comes to an end."

The leaders who are best during this stage are typically very different from those who succeeded in Stages 6 and 1. I call them "civil engineers." While they need to be smart, and ideally they are still strong and inspirational, above all else they need to be able to design and build the system that is productive for most people, or they need to have people working for them who can do that. The different qualities of leaders that are required to succeed in the revolutionary Stages 6 and 1 and those that are required in this rebuilding administrative Stage 2 are exemplified by Winston Churchill and Mao being great "inspirational generals" and lousy "civil engineers." Examples of great leaders at this stage include Konrad Adenauer in Germany, Lee Kuan Yew in Singapore, and Deng Xiaoping in China, who came to power after wars and built systems that produced prosperity well beyond their lifetimes.

The most extraordinary leaders are those who took their countries through Stages 6, 1, and 2—i.e., through the civil war/revolution, through the consolidation of power, and through the building

of the institutions and systems that worked fabulously for a long time after them—and did it at scale. The best ever probably were Tang Taizong (one of the revolutionary founders of the Tang Dynasty in China in the 600s, which was followed by about a century and a half of peace and prosperity that led China to become the world's largest and strongest country); Caesar Augustus (who became the first emperor of Rome in 27 BCE and began roughly 200 years of relative peace and prosperity, in which Rome became the world's largest empire); and Genghis Khan (who founded and led the Mongol Empire starting in 1206, which was followed by over a century of prosperity when it became the world's largest and strongest empire, though failure to establish a sustainable succession produced civil wars, including shortly after his death).

This sequence of rebuilding happens all the time in varying degrees depending on the amount of change that is warranted. In some cases it comes after brutal revolutions when there needs to be a rebuilding of nearly everything, and in other cases it comes when the institutions and systems that are there just need to be modified to suit the new leader.

Stage 3: When There Is Peace and Prosperity

I also call this phase "mid-prosperity." It is the sweet spot of the internal order cycle. It is when people have an abundance of opportunity to be productive, are excited about it, work well together, produce a lot, get rich, and are admired for being successful. In this stage conditions are improving for almost everyone so most of the next generation is better off than most of the prior generation, so there is broad optimism and excitement about the future. History shows us that, when done well, there is wide and almost equal access to education and merit-based placements in jobs. This draws on the widest possible range of the population to access talent and yields a system that most people believe is fair. Successful entrepreneurs, inventors, and adventurers produce new ideas and take their societies to new places and become the heroes who others aspire to be like because of how they come up with revolutionary new ideas, make people's lives better, and are rewarded for it. Debt growth fuels productivity and in turn real income growth, which makes debts easy to service and provides excess profits that make equity returns excellent. Incomes exceed expenses and savings exceed liabilities with the savings financing investment in the future. Stage 3 is an exciting period that has a lot of creativity, productivity, and energy.

Examples of this period include most of the Victorian Era in Britain (covering much of the 19th century, marked by Second Industrial Revolution inventions producing a rapid increase in prosperity); the German Empire in the late 1800s (with rapid industrialization, technological innovation, and a quickly strengthening military); and the 1960s in the United States. For example, the moon shot project exemplified the shared mission. The whole country cheered and was brought closer together when the lunar landing happened.

This is the time for the "inspirational visionary" who can a) imagine and convey an exciting picture of a future that never existed before, b) actually build that future out, and then c) use the prosperity earned to broaden the inclusiveness of it and to invest in the future. They do this while d) maintaining sound finances and e) pursuing excellent international relations, so that they protect or expand their empires without any financially or socially debilitating wars. Examples include:

- In the British Empire's Victorian Age in the mid-to-late 1800s, Prime Minister William Gladstone simultaneously maintained high levels of productivity, imposed strict budget controls that led to strong finances, and supported the general population so much that he was known as "The People's William." He also ran a peaceful and prosperous foreign policy.
- In the German Empire in the late 1800s, Chancellor Otto von Bismarck united the disparate populations of 39 different states and people of different religions to build Germany as a

country and an economic powerhouse. Under him Germany had an economic boom with sound finances while brilliantly navigating international relations so it benefited internally and avoided debilitating major wars.

- Prime Minister Lee Kuan Yew successfully took Singapore through these stages by running the country as prime minister from 1959 to 1990 and mentoring until his death in 2015. He created the principles and shaped the culture to be successful long after him and avoided wars without losing power.
- In the post-war US, John F. Kennedy in his 34 short months as president from January 20, 1961, to November 22, 1963, inspired the country to go to the moon, advanced the civil rights movement, undertook the War on Poverty with Vice President Lyndon Johnson, and kept the United States out of major wars while simultaneously strongly containing opposition to the US Empire.
- In China, Deng Xiaoping transitioned a weak and inefficient communist system to a highly productive state capitalist system, quickly changing the nation's psychology to make these changes with sayings such as "it is glorious to be rich" and "it doesn't matter whether the cat is black or white as long as it catches mice"; built China's economy and finances to be very strong; enormously improved the education and quality of life of most people; dramatically increased life expectancies and reduced poverty rates; successfully led China through internal political conflicts; and strictly maintained China's sovereignty while avoiding major external conflicts.

The longer countries stay in this stage, the longer their good times last.

During this stage the developments to pay attention to that reflect the big risks that naturally develop and undermine the self-sustaining good results are the widenings of the opportunity, income, wealth, and values gaps accompanied by bad and unfair

conditions for the majority, luxurious and unfairly privileged positions for the elites, declining productivity, and bad finances in which excess debts are created. The great empires and great dynasties that were able to sustain themselves stayed in Stage 3 by avoiding these risks. The failure to avoid these risks leads to Stage 4, which is a period of excesses. This is the stage in which the temptation to do everything (and borrow money to do it) can lead to the brink of conflict.

Stage 4: A Period of Excesses

I also call this the "bubble prosperity phase." I will describe it briefly because we touched on these elements before. Classically:

- There is the rapidly increasing debt-financed purchases of goods, services, and investment assets, so debt growth outpaces the capacity of future cash flows to service the debts. So bubbles are created. These debt-financed purchases emerge because investors, business leaders, financial intermediaries, individuals, and policy makers tend to assume that the future will be like the past so they bet heavily on the trends continuing. They mistakenly believe that investments that have gone up a lot are good rather than expensive so they borrow money to buy them, which drives up their prices, which reinforces this bubble process. That is because as their assets go up in value their net worth and spending-to-income level rise, which increases their borrowing capacity, which supports the leveraging-up process, and so the spiral goes until the bubbles burst. Japan in 1988–90, the US in 1929, the US in 2006–07, and Brazil and most other Latin American commodity producers in 1977–79 are classic examples.
- There is a shift in the spending of money and time to more on consumption and luxury goods and less on profitable investments. The reduced level of investments in infrastructure, capital goods, and R&D slows the country's productivity gains

and leads its cities and infrastructure to become older and less efficient.

- There is a lot of spending on the military at this stage to expand and protect global interests, especially if the country is a leading global power.
- The country's balance of payments positions deteriorate, reflecting its increased borrowing and reduced competitiveness. If the country is a reserve currency country, this borrowing is made easy as the result of non-reserve currency country savers having a preference to save in/lend to the reserve currency.
- Wealth and opportunity gaps are large and resentments between classes emerge.

During this phase, the archetypical best leader is the "well-grounded, disciplined leader" who understands and conveys sound fundamental behaviors that yield productivity and sound finances and creates restraints when the crowd wants to overdo things. These leaders are the ones who lead the country to continue to reinvest a significant amount of their earnings and their time into being productive when they become richer. As mentioned, Lee Kuan Yew, the former prime minister of Singapore, ensured that his country and fellow citizens had the culture to become well-educated, disciplined, and of strong character even after becoming successful and rich. However, these leaders are few and far between because fighting the ebullience of the masses is very unpopular. In almost all cases, after becoming rich, the country (and its leaders) become decadent, overspend, borrow to finance excess consumption, and lose competitiveness. This period of decline is exemplified by decadent leaders such as the notorious Emperor Nero (who used a citywide fire in Rome to confiscate land to build an expansive palace), Louis XIV (who expanded the Palace of Versailles while productivity fell and people endured hardships at the height of his power), and the Ming Dynasty's Wanli Emperor (who withdrew from actively governing and focused on the construction of his own immense tomb).

Stage 5: When There Are Bad Financial Conditions and Intense Conflict

The most important influence that transpires in a Big Cycle is that of debt, money, and economic activity. Because I covered that cycle comprehensively in Chapters 3 and 4, I won't explain it here in detail. But to understand Stage 5, you need to know that it follows Stage 3, in which there is peace and prosperity and favorable debt and credit conditions, and Stage 4, in which excess and decadence begin to bring about worse conditions. This process culminates in the most difficult and painful stage—Stage 6—when the entity runs out of money and there is typically terrible conflict in the form of revolution or civil war. Stage 5 is the period during which the interclass tensions that go along with worsening financial conditions come to a head. How different leaders, policy makers, and groups of people deal with conflict has a major impact on whether the country will undergo the needed changes peacefully or violently.

You can see signs of this happening now in a number of countries. Those that have adequate financial conditions (i.e., have incomes that are greater than their expenses and assets that are greater than their liabilities) are in relatively good shape. Those that do not are in relatively bad shape. They want money from the others. The problem is that there are many more who are in bad shape relative to those that are in good shape.

You can also see that these different conditions are big drivers of the differences in what is now happening to most aspects of these countries, states, cities, companies, and people—e.g., their education, healthcare, infrastructure, and well-being. You can also see big cultural differences in how countries approach their stressful conditions, with some approaching them more harmoniously than others who are more inclined to fight.

Because Stage 5 is such a pivotal stage in the internal cycle and because it's the stage that many countries, most importantly the US, are now in, I will devote some time to going through the cause/effect relationships at play during it and the key indicators to watch in examining its progression. Then I will turn more specifically to where the United States stands.

The Classic Toxic Mix

● ***The classic toxic mix of forces that brings about big internal conflicts consists of 1) the country and the people in the country (or state or city) being in bad financial shape (e.g., having big debt and non-debt obligations), 2) large income, wealth, and values gaps within that entity, and 3) a severe negative economic shock.***

That confluence typically brings about disorder, conflict, and sometimes civil wars. The economic shock can come about for many reasons, including financial bubbles that burst, acts of nature (such as pandemics, droughts, and floods), and wars. It creates a financial stress test. The financial conditions (as measured by incomes relative to expenses and assets relative to liabilities) that exist at the time of the stress test are the shock absorbers. The sizes of the gaps in incomes, wealth, and values are the degrees of fragility of the system. When the financial problems occur, they typically first hit the private sector and then the public sector. Because governments will never let the private sector's financial problems sink the entire system, it is the government's financial condition that matters most. When the government runs out of buying power, there is a collapse. But on the way to a collapse there is a lot of fighting for money and political power.

From studying 50-plus civil wars and revolutions, it became clear that the single most reliable leading indicator of civil war or revolution is bankrupt government finances combined with big wealth gaps. That is because when the government lacks financial power, it can't financially save those entities in the private sector that the government needs to save to keep the system running (as most governments, led by the United States, did at the end of 2008), it can't buy what it needs, and it can't pay people to do what it needs them to do. It is out of power.

A classic marker of being in Stage 5 and a leading indicator of the loss of borrowing and spending power, which is one of the triggers

for going into Stage 6, is that the government has large deficits that are creating more debt to be sold than buyers other than the government's own central bank are willing to buy. That leading indicator is turned on when governments that can't print money have to raise taxes and cut spending, or when those that can print money print a lot of it and buy a lot of government debt. To be more specific, when the government runs out of money (by running a big deficit, having large debts, and not having access to adequate credit), it has limited options. It can either raise taxes and cut spending a lot or print a lot of money, which depreciates its value. Those governments that have the option to print money always do so because that is the much less painful path, but it leads investors to run out of the money and debt that is being printed. Those governments that can't print money have to raise taxes and cut spending, which drives those with money to run out of the country (or state or city) because paying more taxes and losing services is intolerable. If these entities that can't print money have large wealth gaps among their constituents, these moves typically lead to some form of civil war/revolution.[3]

At the time of this writing, this late-cycle debt dynamic is now playing out in the United States at both the state and federal levels, with the main difference between them being that state governments can't print money to pay their debts while the federal government can. The federal government and many state and city governments have large deficits, large debts, and large wealth gaps, and the central bank (the Federal Reserve) has the power to print money. So, at the time of this writing, the central bank is printing a lot of money and buying a lot of federal government debt, which finances the government spending that is much bigger than the federal government's intake. That has helped the federal government and those it is trying to help, though it has also cost those who are holding dollars and dollar debt a lot in real purchasing power.

[3] To be clear, when a government's finances are in bad shape that does not necessarily mean it will run out of buying power. But it does mean that there is a much higher risk of that happening than if the government were in a financially strong position.

● ***Those places (cities, states, and countries) that have the largest wealth gaps, the largest debts, and the worst declines in incomes are most likely to have the greatest conflicts.*** Interestingly, those states and cities in the US that have the highest per capita income and wealth levels tend to be the states and cities that are the most indebted and have the largest wealth gaps—e.g., cities like San Francisco, Chicago, and New York City and states like Connecticut, Illinois, Massachusetts, New York, and New Jersey.

Facing these conditions, expenditures have to be cut or more money has to be raised in some way. The next question becomes who will pay to fix them, the "haves" or the "have-nots"? Obviously, it can't be the have-nots. Expenditure cuts are most intolerable for those who are poorest, so there needs to be more taxation of people who can afford to pay more and there is a heightened risk of some form of civil war or revolution. **But when the haves realize that they will be taxed to pay for debt service and to reduce the deficits, they typically leave, causing the hollowing-out process.** This is currently motivating movements from some states to others in the US. If bad economic conditions occur, that hastens the process. These circumstances largely drive the tax cycle.

● ***History shows that raising taxes and cutting spending when there are large wealth gaps and bad economic conditions, more than anything else, has been a leading indicator of civil wars or revolutions of some type.*** To be clear they don't have to be violent, though they can be.

I see these cycles transpiring in my personal interactions. For example, I live in the state of Connecticut, which has the highest per capita income in the country, the largest wealth gap and income gap in the country, and one of the largest per capita debt and unfunded pension obligations in the country. I see how the haves and the have-nots are focused on their own lives and spend little time worrying about the other because they don't have much contact. I have windows into what the lives of both the haves and the have-nots are like because I have contact with the people in our community of haves and because the work my wife does to help disengaged and disconnected high school students in disadvantaged communities brings her into contact with people who live in the communities of the have-nots. I see how terrible the conditions are in those have-not communities and how the haves (who appear rich and decadent to the have-nots) don't feel rich. I see how they are all focused on their own struggles—with the haves struggling with work/life balance, making sure their kids are well-educated, etc., and the have-nots struggling with finding income, food security, avoiding violence, trying to get their kids a quality education, etc.[4]

I see how both groups are more likely to have critical, stereotypical impressions of each other that make them more inclined to dislike each other than to view themselves empathetically as members of one community in which they should help each other. I see how difficult it can be to help each other because of these stereotypes and because the haves don't feel that they have more than enough or that the have-nots deserve their financial support, and I fear what the future might hold because of the existing circumstances and how they are likely to worsen. I have seen close up how COVID-inflicted health and budget shocks have brought to the surface the terrible conditions of the have-nots and are worsening the financial gaps that could bring about the classic toxic mix dynamic.

● ***Averages don't matter as much as the number of people who are suffering and their power.*** Those who favor policies that are good for the

[4] Of course, these two kinds of struggles aren't equivalent. Still, in both cases, I have found that people are focused on their own issues and communities and don't understand the circumstances of those they don't have direct contact with. In many communities, people—and most heartbreakingly the children—are desperately poor and neglected. There is an acute shortage of money for basics, such as adequate school supplies, nutrition, and healthcare, and an environment of violence and trauma that perpetuates a cycle in which children are brought up intellectually and physically malnourished and traumatized; this leaves them disadvantaged as they grow into adulthood, which makes it hard for them to earn a living, which perpetuates the cycle. Consider this fact: a recent study that our foundation funded showed that 22 percent of the high school students in Connecticut—the richest state in the country by income per capita—are either "disengaged" or "disconnected." A disengaged student is one who has an absentee rate of greater than 25 percent and is failing classes. A disconnected student is one who the system can't track because they dropped out. Imagine the consequences in 10 years and the human and social costs of this cycle. Our society has not established limits to how terrible it will allow conditions to get.

whole—e.g., free trade, globalization, advances in technology that replace people—without thinking about what happens if the whole is not divided in a way that benefits most people are missing the fact that the whole is at risk. ● ***To have peace and prosperity, a society must have productivity that benefits most people.*** Do you think we have this today?

What does history show as the path that bankrupt governments can follow to raise productivity that benefits most people? It shows that restructuring and/or devaluing enough of the previously created debt and non-debt obligations helps a lot. That is classic in Stages 5 and 6. Once the restructuring or devaluation reduces the debt burdens, which is typically painful at the time, the reduced debt burdens allow for a rebuilding. ● ***An essential ingredient for success is that the debt and money that are created are used to produce productivity gains and favorable returns on investment, rather than just being given away without yielding productivity and income gains. If it is given away without yielding these gains, the money will be devalued to the point that it won't leave the government or anyone else with much buying power.***

● ***History shows that lending and spending on items that produce broad-based productivity gains and returns on investment that exceed the borrowing costs result in living standards rising with debts being paid off, so these are good policies.*** If the amount of money being lent to finance the debt is inadequate, it is perfectly fine for the central bank to print the money and be the lender of last resort as long as the money is invested to have a return that is large enough to service the debt. History shows and logic dictates that investing well in education at all levels (including job training), infrastructure, and research that yields productive discoveries works very well. For example, big education and infrastructure programs have paid off nearly all the time (e.g., in the Tang Dynasty and many other Chinese dynasties, in the Roman Empire, in the Umayyad Caliphate, in the Mughal Empire in India, in Japan's Meiji Restoration, and in China's educational development programs over the last couple of decades), though they have long lead times. In fact, improvements in education and infrastructure, even those financed by debt, were essential ingredients behind the rises of virtually all empires, and declines in the quality of these investments were almost always ingredients behind empires' declines. If done well, these interventions can more than counterbalance the classic toxic mix.

The classic toxic mix is usually accompanied by other problems. The more of the following conditions that are in place, the higher the probability of having a severe conflict like a civil war or revolution.

+ Decadence

While early in the cycle there is typically more spending of time and money on productive things, later in the cycle time and money go more toward indulgent things (e.g., the finer things, like expensive residences, art, jewelry, and clothes). This begins in Stage 4 when such spending is fashionable, but by Stage 5 it begins to appear grotesque. Often that decadent spending is debt-financed, which worsens the financial conditions. The change in psychology that typically goes along with these changes is understandable. The haves feel that they have earned their money so they can spend it on luxuries if they like, while the have-nots view such spending at the same time they are suffering as unfair and selfish. Besides increasing resentments, decadent spending (as distinct from saving and investing) reduces productivity. ● ***What a society spends money on matters. When it spends on investment items that yield productivity and income gains, it makes for a better future than when it spends on consumption items that don't raise productivity and income.***

+ Bureaucracy

● ***While early in the internal order cycle bureaucracy is low, it is high late in the cycle, which makes sensible and needed decision making more difficult.*** That is because things tend to get more complex as they develop until they reach the point where even obviously good things can't be done—necessitating revolutionary changes. In a legal and contract-based system (which has many benefits), this can become a problem because the law can stand in the way of doing obviously good things. I will give you an example that I'm close to because my wife and I care about it.

Because the US Constitution doesn't make education a federal government responsibility, it has predominantly been a state and local responsibility with school funding coming from revenue raised by local taxes in cities and towns. Though it varies from state to state, typically those children in richer towns in richer states receive a much better education than those in poorer towns in poorer states. This is obviously unfair and unproductive even though most people agree that children should have equal opportunities in education. But because this structure is so ingrained in our political system, it is nearly impossible to fix without a revolutionary reinvention of how we approach it. There are more examples of the bureaucracy standing in the way of doing sensible, productive things than I have time and space to convey here. It is now a big problem in America.

+ Populism and Extremism

Out of disorder and discontent come leaders who have strong personalities, are anti-elitist, and claim to fight for the common man. They are called populists. Populism is a political and social phenomenon that appeals to ordinary people who feel that their concerns are not being addressed by the elites. It typically develops when there are wealth and opportunity gaps, perceived cultural threats from those with different values both inside and outside the country, and "establishment elites" in positions of power who are not working effectively for most people. Populists come into power when these conditions create anger among ordinary people who want those with political power to be fighters for them. Populists can be of the right or of the left, are much more extreme than moderates, and tend to appeal to the emotions of ordinary people. They are typically confrontational rather than collaborative and exclusive rather than inclusive. This leads to a lot of fighting between populists of the left and populists of the right over irreconcilable differences. The extremity of the revolution that occurs under them varies. For example, in the 1930s, populism of the left took the form of communism and that of the right took the form of fascism while nonviolent revolutionary changes took place in the US and the

UK. More recently, in the United States, the election of Donald Trump in 2016 was a move to populism of the right while the popularity of Bernie Sanders, Elizabeth Warren, and Alexandria Ocasio-Cortez reflects the popularity of populism of the left. There are increased political movements toward populism in a number of countries. It could be said that the election of Joe Biden reflects a desire for less extremism and more moderation, though time will tell.

Watch populism and polarization as markers. The more that populism and polarization exist, the further along a nation is in Stage 5, and the closer it is to civil war and revolution. In Stage 5, moderates become the minority. In Stage 6, they cease to exist.

+ Class Warfare

In Stage 5, class warfare intensifies. That is because, as a rule, ● ***during times of increased hardship and conflict there is an increased inclination to look at people in stereotypical ways as members of one or more classes and to look at these classes as either being enemies or allies.*** In Stage 5, this begins to become much more apparent. In Stage 6, it becomes dangerous.

A classic marker in Stage 5 that increases in Stage 6 is the demonization of those in other classes, which typically produces one or more scapegoat classes who are commonly believed to be the source of the problems. This leads to a drive to exclude, imprison, or destroy them, which happens in Stage 6. Ethnic, racial, and socioeconomic groups are often demonized. The most classic, horrific example of this comes from the Nazi's treatment of Jews, who were blamed and persecuted for virtually all of Germany's problems. Chinese minorities living in non-Chinese countries have been demonized and scapegoated during periods of economic and social stress. In the UK, Catholics were demonized and scapegoated in numerous stressful periods, such as the Glorious Revolution and the English Civil War. Rich capitalists are commonly demonized, especially those who are viewed to be making their money at the expense of the poor. Demonizing and scapegoating are a classic symptom and problem that we must keep an eye on.

+ The Loss of Truth in the Public Domain

Not knowing what is true because of distortions in the media and propaganda increases as people become more polarized, emotional, and politically motivated.

In Stage 5, those who are fighting typically work with those in the media to manipulate people's emotions to gain support and to destroy the opposition. In other words, media folks of the left join with others of the left and media folks of the right join with others of the right in the dirty fight. The media goes wild like vigilantes: people are commonly attacked and essentially tried and found guilty in the media, and they have their lives ruined without a judge and jury. A common move among 1930s populists of the left (communists) and of the right (fascists) was to take control of the media and establish "ministers of propaganda" to guide them. The media they produced was explicitly aimed at turning the population against the groups that the governments considered "enemies of the state." The government of the democratically run United Kingdom created a "Ministry of Information" during World War I and World War II to spread government propaganda, and leading newspaper publishers were elevated by the government if they did what the government wanted them to do to win the propaganda war[5] or were vilified and suffered if they didn't cooperate. Revolutionaries did the same distorting of the truth in all sorts of publications. During the French Revolution, newspapers run by revolutionaries pushed anti-monarchist and anti-religious sentiment, but when those revolutionaries attained power, they shut down dissenting newspapers during the Reign of Terror. During times of great wealth gaps and populist thinking, stories that bring down elites are popular and lucrative, especially those that bring down left-leaning elites in right-leaning media outlets and those that bring down right-leaning elites in left-leaning media outlets. History shows that significant increases in these activities are a problem that is typical

[5] Viscount Northcliffe, who controlled just under half of daily newspaper circulation in the UK around World War I, was known for anti-German coverage and was made "Director of Propaganda in Enemy Countries" by the government in 1918.

of Stage 5, and that when combined with the ability to inflict other punishments, the media becomes a powerful weapon.

It is well-recognized this is happening at the time of this writing. The perceived truth in media, both traditional and social, is lower than at any other time in our lifetimes. For example, a 2019 Gallup poll found that only 13 percent of Americans surveyed have "a great deal" of trust in the media and only 41 percent of those surveyed have either a "fair" or "great deal" of trust in the media. That compares with 72 percent who trusted the media in 1976. This is not just a fringe media problem; it is a mainstream media problem and a problem for our whole society. The dramatically decreased trustworthiness has even plagued former icons of journalistic trust such as *The Wall Street Journal* and *The New York Times*, which have seen their trust ratings plunge. In addition to being politically motivated, sensationalistic stories have become commercially rewarding at a time when the media business is in financial trouble. Most of the media folks I speak with share my concerns, though they typically won't share them openly. Still, in reflecting on the problem, Martin Baron, then executive editor of *The Washington Post*, said, "If you have a society where people can't agree on the basic facts, how do you have a functioning democracy?" This dynamic is impeding free speech because people are afraid to speak up because of how they will be attacked in both traditional and social media by distortions that are meant to bring them down.

Even very capable and powerful people are now too afraid of the media to speak up about important matters or run for public office. Since most high-profile people are torn down, most everyone I speak with agrees that it is dangerous to be a high-profile, vocal person who fights for truth and justice, especially if one offends people who are inclined to use the media to fight. Though not discussed in public because of fears of media reprisals, this issue is continuously discussed in private. For example, during a lunch I had not long ago with a general who had held a very high political position and had just left government service, we explored what he would do next. I asked him what he was most passionate about. He said, "Of course helping my country." I asked him whether he would consider running for elected office, and he explained that while he was willing to die for his country he couldn't bring himself to run for public office because of how enemies would use the media and social media to make up lies to harm him and his family. This general and almost everyone I know who we should listen to are afraid to speak openly because they fear that attacks by extremists who oppose them will be enabled and amplified by the sensationalistic media. Many of my friends tell me that I'm crazy to speak so openly about controversial things such as those covered in this book because it is inevitable that some people or groups will try to take me down via the media. I think they are probably right, but I won't let the risks dissuade me.[6]

+ Rule-Following Fades and Raw Fighting Begins

● ***When the causes that people are passionately behind are more***

[6] What can be done? The news media is unique in being the only industry that operates without quality controls or checks on its power. I and most others believe that it would be terrible for our government to regulate it and, at the same time, believe that something has to be done to fix the problem. Perhaps if people protest enough the media could be motivated to create a self-regulatory organization to create and regulate ratings the way the Motion Picture Association did. I don't have a clue about what should be done because this problem isn't in my areas of expertise, and it's not my place to offer suggestions to try to fix the problem; however, it is my responsibility to point out that we are in an era in which sensationalism, commercialism, and political desires to manipulate people's views have superseded accuracy and journalistic integrity as the primary objectives of most of those in the media and that this is like a cancer that threatens our well-being. If you believe that fake and distorted media is a problem and you are interested in watching the media/propaganda for clues about whether and how this is transpiring, here are a few commonly recommended things to look out for. Ask yourself:

1) Does the story consist of emotionally triggering, unsubstantiated accusations, or are the facts substantiated and the sources provided? When the facts are put aside to create an exciting story and the sources are undisclosed, don't believe the story.
2) Does the writer welcome or not welcome replies or arguments that refute what they are asserting, and are they willing or not willing to publish them along with what they published?
3) Are the accusations in the story consistent with what has been identified and proven in the legal system? If people or groups are accused in the media of doing bad things but they haven't been accused and judged to have done bad things in the legal system (which follows a process that tries to weigh the evidence to get at what is true), at least ask yourself why that is and probably don't believe the story.
4) If the writer or outlet has previously shown themselves to be biased, assume that they and their stories are biased.

important to them than the system for making decisions, the system is in jeopardy. Rules and laws work only when they are crystal clear and most people value working within them enough that they are willing to compromise in order to make them work well. If both of these are less than excellent, the legal system is in jeopardy. If the competing parties are unwilling to try to be reasonable with each other and to make decisions civilly in pursuit of the well-being of the whole, which will require them to give up things that they want and might win in a fight, there will be a sort of civil war that will test the relative powers of the relevant parties. In this stage, winning at all costs is the game and playing dirty is the norm. Late in Stage 5 is when reason is abandoned in favor of passion. ● ***When winning becomes the only thing that matters, unethical fighting becomes progressively more forceful in self-reinforcing ways. When everyone has causes that they are fighting for and no one can agree on anything, the system is on the brink of civil war/revolution.***

This typically happens in a couple of ways:

- **Late in Stage 5 it is common for the legal and police systems to be used as political weapons by those who can control them. Also private police systems form—e.g., thugs who beat people up and take their assets, and bodyguards to protect people from these things happening to them.** For instance, the Nazi party formed a paramilitary wing before it came to power that then became an official force when the Nazis were in power. The short-lived British Union of Fascists in the 1930s and the Ku Klux Klan in the US were effectively paramilitary groups as well. Such cases are quite normal, so view their development as a marker of moving to the next stage.
- **Late in Stage 5 there are increasing numbers of protests that become increasingly violent.** Because there is not always a clear line between a healthy protest and the beginnings of a revolution, leaders in power often struggle over how to allow

protests without giving the perceived freedom to revolt against the system. Leaders must manage these situations well. A classic dilemma arises when demonstrations start to cross over into revolution. Both giving the freedom to protest and suppressing protests are risky paths for leaders, as either path could lead the revolution to get strong enough to topple the system. No system allows people to bring down the system—in most, an attempt to do so is treason, typically punishable by death. Nonetheless, it is the job of revolutionaries to bring down systems, so governments and revolutionaries test each other to see what the limits are. When broad-based discontent bubbles up and those in power allow it to grow, it can boil over to the point that when they try to put a lid on it, it explodes. The conflicts in the late part of Stage 5 typically build up to a crescendo that triggers the violent fighting that signifies the transition into what historians stamp as official civil war periods, which I am identifying as Stage 6 in the Big Cycle. ● ***People dying in the fighting is the marker that almost certainly signifies the progression to the next and more violent civil war stage, which will continue until the winners and losers are clearly determined.***

That brings me to my next principle: ● ***when in doubt, get out—if you don't want to be in a civil war or a war, you should get out while the getting is good.*** This is typically late in Stage 5. History has shown that when things get bad, the doors typically close for people who want to leave. The same is true for investments and money as countries introduce capital controls and other measures during such times.

● ***Crossing the line from Stage 5 (when there are very bad financial conditions and intense internal and external conflict exist) to Stage 6 (when there is civil war) occurs when the system for resolving disagreements goes from working to not working.*** In other words, it happens when the system is broken beyond repair, people are violent with each other, and the leadership has lost control.

As you might imagine, it is a much bigger deal to break a system/order and build a new one than it is to make revolutionary changes within an existing system/order. Though breaking a system/order is more traumatic, it isn't necessarily a worse path than operating within a system.

Deciding whether to keep and renovate something old that is not working well or to dispose of it and replace it with something new is never easy, especially when the something new is not clearly known and what is being replaced is as important as the domestic order. Nonetheless, it happens, though typically it is not decided on intellectually; it is more often emotionally driven.

● ***When one is in Stage 5 (like the US is now), the biggest question is how much the system will bend before it breaks.*** The democratic system, which allows the population to do pretty much whatever it decides to do, produces more bending because the people can make leadership changes and only have themselves to blame. In this system regime changes can more easily happen in a peaceful way. However, the "one person, one vote" democratic process has the drawback of having leaders selected via popularity contests by people who are largely not doing the sort of thoughtful review of capabilities that most organizations would do when trying to find the right person for an important job. Democracy has also been shown to break down in times of great conflict.

Democracy requires consensus decision making and compromise, which requires a lot of people who have opposing views to work well with each other within the system. That ensures that parties that have significant constituencies can be represented, but like all big committees of people who have widely different views (and might even dislike each other), the decision-making system does not lend itself to efficient decision making. ● ***The biggest risk to democracies is that they produce such fragmented and antagonistic decision making that they can be ineffective, which leads to bad results, which leads to revolutions led by populist autocrats who represent large segments of the population who want to have a strong, capable leader get control of the chaos and make the country work well for them.***

Also noteworthy: history has shown that during times of great conflict federalist democracies (like the US) typically have conflicts between the states and the central government over their relative powers. That would be a marker to look out for that hasn't yet arisen much in the US; its happening would signify the continued progression toward Stage 6.

There are far too many breakdowns of democracies to explore, let alone describe. While I looked into a number of them to see the patterns, I haven't fully mined them, and I'm not going to dive into them here. I will say that the factors described in the explanations of Stage 5 when taken to the extreme—most importantly, terrible finances, decadence, internal strife and disorder, and/or major external conflict—lead to a dysfunctional set of conditions and a fight for power led by a strong leader. Archetypical examples include Athens from the late 400s to the 300s BCE, the end of the Roman Republic in the century or so preceding 27 BCE,[7] Germany's Weimar Republic in the 1920s, and the weak democracies of Italy, Japan, and Spain in the 1920s and 1930s that turned to autocracies of the right (fascism) to bring order to the chaos.

● ***Different stages require different types of leaders to get the best results.*** **Stage 5 is a juncture in which one path could lead to civil war/revolution and the other could lead to peaceful and, ideally, prosperous coexistence.** Obviously the peaceful and prosperous path is the ideal path, but it is the much more difficult path to pull off. That path requires a "strong peacemaker" who goes out of their way to

---

[7] The Roman Republic and Athens both had democratic elements, but not everyone was able to participate or vote equally. Although democracies have existed for thousands of years, it is only recently that most people were allowed to vote. For example, in the US, African-American men were not universally allowed to vote until 1870, and women of all races until 1920.

bring the country together, including reaching out to the other side to involve them in the decision making and reshaping the order in a way that most people agree is fair and works well (i.e., is highly productive in a way that benefits most people). **There are few such cases in history. We pray for them.** The second type is a "strong fighter" who is capable of taking the country through the hell of civil war/revolution.

Stage 6: When There Are Civil Wars

● ***Civil wars inevitably happen, so rather than assuming "it won't happen here," which most people in most countries assume after an extended period of not having them, it is better to be wary of them and look for the markers to indicate how close one is.*** While in the last section we looked at nonviolent revolutions that took place within the order, in this section we will be looking at the markers and the patterns of civil wars and revolutions that were almost always violent and toppled the old order and replaced it with a new one. **Though there are innumerable examples that I could have examined to understand how they work, I chose what I believe are the 29 most significant ones, which are shown in the following table. I categorized this group into those that produced big changes to the system/regime and those that did not.** For example, the US Civil War was a really bloody civil war that failed to overturn the system/order, so it is in the second group at the bottom of the table, while those that toppled the system/order are at the top. These categories are of course imprecise, but once again we won't let imprecision stand in the way of seeing what we couldn't see if we insisted on being precise. Most of these conflicts, though not all of them, transpired in the archetypical way described in this section.

CONFLICT	COUNTRY	BEGAN IN...	
Dutch Revolt	NLD	1566	Cases that created changes to the system or regime
English Civil War	GBR	1642	
Glorious Revolution	GBR	1688	
American Revolution	USA	1775	
French Revolution	FRA	1789	
Trienio Liberal	ESP	1820	
French Revolution of 1848	FRA	1848	
Meiji Restoration	JPN	1868	
Xinhai Revolution	CHN	1911	
Russian Revolution and Civil War	RUS	1917	
German Revolution/End of Monarchy	DEU	1918	
Rise of Hitler/Political Violence	DEU	1929	
Rise of Japanese Militarists	JPN	1932	
Spanish Civil War	ESP	1936	
Chinese Civil War	CHN	1945	
Jacobite Risings	GBR	1745	Cases that didn't create changes to the system or regime
Pugachev's Rebellion	RUS	1773	
Dutch Patriot Revolt	NLD	1781	
White Lotus Rebellion	CHN	1794	
German Revolutions of 1848	DEU	1848	
Taiping Rebellion	CHN	1851	
Panthay Rebellion	CHN	1856	
US Civil War	USA	1861	
Muslim Rebellion	CHN	1862	
Paris Commune	FRA	1871	
Boxer Rebellion	CHN	1899	
1905 Russian Revolution	RUS	1905	
National Protection War	CHN	1915	
6 February 1934 Crisis	FRA	1934	

A classic example of a civil war breaking the system and having to build a new system is the Russian Revolution/Civil War of 1917. This put into place the communist internal order that eventually entered Stage 5 in the late 1980s, which led it to attempt to make revolutionary changes within the system—called *perestroika* (i.e., restructuring)—which failed and were followed by the collapse of the Soviet Union's order in 1991. The communist domestic order lasted 74 years (from 1917 until 1991). That order was replaced by the new system/order that is now governing Russia, which, after the collapse of the old order, was built in the classic ways described earlier in this chapter in my explanations of Stages 1 and 2.

Another is Japan's Meiji Restoration, which came about as a result of a three-year revolution (1866–69) that happened because the Japanese were closed off to the outside world and failed to advance. The Americans forced the Japanese to open, which prompted a revolutionary group to fight and defeat the rulers (led by the military shogun) in battle, which led to overturning the internal order then run by the four classes—the military, farmers, artisans, and merchants—that had ruled Japan. This old Japanese order run by traditional people was ultra-conservative (e.g., social mobility was outlawed) and was replaced by revolutionaries who were relatively progressive and changed everything by reinstating the powers of a modernizing emperor. Early in this period there were lots of labor disputes, strikes, and riots that resulted from the classic triggers of wealth gaps and bad economic conditions. In the reform process the leadership provided universal elementary education for both boys and girls, adopted capitalism, and opened the country up to the outside world. They did this with new technologies, which led them to become very competitive and gain wealth.

There are many such cases of countries that did the right things to produce revolutionarily beneficial improvements, just as there are many cases of revolutionaries doing the wrong things that inflicted terrible pain on their people for decades. By the way, as a result of its reformations Japan went on to move through the classic stages of the Big Cycle. It became extremely successful and rich. But over time it became decadent, overextended, and fragmented, had an economic depression, and fought expensive wars, all of which led to a classic demise. Its Meiji order and its classic Big Cycle lasted for 76 years from 1869 to 1945.

● ***Civil wars and revolutions inevitably take place to radically change the internal order. They include total restructurings of wealth and political power that include complete restructurings of debt and financial ownership and political decision making.*** These changes are the natural consequence of needing to make big changes that can't be made within the existing system. Almost all systems encounter them. That is because almost all systems benefit some classes of people at the expense of other classes, which eventually becomes intolerable to the point that there is a fight to determine the path forward. When the gaps in wealth and values become very wide and bad economic conditions ensue so that the system is not working for a large percentage of the people, the people will fight to change the system. Those who are suffering the most economically will fight to get more wealth and power from those who have wealth and power and who benefit from the existing system. Naturally the revolutionaries want to radically change the system, so naturally they are willing to break the laws that those in power demand they adhere to. These revolutionary changes typically happen violently through civil wars, though as previously described, they can come about peacefully without toppling the system.

The periods of civil war are typically very brutal. Typically, early on these wars are forceful and orderly struggles for power, and as the fighting and emotions intensify and the sides do anything to win, the levels of brutality accelerate unexpectedly such that the actual levels of brutality that occur in the Stage 6 civil wars and revolutions would have been considered implausible in Stage 5. The elites and moderates generally flee, are imprisoned, or are killed. Reading the stories of civil wars and revolutions, such as the Spanish Civil War, the Chinese Civil War, the Russian Revolution, and the French Revolution, made my hair curl.

How do they transpire? Earlier I described the dynamics of Stage 5 that led to crossing the line into Stage 6. During this stage all of those intensify greatly. I will explain.

How Civil Wars and Revolutions Transpire

As previously described, the cycle of building wealth and wealth gaps that leads to a very small percentage of the population controlling an exceptionally large percentage of the wealth eventually results in the poor majority overthrowing the rich minority via civil wars and revolutions. This has happened more times than one can imagine.

While most of the archetypical civil wars and revolutions shifted power from the right to the left, many shifted wealth and power to the right and away from those on the left. However, there were fewer of them and they were different. They typically happened when the existing orders slipped into dysfunctional anarchies and a large percentage of the population yearned for strong leadership, discipline, and productivity. Examples of revolutions from the left to the right include Germany, Spain, Japan, and Italy in the 1930s; the fall of the Soviet Union in the 1980s to the early 1990s; the 1976 coup in Argentina replacing Isabel Perón with a military junta; and the coup leading to the Second French Empire in 1851. All those that I examined worked or didn't work for the same reason. Like those of the left, these new internal orders succeeded when they produced broad-based economic successes and failed when they did not. Because broad economic prosperity is the biggest reason a new regime succeeds or fails, the long-term trends have been to both greater total wealth and broader distribution of the wealth (i.e., better economic and health outcomes for the average person). That big picture can be easily lost when one is in and experiencing one part of the Big Cycle.

Typically the people who led the civil war/revolution were (and still are) well-educated people from middle-class backgrounds. For example, three of the key revolutionary leaders of the French Revolution were Georges-Jacques Danton, a lawyer raised in a bourgeois family; Jean-Paul Marat, a physician, scientist, and journalist raised in a bourgeois family; and Maximilian Robespierre, a lawyer and statesman also from a bourgeois family. This revolution was initially supported by many liberal aristocrats, like the Marquis de Lafayette, who were raised in moderately well-off families. Similarly, the leaders of the Russian Revolution were Vladimir Lenin, who studied law, and Leon Trotsky, who was raised in a bourgeois family of intellectuals. The Chinese Civil War was led by Mao, who was from a moderately well-off family and studied a variety of subjects such as law, economics, and political theory, and Zhou Enlai, who was from a scholarly middle-class family of civil servants. **These leaders also typically were (and still are) charismatic and able to lead and work well with others to build big, well-run organizations that have the power to bring about the revolutions. If you want to look for the revolutionaries of the future, you might keep an eye on those who have these qualities. Over time they typically evolve from being idealistic intellectuals wanting to change the system to be fairer to brutal revolutionaries bent on winning at all costs.**

While having large wealth gaps during economically difficult times was typically the biggest source of conflict, there were always other reasons for conflict that added up to a lot of opposition to the leadership and the system. Typically in revolutions the revolutionaries with these different grievances joined together to make revolutionary changes; while they looked united during the revolution, after winning the revolution, they typically fought with each other over issues and for power.

As previously mentioned, **during the civil war/revolution stage of the cycle the governments in power almost always had an acute shortage of money, credit, and buying power. That shortage created the desire to grab money from those who had it, which led those who had wealth to move it into places and assets that were safe, which led the governments to stop these movements by imposing capital controls—i.e., controls on movements to other jurisdictions (e.g., other countries), to other currencies, or to assets that are more difficult to tax and/or are less productive (e.g., gold).**

To make matters even worse, when there was internal disorder, foreign enemies were more likely to challenge the country. This happens because domestic conflict causes vulnerabilities that make external wars more likely. Internal conflict splits the people within a country, is financially taxing on them, and demands attention that leaves less time for the leaders to tend to other issues—all things that create vulnerabilities for foreign powers to take advantage of. That is the main reason why internal wars and external wars tend to come close together. Other reasons include: emotions and tempers are heightened; strong populist leaders who tend to come to power at such times are fighters by nature; when there are internal conflicts leaders find that a perceived threat from an external enemy can bring the country together in support of the leader so they tend to encourage the conflict; and being deprived leads people/countries to be more willing to fight for what they need, including resources that other countries have.

● ***Almost all civil wars have had some foreign powers participating in attempt to influence the outcome to their benefit.***

● ***The beginnings of civil wars and revolutions aren't clear when they are happening, though they are obvious when one is deeply in the middle of them.*** While historians assign dates to the beginnings and ends of civil wars, they are arbitrary. The truth is that almost no one at the time knows that a civil war has begun or that it has ended, but they know when they are in them. For example, many historians have designated July 14, 1789, as the day the French Revolution began because a mob stormed an armory and prison called the Bastille. But nobody at the time thought it was the beginning of the French Revolution or had any idea how terribly brutal that civil war and revolution would become. While one might not know what's to come, one can have imprecise markers that help one place where one is, to see the direction that one is moving in, and to know something about what the next stage will be like.

Civil wars are incredibly brutal because they are fights to the death. Everyone is an extremist because everyone is forced to pick a side and fight—also moderates lose out in knife fights.

As for what types of leaders are best for civil wars and revolutions, they are the "inspirational generals"—people who are strong

enough to marshal support and win the various types of battles they have to win. Because the fight is brutal they have to be brutal enough to do whatever is necessary to win.

The time that historians stamp as the civil war period typically lasts a few years and determines the official winners and losers, which is conveyed by who gets to occupy the government buildings in the capital. But like the beginnings, the ends of civil wars/revolutions are not as clearly defined as historians convey. The fighting to consolidate power can go on for a long time after the official civil war has ended.

While civil wars and revolutions are typically extremely painful, they often lead to restructurings that, if done well, can establish the foundation for improved future results. What the future after the civil war/revolution looks like depends on how the next steps are handled.

CONCLUSION

My study of history has taught me that nothing is forever other than evolution, and within evolution there are cycles that are like tides that come in and go out and that are hard to change or fight against. To handle these changes well it is essential to know which stage of the cycle one is in and to know timeless and universal principles for dealing with it. As conditions change the best approaches change—i.e., what is best depends on the circumstances and the circumstances are always changing in the ways we just looked at. For that reason it is a mistake to rigidly believe that any economic or political system is always best because there will certainly be times when that system is not best for the circumstances at hand, and if a society doesn't adapt it will die. That is why constantly reforming systems to adapt well is best. The test of any system is simply how well it works in delivering what most of the people want, and this can be objectively measured, which we can do and will continue to do. Having said that, the lesson from history that comes through most loudly and most clearly is that skilled collaborations to produce productive win-win relationships to both grow and divide the pie well, so that most people are happy, are much more rewarding and much less painful than fighting civil wars over wealth and power that lead to one side subjugating the other side.

CHAPTER 6

THE BIG CYCLE OF EXTERNAL ORDER AND DISORDER

Relationships between people and the orders that govern them work in basically the same ways, whether they are internal or external, and they blend together. In fact, it wasn't long ago that there were no distinctions between internal and external orders because there were no clearly defined and mutually recognized boundaries between countries. For that reason, **the six-stage cycle of going between order and disorder that I described in the last chapter about what happens within countries works the same way between countries, with one big exception:** ● ***international relations are driven much more by raw power dynamics.*** **That is because all governance systems require effective and agreed-upon 1) laws and law-making abilities, 2) law enforcement capabilities (e.g., police), 3) ways of adjudicating (e.g., judges), and 4) clear and specified consequences that both suit crimes and are enforced (e.g., fines and incarcerations), and those things either don't exist or are not as effective in guiding relations between countries as they are in guiding relations within them.**

While attempts have been made to make the external order more rule-abiding (e.g., via the League of Nations and the United Nations), by and large they have failed because these organizations have not had more wealth and power than the most powerful countries. **When individual countries have more power than the collectives of countries, the more powerful individual countries rule. For example, if the US, China, or other countries have more power than the United Nations, then the US, China, or other countries will determine how things go rather than the United Nations. That is because *power prevails*, and wealth and power among equals is rarely given up without a fight.**

When powerful countries have disputes, they don't get their lawyers to plead their cases to judges. Instead, they threaten each other and either reach agreements or fight. **The international order follows the law of the jungle much more than it follows international law.**

There are five major kinds of fights between countries: trade/economic wars, technology wars, capital wars, geopolitical wars, and military wars. Let's begin by briefly defining them.

1. **Trade/economic wars:** Conflicts over tariffs, import/export restrictions, and other ways of damaging a rival economically
2. **Technology wars:** Conflicts over which technologies are shared and which are held as protected aspects of national security
3. **Geopolitical wars:** Conflicts over territory and alliances that are resolved through negotiations and explicit or implicit commitments, not fighting
4. **Capital wars:** Conflicts imposed through financial tools such as sanctions (e.g., cutting off money and credit by punishing institutions and governments that offer it) and limiting foreign access to capital markets
5. **Military wars:** Conflicts that involve actual shooting and the deployment of military forces

Most fights between nations fall under one or more of those

categories (cyber warfare, for example, has a role in all of them). They are over wealth and power and the ideologies pertaining to them. **While most of these types of wars don't involve shooting and killing, they all are power struggles.** In most cases, the first four kinds of war will evolve over time as intense competitions between rival nations until a military war begins. **These struggles and wars, whether or not they involve shooting and killing, are exertions of power of one side over the other. They can be all-out or contained, depending on how important the issue is and what the relative powers of the opponents are. But once a military war begins, all four of the other dimensions will be weaponized to the greatest extent possible.**

As discussed in the last several chapters, all of the factors that drive internal and external cycles tend to improve and worsen together. When things get bad, there are more things to argue over, which leads to greater inclinations to fight. That's human nature, and it is why we have the Big Cycle, which oscillates between good times and bad ones.

● ***All-out wars typically occur when existential issues (ones that are so essential to the country's existence that people are willing to fight and die for them) are at stake and they cannot be resolved by peaceful means. The wars that result from them make it clear which side gets its way and has supremacy in subsequent matters.*** That clarity over who sets the rules then becomes the basis of a new international order.

The following chart shows the cycles of internal and external peace and conflict in Europe going back to 1500 as reflected in the deaths they caused. As you can see, **there were three big cycles of rising and declining conflict, averaging about 150 years each. Though big civil and external wars last only a short time, they are typically the culmination of the longstanding conflicts that led up to them.** While World Wars I and II were separately driven by the classic cycle, they were also interrelated.

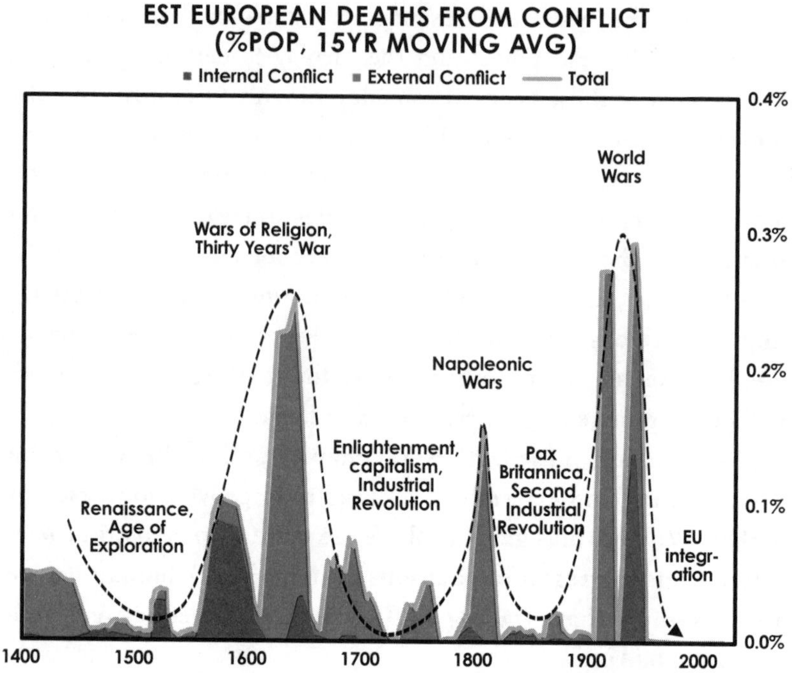

As you can see, **each cycle consisted of a relatively long period of peace and prosperity (e.g., the Renaissance, the Enlightenment, and the Industrial Revolution) that sowed the seeds for terrible and violent external wars (e.g., the Thirty Years' War, the Napoleonic Wars, and the two World Wars).** Both the upswings (the periods of peace and prosperity) and the downswings (the periods of depression and war) affected the whole world. Not all countries prosper when the leading powers do because countries gain at the expense of others. For example, the decline of China from around 1840 to 1949, known as the "Century of Humiliation," came about because the Western powers and Japan exploited China.

As you read on, keep in mind that ● ***the two things about war that one can be most confident in are 1) that it won't go as planned and 2) that it will be far worse than imagined.*** It is for those reasons that so many of the principles that follow are about ways to avoid shooting wars. Still, whether they are fought for good reasons or bad, shooting wars happen. To be clear, while I believe most are tragic and fought for nonsensical reasons, some are worth fighting because the consequences of not fighting them (e.g., the loss of freedom) would be intolerable.

THE TIMELESS AND UNIVERSAL FORCES THAT PRODUCE CHANGES TO THE EXTERNAL ORDER

As I explained in Chapter 2, after self-interest and self-survival, the quest for wealth and power is what most motivates individuals, families, companies, states, and countries. Because wealth equals power in terms of the ability to build military strength, control trade, and influence other nations, ● ***domestic and military strength go hand in hand.*** It takes money to buy guns (military power) and it takes money to buy butter (domestic social spending needs). When a country fails to provide adequate amounts of either, it becomes vulnerable to domestic and foreign opposition. From my study of Chinese dynasties and European empires, I've learned that ● ***the financial strength to outspend one's rivals is one of the most important strengths a country can have.*** That is how the United States beat the Soviet Union in the Cold War. Spend enough money in the right ways, and you don't have to have a shooting war. Long-term success depends on sustaining both the "guns" and the "butter" without producing the excesses that lead to their declines. In other words, a country must be strong enough financially to give its people both a good living standard and protection from outside enemies. The really successful countries have been able to do that for 200 to 300 years. None has been able to do it forever.

Conflict arises when the dominant power begins to weaken or an emerging power begins to approach it in strength—or both. ● ***The greatest risk of military war is when both parties have 1) military powers that are roughly comparable and 2) irreconcilable and existential differences.*** As of this writing, the most potentially explosive conflict is that between the United States and China over Taiwan.

The choice that opposing countries face—either fighting or

backing down—is very hard to make. Both are costly—fighting in terms of lives and money, and backing down in terms of the loss of status, since it shows weakness, which leads to reduced support. When two competing entities each have the power to destroy the other, both must have extremely high trust that they won't be unacceptably harmed or killed by the other. Managing the prisoner's dilemma well, however, is extremely rare (see the addendum to Chapter 2 for a full explanation).

While there are no rules in international relations other than those the most powerful impose on themselves, some approaches produce better outcomes than others. Specifically, those that are more likely to lead to win-win outcomes are better than those that lead to lose-lose outcomes. Hence this all-important principle: ● ***to get more win-win outcomes one needs to negotiate with consideration given to what is most important to the other party and to oneself, and know how to trade them.***[1,2]

Skilled collaborations to produce win-win relationships that both increase and divide up wealth and power well are much more rewarding and much less painful than wars that lead to one side subjugating the other. Seeing things through your adversary's eyes and clearly identifying and communicating your red lines to them (i.e., what cannot be compromised) are the keys to doing this well. ● ***Winning means getting the things that are most important without losing the things that are most important, so wars that cost much more in lives***

---

[1] To give an oversimplified example of a win-win approach, if each country picks the top 10 things that they want to get or want to be protected against and allocates 100 points in total to these to express how much they want these things, they could determine what the best trades would be. For example, I expect that high on China's list would be the reunification with Taiwan—so high in fact that they would go to war for it. I can't imagine that preventing that from happening peacefully would be nearly as high on the US's list, whereas something on the US's list would be very high so that they should be willing to trade it to make both sides happy.

[2] Though it might sound naïve, I wish the power of thoughtful disagreement could be tapped to deal with the US-China wars. For example, I visualize how wonderful it would be if leaders or representatives of each country were to have a series of publicly aired thoughtful disagreements, like presidential debates, that the populations of both countries could listen to in order to gain both sides' perspectives. I'm sure it would make us much more knowledgeable and empathetic, and improve the chances of peaceful resolutions.

and money than they provide in benefits are stupid. But "stupid" wars still happen all the time for reasons that I will explain.

It is far too easy to slip into stupid wars because of a) the prisoner's dilemma, b) a tit-for-tat escalation process, c) the perceived costs of backing down for the declining power, and d) misunderstandings existing when decision making has to be fast. Rival great powers typically find themselves in the prisoner's dilemma; they need to have ways of assuring the other that they won't try to kill them lest the other tries to kill them first. Tit-for-tat escalations are dangerous in that they require each side to escalate or lose what the enemy captured in the last move; it is like a game of chicken—push it too far and there is a head-on crash.

Untruthful and emotional appeals that rile people up increase the dangers of stupid wars, so it is better for leaders to be truthful and thoughtful in explaining the situation and how they are dealing with it (this is especially essential in a democracy, in which the opinions of the population matter). The worst thing is when leaders are untruthful and emotional in dealing with their populations, and it is worse still when they take over the media.

By and large, the tendency to move between win-win relationships and lose-lose relationships happens in a cyclical way. People and empires are more likely to have cooperative relationships during good times and to fight during bad times. When the existing great power is declining in relation to a rising power, it has a natural tendency to want to maintain the status quo or the existing rules, while the rising power wants to change them to be in line with the changing facts on the ground.

While I don't know about the love part of the saying "all is fair in love and war," I know the war part is right. As an example, in the American Revolutionary War, when the British lined up in rows for the fight and the American revolutionaries shot at them from behind trees, the British thought that was unfair and complained. The revolutionaries won believing the British were foolish and that the cause of independence and freedom justified changing the rules of war. That's just how it is.

This leads me to one final principle: ● ***have power, respect power, and use power wisely.*** Having power is good because power will win out over agreements, rules, and laws all the time. When push comes to shove, those who have the power to either enforce their interpretation of the rules and laws or to overturn them will get what they want. It is important to respect power because it's not smart to fight a war that one is going to lose; it is preferable to negotiate the best settlement possible (that is unless one wants to be a martyr, which is usually for stupid ego reasons rather than for sensible strategic reasons). It is also important to use power wisely. Using power wisely doesn't necessarily mean forcing others to give you what you want—i.e., bullying them. It includes the recognition that generosity and trust are powerful forces for producing win-win relationships, which are fabulously more rewarding than lose-lose relationships. In other words, it is often the case that using one's "hard powers" is not the best path and that using one's "soft powers" is preferable.[3]

When thinking about how to use power wisely, it's also important to decide when to reach an agreement and when to fight. To do that, a party must imagine how its power will change over time. It is desirable to use one's power to negotiate an agreement, enforce an agreement, or fight a war when one's power is greatest. That means that it pays to fight early if one's relative power is declining and fight later if it's rising.

If one is in a lose-lose relationship, one has to get out of it one way or another, preferably through separation, though possibly through war. To handle one's power wisely, it's usually best not to show it because it will usually lead others to feel threatened and build their

[3] For example, though I always had the ownership power to make decisions at Bridgewater autocratically, I chose not to use that power. Instead, I created and operated an idea-meritocratic system (which I described in *Principles: Life and Work*). I also chose to be far more generous with the people I worked with than I had to be while maintaining extremely high standards because I knew that operating that way would produce the amazing relationships and outcomes that we experienced—far better than if I had used my "hard powers" more forcefully. So, it's important to remember that great relationships give one great powers and that they are wonderful rewards in and of themselves. There is nothing more powerful and rewarding for the individual and the collective than the cooperation of capable people who care for each other and who will give each other all they can.

own threatening powers, which will lead to a mutual escalation that threatens both. Power is usually best handled like a hidden knife that can be brought out in the event of a fight. But there are times when showing one's power and threatening to use it are most effective for improving one's negotiating position and preventing a fight. Knowing what matters most and least to the other party, especially what they will and won't fight for, allows you to work your way toward an equilibrium that both parties consider a fair resolution of a dispute.

Though it is generally desirable to have power, it is also desirable to not have power that one doesn't need. That is because maintaining power consumes resources, most importantly your time and your money. Also, with power comes the burden of responsibilities. I have often been struck by how much happier less powerful people can be relative to more powerful people.

CASE STUDY: WORLD WAR II

Now that we have covered the dynamics and principles that drive the external order and disorder cycle, which were derived by looking at many cases, I'd like to briefly look at the World War II case because it provides the most recent example of the iconic dynamic of going from peace to war. Though it is only one case, it clearly shows how the confluence of the three big cycles—i.e., the overlapping and interrelated forces of the money and credit cycle, the internal order/disorder cycle, and the external order/disorder cycle—created the conditions for a catastrophic war and laid the groundwork for a new world order. While the stories from this period are very interesting in and of themselves, they are especially important because they provide lessons that help us think about what is happening now and what might be ahead. Most importantly, the United States and China are in an economic war that could conceivably evolve into a military war and comparisons between the 1930s and today provide valuable insights into what might happen and how to avoid a terrible war.

THE PATH TO WAR

To help convey the picture of the 1930s, I will run through the geopolitical highlights leading up to the official start of the war in Europe in 1939 and the bombing of Pearl Harbor in 1941. Then I will quickly move through the war and the start of the new world order in 1945, with the US at the peak of its power.

The global depression that followed the Great Crash of 1929 led to almost all countries having big internal conflicts over wealth. This caused them to turn to more populist, autocratic, nationalistic, and militaristic leaders and policies. These moves were either to the right or to the left and occurred in varying degrees, according to the countries' circumstances and the strengths of their democratic or autocratic traditions. In Germany, Japan, Italy, and Spain, extremely bad economic circumstances and less well-established democratic traditions led to extreme internal conflicts and a turn to populist/autocratic leaders of the right (i.e., fascists), just as at different points in time the Soviet Union and China, which also endured extreme circumstances and had no experience with democracy, turned to populist/autocratic leaders of the left (i.e., communists). The US and the UK had much stronger democratic traditions and less severe economic conditions, so they became more populist and autocratic than they had been, but not nearly as much as other nations.

Germany and Japan

While Germany had previously been saddled with tremendous reparation debts following World War I, by 1929 it was beginning to emerge from under their yoke via the Young Plan, which provided for considerable debt relief and the departure of foreign troops from Germany by 1930.[4] But the global depression hit Germany hard, leading

[4] Specific developments and detail on this period are explained in my book *Principles for Navigating Big Debt Crises.*

to nearly 25 percent unemployment, massive bankruptcies, and extensive poverty. As is typical, there was a struggle between populists of the left (communists) and populists of the right (fascists). Adolf Hitler, the leading populist/fascist, tapped into the mood of national humiliation to build a nationalistic furor, casting the Treaty of Versailles and the countries that imposed it as the enemy. He created a 25-point nationalistic program and rallied support around it. In response to internal fighting and the desire to restore order, Hitler was appointed chancellor in January 1933, drawing large support for his Nazi Party from industrialists who feared the communists. Two months later, the Nazi Party won the most support and the most seats in the German Parliament (the Reichstag).

Hitler refused to pay any further reparation debts, left the League of Nations, and took autocratic control of Germany in 1934. Holding the dual roles of chancellor and president, he became the country's supreme leader. In democracies there are always some laws that allow leaders to grab special powers; Hitler seized them all. He invoked Article 48 of the Weimar Constitution to put an end to many civil rights and suppress political opposition from the communists, and forced the passage of the Enabling Act, which allowed him to pass laws without the approval of the Reichstag and the president. He was ruthless against any opposition—he censored or took control of newspapers and broadcasting companies, created a secret police force (the Gestapo) to root out and crush opposition, deprived Jews of their rights of citizenship, seized the Protestant Church's finances, and arrested church officials who opposed him. Declaring the Aryan race superior, he prohibited non-Aryans from serving in government.

Hitler took that same autocratic/fascist approach to rebuilding Germany's economy, coupled with big fiscal and monetary stimulation programs. He privatized state-owned businesses and encouraged corporate investment, acting aggressively to raise Aryan Germans' living standards. For example, he set up Volkswagen to make cars affordable and accessible, and he directed the building of the Autobahn. He financed this substantially increased government spending by forcing banks to buy government bonds. The debts that were produced were paid back by the earnings of companies and the central bank (the Reichsbank) monetizing debt. These fiscal policies by and large worked well in achieving Hitler's goals. This is another example of how borrowing in one's own currency and increasing one's own debt and deficits can be highly productive if the money borrowed is put into investments that raise productivity and produce more than enough cash flow to service the debt. Even if it doesn't cover 100 percent of the debt service, it can be very cost-effective in achieving the economic goals of the country.

As for the economic effects of these policies, when Hitler came to power in 1933 the unemployment rate was 25 percent. By 1938 it was nil. Per capita income increased by 22 percent in the five years after Hitler took power, and real growth averaged over 8 percent per year between 1934 and 1938. As shown in the following charts, German equities rallied nearly 70 percent in a steady trend between 1933 and 1938, until the onset of the hot war.

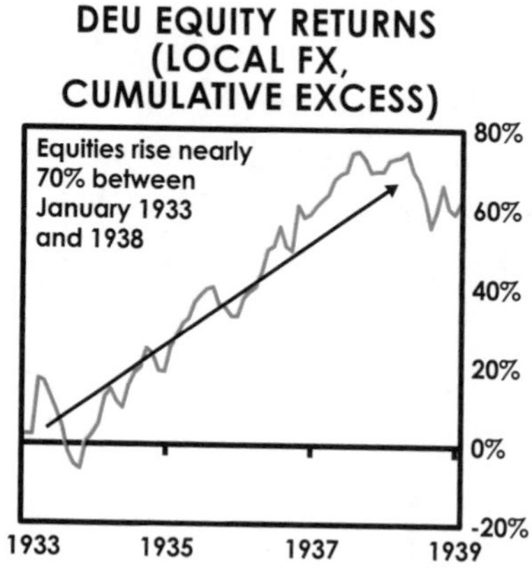

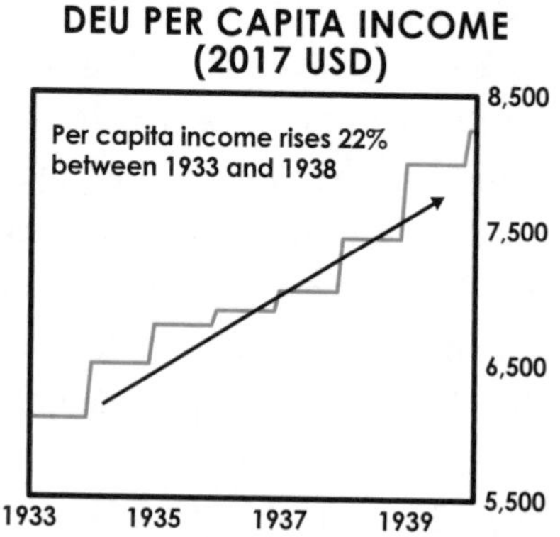

In 1935, Hitler began to build the military, making military service compulsory for Aryans. Germany's military spending increased much faster than any other country because **the German economy needed more resources to fuel itself and it intended to use its military power to seize them.**

Like Germany, **Japan was also hit exceptionally hard by the depression and became more autocratic in response**. Japan was especially vulnerable to the depression because, as an island nation without adequate natural resources, it relied on exports for income to import necessities. When its exports fell by around 50 percent between 1929 and 1931, Japan was economically devastated. **In 1931, Japan went broke**—i.e., it was forced to draw down its gold reserves, abandon the gold standard, and float its currency, which depreciated it so greatly that Japan ran out of buying power. **These terrible conditions and large wealth gaps led to fighting between the left and the right. By 1932, there was a massive upsurge in right-wing nationalism and militarism, in the hope that order and economic stability could be forcibly restored. Japan set out to get the natural resources (e.g., oil, iron, coal, and rubber) and human resources (i.e., slave labor) it needed by seizing them from other countries, invading Manchuria in 1931 and spreading out through China and Asia. As with Germany, it could be argued that Japan's path of military aggression to get needed resources was more cost-effective than relying on classic trading and economic practices.** In 1934, there was severe famine in parts of Japan, causing even more political turbulence and reinforcing the right-wing, militaristic, nationalistic, and expansionistic movement.

In the years that followed, Japan's top-down fascist command economy grew stronger, building a military-industrial complex to protect its existing bases in East Asia and northern China and support its excursions into other countries. As was also the case in Germany, while most Japanese companies remained privately held, their production was controlled by the government.

What is fascism? Consider the following three big choices that a country has to make when selecting its approach to governance: 1) bottom-up (democratic) or top-down (autocratic) decision making, 2) capitalist or communist (with socialist in the middle) ownership of production, and 3) individualistic (which treats the well-being of the individual with paramount importance) or

collectivist (which treats the well-being of the whole with paramount importance). Pick the one from each category that you believe is optimal for your nation's values and ambitions and you have your preferred approach. Fascism is autocratic, capitalist, and collectivist. Fascists believe that top-down autocratic leadership, in which the government directs the production of privately held companies such that individual gratification is subordinated to national success, is the best way to make the country and its people wealthier and more powerful.

The US and the Allies

In the US, debt problems became ruinous for American banks after 1929, which curtailed their lending around the world, hurting international borrowers. At the same time, the depression created weak demand, which led to a collapse of US imports and other countries' sales to the US. As incomes weakened, demand fell and more credit problems occurred in a self-reinforcing downward economic spiral. The US responded by turning protectionist to safeguard jobs, raising tariffs via the passage of the Smoot-Hawley Tariff Act in 1930, which further depressed economic conditions in other countries.

● ***Raising tariffs to protect domestic businesses and jobs during bad economic times is common, but it leads to reduced efficiency because production does not occur where it can be done most efficiently.*** **Ultimately, tariffs contribute to greater global economic weakness, as tariff wars cause the countries that impose them to lose exports. Tariffs do, however, benefit the entities that are protected by them, and they can create political support for the leaders who impose them.**

The Soviet Union had yet to recover from its devastating 1917–22 revolution and civil war, a lost war to Germany, a costly war with Poland, and a famine in 1921, and it was wracked by political purges and economic hardships throughout the 1930s. China also suffered from civil war, poverty, and a famine in 1928–30. **So, when things worsened in 1930 and tariffs began, bad conditions became desperate conditions in those countries.**

To make matters worse, there were droughts in the US and in the Soviet Union in the 1930s. ● ***Harmful acts of nature (e.g., droughts, floods, and plagues) often cause periods of great economic hardship that when combined with other adverse conditions lead to periods of great conflict.*** In combination with extreme government policies, millions died in the USSR. At the same time, internal political fighting and fears of Nazi Germany led to purges of hundreds of thousands of people who were accused of spying and shot without trials.

● ***Deflationary depressions are debt crises caused by there not being enough money in the hands of debtors to service their debts. They inevitably lead to the printing of money, debt restructurings, and government spending programs that increase the supply of, and reduce the value of, money and credit. The only question is how long it takes for government officials to make this move.***

In the case of the US, it took three and a half years from the crash in October 1929 until President Franklin D. Roosevelt's March 1933 actions. In Roosevelt's first 100 days in office, he created several massive government spending programs that were paid for by big tax increases and big budget deficits financed by debt that the Federal Reserve monetized. He instituted jobs programs, unemployment insurance, Social Security supports, and labor- and union-friendly programs. After his 1935 tax bill, then popularly called the "Soak the Rich Tax," the top marginal income tax rate for individuals rose to 75 percent (versus as low as 25 percent in 1930). By 1941, the top personal tax rate was 81 percent, and the top corporate tax rate was 31 percent, having started at 12 percent in 1930. Roosevelt also imposed a number of other taxes. Despite all of these taxes and the pickup in the economy that helped raise tax revenue, budget deficits increased from around 1 percent of GDP to about 4 percent of GDP because the spending increases were so large.[5] **From 1933 until the end of 1936 the stock market returned over 200 percent, and the**

[5] Specific developments through the Great Depression are explained in great detail in my book *Principles for Navigating Big Debt Crises.*

economy grew at a blistering average real rate of about 9 percent.

In 1936, the Federal Reserve tightened money and credit to fight inflation and slow an overheating economy, which caused the fragile US economy to fall back into recession and the other major economies to weaken with it, further raising tensions within and between countries.

Meanwhile in Europe, the conflict in Spain between the populists of the left (the communists) and the populists of the right (the fascists) flared into the brutal Spanish Civil War. Right-wing Franco, with the support of Hitler, succeeded in purging left-wing opposition in Spain.

● ***During periods of severe economic distress and large wealth gaps, there are typically revolutionarily large redistributions of wealth.*** **When done peacefully these are achieved through large tax increases on the rich and big increases in the supply of money that devalue debtors' claims, and when done violently they are achieved by forced asset confiscations.** In the US and the UK, while there were redistributions of wealth and political power, capitalism and democracy were maintained. In Germany, Japan, Italy, and Spain they were not.

● ***Before there is a shooting war there is usually an economic war.*** As is also typical, before all-out wars are declared there is about a decade of economic, technological, geopolitical, and capital wars, during which the conflicting powers intimidate each other, testing the limits of each other's power. While 1939 and 1941 are known as the official starts of the wars in Europe and the Pacific, the conflicts really began about 10 years before that. **In addition to the economically motivated conflicts within countries and the political shifts that arose from them, all of these countries faced increased external economic conflicts as they fought for greater shares of a shrinking economic pie.** Because power, and not law, rules international relations, Germany and Japan became more expansionist and increasingly began to test the UK, the US, and France in the competition over resources and influence over territories.

Before going on to describe the hot war, I want to elaborate on

the common tactics used when economic and capital tools are weaponized. They have been and still are:

1. **Asset freezes/seizures:** Preventing an enemy/rival from using or selling foreign assets they rely on. These measures can range from asset freezes for targeted groups in a country (e.g., the current US sanctions of the Iranian Revolutionary Guard or the initial US asset freeze against Japan in World War II) to more severe measures like unilateral debt repudiation or outright seizures of a country's assets (e.g., some top US policy makers have been talking about not paying our debts to China).
2. **Blocking capital markets access:** Preventing a country from accessing their own or another country's capital markets (e.g., in 1887 Germany banned the purchase of Russian securities and debt to impede Russia's military buildup; the US is now threatening to do this to China).
3. **Embargoes/blockades:** Blocking trade in goods and/or services in one's own country and in some cases with neutral third parties for the purpose of weakening the targeted country or preventing it from getting essential items (e.g., the US's oil embargo on Japan and cutting off its ships' access to the Panama Canal in World War II) or blocking exports from the targeted country to other countries, thus cutting off their income (e.g., France's blockade of the UK in the Napoleonic Wars).

If you're interested in seeing how these tactics have been applied from 1600 until now, they are available at economicprinciples.org.

THE HOT WAR BEGINS

In November 1937, Hitler secretly met with his top officials to announce his plans for German expansion to gain resources and bring together the Aryan race. Then he put them into action, first annexing Austria and then seizing a part of what was then Czechoslovakia that contained oil resources. Europe and the US watched warily, not wanting to get drawn into another war so soon after the devastation of World War I.

As with all wars, the unknowns were far greater than the knowns because a) rival powers go into wars only when their powers are roughly comparable (otherwise it would be stupidly suicidal for the obviously weaker power) and b) there are way too many possible actions and reactions to anticipate. The only thing that is known at the outset of a hot war is that it will probably be extremely painful and possibly ruinous. As a result, smart leaders typically go into them only if the other side has pushed them into a position of either fighting or losing by backing down. For the Allies, that moment came on September 1, 1939, when Germany invaded Poland.

Germany looked unstoppable; in short order it captured Denmark, Norway, the Netherlands, Belgium, Luxembourg, and France, and strengthened its alliances with Japan and Italy, which had common enemies and were ideologically aligned. By seizing territory rapidly (e.g., oil-rich Romania), Hitler's army was able to conserve its existing oil resources and gain new ones quickly. The thirst for, and acquisition of, natural resources remained a major driver of the Nazi war machine as it pushed its campaigns into Russia and the Middle East. War with the Soviets was inevitable; the only question was when. Although Germany and the USSR had signed a non-aggression pact, Germany invaded Russia in June 1941, which put Germany in an extremely costly war on two fronts.

In the Pacific in 1937, Japan expanded its occupation of China, brutally taking control of Shanghai and Nanking, killing an estimated 200,000 Chinese civilians and disarmed combatants in the capture of Nanking alone. While the US remained isolationist, it did provide Chiang Kai-shek's government with fighter planes and pilots to counter the Japanese, putting a toe in the war. Conflicts between the US and Japan began to flare. A Japanese soldier struck the US consul, John Moore Allison, in the face in Nanking and Japanese fighter planes sank a US gunship.

In November 1940, Roosevelt won re-election after campaigning on the promise to keep the US out of the war, even though the US was already taking economic actions to protect its interests, especially in the Pacific, using economic supports to help countries it sympathized with and economic sanctions against those it did not. Earlier in 1940, Secretary of War Henry Stimson had initiated aggressive economic sanctions against Japan, culminating in the Export Control Act of 1940. In mid-1940, the US moved the US Pacific Fleet to Hawaii. In October, the US ramped up the embargo, restricting "all iron and steel to destinations other than Britain and nations of the Western Hemisphere." The plan was to cut Japan off from resources in order to force them to retreat from most of the areas they had taken over.

In March 1941, Congress passed the Lend-Lease Act, which allowed the US to lend or lease war supplies to the nations it deemed to be acting in ways that were "vital to the defense of the United States," which included Great Britain, the Soviet Union, and China. Helping the Allies was good for the US both geopolitically and economically because it made a lot of money selling weapons, food, and other items to these soon-to-be-allied countries who were struggling to maintain production while waging war. But its motivations weren't entirely mercenary. Great Britain was running out of money (i.e., gold), so the US allowed them to postpone payment until after the war (in some cases waiving payment entirely). Although not an outright declaration of war, Lend-Lease effectively ended the United States' neutrality.

● ***When countries are weak, opposing countries take advantage of their weaknesses to obtain gains.*** France, the Netherlands, and Great Britain all had colonies in Asia. Overstretched by the fighting in Europe, they were unable to defend them against the Japanese. Starting in September 1940, Japan invaded several colonies in Southeast Asia, beginning with French Indochina, adding what it called the Southern Resource Zone to its Greater East Asia Co-Prosperity Sphere. In 1941, Japan seized oil reserves in the Dutch East Indies.

This Japanese territorial expansion was a threat to the US's own Pacific ambitions. In July and August 1941, Roosevelt responded by freezing all Japanese assets in the United States, closing the Panama Canal to Japanese ships, and embargoing oil and gas exports to Japan. This cut off three-fourths of Japan's trade and 80 percent of its oil. Japan calculated that it would run out of oil in two years. This put Japan in the position of having to choose between backing down or attacking the US.

On December 7 and 8, 1941, Japan launched coordinated attacks on US military forces at Pearl Harbor and in the Philippines. This marked the beginning of the declared war in the Pacific, which brought the US into the war in Europe too. While Japan didn't have a widely recognized plan to win the war, the most optimistic Japanese leaders believed that the US would lose because it was fighting a war on two fronts and because its individualistic/capitalist political system was inferior to Japan's and Germany's authoritarian/fascist systems with their command military-industrial complexes. They also believed that they had the greater willingness to endure pain and die for their country, which is a big driver of which side wins. ● ***In war one's ability to withstand pain is even more important than one's ability to inflict pain.***

WARTIME ECONOMIC POLICIES

Just as it is worth noting what classic economic war tactics are, it is also worth noting what classic wartime economic policies are within countries. These include government controls on just about everything as the country shifts its resources from profit making to war making—e.g., the government determines a) what items are allowed to be produced, b) what items can be bought and sold in what amounts (rationing), c) what items can be imported and exported, d) prices, wages, and profits, e) access to one's own financial assets, and f) the ability to move one's own money out of the country. Because wars are expensive, classically the government g) issues lots of debt that is monetized, h) relies on non-credit money such as gold for international transactions because its credit is not accepted, i) governs more autocratically, j) imposes various types of economic sanctions on enemies, including cutting off their access to capital, and k) experiences enemies imposing these sanctions on them.

When the US entered the European and Pacific wars after the attack on Pearl Harbor, classic wartime economic policies were put in place in most countries by leaders whose more autocratic approaches were broadly supported by their populations. The following table shows those economic controls in each of the major countries.

WARTIME ECONOMIC CONTROLS

	Rationing	Production Controls	Price/Wage Controls	Import or Export Restrictions	Takeover of Central Bank
Allies					
United States	Yes	Yes	Yes	Yes	Yes
United Kingdom	Yes	Yes	Yes	Yes	Partial
Axis					
Germany	Yes	Yes	Yes	Yes	Yes
Japan	Yes	Yes	Yes	Yes	Yes

The market movements during the hot war years were heavily affected by both government controls and how countries did in battles as the odds of winning and losing changed. The next table shows the controls over markets and capital flows that were put in place by the major countries during the war years.

REGULATIONS IMPACTING ASSETS

	Market Closures	Asset Price Controls	Asset Ownership Restrictions	FX Controls	Top Marginal Tax Rate	Limits on New Issuance	Limits on Corp Profits
Allies							
United States	No	Yes	Yes	Yes	94%	—	Yes
United Kingdom	Yes	Yes	Yes	Yes	98%	Yes	Yes
Axis							
Germany	Yes	Yes	Yes	Yes	60%	Yes	Yes
Japan	Yes	Yes	Yes	Yes	74%	Yes	Yes

Stock market closures were common in a number of countries, leaving investors in stocks stuck without access to their capital. I should also note that money and credit were not commonly accepted between non-allied countries during the war because of a justifiable wariness about whether the currency would have any value. As noted earlier, gold—or, in some cases, silver or barter—is the coin of the realm during wars. At such times, prices and capital flows are typically controlled, so it is difficult to say what the real prices of many things are.

Because losing wars typically leads to a total wipeout of wealth and power, movements of those stock markets that remained open in the war years were largely driven by how countries did in key battles as these results shifted the probability of victory or defeat for each side. For example, German equities outperformed at the beginning of World War II as Germany captured territory and established military dominance, while they underperformed after Allied powers like the US and the UK turned the tide of the war. After the 1942 Battle of Midway, Allied equities rallied almost continuously until the end of the war, while Axis equities were flat or down. As shown, both the German and Japanese stock markets were closed at the end of the war, didn't reopen for around five years, and were virtually wiped out when they did, while US stocks were extremely strong.

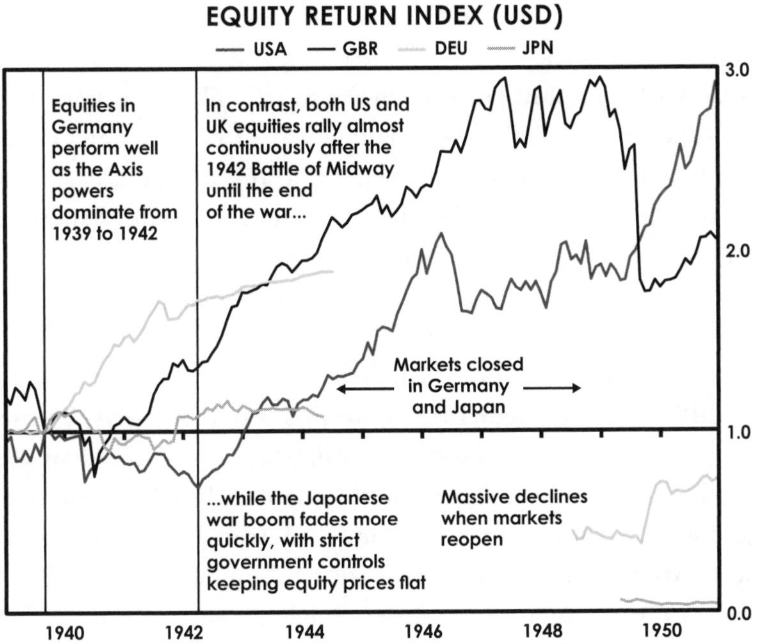
EQUITY RETURN INDEX (USD)
USA
GBR
DEU
JPN
Equities in Germany perform well as the Axis powers dominate from 1939 to 1942
In contrast, both US and UK equities rally almost continuously after the 1942 Battle of Midway until the end of the war...
Markets closed in Germany and Japan
...while the Japanese war boom fades more quickly, with strict government controls keeping equity prices flat
Massive declines when markets reopen
3.0
2.0
1.0
0.0
1940
1942
1944
1946
1948
1950

Protecting one's wealth in times of war is difficult, as normal economic activities are curtailed, traditionally safe investments are not safe, capital mobility is limited, and high taxes are imposed when people and countries are fighting for their survival. Protecting the wealth of those who have it is not a priority relative to the need to redistribute wealth to get it to where it is needed most. As for investing, sell out of all debt and buy gold because wars are financed by borrowing and printing money, which devalues debt and money, and because there is a justifiable reluctance to accept credit.

CONCLUSION

Every world power has its time in the sun, thanks to the uniqueness of their circumstances and the nature of their character and culture (e.g., they have the essential elements of a strong work ethic, smarts, discipline, education, etc.), but they all eventually decline. Some do so more gracefully than others, with less trauma, but they nevertheless decline. Traumatic declines can lead to some of the worst periods in history, when big fights over wealth and power prove extremely costly both economically and in human lives.

Still, the cycle needn't transpire this way if countries in their rich and powerful stages stay productive, earn more than they spend, make the system work well for most of their populations, and figure out ways of creating and sustaining win-win relationships with their most significant rivals. A number of empires and dynasties have sustained themselves for hundreds of years, and the United States, at 245 years old, has proven itself to be one of the longest-lasting.

In Part II, I will turn to the US, the two reserve currency empires that preceded it, and the one that may someday follow it. As we continue, I hope this explanation of the archetypical Big Cycle and the three cycles that make it up will help you see the patterns of history and what they portend. But before we delve more deeply into the history, I'd first like to share how these big three cycles figure into my approach as an investor.

CHAPTER 7

INVESTING IN LIGHT OF THE BIG CYCLE

The game I play for handling both my life and my career is to try to figure out how the world works, develop principles for dealing with it well, and then place my bets. The research that I'm sharing with you in this book was done for that purpose. Naturally, when I look at all that we've covered up to this point, I think about how it applies to my investing. For me to be comfortable that I am doing that well, I need to know how my approach would have worked through time. If I can't confidently explain what happened in the past, or at least have a strategy for dealing with it in light of what I don't know, I consider myself dangerously negligent.

As you saw from my study of the last 500 years up to now, there were Big Cycles of great accumulations and great losses of wealth and power, and of these, the greatest contributing factor was the debt and capital markets cycle. From an investor's perspective, this could be called the Big Investing Cycle. I felt that I needed to understand these cycles well enough to tactically move or diversify my portfolio to be protected against them and/or to profit from them. By understanding them, and ideally realizing where countries are in their cycles, I can do that.

Over my roughly 50 years as a global macro investor, I discovered

many timeless and universal truths that form my principles for investing. While I won't get deeply into all of them here, but will discuss most of them in my next book, *Principles: Economics and Investing*, I will convey one important principle.

● ***All markets are primarily driven by just four determinants: growth, inflation, risk premiums, and discount rates.***

That is because all investments are exchanges of lump-sum payments today for future payments. What these future cash payments will be is determined by growth and inflation, what risk investors are willing to take in investing in them as compared to having cash in hand is the risk premium, and what they are worth today, which is called their "present value," is determined by the discount rate.[1]

How these four determinants change drives how investment returns change. Tell me what each of these determinants is going to do and I can tell you what the investments are going to do. Knowing this tells me how to connect what is happening in the world to what is happening in the markets and vice versa. It also shows me how to balance my investments so that my portfolio doesn't have any bias to any environment, which is what produces good diversification.

Governments influence these factors through their fiscal and monetary policies. As a result, interactions between what governments want to happen and what is actually happening are what drive the cycles.[2] For example, when growth and inflation are too low, central banks create more money and credit growth, which creates

[1] The discount rate is the interest rate that one uses to assess what an amount of money in the future is worth today. To calculate it, one compares what amount of money today, invested at that interest rate (i.e., the discount rate), would be worth a certain amount at a specific time in the future.

[2] If governments and their systems break down, non-government-directed forces take over, which is a whole other story that I won't get into now.

buying power, which causes economic growth to pick up at first and then, with a lag, inflation to pick up as well. When central banks constrain money and credit growth, the opposite happens: economic growth and inflation both slow down.

There is a difference between what central governments and central banks do in order to drive market returns and economic conditions. Central governments determine where the money they use comes from and goes to because they can tax and spend, but they can't create money and credit. Central banks on the other hand can create money and credit but can't determine what the money and credit go into in the real economy. These actions from central governments and central banks influence the purchases and sales of goods, services, and investment assets, driving their prices up or down.

To me each investment asset reflects these drivers in its own way that is logical in light of the effects on its future cash flows. Each investment asset is a building block for a portfolio, and the challenge is to put together a portfolio well in light of these things. For example, when growth is stronger than expected, all else being equal, stock prices will likely rise, and when growth and inflation are higher than expected, bond prices will likely fall. **My goal is to put these building blocks together in a portfolio that is well-diversified and tactically tilted based on what is happening or is going to happen in the world that is affecting these four drivers.** These building blocks can be broken out by country, by environmental bias, and all the way down to the level of individual sectors and companies. When this concept is put into a well-balanced portfolio, it looks like the following graphic. It is through this lens that I look at the history of events, the history of the markets, and the behavior of portfolios.

THE BUILDING BLOCKS OF A WELL-DIVERSIFIED PORTFOLIO

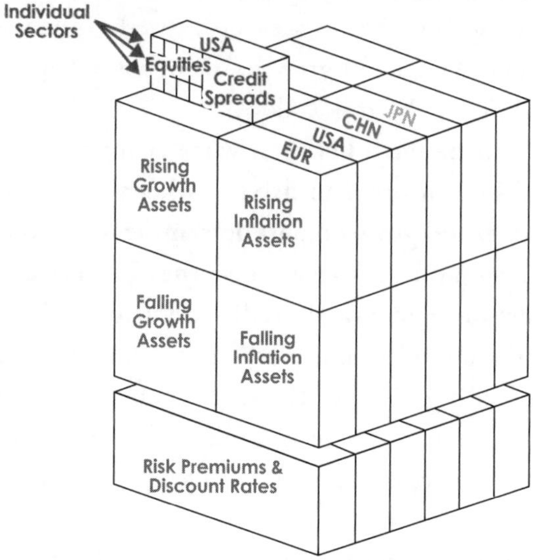

I understand that my approach is different from that of most investors for two reasons. First, most investors don't look for historically analogous periods because they think history and old investment returns are largely irrelevant to them. Second, they don't look at investment returns through the lens I just described. I believe that these perspectives give me and Bridgewater a competitive advantage, but it's up to you to take or leave them as you like.

Most investors base their expectations on what they have experienced in their lifetimes and a few more diligent ones look back in history to see how their decision-making rules would have worked back to the 1950s or 1960s. There are no investors I know and no senior economic policy makers I know—and I know many and I know the best—who have any excellent understandings of what happened in the past and why. Most investors who look at longer-term returns look at those in the US and the UK (the countries that won World War I and World War II) as being representative. That is because there are not many stock and bond markets that survived World War II. But these countries and time periods are not representative because of their survivorship bias. In looking at the returns of the US and the UK, one is looking at uniquely blessed countries in the uniquely peaceful and productive time that is the best part of the Big Cycle. Not looking at what happened in other countries and in times before yields a distorted perspective.

Reasoning logically from what we know about Big Cycles, when we extend our perspective just a few decades further back and look at what happened in different places, we get a shockingly different perspective. I'm going to show you this because I think you should have it.

In the 35 years before 1945, virtually all wealth was destroyed or confiscated in most countries, and in some countries many capitalists were killed or imprisoned because of anger at them when the capital markets and capitalism failed along with other aspects of the old order. If we look at what happened over the past few centuries, we see that such extreme boom/bust cycles happened regularly—there were regular cycles of capital and capitalist boom periods (such as the Second Industrial Revolution and the Gilded Age that happened in the late 19th and early 20th centuries) that were followed by transition periods (like the 1900–10 period of rising internal conflict and rising international conflict over wealth and power) that led to great conflict and economic bust periods (similar to those that happened between 1910 and 1945). We can also see that the cause/effect relationships that were behind the movements of those boom and bust periods are now more aligned with the late-cycle bust and restructuring periods than the early-cycle boom and building periods.

My goal was simply to see and try to understand what happened in the past and do a good job of showing it to you. That is what I will now try to do. I will start in 1350, though the story begins long before.

THE BIG CYCLE OF CAPITALISM AND MARKETS

Up until around 1350, lending with an interest rate was prohibited by both Christianity and Islam—and in Judaism it was banned within the Jewish community—because of the terrible problems it caused,

with human nature leading people to borrow more than they could pay back, which created tensions and often violence between borrowers and lenders. As a result of this lack of lending, currency was "hard" (gold and silver). A century or so later, in the Age of Exploration, explorers went around the world collecting gold and silver and other hard assets to make more money. That's how the greatest fortunes were built at the time. The explorers and those who backed them split the profits. It was an effective incentive-based system for getting rich.

The alchemy of lending as we know it today was first created in Italy around 1350. Rules for lending changed and new types of money were made: cash deposits, bonds, and stocks that looked pretty much like we know them today. Wealth became promises to deliver money—what I call "financial wealth."

Think about what a huge impact the inventions and developments of bond and stock markets had. Before then, all wealth was tangible. Think about how much more "financial wealth" was created by creating these markets. To imagine the difference, consider how much "wealth" you would now have if your cash deposits and stock and bond promises to pay you in the future didn't exist. You wouldn't have much at all. You'd feel broke, and you'd behave differently—for example, you'd build up more savings in tangible wealth. That is pretty much what it was like before cash deposits, bonds, and stocks were created.

With the invention and growth of financial wealth, money was not constrained by a link to gold and silver. Because money and credit, and with them spending power, were less constrained, it was common practice for entrepreneurs who came up with good ideas to create companies and borrow money and/or sell a piece of those companies by selling stock to get money to buy what they needed. They could do this because promises to pay became money that took the form of journal entries. Around 1350 those who could do this, most famously the Medici family in Florence, could create money. If you can create credit—let's say five times as much as there is actual money (which banks can do)—you can produce a lot of buying power so you don't need as much of the other type of money (gold and silver) anymore. The creation of new forms of money was and still is a kind of alchemy. Those who could create it and use it—bankers, entrepreneurs, and capitalists—became very rich and powerful.[3]

This process of expanding financial wealth has continued up to today, with financial wealth becoming so large that the hard money (gold and silver) and other tangible wealth (e.g., property) have become relatively unimportant. But of course the more promises there are in the form of financial wealth the greater the risk there is that these promises can't be kept. That's what makes the classic big debt/money/economic cycle.

Think about how much financial wealth there is now relative to real wealth and imagine if you and others who are holding it actually tried to convert it into real wealth—that is, sell it and buy stuff. It would be like a run on a bank. It couldn't happen. The bonds and stocks are too sizable in value relative to what they could buy. But remember that with fiat money the central banks can print and provide the money needed to meet the demand. That is a timeless and universal truth.

Also remember that paper money and financial assets (e.g., stocks and bonds) that are essentially promises to pay aren't of much use; it is only what they buy that is of use.

As discussed in detail in Chapter 3, **when credit is created, buying power is created in exchange for a promise to pay back, so it is near-term stimulating and longer-term depressing.** That creates cycles. Throughout history the desire to obtain money (by borrowing or selling stock) and the desire to save it (by investing through lending or buying stock) have been in a symbiotic relationship. **This has led to growth in the form of buying power and eventually to many more promises to pay than can be delivered and broken-promises crises in the form of debt-default depressions and stock market crashes.**

That is when the bankers and capitalists are hanged both figuratively and literally, vast amounts of wealth and lives are wiped out, and vast amounts of fiat money (money that can be printed and has no intrinsic value) are printed to try to relieve the crisis.

---

[3] You can see this kind of alchemy at work today in the form of digital currency.

THE MORE COMPLETE PICTURE OF THE BIG CYCLE FROM AN INVESTOR'S PERSPECTIVE

While it would be too burdensome for me and you to go through all the relevant history between 1350 and now, I will show you what the picture would have looked like if you had started investing in 1900. But before I do so I want to explain how I think about risk because I'm going to highlight these risks in what I show you.

As I see it, **investment risk is failing to earn enough money to meet your needs**. It's not volatility measured by standard deviation, which is the almost exclusively used measure of risk.

To me, **the three biggest risks most investors face are that their portfolios won't provide the returns needed to meet their spending needs, that their portfolios will face ruin, and that a large share of their wealth will be taken away (e.g., through high taxes)**.

While the first two risks sound analogous, they are in fact different because it is possible to have average returns that are higher than required but also experience one or more periods of devastatingly high losses.

To gain perspective, I imagined that I was dropped into 1900 to see how my investments would have done in every decade since. I chose to look at the 10 greatest powers as of 1900 and skip less-established countries, which were more prone to bad outcomes. Virtually any one of these countries was or could have become a great, wealthy empire, and they were all reasonable places for one to invest, especially if one wanted to have a diversified portfolio.

Seven of these 10 countries saw wealth virtually wiped out at least once, and even the countries that didn't see wealth wiped out had a handful of terrible decades for asset returns that virtually destroyed them financially. Two of the great developed countries—Germany and Japan, which at times one easily could have bet on as being winners—had virtually all their wealth and many lives destroyed in the World Wars. I saw that many other countries had similar results. The US and the UK (and a few others) were the uniquely successful cases, but even they experienced periods of great wealth destruction.

If I hadn't looked at these returns in the period before the new world order began in 1945, I wouldn't have seen these periods of destruction. And had I not looked back 500 years around the world, I wouldn't have seen that this has happened repeatedly almost everywhere.

The numbers shown in this table are annualized real returns for each decade, which means that for the decade as a whole the losses are about eight times greater than shown and the gains are about 15 times greater.[4]

A LOOK AT ASSET RETURNS ACROSS THE GREAT POWERS
(Real Returns, 10-Year Window, Ann)

	UNITED STATES			GREAT BRITAIN			JAPAN			GERMANY		
	Equity	Bond	Cash	Equity	Bond	Cash	Equity	Bond	Cash	Equity	Bond	Cash
1900–10	9%	0%	1%	3%	2%	2%	4%	1%	4%	3%		2%
1910–20	-2%	-4%	-3%	-6%	-7%	-5%	1%	-5%	-4%	-14%	-10%	-14%
1920–30	16%	7%	5%	10%	8%	7%	-3%	12%	10%	-24%	-95%	-86%
1930–40	0%	7%	3%	1%	5%	1%	6%	4%	-1%	7%	11%	6%
1940–50	3%	-2%	-5%	3%	-1%	-4%	-28%	-34%	-33%	-4%	-16%	-19%
1950–60	16%	-1%	0%	13%	-1%	-1%	27%	-1%	5%	26%	5%	2%
1960–70	5%	-1%	2%	4%	0%	2%	8%	8%	2%	3%	5%	1%
1970–80	-2%	-1%	-1%	-4%	-3%	-3%	3%	-2%	-1%	-7%	4%	0%
1980–90	13%	9%	4%	16%	8%	5%	19%	9%	4%	10%	6%	3%
1990–00	14%	6%	2%	12%	8%	5%	-7%	9%	2%	13%	7%	3%
2000–10	-3%	8%	0%	0%	4%	2%	-3%	4%	1%	-2%	6%	2%
2010–20	11%	4%	-1%	5%	5%	-1%	10%	2%	0%	7%	5%	-1%

[4] When compounded over a decade, gains are greater than losses because you keep building off of gains; whereas as you experience losses and approach zero, future percent losses matter less in dollar terms. The comparison of annualizing gains versus losses represents compounding from 10 percent annualized gains and -5 percent annualized losses on average. At more extreme changes the multipliers change from there.

A LOOK AT ASSET RETURNS ACROSS THE GREAT POWERS
(Real Returns, 10-Year Window, Ann)

	FRANCE			NETHERLANDS			ITALY		
	Equity	Bond	Cash	Equity	Bond	Cash	Equity	Bond	Cash
1900–10	1%	3%	2%	5%	1%	1%		3%	4%
1910–20	-7%	-8%	-6%	1%	-6%	-3%	-9%	-8%	-6%
1920–30	-2%	-1%	-4%	1%	11%	6%	-6%	-5%	-1%
1930–40	-10%	2%	0%	2%	6%	3%	4%	5%	5%
1940–50	-20%	-22%	-23%	2%	-3%	-6%	-13%	-30%	-30%
1950–60	17%	0%	-2%	14%	0%	-2%	20%	2%	1%
1960–70	0%	2%	1%	2%	0%	0%	0%	2%	0%
1970–80	-2%	-3%	0%	-3%	2%	-2%	-13%	-8%	-1%
1980–90	16%	9%	5%	16%	7%	5%	15%	4%	6%
1990–00	13%	10%	5%	20%	7%	4%	9%	15%	6%
2000–10	-2%	5%	1%	-6%	5%	1%	-4%	5%	1%
2010–20	7%	6%	-1%	8%	5%	-1%	3%	8%	-1%

	RUSSIA			CHINA			AUSTRIA-HUNGARY		
	Equity	Bond	Cash	Equity	Bond	Cash	Equity	Bond	Cash
1900–10	-2%	3%	4%	7%	6%	3%	4%	3%	2%
1910–20	-100%	-100%	-36%	3%	1%	4%	-9%	-10%	-8%
1920–30				9%	6%	1%	-6%	-44%	-44%
1930–40				2%	-7%	-6%			
1940–50				-100%	-100%	-73%			
1950–60									
1960–70									
1970–80									
1980–90									
1990–00									
2000–10	15%		-2%	4%		1%			
2010–20	7%	4%	1%	2%	2%	0%			

[5]

[5] For China and Russia, bond data pre-1950 is modeled using hard currency bond returns held as though hedged back to local currency by a domestic investor; stocks and bonds modeled as full default at time of revolution. Annualized returns assume a full 10-year period even if markets closed during the decade.

Perhaps this next chart paints a clearer picture, as it shows what percentage of countries saw losses of a 60/40 stock/bond portfolio over five-year periods.

SHARE OF PORTFOLIOS LOSING X% OVER 5 YEARS BY COUNTRY (60/40 PORTFOLIO, REAL RETURNS)

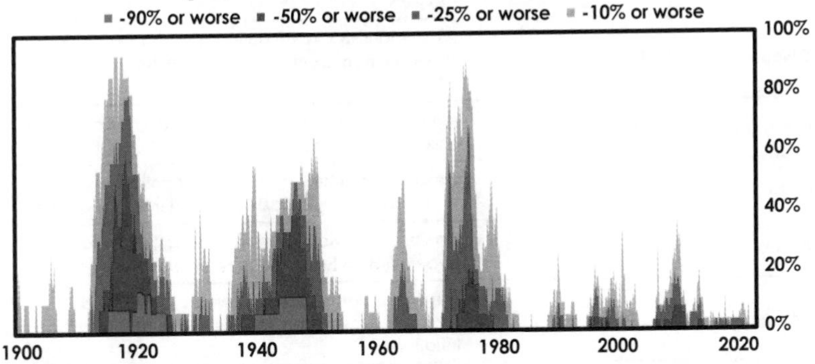

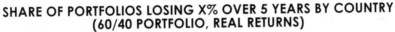

The following table shows the worst cases of investing in major countries in detail. You will note that the US doesn't appear on this table because it wasn't among the worst cases. **The US, Canada, and Australia were the only countries that didn't experience sustained periods of losses.**

WORST INVESTOR EXPERIENCES (ACROSS MAJOR COUNTRIES)
Major Cases of 60/40 Real Returns Below -40% over a 20-Year Window

Country	20yr Window	Worst 20yr Return (Real, Cumul)	Detail
Russia	1900–1918	-100%	The Russian Civil War ended with communist rule, debt repudiation, and the destruction of financial markets.
China	1930–1950	-100%	Asset markets closed during WWII and were destroyed when communist rule took hold in the late 1940s.
Germany	1903–1923	-100%	Weimar Republic hyperinflation led to a collapse in assets following WWI.
Japan	1928–1948	-96%	Japanese markets and currency collapsed as markets reopened post-WWII and inflation soared.
Austria	1903–1923	-95%	Similar to Weimar Germany (though less infamous); hyperinflation led to poor asset returns post-WWI.
France	1930–1950	-93%	The Great Depression, followed by WWII and German occupation, led to poor returns and high inflation.
Italy	1928–1948	-87%	Similar to those of other Axis powers, Italian markets collapsed as WWII concluded.
Italy	1907–1927	-84%	Post-WWI, Italy suffered from economic depression and high inflation, helping lead to Mussolini's rise.
France	1906–1926	-75%	The early 20th century saw WWI, followed by France's inflationary currency crisis in the early 1920s.
Italy	1960–1980	-72%	Italy endured a series of recessions, high unemployment rate and inflation, and currency declines in the 1960–70s.
India	1955–1975	-66%	Post-independence, a series of major droughts caused weak Indian economic growth and high inflation.
Spain	1962–1982	-59%	The post-Franco transition to democracy coupled with the inflationary 1970s strained Spain's economy.
Germany	1929–1949	-50%	The Great Depression followed by the devastation of WWII led to a terrible period for German assets.
France	1961–1981	-48%	Like other European nations, the 1960–70s saw weaker growth, currency declines, and high inflation.
UK	1901–1921	-46%	The early 20th century saw World War I, followed by the depression of 1920–21.

[6]

[6] Cases of poor asset returns in smaller countries such as Belgium, Greece, New Zealand, Norway, Sweden, Switzerland, and across the emerging world are excluded from this table. Note that for conciseness the worst 20-year window is shown for each country/time period (i.e., including Germany in 1903–23 precludes including Germany from 1915–35). For our 60/40 portfolios, we assumed monthly rebalancing across the 20-year window.

Naturally I think about how I would have approached these periods if I had been living through them. I'm certain that even if I had seen the signs of things coming that I'm passing along in this book I never would have confidently predicted such bad outcomes—as noted earlier, seven of 10 countries saw their wealth wiped out. In the early 1900s, even those looking back over the past few decades would never have seen it coming because there were plenty of reasons to be optimistic based on what had happened during the second half of the 19th century.

People today often assume that World War I must have been easy to foresee in the years leading up to it, but that wasn't the case. Before the war, there had been about 50 years of almost no conflict between the world's major powers. During those 50 years the world experienced the greatest innovation and productivity growth rates it had ever seen, which led to enormous wealth and prosperity. Globalization was at new highs, with global exports up several multiples in the 50 years prior to World War I. Countries were more interconnected than ever. The US, France, Germany, Japan, and Austria-Hungary were rapidly rising empires, experiencing dizzying technological advancement. The UK was still the dominant global power. Russia was rapidly industrializing. Of those countries shown in the table of worst investor experiences, only China was obviously in decline. Strong alliances among European powers were seen at the time as a means of keeping the peace and maintaining the balance of power. Going into 1900 things looked great, except for the fact that wealth gaps and resentments were increasing and debts had become large.

Between 1900 and 1914 these conditions worsened and international tensions increased. Then came the periods of terrible returns I just described.

But it was worse than just terrible returns.

In addition, the impacts on wealth of wealth confiscations, confiscatory taxes, capital controls, and markets being closed were enormous. Most investors today don't know of such things and consider them implausible because they wouldn't have seen them by looking back on the past few decades. The following table shows in which decades these events occurred. Naturally the most severe cases of wealth confiscation came during periods in which there were large wealth gaps and internal conflict over wealth when economic conditions got bad and/or there was a war.

PERIODS OF WEALTH CONFISCATION

	1900	1920	1940	1960	1980	2000
UK						
USA	Yes	Yes				
China			Yes	Yes		
Germany		Yes				
France						
Russia	Yes	Yes	Yes			
Austria-Hungary						
Italy		Yes				
Netherlands						
Japan			Yes			

PERIODS OF STRICT/RISING CAPITAL CONTROLS

	1900	1920	1940	1960	1980	2000
UK	Yes	Yes	Yes	Yes		
USA	Yes	Yes				
China			Yes	Yes	Yes	
Germany	Yes	Yes	Yes	Yes		
France	Yes			Yes		
Russia	Yes	Yes	Yes	Yes	Yes	Yes
Austria-Hungary	Yes					
Italy		Yes				
Netherlands				Yes		
Japan		Yes		Yes		

[7]

[7] While this diagram is not exhaustive, I include instances where I could find clear evidence of each occurring in the 20-year period. For this analysis, wealth confiscation was defined as extensive seizure of private assets, including large-scale forced, non-economic sales by a government (or revolutionaries in the case of revolution). Relevant capital controls were defined as meaningful restrictions on investors moving their money to and from other countries and assets (although this does not include targeted measures directed only at single countries, such as sanctions).

The next chart shows the share of major countries that shut their stock markets through time. Wartime stock market closures were common, and of course communist countries shut their stock markets over a generation.

STOCK MARKET CLOSURES ACROSS MAJOR ECONOMIES

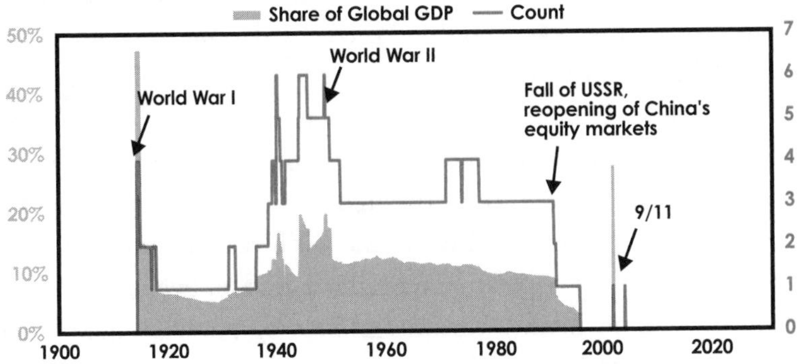

The bad parts of all the cycles that took place prior to 1900 were similarly bad. To make matters even worse, **these periods of internal and external fighting over wealth and power led to many deaths.**

DEATHS IN MAJOR VIOLENT CONFLICTS (%POPULATION)
INTERNAL AND EXTERNAL

	1900	1910	1920	1930	1940	1950	1960	1970	1980	1990	2000	2010
UK	0%	2%	0%	0%	1%	0%	0%	0%	0%	0%	0%	0%
USA	0%	0%	0%	0%	0%	0%	0%	0%	0%	0%	0%	0%
China	0%	0%	1%	2%	3%	1%	1%	1%	0%	0%	0%	0%
Germany	0%	3%	0%	9%	15%	0%	0%	0%	0%	0%	0%	0%
France	0%	4%	0%	0%	1%	0%	0%	0%	0%	0%	0%	0%
Russia	0%	4%	5%	10%	13%	0%	0%	0%	0%	0%	0%	0%
Austria-Hungary	0%	2%										
Italy	0%	2%	0%	0%	1%	0%	0%	0%	0%	0%	0%	0%
Netherlands	0%	0%	0%	1%	2%	0%	0%	0%	0%	0%	0%	0%
Japan	0%	0%	0%	1%	4%	0%	0%	0%	0%	0%	0%	0%

Even for the lucky investors who were in countries that won the wars (such as the US, which was twice the biggest winner), there were two further headwinds: market timing and taxes.

Most investors sell near the lows when things are bad because they need money and because they tend to panic; they tend to buy near the highs because they have plenty of money and they are drawn into the euphoria. This means that their actual returns are worse than the market returns I showed. A recent study showed that US investors underperformed US stocks by around 1.5 percent a year between 2000 and 2020.

As for taxes, this table estimates the average impact of taxes for investors in the S&P 500 over all 20-year periods (using average tax rates for the top quintile today throughout the analysis period). The different columns represent different ways of investing in the US stock market, including a tax-deferred retirement account (where tax is paid only at the end of the investment) and holding physical equities and reinvesting dividends annually like if stocks were held in a brokerage account. While these different implementations have different tax implications (with retirement accounts least impacted), all of them show a significant impact, especially in real returns, where taxes can erode a significant portion of returns. US investors lost about a quarter of their real equity returns on average to taxes in any given 20-year period.

IMPACT OF TAXES ON ROLLING 20-YEAR S&P TOTAL RETURNS

	Pre-Tax	Post-Tax (401[k])	Post-Tax (Brokerage)
Avg Ann Total Return	9.5%	8.2%	7.9%
Avg Drag from Taxes (Ann Total Return)		-1.3%	-1.6%
Avg Drag from Taxes (% of Total Returns)		-14%	-17%
Avg Ann Real Return	6.2%	4.9%	4.6%
Avg Drag from Taxes (Ann Real Return)		-1.2%	-1.6%
Avg Drag from Taxes (% of Real Returns)		-20%	-26%

[8]

[8] Tax impact for 401(k) method applies a 26 percent income tax rate (effective average federal tax rate for top quintile from the Congressional Budget Office as of 2017) at the conclusion of each 20-year investment period (i.e., tax-free investment growth). Tax impact for brokerage method separately taxes dividends (at the same 26 percent income tax rate) and capital gains, paying taxes on all capital gains (at a 20 percent rate) from both principal and dividend reinvestment at the conclusion of each 20-year investment period and netting losses against any gains.

REVIEWING THE BIG CAPITAL MARKETS CYCLE

Earlier, I explained how the classic big debt and capital markets cycle works. To reiterate, **in the upwave, debt is increased and financial wealth and obligations rise relative to tangible wealth to the point that these promises to pay in the future (i.e., the values of cash, bonds, and stocks) can't be met. This causes "run on the bank"-type debt problems to emerge, which leads to the printing of money to try to relieve the problems of debt defaults and falling stock market prices, which leads to the devaluation of money and in turn to financial wealth going down relative to real wealth, until the real (inflation-adjusted) value of financial assets returns to being low relative to tangible wealth. Then the cycle begins again.** That is a very simplified description, but you get the idea—during the downwave in this cycle there are negative real returns of financial assets relative to real assets and there are bad times. It is the anti-capital, anti-capitalist part of the cycle that continues until the opposite extreme is reached.

This cycle is reflected in the following two charts. The first shows the value of total financial assets relative to the total value of real assets. The second shows the real return of money (i.e., cash). I use US numbers rather than global numbers because they are the ones that are most continuous since 1900. **As you can see, when there is a lot of financial wealth relative to real wealth it reverses and real returns of financial wealth, especially cash and debt assets (like bonds), are bad. That is because interest rates and returns for debt holders have to be low and bad in order to provide the relief to the debtors who have too much debt and in order to try to stimulate more debt growth as a way of stimulating the economy.** This is the classic late-cycle part of the long-term debt cycle. It occurs when printing more money is used to reduce debt burdens and new debts are created to increase purchasing power. This devalues the currency relative to other storeholds of wealth and relative to goods and services. **Eventually as the value of financial assets declines until**

they become cheap relative to real assets, the opposite extreme is reached and reverses, which is when peace and prosperity return, the cycle goes into its up phase, and financial assets have excellent real returns.

USA FINANCIAL ASSETS SHARE OF TOTAL ASSETS

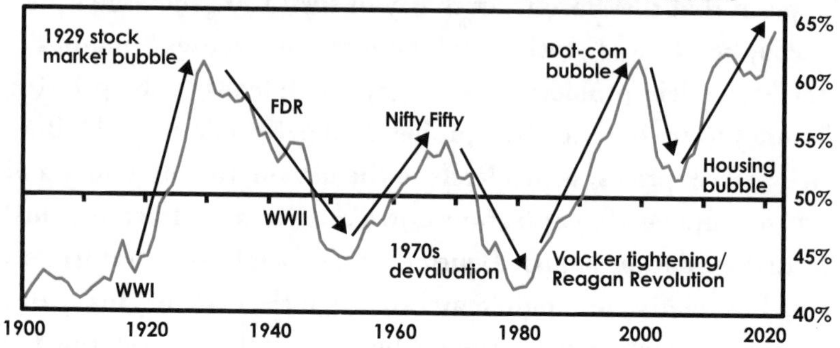

REAL RETURN OF BILLS (VS CPI)

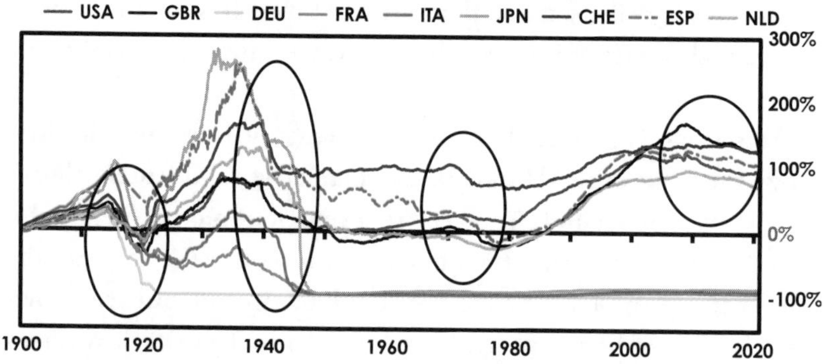

As explained earlier, during periods of the devaluation of money, hard money and hard assets rise in value relative to cash. For example, the next chart shows that periods when the value of the classic 60/40 stock/bond portfolio declined were periods when gold prices rose. I am not saying anything about gold being a good or bad investment. I am simply describing economic and market mechanics and how they have been manifest in past market movements and investment returns for the purpose of sharing my perspective on what happened and what could happen and why.

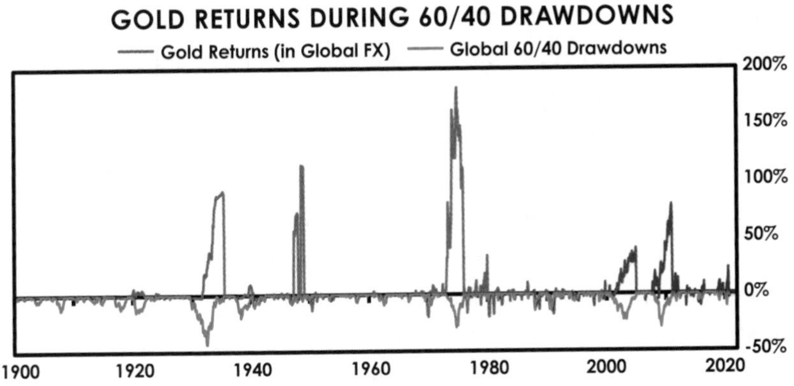

One of the most important questions investors need to regularly ask themselves is whether the amount of interest that is being paid more than makes up for the devaluation risk they face.

The classic big debt/money/capital markets cycle, which has repeated through time and in all places and is reflected in the charts I just showed you, is seen in the relative values of 1) real/tangible money and real/tangible wealth and 2) financial money and financial wealth. Financial money and financial wealth are valuable only to the extent that they get you the real money and real wealth that have real (i.e., intrinsic) value. The ways these cycles have always worked is that, in their rising phases, the amounts of financial money and financial wealth (i.e., created debt and equity assets) are increased relative to the amounts of real money and real wealth that they are claims on. They are increased because a) it is profitable for those capitalists who are in the business of creating and selling financial assets to produce and sell them, b) increasing money, credit, and other capital market assets is an effective way for policy makers to create prosperity because it funds demand, and c) it creates the illusion that people are wealthier because the stated values of financial investments go up when the value of the money and debt assets goes down. In this way central governments and central bankers have always created many more claims on real money and real wealth than could ever be turned in for real wealth and real money.

In the rising parts of the cycle, stocks, bonds, and other investment assets go up as interest rates go down because falling interest rates make asset prices rise, all else being equal. Also putting more money in the system raises the demand for financial assets, which lowers risk premiums. When these investments go up because of lower interest rates and more money in the system, that makes them seem more attractive at the same time as interest rates and the future expected returns of financial assets are going down. The more outstanding claims there are relative to what there are claims on, the more risk there is. This should be compensated for by a higher interest rate, but it typically isn't because at that moment conditions seem good and memories of debt and capital market crises have faded.

The charts that I showed you before to convey the cycles would not be complete in painting the picture without some interest rate charts. Interest rates are shown in the next four charts that go back to 1900. They show real (i.e., inflation-adjusted) bond yields, nominal (i.e., not inflation-adjusted) bond yields, and nominal and real cash rates for the US, Europe, and Japan at the time of my writing. As you can see they were much higher and now they are very low. Real yields of reserve currency sovereign bonds, at the time of my writing this, are near the lowest ever, and nominal bond yields are around 0 percent, also near the lowest ever. As shown real yields of cash are even lower, though not as negative as they were in the 1930–45 and 1915–20 great monetization periods. Nominal cash yields are near the lowest ever.

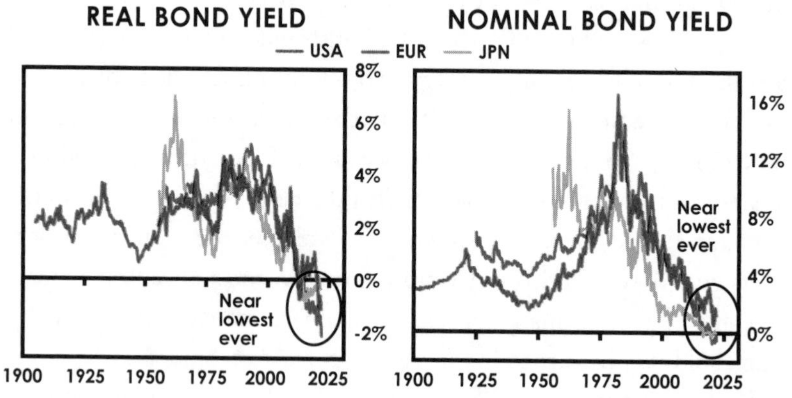

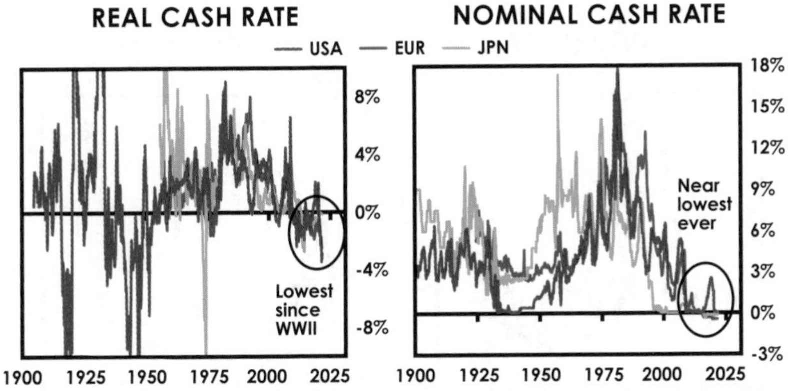

What does this mean for investing? The purpose of investing is to have money in a storehold of wealth that one can convert into buying power at a later date. When one invests, one gives a lump-sum payment for payments in the future. Let's look at what that deal, as of this writing, looks like. If you give \$100 today, how many years do you have to wait to get your \$100 back and then start collecting the reward on top of what you gave? In US, Japanese, Chinese, and European bonds you could have to wait roughly 45 years, 150 years, and 30 years[9] respectively to get your money back (likely getting low or nil nominal returns) and in Europe at the time of this writing you would likely never get your money back given negative nominal interest rates. However, because you are trying to store buying power you have to take into consideration inflation. At the time of this writing, in the US and Europe, you may never get your buying power back (and in Japan it will take over 250 years). In fact, in these countries with negative real interest rates, you are almost guaranteed to have a lot less buying power in the future. Rather than get paid less than inflation, why not instead buy stuff—any stuff—that will equal inflation or better? I see a lot of investments that I expect to do significantly better than inflation. The following charts show these payback periods for holding cash and bonds in the US, in both nominal and real terms. As shown, it is the longest ever and obviously a ridiculous amount of time.

[9] Based on August 2021 levels of 30-year nominal bond yields (treated as a perpetuity).

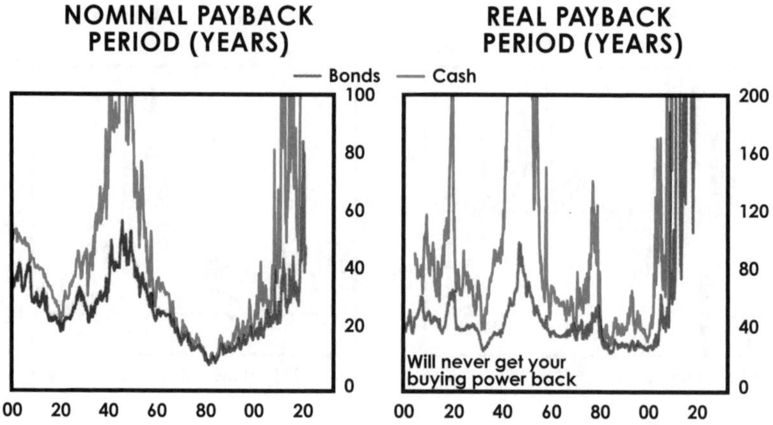

CONCLUSION

What I showed you here was the Big Cycle from an investor's perspective since 1900. In looking around the world going back 500 years and in China going back 1,400 years I saw basically the same cycles occur repeatedly for basically the same reasons.

As discussed earlier in the book, the terrible periods in the years prior to the 1945 establishment of the new world order are typical of the late Big Cycle transition stage when revolutionary changes and restructurings occur. While they were terrible, they were more than matched by terrific upswings that came after the painful transition from the old order to the new order. Because these things have happened many times before, and because I can't say for sure what will happen in the future, I can't invest without having protections against these sorts of things happening and my being wrong.

PART II

HOW THE WORLD HAS WORKED OVER THE LAST 500 YEARS

CHAPTER 8

THE LAST 500 YEARS IN A TINY NUTSHELL

In Part I, I described how I believe the perpetual-motion machine works. In Part II, I will show you what this perpetual-motion machine has produced over the last 500 years of history. Just as I did in Part I, I'll start by conveying everything in a tiny nutshell. This chapter will set the stage for the remaining chapters of Part II, which will cover in detail how the Big Cycle played out in the Dutch, British, American, and Chinese cases. Finally, in Part III, I will attempt to squint into the future by sharing with you what my model says about a number of the leading countries today. But before we get there, we need to go back to 1500 to get a better picture of what the world was like when this story begins.

THE WORLD IN 1500

The world was very different in 1500 yet it operated the same way it does now. That's because while things have evolved a lot since 1500, they've done so in the same ways they always have, with evolutionary uptrends producing advancements and big cycles creating swings and bumps around the uptrends.

A few of the most important ways that the world was different in 1500 were:

The World Was Much "Bigger" Then. Five hundred years ago one could travel about 25 miles in a day on horseback. Today it is possible to travel to the other side of the world in the same amount of time. The Apollo astronauts traveled to the moon and back much faster than it took a traveler to get from Paris to Rome in 1500. As a result, the geographic areas of relevance—e.g., who could impact whom—were much smaller so the world seemed much bigger. Europe was one world, Russia was another, and China and the areas around it were an even more remote world. States that in retrospect seem tiny and numerous did not seem that way at all at the time. Because national boundaries didn't exist as they do today, there were almost constant fights with neighbors over wealth and power in their neighborhoods.

But in 1500, that picture was changing quickly. The European powers were well into their Age of Exploration, which was led by the Portuguese and the Spanish and brought them into contact with faraway empires. Like all periods of great evolution, the Age of Exploration was enabled by technological developments that could make people rich—in this case, the invention of ships that could travel the world to accumulate riches by trading with and taking wealth from those who the explorers encountered. At the time, wealthy rulers funded the expeditions in exchange for a share of the bounty that the explorers brought back with them.

Countries Didn't Exist—Instead, Territories Were Run by Families. Back in 1500, there were no sovereign states with borders and ruling orders. They hadn't been invented yet. Instead there were **big family estates called kingdoms and dynasties run by kings and emperors that almost constantly fought with their neighbors for**

wealth and power. When a kingdom conquered, grew, and encompassed enough area, it was called an empire. Because the ruling order was centered around families, kingdoms and dynasties at that time could inherit other lands if their rulers died and there was no closer relative, similar to how one would inherit property or a family company today. Arranged marriages were logical ways the empire could stay in the hands of a tighter family group rather than branching off and dissipating over the generations.

Religions and Religious Leaders Were Much More Powerful—and Science as We Know It Today Didn't Exist. In most of the world, the elites (i.e., that small percentage of the population who had most of the wealth and power) consisted of monarchs who supposedly gained their power from the divine, the clergy who represented the divine, and the landowning nobles who oversaw the peasants and largely treated them like oxen working the land. The monarchs had ministers, bureaucracies, and militaries that controlled and defended their territories for them.

Though the Europeans and the Chinese were on opposite sides of the world and had virtually no contact with each other, they operated in essentially the same way, though China's institutions were bigger, more developed, and less religious than Europe's.

The World Was Much Less Egalitarian. The ideas that a) all people should be treated equally and b) judged by the law didn't exist at the time. This was true both within kingdoms and between them; in both cases, power through arms and violence ruled the day. Up until the 1300s and 1400s, serfdom (i.e., peasants being essentially treated as the property of their rulers) existed in most of Western Europe, which meant that the only way for most people to assert their power was through revolt. While this had largely changed by 1500, the rights afforded to common people remained weak until the Enlightenment in the 1700s.

THE WORLD'S EMPIRES IN 1500

Europe

- **The Habsburg family dynasty controlled Spain and all the territories that Spain controlled plus a collection of territories that formed the Holy Roman Empire. This included parts of what we now call the Netherlands, Belgium, Italy, Germany, and Austria.** It was the Western world's most powerful empire.
- **The Valois (later Bourbon) family dynasty, which was the main rival to the Habsburgs, controlled France.** This led to a lot of fighting between the families.
- **The Tudor dynasty controlled England**, which was not yet an important force in Europe though it was growing in strength.
- **Florence, Venice, and Milan, which were frequently run as republics with prominent families**, were where the action was. Most of the financial, commercial, intellectual, and artistic innovation coming out of Europe in 1500 originated in these states. They were very rich and played a central role in shaping Europe and the Western world at this time and for centuries to come because of the revolutionary ideas they fostered, ideas I will explore in more detail later.
- **The Papal States were run by the pope and the Catholic Church.** Throughout Christian Europe, relationships between monarchs, nobles, and the church followed the typical formula of elites working in mutually supportive ways to drive the ruling orders to their benefit. As a result of this, the church acquired vast wealth, which it got mostly from poor peasants who gave money to the church (through the system of tithes) and worked without pay on church agricultural lands.
- **The Rurik dynasty, and later the Romanovs, ruled Russia,**

which was a peripheral power at the time and seemed remote to Europeans.

- **The Ottoman Empire, named after its ruling family,** was centered in Constantinople, which it had conquered in 1453.

Additionally there were many hundreds, perhaps thousands, of family-run states across Europe. They fought all the time because each had to constantly defend and fight one's neighbors. Allies and enemies were always important and constantly changing. This map shows the major powers in Europe in 1550. There were many more small states we couldn't fit on this map.

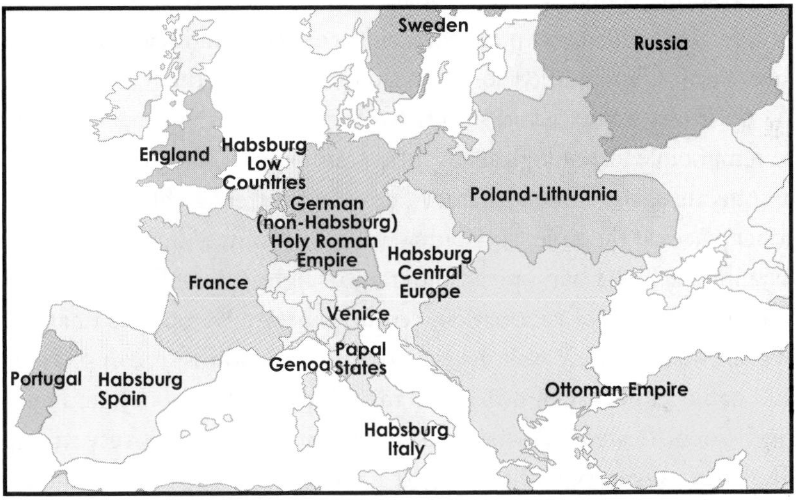

Asia

The Ming Dynasty controlled almost all of China and was the most advanced and powerful empire in the world. Like European empires, it was family-controlled with an emperor who had the "mandate of heaven." The emperor oversaw a bureaucracy that was run and protected by ministers and military leaders who worked in

symbiotic—though sometimes contentious—relationships with landowning noble families who oversaw peasant workers. In 1500 the Ming Dynasty was approaching its peak and was leaps and bounds ahead of Europe in wealth, technology, and power. It had enormous cultural and political influence all over East Asia and Japan.[1]

At the time, Confucian scholars were then seen to be near the top of the social hierarchy, which helped them get ahead in politics. To get ahead one needed to study Confucianism in depth and pass highly competitive exams. Political decisions were frequently based on ruler's interpretations of Confucian ideals. "Neo-Confucianism," which was dominant at the time, shifted the focus of the belief system toward a more rational, philosophical, academic, and humanistic form. This way of thinking, which was practical, evidence-based, and scientific, was a key reason China pulled so far ahead of Europe in the Middle Ages. At the time, scholars and scientists had significant power, which led to remarkable technological advances (gun powder, the printing press, architecture, and more). Literacy rates were extremely high relative to other places at the time, and China was also advanced in medicine. For example, it had a widespread program of fighting smallpox infection via an early form of vaccination, centuries before Europe. Its financial system was relatively well developed with early forms of corporations and banks, a history of using (and misusing) printed money, and relatively sophisticated financial markets. And it was militarily very strong. The Ming Dynasty had the largest navy in the world and a standing army of a million troops.

In his wonderful book, *The Rise and Fall of the Great Powers*, historian Paul Kennedy described it well:

> "Of all the civilizations of premodern times, none appeared more advanced, none felt more superior than that of China.

[1] By the way, the existence of familial relationships in a Chinese dynasty should not be mistaken for loving and caring relationships, as, just like in Europe, fights between family members for control of dynasties were brutal and often to the death.

> Its considerable population, 100–130 million compared with Europe's 50–55 million in the fifteenth century; its remarkable culture; its exceedingly fertile and irrigated plains, linked by a splendid canal system since the eleventh century; and its unified, hierarchic administration run by a well-educated Confucian bureaucracy had given a coherence and sophistication to Chinese society which was the envy of foreign visitors."

Ironically and typically, the enormity of the Ming Dynasty's wealth and power is one possible explanation of what eventually led to its fall. Believing that they did not need anything else, the emperors put an end to China's exploration of the world, closed its doors, and retired to lives of pleasure, and turned over the running of government to their ministers and eunuchs, which led to dysfunctional infighting, corruption, weakness, and vulnerability to attack. There was a shift away from pragmatic scientific study and innovation toward pedantic scholarship. As we'll see in Chapter 12, this helped drive the decline of China relative to Europe.

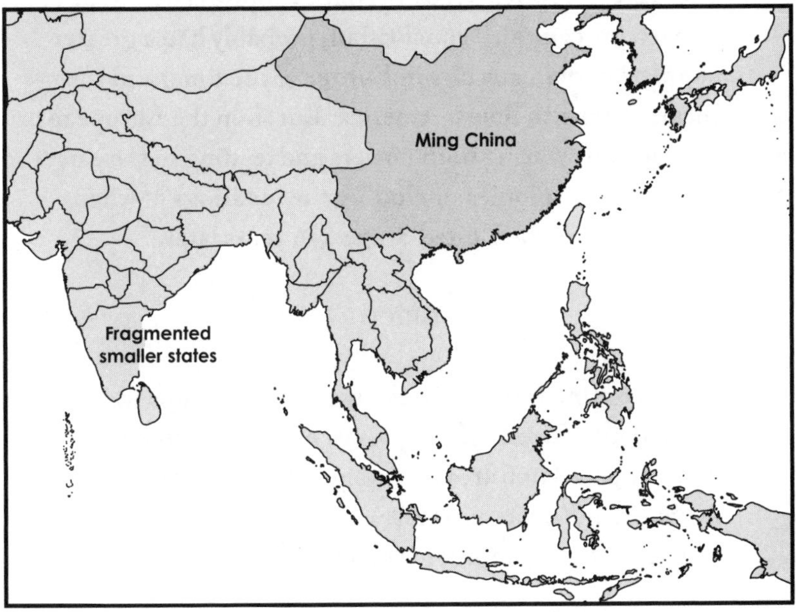

Across the rest of Asia, the story in 1500 was one of fragmentation. India was divided among several kingdoms, including the Delhi Sultanate in the north and the Hindu Vijayanagara Empire in the south. It was not an empire of note, though it was about to be, as in the 1520s the Mughal Empire began its conquest of India, eventually leading it to be among the world's most powerful. Likewise **Japan in 1500 was divided into many entities, experienced civil war, and was isolated, so it too was not a power of note.**

The Middle East

- **The Ottoman Empire, mentioned before, also came to control much of the Middle East by the mid-1500s, with a key rival in the new Safavid dynasty of Persia (modern-day Iran).**

The Americas

- **The largest empires were the Aztec Empire centered in Mexico (its capital, Tenochtitlán, probably had a greater population than any city in Europe at the time) and the Incan Empire in South America. But soon the Europeans arrived, devastating both powers and leading to the emergence of new colonies, including the seedlings of what would become the United States 276 years later.**

Africa

- **A vast continent three times bigger than Europe was divided into dozens of kingdoms, often separated by large, sparsely populated areas.** The biggest in the year 1500 was the Songhai Empire in West Africa, which had a reputation as a center of trade and Islamic scholarship.

That was the lay of the land in 1500. **The world order was about to change in very big ways.**

WHAT HAS HAPPENED SINCE 1500

As you might imagine, there are far too many important things that have happened since 1500 for me to fit into this tiny nutshell. However, I can hit the highlights of the story of how the world changed from 1500 until now, with an emphasis on the key themes and shifts I will be expanding on in the following chapters. The most important changes were the changes in thinking that led to people changing behaviors, particularly about how wealth and power should be shared. They were what made the story transpire as it did. It is easy to identify the biggest periods of change because they are generally called "revolutions" and "ages" (though sometimes they are called other things).

When reading this short summary of the last 500 years, notice both the evolutions and the cycles. You will see that there were both 1) several revolutions in ways of thinking that led to tremendous evolution and progress over hundreds of years and 2) many cycles of peaceful and prosperous periods alternating with depressions and wars that marked the ends of old orders and beginnings of new ones.

The Commercial Revolution (1100s–1500s)

The Commercial Revolution was the move away from a solely agriculture-based economy to one that included trade in a variety of goods. This evolution began in the 12th century, and by 1500, it was centered in the Italian city-states due to a confluence of two factors that enabled them to become terrifically wealthy. First, the wars between Christian Europe and the Ottoman Empire significantly slowed land trade (especially for spices and luxuries) between Europe and the rest of the world, which created a significant opening for maritime trade. Second, a number of Italian city-states developed republican governments modeled after the Roman Republic. Their governments were more inventive and responsive than those in the rest of Europe, which allowed a strong merchant class to develop.

Venice was a prime example of this, as its governance system was designed with multiple checks and balances to ensure that there was a more meritocratic approach to government than existed in the rest of Europe. Venice's leader—called the doge—did not have the right to name a successor and was restricted from bringing family members into government. New doges were chosen by vote by a series of committees whose members, in some cases, were chosen by lot from among several hundred aristocratic families. The Italians produced well-functioning capital markets, supported by new advances in bookkeeping and impartial institutions to enforce contracts. While private and government borrowing weren't new, leading up to 1500, they tended to take place as bilateral deals between wealthy citizens, and defaults on creditors (or the expulsion and even execution of them) were extremely common. Because those who made money from trade—the merchant class—could benefit from a well-functioning financial system in which savings could be put into investments that fueled productivity, they created a number of financial innovations, including credit markets.

With the proceeds from trade flowing in and a need for standardized coinage, coins minted in the Italian city-states, especially Florence's gold florin, were of solid value, were well-recognized as such, and, as a result, began to be accepted as global currencies. On the basis of their solid currencies, these city-states developed effective lending and a publicly traded bond market. Venice established a perpetual bond early in the 12th century with a 5 percent coupon that the government would either issue (i.e., borrow) or purchase back depending on the finances/needs of the time. Venice's merchants owned the bonds and had significant influence on the government, so default could only be a last resort. The centuries in which the bond existed without defaults gave lenders confidence in it and institutions for trading bonds in secondary markets made it a liquid form of investment.

The ability to borrow quickly at reasonable rates was an enormous boon to Venice. Though Venice eventually defaulted after losing a series of wars around 1500, liquid bond markets caught on elsewhere including in the Netherlands and in the UK.

The Renaissance (1300s–1600s)

A new way of thinking in many respects modeled after the ancient Greeks and Romans started in Italian city-states around 1300 and passed through Europe until the 1600s, in a period known as the Renaissance. Renaissance thinkers made a big pivot toward using logical reasoning instead of divine intention as the way to explain how the world works. This shift contributed to dizzyingly fast discoveries that led to artistic and technological advances in Europe. It began in the city-states of northern Italy where the Commercial Revolution had created riches that led to advances in trade, production, and banking enabled by intellectualism and creativity. **The Renaissance was one of history's greatest cases of a self-reinforcing cycle I described in Chapter 5: peaceful periods in which creativity and commerce reinforce each other to produce an economic boom and great advancements.**

In the middle of it, and propelling it forward, were people and families like the Medici, who were merchants and bankers, not feudal kings. They used their riches to support the arts, architecture, and science.[2] Alongside the flourishing in art and architecture were huge advances in science, technology, and business. **Knowledge and ideas spread rapidly because of the invention of the printing press in the mid-15th century.**

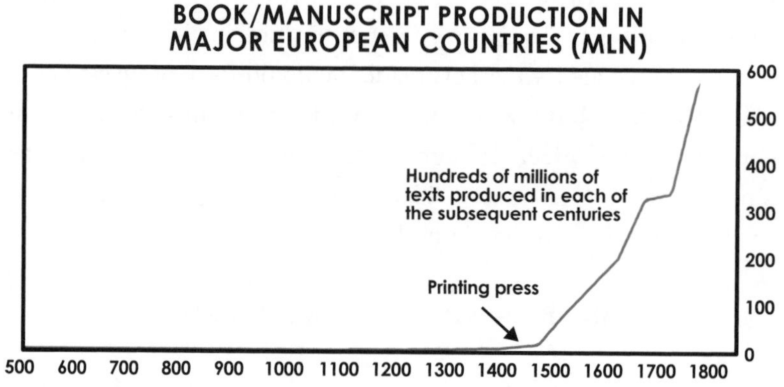

By the way, many of the European Renaissance innovations had already been in place in China for centuries because the Chinese discovered the key elements to produce it—e.g., the printing press, the scientific method, and the meritocratic placements of people in jobs—much earlier. One can think of China's Neo-Confucianism, described earlier, as being like China's Renaissance because, as in Europe's Renaissance, it led to more logic- and evidence-based thinking and more inventive rather than religious worldviews.

[2] The Medici family, who ruled and developed Florence during the period (though Florence technically remained a republic for much of their rule), acquired their wealth and power as business leaders and bankers. The Medici used their wealth, power, and smarts to acquire more wealth and power and to contribute enormously to the arts and sciences. They also acquired significant political power in Europe. For example, to gain power and/or to provide public service, four popes came from the Medici family during their reign. A number of Medici were themselves artists and political leaders who looked to help not only the rich but also the middle and poorer classes in the city. However, like many multigenerational families and monarchies, after a few generations a weak head of the family and leader of the state, together with perceived excesses at a time of economic stress, led to a revolution. The Medici lost control of Florence on several occasions. While the Medici returned to power over the subsequent three centuries and the Renaissance continued, they struggled and failed in the mid-16th century as a result of wars, changing trade routes, and bad loan making, which damaged their finances, and of changes in social norms and political practices.

As the new ideas spread across Europe in the late 16th and early 17th centuries, luminaries such as Shakespeare and Francis Bacon in England, Descartes in France, and Erasmus in the Netherlands had broad impacts. Living standards rose dramatically, though much more for the elites than for peasants. In Italy, this period of relative peace and prosperity eventually led to excesses, decadence, and decline as the city-states became less competitive and their financial conditions deteriorated.

The Age of Exploration and Colonialism (1400s–1700s)

The Age of Exploration began in the 1400s when Europeans traveled all over the world in search of wealth, creating widespread contact between many different peoples for the first time and beginning to shrink the world. It roughly coincided with the Renaissance because the technological marvels of the Renaissance translated into advancements in shipbuilding and navigation, and the riches that those ships brought back financed further Renaissance advancements.

Ruling families supported these money-making explorations and split the profits with explorers. For example, Henry the Navigator, the brother of the head of the Portuguese royal family, sponsored some of the earliest voyages and established a trading empire in Africa and Asia. Spain followed suit, swiftly conquering and colonizing significant portions of the Western Hemisphere, including the precious-metal-rich Aztec and Incan empires. Though Portugal and Spain were rivals, the unexplored world was huge, and when they had disputes, they were successfully mediated. Spain's integration into the Habsburg Empire and its control over highly profitable silver mines made it stronger than Portugal in the 1500s, and for a roughly 60-year period starting in the late 1500s the Habsburg king ruled Portugal as well. Both translated their wealth into golden ages of art and technology. The Spanish Empire grew so large it became known as "the empire on which the sun never sets"—an expression that would later be used to describe the British Empire.

As European nations found ways to make their explorations more profitable, the rise of global trade transformed their economies. Most notably, the flow of new riches (particularly silver) to Europe fueled a rise in prices for basic goods and services. Referred to as the Spanish Price Revolution, **Europe went from hundreds of years of steady prices to a doubling of prices every few decades, a reminder of how big shifts can have economic impacts that seem unimaginable based on one's most recent experiences.**

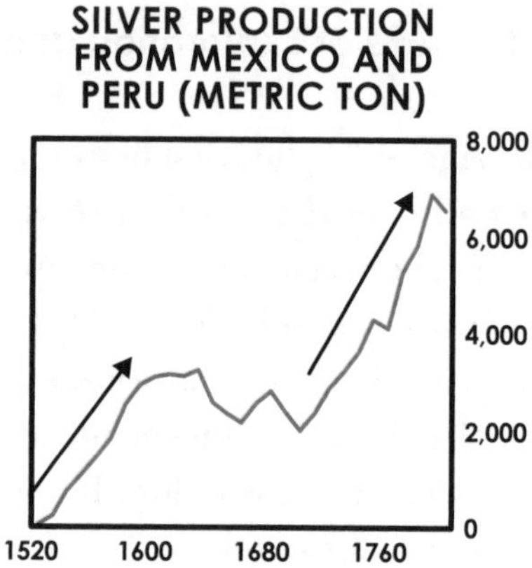

Eventually this push toward exploration led Europe to trade with—and exploit—Asia, most notably China, Japan, and the Indian subcontinent. The Portuguese were the first of these explorers to approach China in 1513, though other European explorers like Marco Polo had been in contact before. Europeans were dazzled by the quality of Chinese porcelain, silk, and other goods, which became highly sought after, but the Chinese weren't interested in buying European goods, which they considered inferior. However they eagerly accepted silver, which was money in China as well as in Europe, as payment. As we'll cover later, China struggled for centuries with shortages of the precious metals it needed to have a sufficient supply of money. However the Europeans didn't have enough silver to trade and the Chinese weren't interested in other goods, which eventually led to the Opium Wars and other interesting stories that we will explore later.

China's Ming Dynasty had its own version of the Age of Exploration but abandoned it. Starting in the early 1400s, Ming Dynasty Emperor Yongle empowered his most trusted admiral, Zheng He, to lead seven major naval expeditions—"treasure voyages"—around the world. Though not colonizing expeditions (and historians debate the extent to which they were commercial), these naval missions helped project China's power abroad. Yongle's navy was the largest and most sophisticated in the world, featuring larger and better-constructed ships than any country in Europe would produce for at least a century.

China's international influence, as indicated by the number of foreign cities engaged in formal tributary relationships with the mainland, increased rapidly. However, the Ming emperors chose to end these voyages and pulled the empire into itself. It remains a matter of conjecture whether that is because Yongle's military and naval expeditions were expensive or because the emperors believed that they had all they needed within China so there was no need for this exploration.

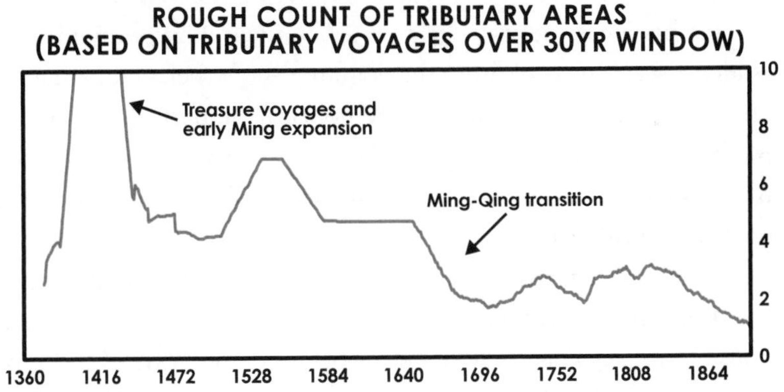

The result of this pullback was an Age of Isolationism in China and in Japan as well, where it was called *Sakoku*. For the next several centuries, China and Japan broadly moved away, in fits and starts, from openness toward foreigners and toward distance and isolation.

The Reformation (1517–1648)

Beginning in the 1500s in Europe, Protestant religious movements initiated a revolution against the Roman Catholic Church, which contributed to a series of wars and the bringing down of the then-existing European order. As previously explained, at the time, the existing order consisted of monarchs, nobles, and the church in symbiotic relationships. The Reformation took aim at the power and corruption of the Roman Catholic Church and sought an independent religion in which people dealt with God directly rather than one mediated by the church's rules. At the time, many Catholic bishops and other senior clergy lived like princes in palaces and the church sold "indulgences" (a supposed reduction in time people would have to spend in purgatory). The Roman Catholic Church was a nation as much as it was a religion, directly governing a sizable share of modern Italy (the Papal States).

The Reformation started in 1517, when Martin Luther published his *Ninety-Five Theses*, challenging the papal monopoly on the interpretation of the Bible and on papal power in general. When he refused to recant his ideas, he was declared a heretic and excommunicated. His ideas—and those of other theologians—nonetheless took hold in large parts of Europe, thanks to the political support of key nobles, as well as the new printing press technology. **That move, together with the usual constant fighting for power, broke down the existing European world order.**

In virtually all the major Christian powers, the immediate impact of the Reformation was increased internal conflict and instability, and the instability extended between countries too. **The Wars of Religion were intertwined with the wars against the existing orders and existing elites. They included an extended civil war in France in which an estimated 3 million people died and later contributed to an extended civil war in the UK. In the end, the Reformation led to Protestants earning substantial rights and freedoms. It also undermined the power of the Holy Roman Empire and the Habsburgs, left Germany**

with deep divisions that would continue to build through the end of the incredibly brutal Thirty Years' War in the mid-1600s, and led to civil wars for over a hundred years. As is typical, the big war led to a new order, which was followed by a period of peace and prosperity.

The New World Order Following the Thirty Years' War (1648)

On its surface, the Thirty Years' War pitted Protestant countries against Catholic ones; however, the full story was more complicated with wider geopolitical interests related to wealth and power playing a role of who lined up with whom. At the end of the war the new order was laid out at the Peace of Westphalia. The most important breakthroughs that came from it were the establishment of geographic borders and the sovereign rights of the people within those borders to decide what happens in their domains. Like most periods after major wars and the establishment of new orders, there was an extended time of peace between countries, with the Dutch emerging from the chaos as the leading global economic power. However, the battles for wealth and power—most importantly between declining monarchies and their subjects—continued across the continent.

The Invention of Capitalism (1600s)

Beginning with the Dutch, the development of publicly available and popularly used equity markets allowed savers to effectively transfer their buying power to entrepreneurs who could put that buying power to productive and profitable use. This significantly improved the allocation of resources and was stimulative to economies because it produced new buying power. It also produced the capital markets cycles. While there were many elements involved in the creation of capitalism, a series of related economic and financial developments—most notably the developments of publicly traded stock and bond markets such as the opening of the Amsterdam Stock

Exchange in 1602 and the Bank of England's first government bond issuance (to fund the war with France) in 1694—are associated with it. Along with the advances of the Scientific Revolution, the invention of capitalism was a key reason behind the shift from slow real GDP growth to the faster growth, as seen in the chart I showed in Chapter 1. We will explore this innovation and its tremendous impact in more detail in the following chapter.

The Scientific Revolution (1500s–1600s)

The Scientific Revolution was an extension of the Renaissance-era shift from finding truth in religion to finding truth in logical reasoning and the Reformation's drive to question authority and think for oneself. These factors led to the development of the scientific method, which improved humanity's understanding of the world, establishing protocols by which scientific discoveries could be investigated and proven and ushering in many discoveries that raised living standards.

The scientific method was pioneered by Francis Bacon in the early 1600s, though many important advances in astronomy—particularly the work of Copernicus and Galileo—took place earlier, in the 1500s. These discoveries vastly expanded European knowledge about the solar system for the first time since the Greco-Roman period and were paralleled by many others across anatomy, mathematics, physics (e.g., Isaac Newton's laws of motion), and many other fields. European governments began to support and sponsor this research, with the most famous example being the Royal Society in the UK, which was founded in 1660 and proved instrumental in promoting the exchange of ideas and discoveries (Newton was its president from 1703 to 1727). Over the centuries to come, the discoveries of the Scientific Revolution helped unleash economic growth and greater competitiveness for the major European powers, particularly the UK. The ideas and methods that underpinned the revolution were applied to more and more fields through the movement known as the Enlightenment.

The First Industrial Revolution (1700s–1800s)

Beginning in the UK in the 1700s, freeing people to be inventive and productive and providing them with capital led many societies to shift to new machine-based manufacturing processes, creating the first sustained and widespread period of productivity improvement in thousands of years. These improvements began with agricultural inventions that increased productivity, which led to a population boom and a secular shift toward urbanization as the labor intensity of farming declined. As people flocked to cities, industry benefited from the steadily increasing supply of labor, creating a virtuous cycle and leading to shifts in wealth and power both within and between nations. The new urban populations needed new types of goods and services, which required the government to get bigger and spend money on things like housing, sanitation, and education, as well as on the infrastructure for the new industrial capitalist system, such as courts, regulators, and central banks. Power moved into the hands of central government bureaucrats and the capitalists who controlled the means of production.

Geopolitically, these developments most helped the UK, which pioneered many of the most important innovations. The UK caught up to the Netherlands in output per capita around 1800, before overtaking them in the mid-19th century, when the British Empire approached its peak share of world output (around 20 percent).

The Enlightenment and the Age of Revolutions (1600s–1700s)

Also known as the Age of Reason, the Enlightenment was essentially the scientific method applied to how humans should behave. This way of thinking became widespread in Europe in the 1700s and 1800s and was an extension of the diminishing of the rights of the monarchy and the church and the increasing of the rights of the individual that characterized earlier intellectual movements. New fields like economics expanded thanks to thinkers like Adam

Smith, while figures like John Locke and Montesquieu pushed political philosophy in new directions. In particular, the Enlightenment ideas of these and other figures promoted rationality and individual liberties and undermined monarchic and religious powers, creating a movement toward overthrowing monarchies known as the Age of Revolutions. This wave of revolutions included the American, French, Spanish, German, Portuguese, and Italian. As is typical, this era of upheaval led some nations to seek out strong leaders who could bring order to the chaos. In the case of France, that leader was Napoleon, who changed the course not just of French history but of European history as he sought to conquer all of Europe. Napoleon was the classic great benevolent dictator who converted chaos into order and prosperity, and expanded the empire with his military prowess. As is often the case, he overreached and failed.

The Napoleonic Wars and the New World Order that Followed (1803–1815)

The Napoleonic Wars lasted from 1803 to 1815, when Great Britain and its allies defeated Napoleon and his allies. As is usual, the victors got together to create a new world order, which was hashed out at the Congress of Vienna. It drew new boundaries to ensure that no European power would become too dominant, based on balance of power concepts that would avoid war. The British emerged as the world's leading empire, and as is typical after the war and the establishment of a new order, there was an extended period of peace and prosperity—the Pax Britannica.

Western Powers Move into Asia (1800s)

The British and other Western powers brought their gunboats to India, China, and Japan in the mid-1700s and into the 1800s, causing dramatic disruptions to the course of their histories. At the time, both China and Japan were isolationist. India was controlled by the Mughal Empire, which had expanded into a significant power in South Asia but experienced rapid decline in the 1700s. The Western powers, which were significantly more advanced militarily at this time, wanted to force trade on all three. The Chinese attempted to fight the British but lost; the Japanese saw this and opened themselves for trade after US Commander Matthew Perry sailed four warships into Tokyo Bay in 1853. **These developments led to the eventual fall of the Qing Dynasty, the resignation of the Japanese government, and the continued control of India by the British. Especially in Japan and China, it also led to the realization that they needed to modernize, which prompted the Meiji Restoration (in Japan) and the Self-Strengthening Movement (in China). This move was very successful in Japan and not successful in China, which continued to suffer in what the Chinese call the Century of Humiliation.**

Second Industrial Revolution (1850s–early 1900s)

Beginning in the mid-1800s, a second big wave of innovation took place, centered at first around steam-powered locomotion (e.g., railroads) and then electricity, telephones, interchangeable manufacturing parts, and other innovations at the turn of the 20th century. Whereas the First Industrial Revolution was centered on the UK, the Second Industrial Revolution primarily benefited the United States. **As is typical, this period produced both great wealth and great wealth gaps and excesses in the capital markets, leading to an era known as the Gilded Age in the US.**

Invention of Communism (1848)

The invention and development of communism in the mid-1800s came as a reaction against both capitalism and the wealth gaps it created and the benefits of the Industrial Revolutions going more to the owners of the new technologies than to the workers. Conflicts between communists and the established powers intensified around the turn of the century and led to a number of major revolutions in the 20th century, including in both Russia and China where communist governments took power.

That brings us to the 20th century, which had two big cycles of boom, busts, wars, and new orders, the second of which we appear to be in the late stages of. Because I review these comprehensively in Chapters 10 through 13, and because they are much more familiar to most readers, I will end this overview here and dive now into the story of the Dutch and how they rose to become the first global reserve currency empire.

CHAPTER 9

THE BIG CYCLE RISE AND DECLINE OF THE DUTCH EMPIRE AND THE GUILDER

After a series of attempted revolts in the mid-1500s, the Dutch, who were under the control of Habsburg Spain, finally became powerful enough to gain de facto independence in 1581. From 1625 until their collapse in 1795, the Dutch gained enough wealth and power to eclipse both the Habsburgs and China as the world's richest empire.

The Dutch Empire rose for all the classic reasons explained in earlier chapters, peaking around 1650 in what is now remembered as the Dutch Golden Age. While its small population and territorial footprint prevented it from being the dominant military power on the European continent, it more than made up for that through a combination of economic strength, financial sophistication, and a strong navy that could protect its large empire of trading posts and colonies around the world. This allowed its currency, the Dutch guilder, to emerge as the first global reserve currency.

The following chart shows the eight powers that fueled the Dutch ascent and eventual decline.

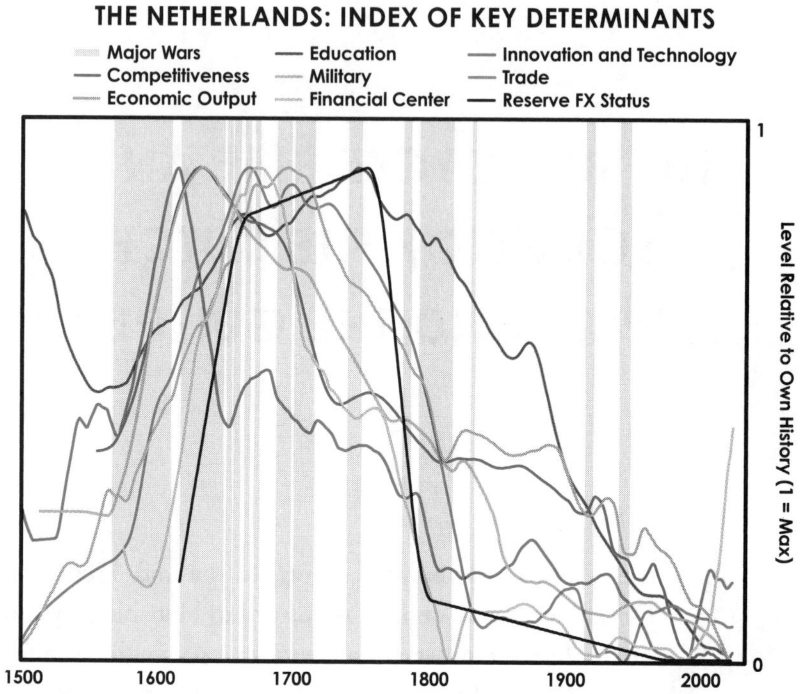

What the chart doesn't show is the decline of the prior leading power, the Habsburg Empire, which you can see in the next chart depicting the entire arc of the Dutch Empire with key events noted. The numbers mark the approximate times of the six stages of the internal order cycle.

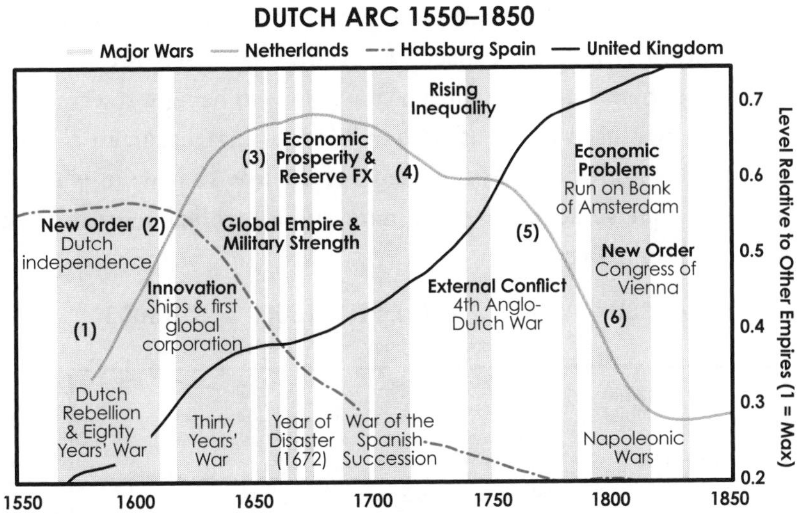

The story begins with the decline of the Spanish Habsburgs, which initiated the first stage of the Dutch Big Cycle.

The Transition from the Spanish/Habsburg Empire to the Dutch Empire

New empires rise when old ones become weak and decadent. The story of the Dutch Empire began when the Habsburg Empire became weak, decadent, and overextended in all the classic ways.

From 1519 until 1556, the Holy Roman emperor and head of the Habsburg Empire was Charles V. The union of territories he controlled—which included most of modern-day Netherlands, Belgium, Italy, Germany, Austria, and Spain—made the Habsburg Empire the most powerful family empire in Europe. **Spain was especially**

strong[1] because of the wealth and power it acquired in the Age of Exploration. The Spanish fleet was clearly the most powerful navy in Europe. Spanish silver coinage came close to being a reserve currency—it was used as far afield as China. Things began to change around the mid-1500s as **the seeds of decline that were planted in the top phase began to germinate and a revolutionary shift in power began to brew.**

HABSBURG SPAIN'S ARC IN THE 1500S AND 1600S

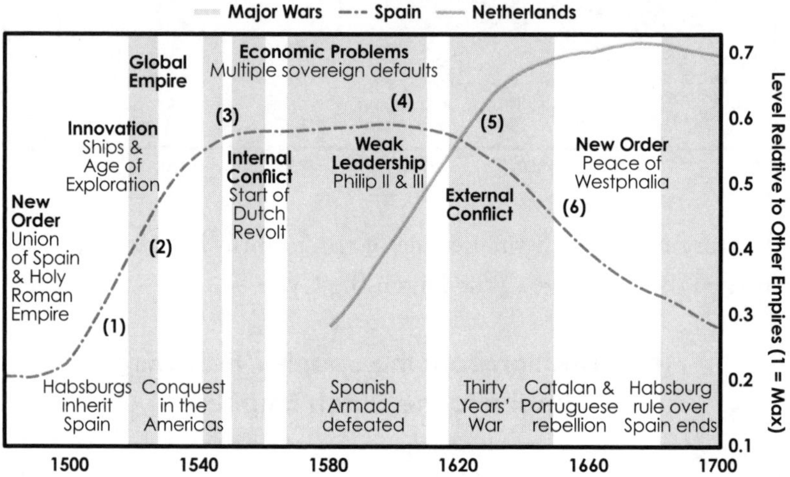

[1] By 1500, the territory of modern-day Spain was increasingly unified following more than 500 years of conflict between Christian kingdoms and Muslim powers that had ruled most of the area since the 700s. The two largest kingdoms, Castile and Aragon, were joined together following the marriage of their rulers in 1469, and in 1492 they conquered Spain's last Muslim kingdom in Granada. The emergent Spanish power had a strong military and very close ties to the Catholic Church—significant portions of the Reconquista of Muslim Spain took the form of papally supported crusades, and religious and monarchic authorities were often closely aligned, as in the Spanish Inquisition.

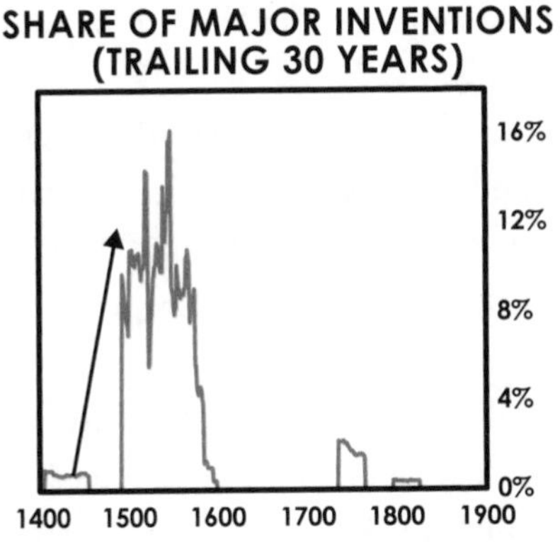

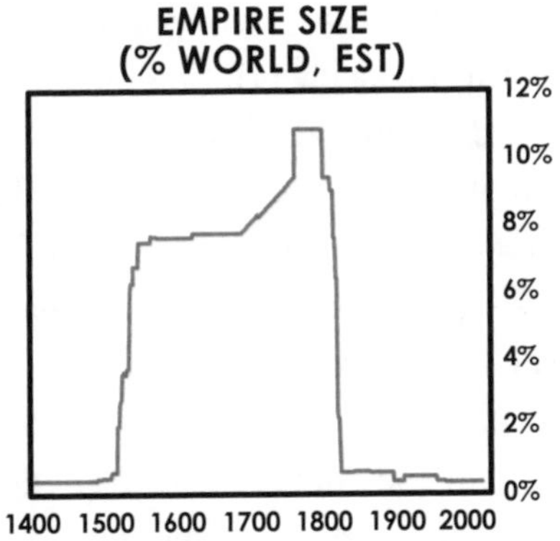

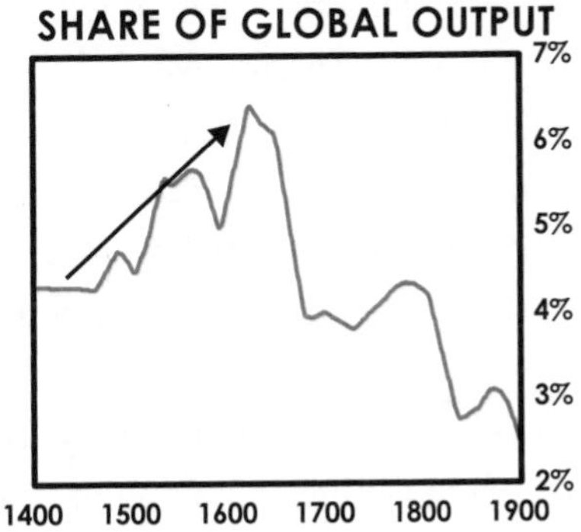

The decline of the Habsburgs happened in many of the classic ways. There were revolutions against the elites who held wealth and power by those without them, challenging the existing order. For example, as I explained in the previous chapter, new religious ideas surfaced in the form of the Reformation, a revolution against the Roman Catholic Church, which was perceived as decadent and exploitative. At the time, the Catholic Church and the Holy Roman Empire were a rich and powerful political force that was integral to the existing order. **The revolution started when a collection of religious opposition groups known generally as Protestantism challenged the system.** Martin Luther published his *Ninety-Five Theses* in 1517, challenging the papal interpretation of the Bible and papal power in general. When Luther refused to recant, he was declared a heretic and excommunicated. His ideas nonetheless took hold in large parts of Europe, thanks to the political support of key nobles, as well as Europe's new printing press technology.

This came at an economically difficult time, when conflicts were intensifying, leading to instability and terrible civil wars,[2] eventually culminating in the brutal Thirty Years' War in the mid-1600s. Its biggest negative impact was on the Holy Roman Empire and the Habsburgs.

Charles V failed to prevent the revolutionary impacts of the Reformation and with it the damage to the existing order. He was forced to sign the Peace of Augsburg in 1555, which weakened the Holy Roman Empire and the Habsburg dynasty. He abdicated and divided his holdings in two: the Holy Roman Empire, which he passed to his brother Ferdinand, and most of the rest of the Habsburg Empire—most importantly Spain, but also the Netherlands, Belgium, significant portions of Italy, and Spanish colonies abroad—which he passed on to his son Philip II. From that point forward, the decline followed the classic script:

- **The empire was overextended militarily.** Not only did Spain face a lengthy revolt against its unpopular rule in the Netherlands, it also fought with the Ottoman Empire, various Italian states, the French, and the British. These wars were costly and chipped away at the Habsburg family dynasty even before the Thirty Years' War.
- **Terrible national finances caused the classic toxic mix of increased taxation, money printing, and rising debt.** Philip II defaulted on debts four times during his reign.
- **The lower and middle classes suffered from rising food prices**, which were increasing at an unprecedented rate from the Spanish Price Revolution.
- **Internal conflict grew**, for all the previously mentioned reasons.

[2] For example, the Wars of Religion in France led to millions of deaths from 1550 to 1600, while England violently switched faiths at several points in the 1500s as new monarchs came to the throne. Even later on, the devastating English Civil Wars of the mid-1600s were significantly driven by religious strife.

- **Leadership deteriorated.** Philip II and his son Philip III preferred lavish living to governing and ultimately used money printing to cover the large deficits, which led to high inflation and economic pain. Those around them behaved similarly.

This chart shows the value of the most popular commonly circulating coin in silver terms. Adding cheap base metals to the monetary supply was the popular way to "print" and devalue money at the time. You can see it started in the early 1600s.

SPANISH MARAVEDI COIN (GRAMS OF SILVER, INDEXED)

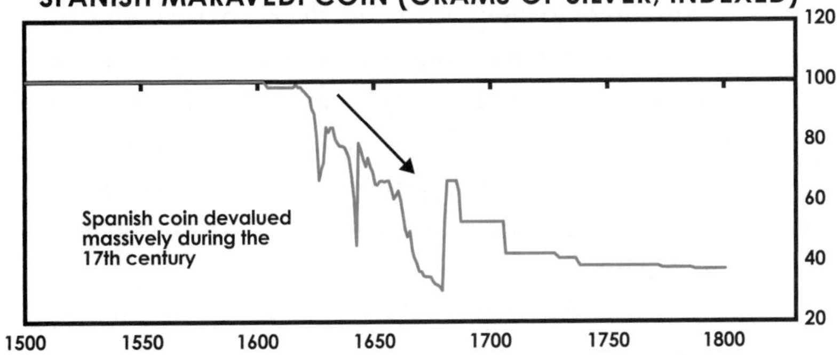

The events of the 1500s were not the end of the Habsburg Empire, nor even to its claim to control the Netherlands—that wouldn't happen until the end of the Thirty Years' War in 1648. But they did create the conditions that allowed the Dutch to rise.

THE RISE

From 1581 until around 1625, the Dutch Empire was built following the classic steps of a rising empire outlined in Chapter 1. More specifically:

- Led by William the Silent, the Dutch successfully revolted against Spain in the Eighty Years' War, which resulted in the

Dutch Republic asserting its independence in 1581. William, who was basically the father of the Netherlands, was a skilled military commander and united the various Dutch provinces against the Spanish.

- While the Spanish and the Dutch continued to fight over the subsequent decades, the Dutch were able to gain independence and the seeds were sown for the rise of a more unified Dutch Republic (particularly as Philip II cut off trade with the Dutch, forcing them to expand abroad on their own).
- **Because the republic was set up to allow each of the underlying provinces to maintain a high degree of sovereignty, the rise of the Dutch Empire was driven by a collective of statesmen rather than by a single monarch or leader.** Though nobles held the most important roles, this system created checks and balances and a partnership that proved effective.
- **Dutch values and culture emphasized education, saving, merit, and tolerance.**
- The break from Spain allowed the Dutch to create a **more open and inventive society.**
- **The Dutch invented ships that could go around the world to collect riches, capitalism that could finance these and other productive endeavors, and many more breakthroughs that made them rich and powerful. The Dutch created the world's first mega-corporation, the Dutch East India Company, which accounted for about one-third of world trade.**[3] **Dutch openness to new ideas, people, and technology helped them rise quickly.**
- To support trade **the Dutch government increased military investments**, which allowed the country to control still more trade by holding off the British in a number of military conflicts.
- **The Dutch also created the world's first reserve currency other than gold and silver, the Dutch guilder, supported by**

[3] Rough estimate based on my calculations.

an innovative banking and currency system put into place via the establishment of the Bank of Amsterdam.[4]

As a result of these classic and sound fundamental steps, the Dutch became rich—income per capita in the Netherlands rose to over twice that of most other European powers. The Dutch continued to invest heavily in education and infrastructure to build on their successes. Dutch literacy rates reached twice the world average. They continued to develop their capital markets and **Amsterdam became the world's most important financial center**. The Dutch did all of this with a population of only 1–2 million people.

The following charts provide some perspective on the unique nature of Dutch education, innovation, and trade in the 1600s and the impact these forces had on Dutch incomes, all of which we will explore later in this chapter.

In short, the Dutch were superbly educated people who were very hardworking and inventive—in fact, they came up with about a quarter of all major inventions in the world when they were at their peak, a spike that began shortly before Dutch independence from Spain.

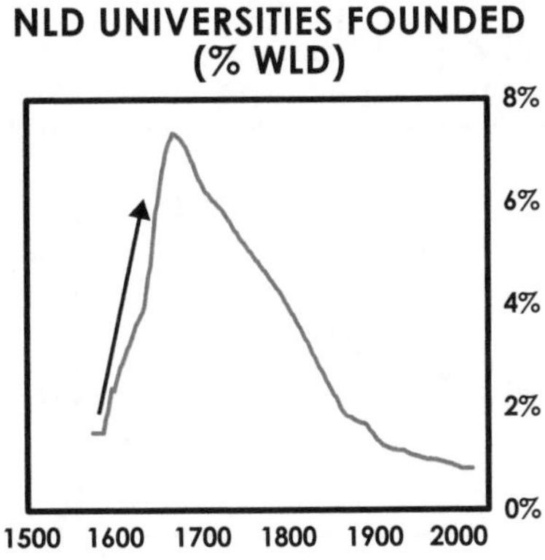

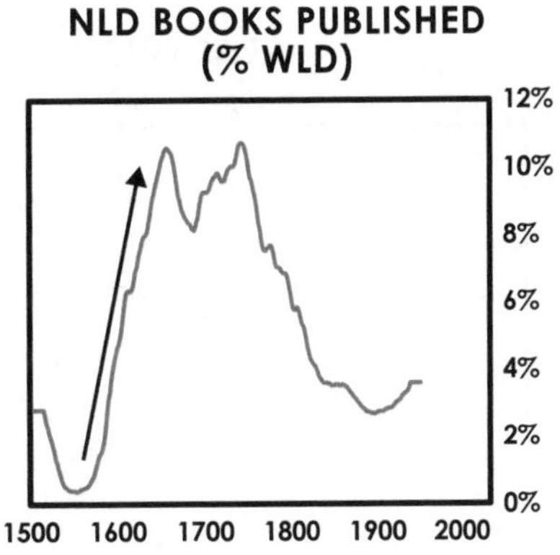

[4] In this chapter, when talking about the "guilder," we are generally referring to guilder bank notes, which were used at the Bank of Amsterdam, rather than to the physical coin (also called "guilder"), which was made of a precious metal (i.e., Type 1 money).

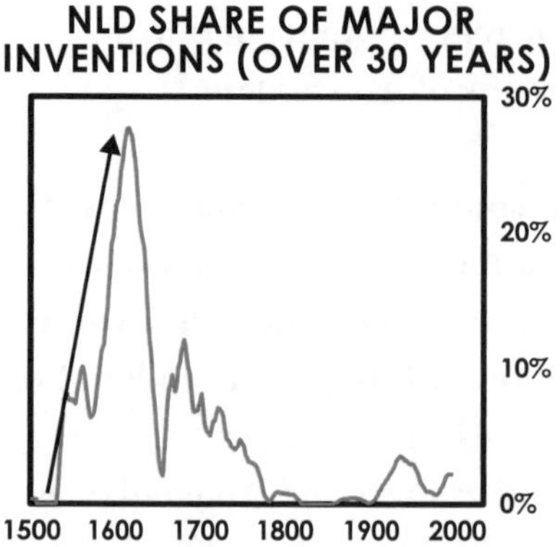

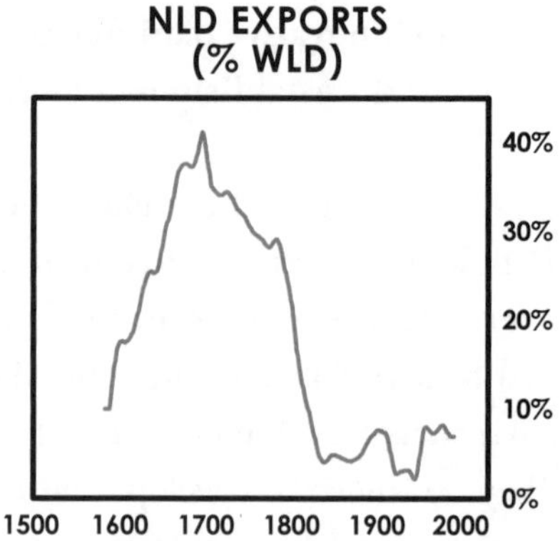

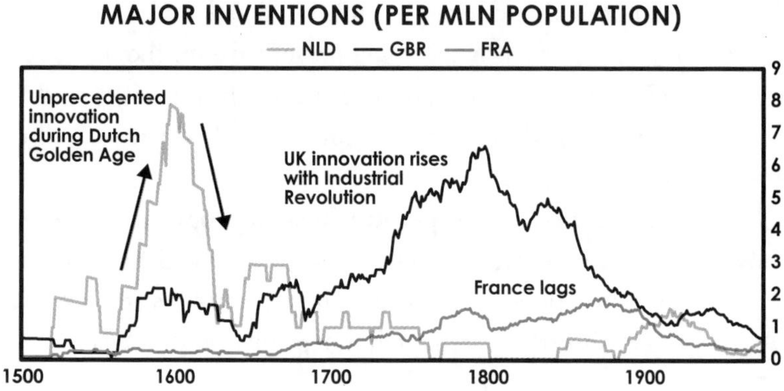

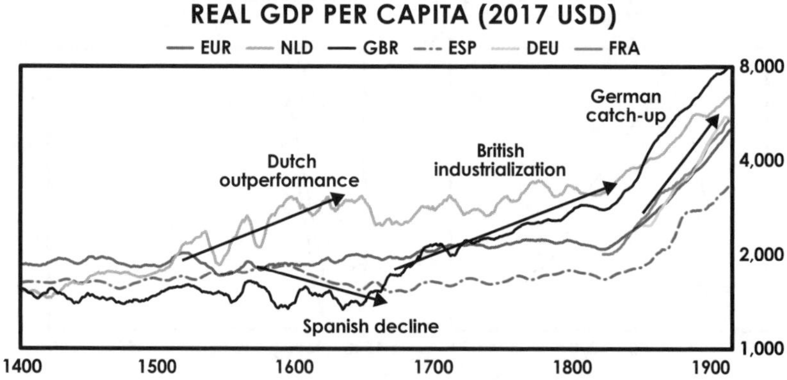

To reiterate, the two most important inventions they came up with were 1) uniquely effective sailing ships that could take them all around the world, which, with the military skills they acquired

from the fighting they did in Europe, allowed them to collect great riches, and 2) the capitalism that fueled these endeavors.

The Capital Markets Cycle of the Dutch

The Dutch invented capitalism as we know it. This was great for the Dutch and great for the world, but like most great inventions, it brought with it some potentially deadly consequences. While production, trade, and private ownership had existed before, **the ability of large numbers of people to collectively buy ownership in money-making endeavors through public equity markets did not exist. The Dutch created that when they invented the world's first publicly listed company (the Dutch East India Company) and the first stock exchange in 1602.**

Like most inventions, these capital market developments arose out of necessity and self-interest. The voyages across the world in search of new trade routes were risky ventures, so it made sense for merchants to sell some of the risk associated with the voyage to others in exchange for a share of the future profits. At the time the Dutch introduced equity shares in their voyages in the mid-1500s, it was revolutionary. Until 1600, these shares were held by only a small number of merchants, largely lacked transparency, and were illiquid, so their attractiveness to outside investors was limited.

The formation of the Amsterdam Stock Exchange in August 1602 and the listing of the Dutch East India Company spread share ownership much wider (more than one in 50 Dutch adults owned shares), and the exchange's clear rules about ownership and transfer of shares made the market much more transparent. **The Dutch East India Company was an equally revolutionary invention. The world's first transnational corporation, it had many of the features you see in companies today**—shareholders, a corporate logo, a board of directors, etc. Capital markets enabled investors to save, merchants to raise funds, and everyone to have a liquid market in which transfers of capital could happen easily and efficiently, fueling a new era of wealth accumulation. At their peak in the early 1700s, Dutch East India Company dividends accounted for nearly $1 out of every $100 of total Dutch GDP.

Importantly, the Dutch outcompeted the Spanish and the Portuguese, which led them to win the main prize—a higher share of the trading between Europe and Asia, particularly China and Indonesia, which was very profitable.

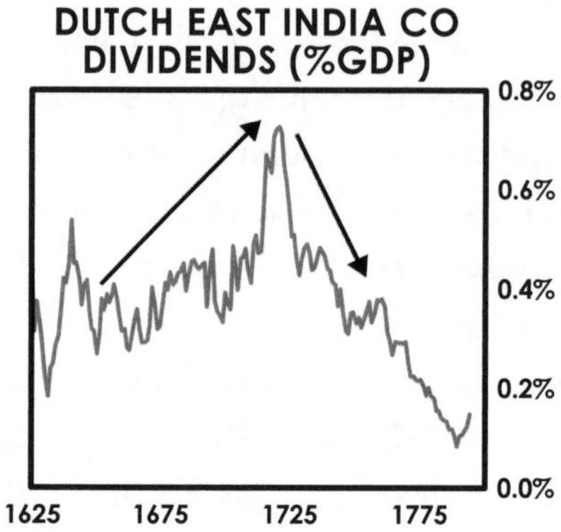

In addition to creating an equity market, the Dutch developed an innovative banking system, which grew rapidly and began to finance international trade for Dutch and non-Dutch merchants. Prior to the Dutch banking innovations, the international currency situation was a mess. In the late 1500s, around 800 different foreign and domestic coins circulated in the Netherlands, many of which were debased (i.e., had a lowered content of precious metal in the coins) and difficult to distinguish from counterfeits. This created uncertainty over the value of money, which made international trade slower and more expensive.

In 1609, the Bank of Amsterdam was established as an exchange bank to protect commercial creditors from unreliable commodity money in general circulation. The Bank of Amsterdam undertook activities that would generate monetary stability and put the Netherlands' coinage, the bank's letters of credit, and the Dutch financial system at the center of global finance. Notably, this bank guilder, though backed by hard currency, was essentially Type 2 money. That set up the guilder as a true reserve currency, the first of its kind.

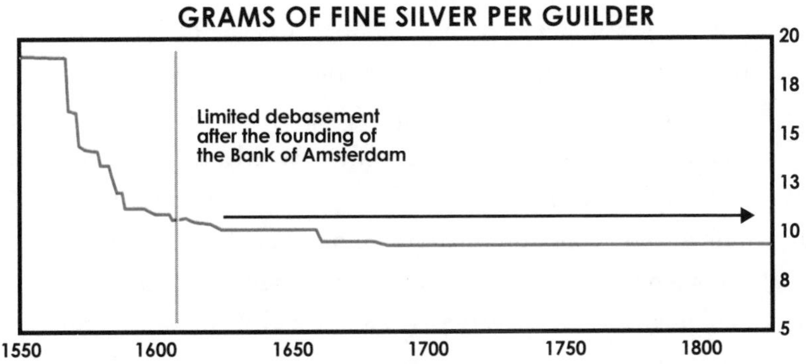

As a result of this system, the guilder remained effective as both a medium of exchange and a storehold of wealth. **Bank of Amsterdam bills of exchange improved their status as a reserve currency. Baltic and Russian trade relied solely on guilders and Bank of Amsterdam bills of exchange for pricing and contract settlement.**[5]

The New World Order: The Thirty Years' War and the Peace of Westphalia

Then came the Thirty Years' War (1618–48). While the Dutch played a relatively minor role in the Europe-wide conflict, it is worth covering this war in some detail given its importance to the internal and external orders of Europe more broadly. It is also a classic case of how internal and external orders work together.

All the classic balance of power dynamics came into play. In this case, the Thirty Years' War was a classic fight over wealth and power, just a lot longer one. On one side was the Catholic emperor of Habsburg Austria, who was allied with the German Catholic territories (most

[5] By 1650, it was fairly common for, say, a merchant in London to pay for goods imported from Moscow with a bill drawn on their deposit in Amsterdam. Both the number of accounts and deposit base of the bank rose continually through 1650.

prominently Bavaria), as well as with Spain and the Papal States. On the other side were the German Protestant nobles, allied at different points in time with Denmark, the Netherlands, Sweden, and France. The fighting was about money, religion (Protestants versus Catholics), and geopolitics. The alliances were pretty complex. For example, the French monarchy—despite being Catholic and having Cardinal Richelieu[6] driving policy—was allied (first secretly, then openly) with both Lutheran Sweden and largely Calvinist Netherlands. That is because money and geopolitics mattered more than religious ideologies.

The Habsburgs lost the war. That left them in a meaningfully weakened position. The treaty that established the new international order, the Peace of Westphalia, expanded the autonomy of the individual princes of the Holy Roman Empire, further eroding the limited authority of the Austrian emperor over the other states. More importantly, **the deal that was cut at Westphalia invented countries as we know them, which is to say it allowed sovereignty of the state with the ability to make choices within its geographic borders** (e.g., their religions, their languages, and all their rules) and instituted respect for those boundaries so that no longer would borderless, free-flowing power grabs occur (without, of course, the understanding that you'd be starting a major war). The emergence of the concept of states led to nationalism and the pursuit of national interests, which reshaped the concept of the balance of power between rival states. **It also made the religious authorities much less powerful.**

---

[6] Cardinal Richelieu was the most important leader in France at the time, serving as chief minister from 1624 until 1642. Richelieu was a brilliant man who provided advice to the two rivals for control of the monarchy in France: the queen mother and her young son Louis XIII. (You can't make this stuff up.) Richelieu had his own particular view of how an internal order should work, which was that the state should be all-powerful—more important than what the monarchy, church, or nobility wanted. Besides being a great big-picture thinker, he was a great administrator who made the system work well. He improved efficiency throughout the kingdom, effectively collecting taxes and controlling power over the nobility and local authorities. He created the notions of national interest and balance of power—e.g., focusing policy on the goal of having France balance the Habsburg hegemony. This wasn't that long after Machiavelli's theories first circulated. His concept of keeping Central Europe divided and balanced (because united it would dominate other areas) worked from 1624 until the French Revolution (for more, see Henry Kissinger's *World Order*).

The Peace of Westphalia reflected what I call the "exhaustion of war," which contributed to a long period of peace and prosperity that followed. Like all big wars, the Thirty Years' War produced devastating losses of life, property, and wealth. One quarter of the population of Europe died from combat, disease, or starvation. **Because wars are so much more terrible than even those who are eager for them can imagine, they lead to treaties that redefine the order and are followed by periods of peace, until the next big war happens.**

The Dutch benefited greatly from the new balance of power and period of relative stability; probably most importantly, it protected them from the threat of Habsburg domination.

It is also the case that ● ***wars are devastating financially; that is true for the winners and much more so for the losers.*** For example, France, though a "winner" and only indirectly involved for much of the war, experienced such bad financial problems and instability as a result that it was faced with widespread rebellions. The losing Habsburg Empire was even more devastated. Relative to the French and Spanish, the Dutch were less financially hurt. They benefited from the peace that fostered the Dutch Golden Age. The Dutch also benefited from the military developments that occurred in the war because, when coupled with the shipping capabilities of the Dutch East India Company, this strong shipping and military combination expanded Dutch power around the world.

THE TOP

The Dutch Golden Age led the Dutch to shift their attentions to "living the good life" in a way that weakened their finances. Other powers rose too and began to challenge them. The arrival of capitalism, combined with the new approaches of the Enlightenment, led to an economic transformation called the Industrial Revolution, which was centered in Britain. The Dutch, who had been the unparalleled leaders in innovation, trade, and wealth in the 1600s, failed to keep up. Eventually the cost of maintaining a declining and overextended empire became unsustainable.

This chart shows a number of key steps.

DUTCH STANDING RELATIVE TO OTHER GREAT POWERS (EST)

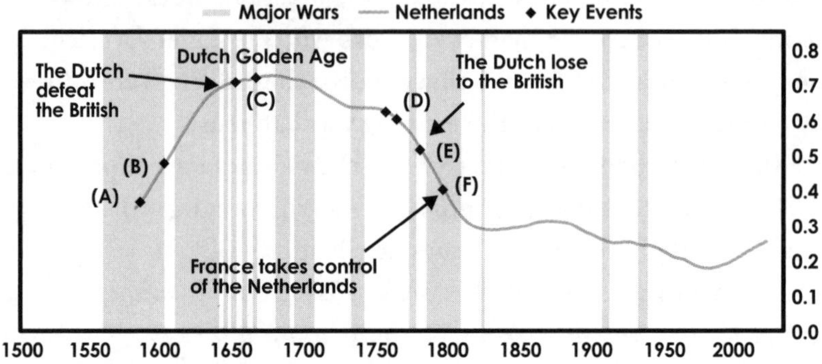

(A) The Dutch declare independence from Spain
(B) Dutch East India Co, Bank of Amsterdam, and stock exchange founded
(C) First and Second Anglo-Dutch Wars
(D) Seven Years' War and Shadow Banking Crisis of 1763
(E) Fourth Anglo-Dutch War, run on the Bank of Amsterdam
(F) Dutch East India Co nationalized, downfall of the Dutch Empire

At the top, the Dutch saw a reversal of many of the classic ingredients we discussed earlier:

- The Dutch **educational and technological edge eroded**.
- The Dutch became **uncompetitive** in general and via the decline of the Dutch East India Company.
- **In the 1700s, the Industrial Revolution led the British to overtake the Dutch as the preeminent economic and financial power in Europe.**
- Slower economic growth relative to other powers made it more difficult to pay for and maintain its vast empire (especially one controlled by such a small nation). Increasing military conflicts (in attempts to protect their vast wealth around the world) left the Dutch **overextended and overindebted**.
- This all set the stage for the **decline in the guilder's reserve**

currency status, which ultimately deteriorated after the Dutch **lost a war** (and with it, important assets) to the British.
- With the Dutch Empire weakened, its **financial center eroded**, especially after a series of debt crises and a run on the central bank and currency.

Even though the Peace of Westphalia brought relative peace and stability to Europe, the Dutch were still engaged in a number of conflicts throughout their time as an empire, as opponents saw their weaknesses and attacked, especially via naval wars fought over trade. Here is a brief summary of the wars the Dutch fought to build and then to hold on to its empire:

- **Eighty Years' War (1566–1648)**: This was the revolt by Protestant Netherlands against Catholic Spain. The Dutch first declared independence in 1581, but their full independence was not realized until the Peace of Westphalia (1648) ended both the Thirty Years' War and the Eighty Years' War.
- **The First Anglo-Dutch War (1652–54)**: This was a trade war that began when the English Parliament passed the Navigation Act of 1651, mandating that all goods from its American colonies be carried by English ships. The war was largely a stalemate and failed to resolve the trade rivalry between the nations.
- **The Dano-Swedish War (1657–60)**: This began when Sweden declared war on Denmark, a Dutch ally, threatening the highly profitable Baltic trade routes. The Dutch defeated the Swedish.
- **The Second Anglo-Dutch War (1665–67)**: England and the Netherlands fought over another trade dispute, which ended with a Dutch victory.
- **The Franco-Dutch War (1672–78) and the Third Anglo-Dutch War (1672–74)**: These were also fights over trade. The Dutch foiled French plans to conquer the Netherlands and forced them to reduce some of their tariffs, but at a tremendous cost.

- **The Fourth Anglo-Dutch War (1780–84)**: The British began the war in retaliation for Dutch support of the colonies in the American Revolution. It ended in a significant defeat for the Dutch, ushering in the end of the guilder as a reserve currency.

Ironically, it was a military victory, one that began nearly a century of peace, that led power to shift away from the Netherlands. In 1688, William III of Orange married Mary II, who was the daughter of the unpopular king of England, and successfully invaded England and took power. This was known as the Glorious Revolution and created a new internal order for Great Britain. While it was undoubtedly good for the Dutch in the short run to have William III on the British throne, **the second-order consequences of economic integration and military cooperation played a major role in the decline of Dutch economic power and the guilder over the next century.**

After 1688, as Great Britain became more competitive, Dutch merchants shifted their operations to London, hastening its rise as an international center of finance. The alliance also gave English merchants access to Dutch trade. William III moved to England instead of focusing his attention on ruling the Netherlands. When he died heirless in 1702, the direct connection between the two nations was broken, and the various Dutch provinces that had been unified under him began to splinter. While England and the Netherlands continued to have military partnerships against the French during most of the 80-plus years leading up to the Fourth Anglo-Dutch War, by the mid-1700s they were beginning to bump into each other in many of the same markets.

By the mid-18th century, the Dutch Empire was no longer the world's leading empire. Britain especially had learned from Dutch innovations and made their own investments in education to strengthen their people's capabilities. These abilities, coupled with the use of capitalism, led to the advancements that made up the Industrial Revolution, which brought about constant improvements on existing concepts to make production more efficient, such as standardizing inputs and moving production from individual artisans to factories. It also led to transformative new inventions. This allowed the British to become more productive, capture more trade, and build military might.

Additionally, and as is classic, **as the Dutch became extremely wealthy, they became less competitive**—for example, their wages were generally higher than those in other parts of Europe. The Dutch East India Company lost its competitive edge as well. For example, it was ineffective in trading popular new products like tea. **Dutch economic growth slowed relative to other powers, which made it more difficult for the Dutch to pay for and maintain their vast empire.** Increasing military conflicts to protect their vast wealth left them **overextended**.

Thus, from around 1725 through around 1800 the financial decline unfolded in the classic ways. These charts do a good job of conveying both the ascent and the decline of the Bank of Amsterdam.

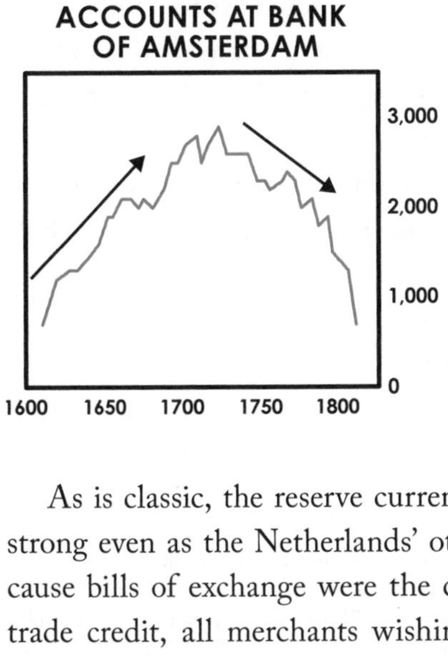

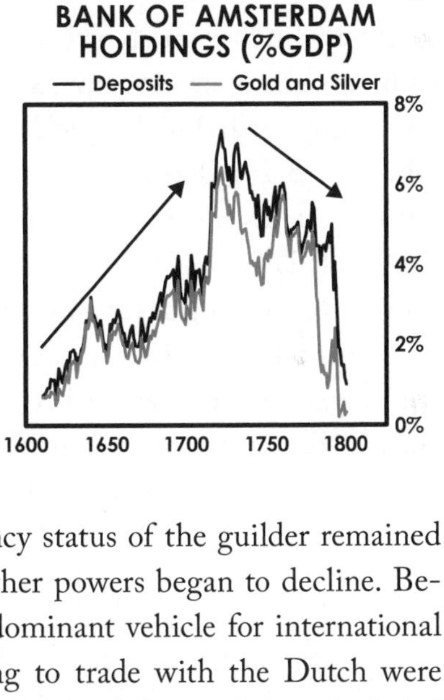

As is classic, the reserve currency status of the guilder remained strong even as the Netherlands' other powers began to decline. Because bills of exchange were the dominant vehicle for international trade credit, all merchants wishing to trade with the Dutch were forced to open an account at the Bank of Amsterdam, which led to **around 40 percent of global trade being settled in Amsterdam using bank guilders**. The importance of the Dutch in trade and financial transactions, the Bank of Amsterdam's policies that made the guilder very effective as both a medium of exchange and a storehold of wealth, and the fact that Dutch commercial entities and banks insisted on its usage all cemented the guilder's place as the first global reserve currency.[7] This gave the Dutch the "extraordinary privilege" of being able to get into a lot of debt.

THE DECLINE

Around 1750 the British (and the French) became stronger than the Dutch, both because their own power had grown and because the Dutch had become weaker. As is classic, the Dutch a) became more indebted, b) experienced a lot of internal fighting over wealth,[8] and c) weakened militarily. All this made them vulnerable to decline and attack.

As earnings from abroad fell, wealthy Dutch savers moved their cash into British investments, which were more attractive due to their strong growth and higher yields.[9] Despite this, the guilder remained widely used as a global reserve currency. As explained earlier, reserve currency status classically lags the decline of other key drivers of the rise and fall of empires. Then, **as is typical, a rising great power challenged the existing great power in a war.**

Starting in the 1770s, the English began to interfere with Dutch shipping, escalating the conflict after the Dutch traded arms with the colonies during the American Revolution. In retaliation, the English delivered a massive blow to the Dutch Navy in the Caribbean in 1781,

[7] Available payment data supports the claim that the guilder accounted for a large share of global trade: the annual value of payments made through the bank peaked in the 1760s at about 1.5 times the Dutch Republic's annual GDP (with some estimates more than double that). Similar ratios for the United Kingdom in 1868 and the United States in 1955 were 3.6 and 2.7, respectively.

[8] A good example of this is the popularity of the Patriot Movement in the Netherlands around this time.

[9] There was a general rise in foreign investment by the Dutch during this period. Examples include Dutch purchases of stock in the British East India Company and the City of London selling term annuities (bonds) to Dutch investors. For a further description, see Hart, Jonker, and van Zanden, *A Financial History of the Netherlands*.

taking over Dutch territories there and in the East Indies as well. Having lost half its ships and access to its key trade routes, the Dutch East India Company had to borrow heavily from the Bank of Amsterdam to stay alive. Rival powers took the Dutch defeat as an opportunity to grab still more of the Dutch shipping business. British blockades in the Netherlands and in the East Indies caused a liquidity crisis. The financial consequences of these events can be seen in the following charts.

DUTCH EAST INDIA COMPANY BALANCE SHEET (%GDP)

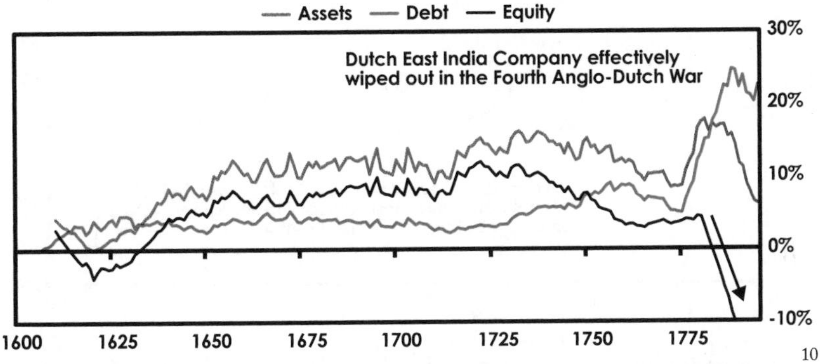

[10]

DUTCH EAST INDIA COMPANY PROFIT & LOSS (GUILDER, MLN)

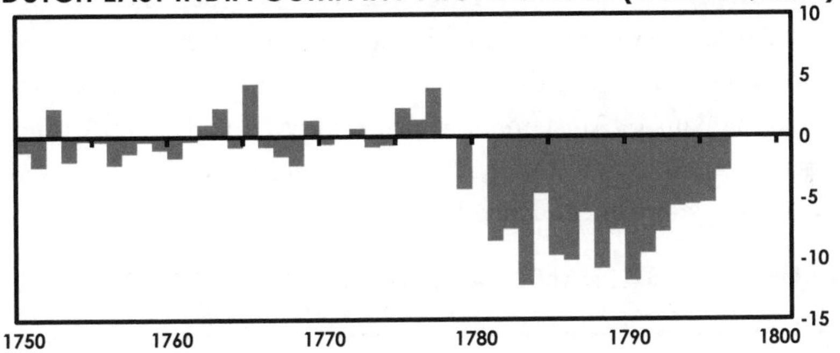

Financial losses and large debts led to the classic move by the central bank to print more money. As the Bank of Amsterdam printed more and more paper money to provide loans to the Dutch

[10] This chart only shows the financial results from the Dutch East India Company reported *in patria*, i.e., the Netherlands. It does not include the parts of the revenue and debt from its operations in Asia but does include its revenue from goods it sourced in Asia and sold in Europe.

East India Company, it soon became clear that there would not be enough gold and silver to cover all the paper claims on it. That led to the classic "run on the bank" dynamic, in which investors exchanged their paper money for precious metals. With the bank's store of precious metals exhausted, the supply of guilders soared, even as demand for them fell, as shown in the following chart.

BANK OF AMSTERDAM HOLDINGS (%GDP)

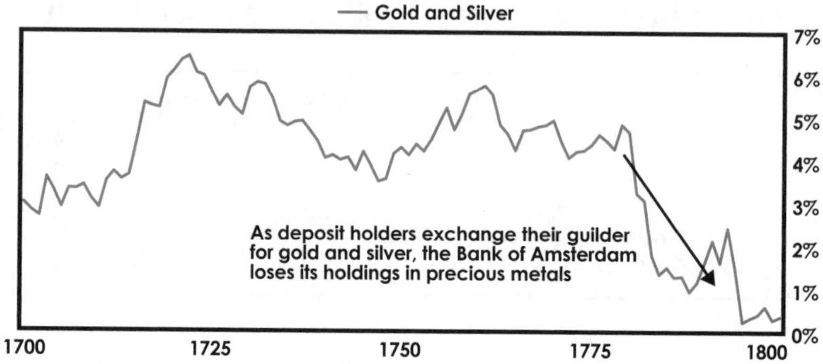

The next chart shows this explosion of loans on the bank's balance sheet throughout the Fourth Anglo-Dutch War. (For reference, the full balance sheet at the start of the war was about 20 million bank guilders outstanding, so this represented a roughly 50 percent expansion in the Bank of Amsterdam's balance sheet.) The Bank of Amsterdam had no choice; the Dutch East India Company was too big to fail because the government depended on loans from the company.

BANK OF AMSTERDAM LOANS OUTSTANDING (GUILDER, MLN)

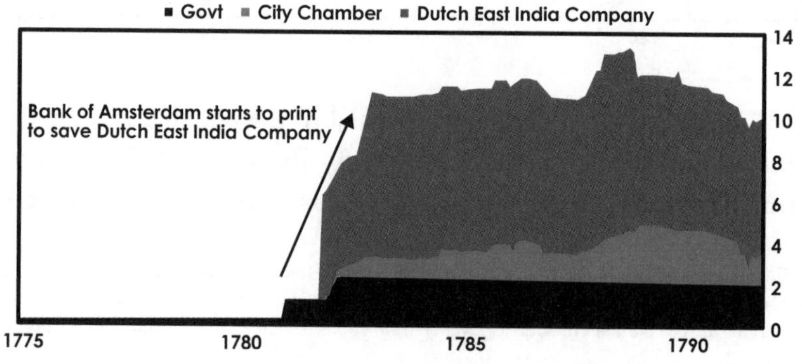

Interest rates rose and the Bank of Amsterdam had to devalue, undermining the credibility of the guilder as a storehold of wealth.[11] As a result, the British pound replaced the Dutch guilder as the leading reserve currency.

What happened to the Dutch was classic, as described in Chapter 1's summary of why empires rise and fall and Chapter 3's description of how money, credit, and debt work. **The Bank of Amsterdam started with a Type 1 monetary system (precious metal) that morphed into a Type 2 monetary system (paper money linked to precious metal).** As usual, this transition occurred at a time of financial stress and military conflict. It was risky because the transition decreased trust in the currency and added to the risk of a bank-run-like dynamic, which is exactly what occurred. Bank of Amsterdam deposits (i.e., holdings of short-term debt) had been a reliable storehold of wealth for nearly two centuries. They began to trade at large discounts to guilder coins (which were made of gold and silver). The bank used its holdings of coin and precious metals (i.e., its reserves) to buy its currency on the open market to support the value of deposits, but it lacked adequate foreign currency reserves to do this indefinitely. Accounts backed by coins held at the bank plummeted from 17 million guilder in March 1780 to only 300,000 guilder in January 1783 as owners of these gold and silver coins demanded them back. The bank run marked the end of the Dutch Empire and the guilder as a reserve currency. In 1791 the bank was taken over by the City of Amsterdam, and in 1795 the French revolutionary government overthrew the Dutch Republic, establishing a client state in its place. After being nationalized in 1796, rendering its stock worthless, the Dutch East India Company's charter expired in 1799.

The following charts show the exchange rates between the guilder and the pound and gold. As it became clear that the bank no longer had any credibility, investors fled to other assets and currencies.[12]

---

[11] The Bank of Amsterdam was ahead of its time and used ledgers instead of real "paper money." See Quinn & Roberds, "The Bank of Amsterdam Through the Lens of Monetary Competition."

[12] Historical data suggests that by 1795 bank deposits were trading at a -25 percent discount to actual coin. See Quinn & Roberds, "Death of a Reserve Currency."

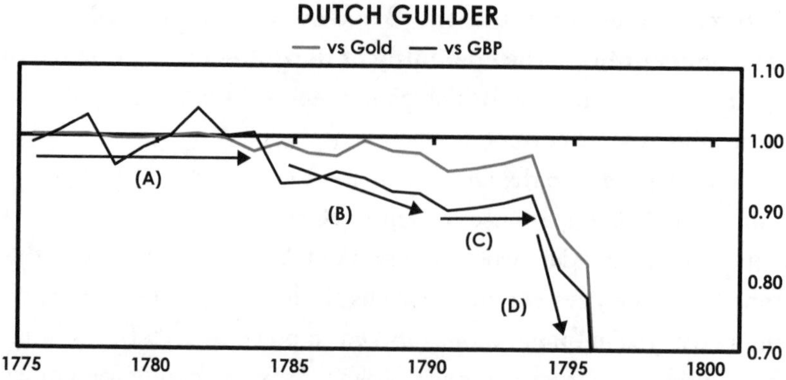

(A) Guilder stable through most of the decline era
(B) Fourth Anglo-Dutch War leads to money printing and initial pressure on the guilder (run on the Bank of Amsterdam)
(C) Short period of stabilization as investors seek safe havens at the start of the French Revolution
(D) The French overthrow the Dutch; accounts at the bank basically wiped out [13]

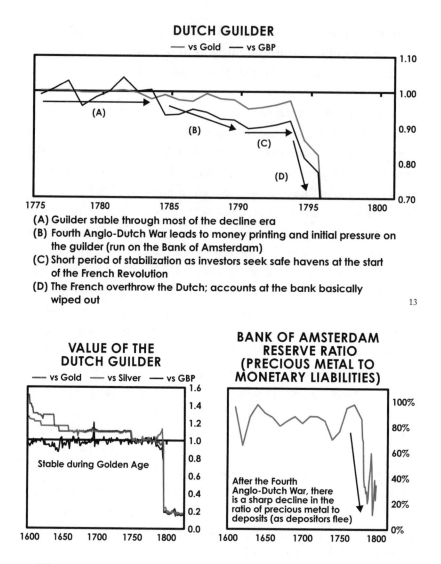

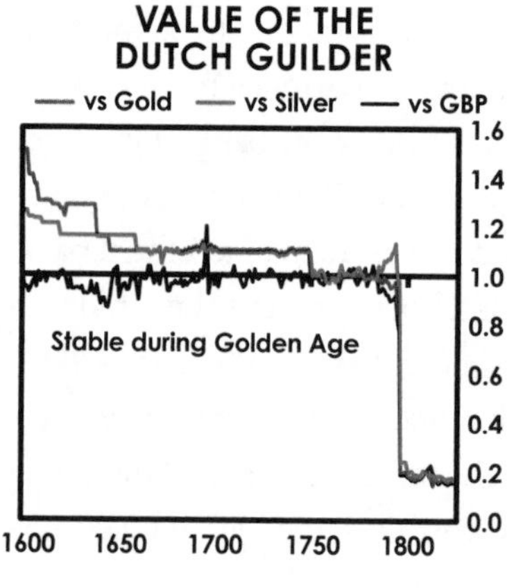

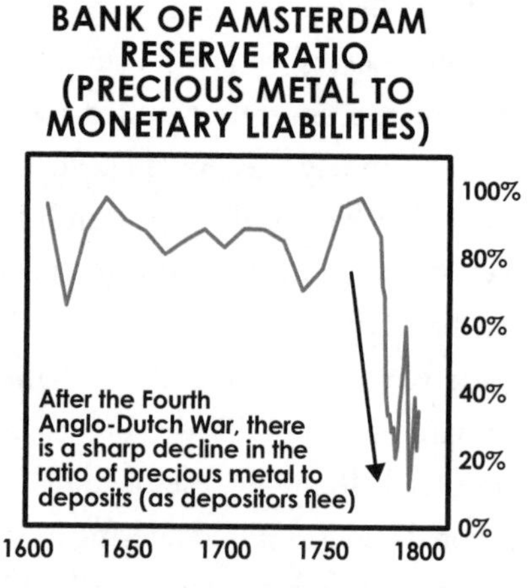

The next chart shows the returns of holding Dutch East India Company stock starting in various years. As with most bubble companies, it

[13] To fully represent the likely economics of a deposit holder at the Bank of Amsterdam, we assumed depositors each received their pro-rated share of precious metal still in the bank's vaults when it closed (that was roughly 20 percent of the fully backed amount, thus the approximately 80 percent total devaluation).

did great at first and seemed to have great fundamentals. This attracted still more investors even after those fundamentals began to weaken. Ultimately its failed fundamentals and excessive debt burdens broke it.

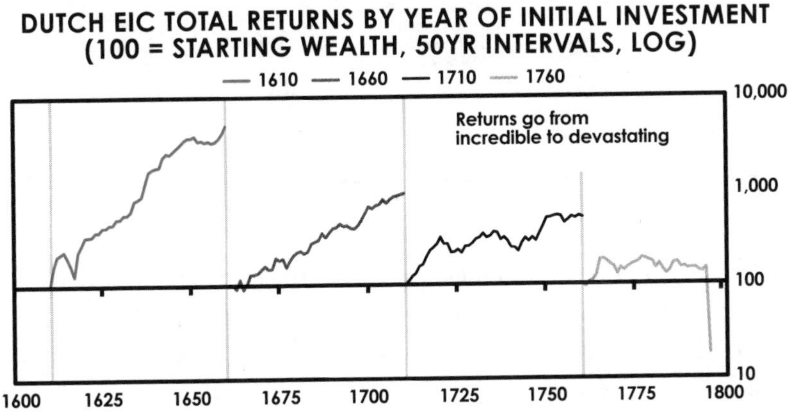

As is typical, the returns of investment assets in the declining empire fall relative to the returns of investing in the rising empire. Returns on investment in the British East India Company, for example, far exceeded those in the Dutch East India Company, and the returns on Dutch government bonds were terrible relative to British government bonds.

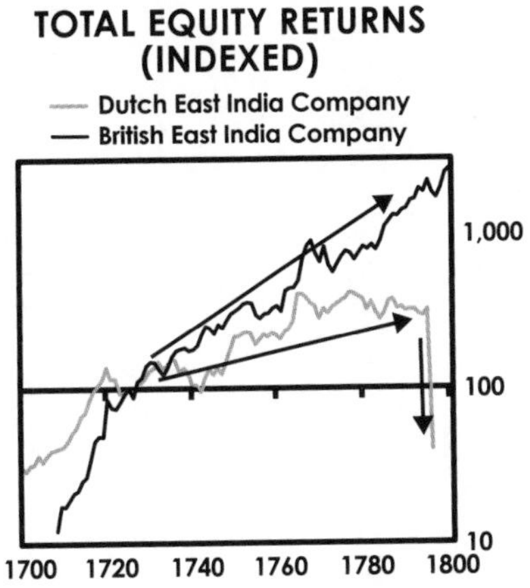

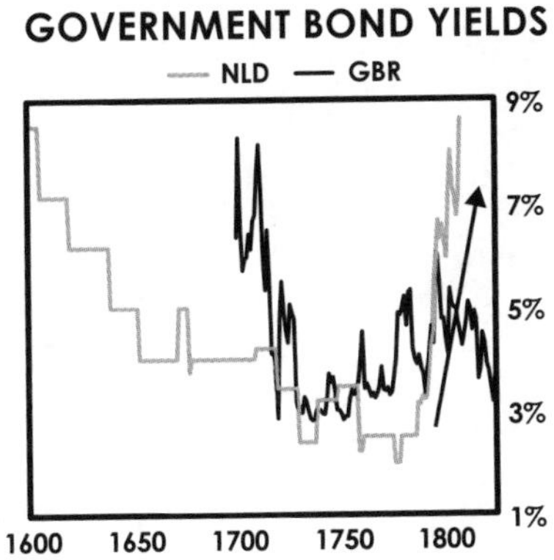

DUTCH BOND PRICES (TERM ANNUITIES)

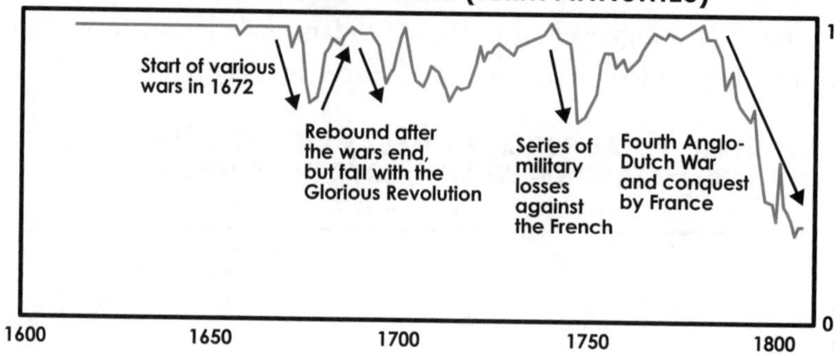

The decline of the Dutch Empire led to the next Big Cycle in world history: the rise and decline of the British Empire and its reserve currency. That story—which is basically the same story, just a century or so later in a more technologically evolved form with people in different clothes speaking a different language—is told in the next chapter.

CHAPTER 10

THE BIG CYCLE RISE AND DECLINE OF THE BRITISH EMPIRE AND THE POUND

Changes in the world order come about when two or more countries (or alliances of countries) of comparable power fight and one wins and becomes dominant enough to set the new rules, which is the new world order. Before this happens, the rising country needs to get itself into a comparable position of strength relative to the reigning country, so the story of any great country's rise begins long before it becomes a great power. Likewise, the story of its decline extends long after it ceases to be a great power. That is reflected in the arc chart that shows the simplified version of the cycles of the Dutch, British, American, and Chinese empires that I shared with you before and share here again.

CHANGES TO THE WORLD ORDER (CONCEPTUAL EXAMPLE)

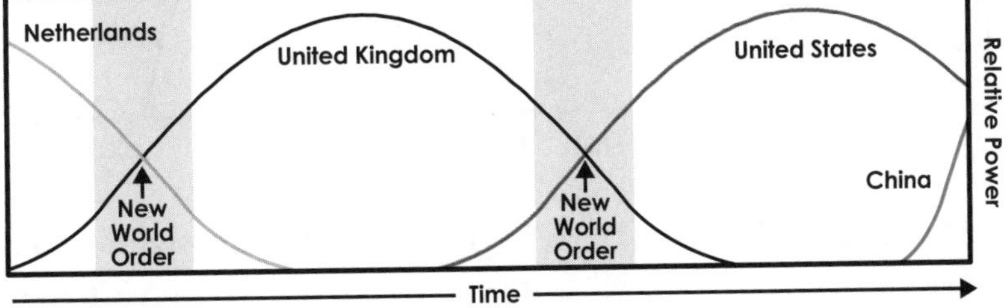

The rise of the British Empire started long before it became preeminent, as it first had to build its educational, institutional, and technological strengths to become more competitive and then challenge and defeat the Dutch. This chart shows my gauges of the eight measures of power for the British Empire from 1600 to the present. As shown, competitiveness, education, and innovation and technology levels rose sharply in the early 1600s and continued to increase steadily from 1600 to 1800, which paid off from 1700 to 1900 as the UK's output, share of world trade, and military expanded together. With the typical lag, the development of Britain's financial markets and its financial center (London) to become world leaders followed, and, with a greater lag, the pound overtook the guilder as the global reserve currency.

UNITED KINGDOM: INDEX OF KEY DETERMINANTS

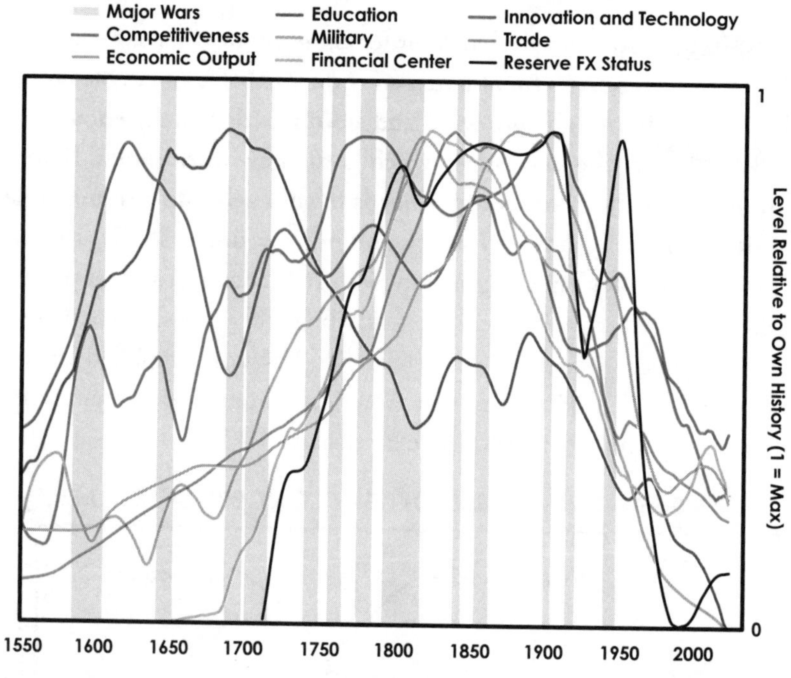

While the fall of the Dutch in the late 1700s removed the UK's primary trade and financial competitor, Britain's rise wasn't complete until the early 1800s because it had one last great rival power to

defeat—France, led by Napoleon. You see, Napoleon was on a tear to conquer Europe and be the greatest power via the Napoleonic Wars. This created the usual sort of great power rivalry and balance of power struggle dynamic that I described in the addendum to Chapter 2, with all the alliances and escalation building to a great crescendo. Later in this chapter, I will briefly drop into the French story, also an iconic one, as part of explaining the rise of the British Empire. But for now I will simply jump to the punchline, which is that **Britain won through effective economic as well as military warfare. Then, following the classic Big Cycle script of what happens after wars that establish the dominant power, there was a new world order set out by the winners followed by a long period—in this case 100 years—of relative peace and prosperity. That is when the British Empire became the greatest empire ever.** At its peak, with only 2.5 percent of the world's population in the UK, the British empire produced over 20 percent of the world's income and controlled over 20 percent of the world's land mass and over 25 percent of the global population.

But I'm getting ahead of myself. As shown in the previous chart, the story of Britain's rise began around 1600, so we should start there. The following chart shows the arc and the timing of key events. The numbers mark the approximate times of the six stages of the internal order cycle.

UK ARC 1600–PRESENT

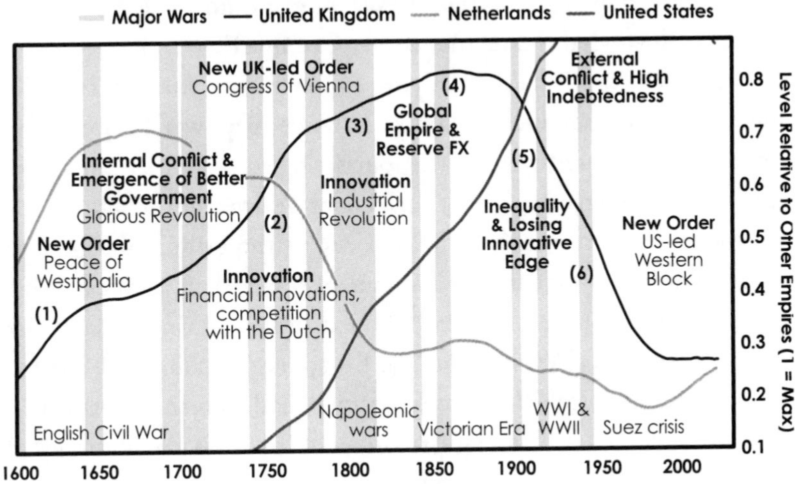

THE RISE

To set the stage for the UK's rise, we need to describe its situation, as well as the broader backdrop of Europe, at the end of the 1600s. For both, the early 17th century had massive conflicts that radically changed or overturned all the prior orders. As explained in the last chapter, **in Europe there was great devastation and change that resulted from the Thirty Years' War because it was a war between ideologies, religions, and economic classes that created a new European order through the Peace of Westphalia. This treaty established countries as we know them and created a fractured Europe, which led to different choices in different countries**. Great Britain had its own turmoil over wealth and power that took the forms of the English Civil War, which was a brutally violent continuation of the centuries-long battles between classes, and the Glorious Revolution, which less violently led to William III, a Dutch ruler, becoming the king of England. What these conflicts have in common is that they weakened the monarchy and strengthened Parliament. They also established terms for the relationships between the kingdoms of England, Scotland, and Ireland. **The English Civil War specifically led to the king (Charles I) being tried and executed and the monarchy being replaced by the Commonwealth of England under the rule of the general who led the revolt, Oliver Cromwell.**

These conflicts established rule of law rather than rule of the monarchy and they created a new balance of power between the king and Parliament that set the foundation for Great Britain's later rise. That is because a strong Parliament allowed for a moderately meritocratic selection of national leaders, as the prime minister had to command the confidence of Parliament rather than just be a favorite of the royal court. Statesmen who led Britain during its later rise and peak—such as William Pitt the Elder and his son, Will Pitt the Younger, Robert Peel, William Gladstone, and Benjamin Disraeli—were strong forces for shaping Britain. They all came from families of merchants, not the landed gentry.

This revolutionary strengthening of Parliament was heavily influenced by the new Enlightenment thinking about who should have what powers and how governments should work that had spread throughout Europe starting in the late 1600s. That was shaped by the earlier scientific thought of Englishman Francis Bacon (1561–1626). **At the core of this new, human-centric philosophy was the idea that society should be based on reason and science and that the government's power comes from the people, not from God.**

Debate and skepticism were encouraged. Improvements in basic education (which caused literacy rates to rise), the dissemination of ideas via printed materials (the first encyclopedias and dictionaries were printed en masse at this time), and a growing number of transnational elites (who were well-read and cultivated cross-border contacts) created a new and wider "public sphere" of political and social thought. The key thinkers during this time produced ideas and concepts that are still important in the Western world.

Enlightenment ideas influenced different countries in different ways, ranging from more autocratic monarchs like Catherine the Great in Russia to the more representative form of government adopted by America's Founding Fathers. **The UK particularly reaped the benefits of the Enlightenment's strong political institutions and rule of law alongside the Enlightenment's emphasis on science, which supported major discoveries.**

While these strengths did not bring about immediate prosperity, **over time the British system's respect for the rule of law, combined with strong education, gave it the foundation to gain competitive advantages in commerce and innovations that followed and led to the rise of the British Empire.**

At the same time, **England became financially strong as it created a powerful and centralized fiscal authority that allowed the state to raise significantly more revenue than its international rivals. By the 18th century, the tax burden in Britain was almost twice that of France. The creation of the Bank of England in 1694 helped standardize and increase the liquidity of UK government**

debt, improving its ability to borrow. Consistent with these reforms, government bond yields fell drastically, both outright and relative to other countries over the early 1700s.

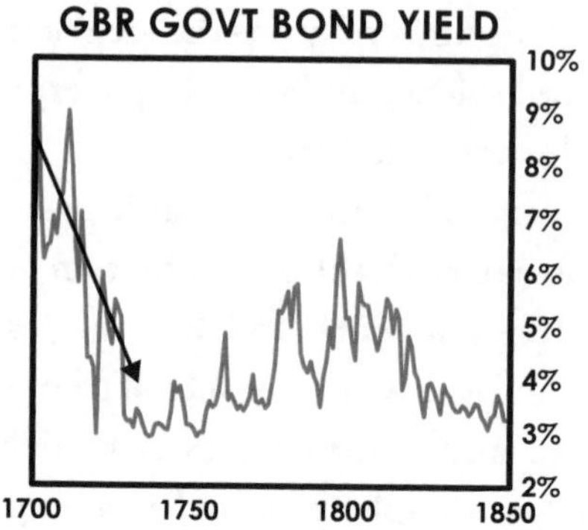

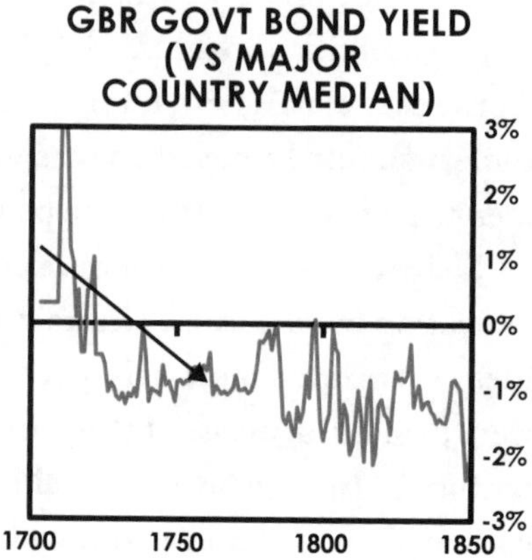

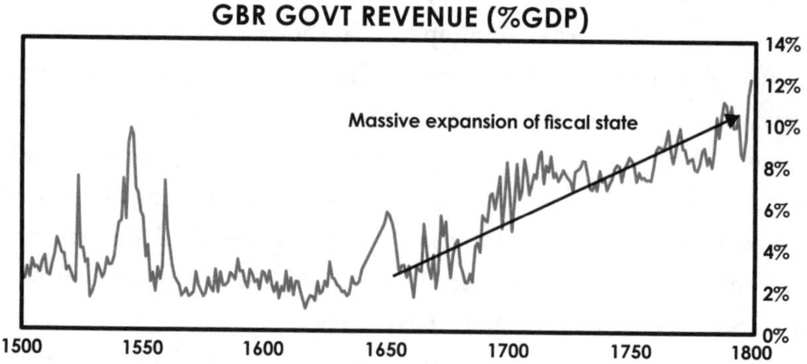

By the early 1700s, there were many other classic signs of an empire on the rise. In these charts, you can see Britain's leadership in innovation compared to its main rivals at the time.

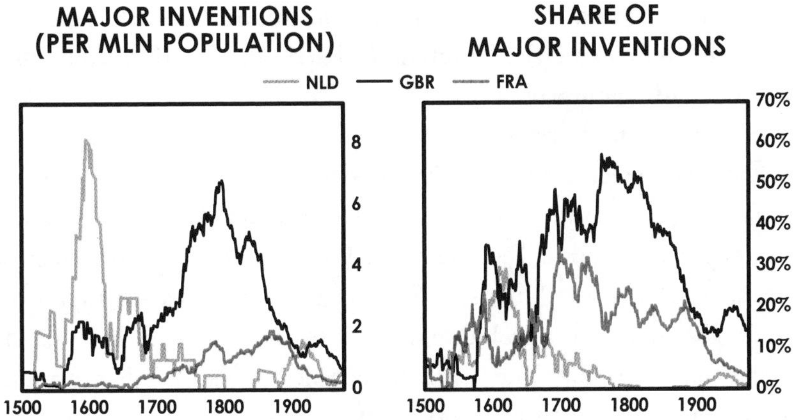

The Industrial Revolution

A well-educated population together with a culture of inventiveness and the availability of capital to financially support the developments of new ideas—especially about how machines could more efficiently do what many were laboring to do—created a great wave of competitiveness and prosperity. England's geological endowments of iron and coal gave it a great boost in producing this economic transformation known as the First Industrial Revolution. As described in Chapter 8, this shift changed Europe from a primarily rural and agrarian society in which most people were poor and power resided with landowning elites to an urban and industrial society in which people as a whole got a lot richer (though benefits disproportionately accrued to the elites) and power resided with central government bureaucrats and capitalists. Geopolitically, these strengths led it to overtake the Dutch as the preeminent

economic and financial power in Europe around 1750, 30 years before the UK defeated the Dutch in the battle and clearly became the world's leading empire.

The productivity revolution started with agriculture. Agricultural inventions increased productivity, which reduced the labor intensity of farming. It also made food more plentiful and cheaper, which led to a population boom. Together these forces led to people flocking to cities, which benefited industry from the steadily increasing supply of labor. The Industrial Revolution was driven not only by the creation of brand-new inventions like the steam engine but also by adapting and improving on existing concepts to make production more efficient, such as standardizing inputs and moving production from individual artisans to factories. Ample labor, energy, and connected global markets together helped support the burst of innovation. This list gives a sense of the timing and pace of innovation in the UK:

- 1712: Steam engine invented.
- 1719: Silk factory established.
- 1733: Flying shuttle (basic weaving machine) invented.
- 1764: Spinning jenny (multi-spindle weaving machine) invented.
- 1765: Separate condenser (for steam engines) invented.
- 1769: Water frame (hydraulic power for weaving machines) invented; steam engine upgraded.
- 1785: Power loom invented; iron refining developed.
- 1801: Steam-powered locomotive on wheels invented.
- 1816: Steam-powered locomotive on rail patented.
- 1825: Railway construction initiated on a line connecting Manchester and Liverpool.

Through these revolutionary changes to agriculture and industry Europe became urban and industrial, with goods made by machines in city factories. The new urban population required new types of goods and services, which required the government to get bigger and spend money on things like housing, sanitation, and education, as well as to set up the infrastructure for the new industrial capitalist system to flourish, such as courts, regulators, and central banks. **Power was in the hands of central government bureaucrats and capitalists who controlled the means of production.**

This was most true in the **United Kingdom, which pioneered many of the most important innovations and which used the new methods of production to pull ahead of other nations and become the world's leading superpower**. As reflected in output per capita, the UK's living standards caught up to those in the Netherlands by around 1800 and overtook them in the mid-19th century, when the UK approached the zenith of its share of world output (around 20 percent). In parallel to this economic growth—and helping to reinforce it—the UK became the world's dominant trading nation, pulling decisively ahead of the Dutch in the late 1700s and maintaining that position through the 19th century. At the same time there was an acceleration in the output of all countries through most of the 1800s. Most countries in the world were then in Stages 3 and 4 of the internal order cycle.

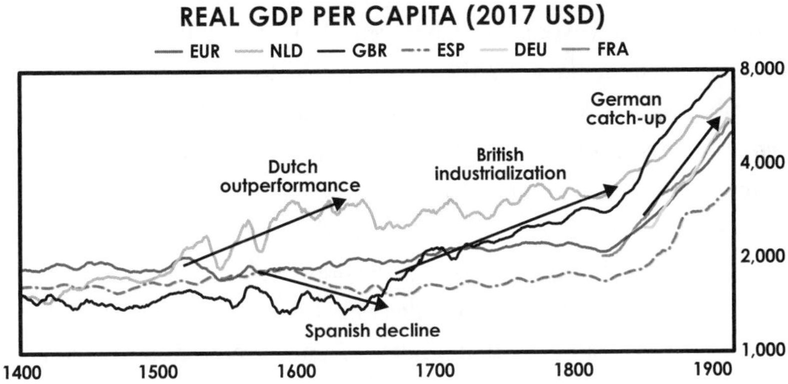

Naturally as it became a world economic power the UK needed to be able to fight militarily to both protect and assert its interests. **The UK's military strength—especially its navy—helped it establish its colonies and take over those of other European powers, as well as secure its control over global trade routes. The profitability**

of the empire more than paid for its military spending because it supported economic activities. Thanks to the Bank of England's financial innovations and the guilder's collapse, **London became the world's financial center and the pound sterling the world's reserve currency. In other words, Great Britain followed the classic Big Cycle steps of a rising empire.**

Britain also took the Netherlands' mantle as the top trader with China. With the Industrial Revolution, Europe no longer demanded nearly as much in the way of manufactured luxury goods from China, but instead sought a commodity—tea. China, for its part, wasn't interested in European goods and continued to seek payment in precious metals. That sowed the seeds of the great British-Chinese conflict that led to the Opium Wars and China's Century of Humiliation. Who would have imagined that?

The story of Britain's rise is obvious in retrospect. It's easy to look back and describe what happened. It's another thing to position oneself well for it by anticipating it and seeing it happen at the time. I wonder what I would have thought at the time. I wonder whether in looking at the readings of my indicators and systems and thinking about the situations whether I would have bet well. That is why it is so important to me to have the data and the decision rules to see what I would have actually done and what the results would have been. I can now see what the indicators would have shown at the time and know that they would have painted the picture I just described, and I can see from that that the picture would not have been crystal clear that the British Empire would have gone on to become the dominant world empire. If I were alive in the early 1700s and looking at my indicators, I would have seen the Dutch still at their peak and Bourbon France as a major power on the rise also, and I would have seen bullish conditions for them both at that time.

Why Not the French?

In the early 1700s, France was a center of education and learning, a hub of the Enlightenment with famous thinkers like Voltaire and

Montesquieu, and a home to a booming publishing industry, so my indicators would have shown the French as being just as strong as the Dutch and British powers. From 1720 to 1780, the number of books on the arts and science published in Paris doubled. As the quantity of information increased, so did people's literacy; over the course of the 18th century literacy rates in France close to doubled.

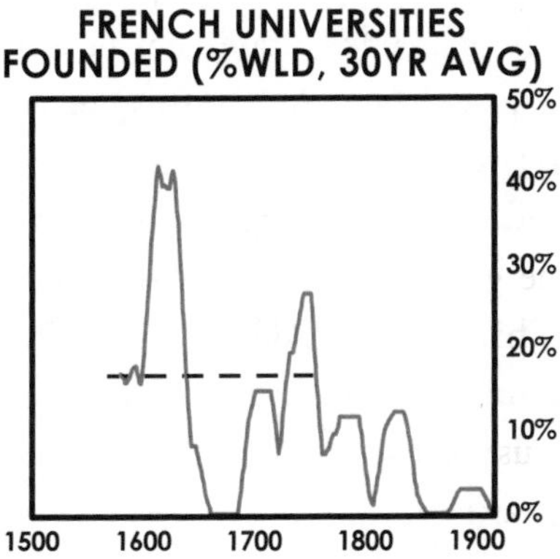

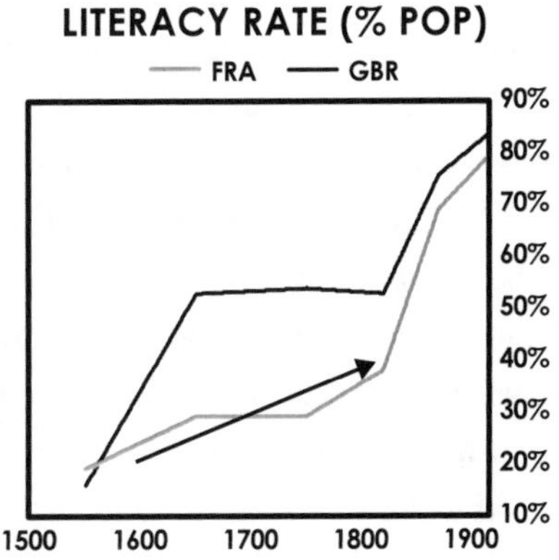

France also would have shown up as economically strong in the early stage of a big debt cycle upswing. It was just before an investment boom was about to turn into a bubble which later turned into a bust. At the time, France's most famous economist was John Law (a Scotsman by birth) who thought the creation of new money would stimulate the economy. In 1716 he created a national bank with the ability to issue paper money backed by land, gold, silver, and state bills. That began the upswing in the cycle. The original capital for this bank, Banque Générale, was provided by shareholders, who also sat on the bank's board. France had had a stock market since 1673, when Finance Minister Jean-Baptiste Colbert's Ordinance of Trade was codified into commercial law,[1] so it had all the ingredients for a classic capital markets upswing. At the same time, Law also created

[1] This law created monopolistic joint-stock companies to trade in both the East and West Indies. Colbert's ordinance was motivated by the desire to fund the trading companies using private funds, and not through the government.

the Company of the West. The Company of the West, or the Mississippi Company, was a trading company with monopoly rights in French Louisiana (half of the present-day United States). Law allowed French government debt to be used to purchase shares in the Mississippi Company. With a new company that had an exciting story about exploiting the opportunities of the new frontier and a bank and government finances supporting this endeavor, all the right ingredients were in place. As the company expanded, state debt holders jumped at the ability to convert their debt into equity. This created what was perceived to be a great investment. Would you have bought in? Would I have bought in? If we didn't would we have had regrets? The stock soared, eventually becoming a bubble in the classic ways these things happen. When it burst, both shares and bills rapidly lost their value because of the classic reason of the outstanding claims on real assets being much greater than the real assets that were backing up the claims.

Naturally people in France fled from the depreciating paper money toward hard currency coinage. New laws prohibited charging interest rates above 5 percent, which meant that only the most credit-worthy borrowers and most stable investments could receive capital. As a result, it became nearly impossible for new businesses to receive funding. There wasn't enough real money.

On top of that, and quite typically, expensive wars made financial conditions worse. A partial list of wars that France was in follows:

- **War of the League of Augsburg (1688–97)**: France, under the leadership of Louis XIV, expanded into modern-day western Germany, spurring war against England, Spain, Austria, and a number of German states.
- **War of the Spanish Succession (1701–14)**: France, allied with Spain, fought an alliance of England, Austria, and the Netherlands to contest the inheritance of the Spanish throne. The war ended with the French heir taking the throne of Spain, but with various concessions made to the other powers

(including giving up Spanish territory in Italy and Belgium to Austria, and France giving England and the Netherlands colonial and trade concessions).

- **War of the Austrian Succession (1740–48)**: France, in alliance with Spain, Prussia, and other German principalities, fought against Austria and the UK, in support of the German princes' territorial ambitions against Austria.
- **Seven Years' War (1756–63)**: France, allied with Austria, Sweden, and Russia, fought against Britain and Prussia over German territories and French and British colonies abroad, particularly in North America. (This war is also known as the French and Indian War.)
- **American Revolution (1775–83)**: France and Spain allied with the American revolutionary forces against the British government.

While a number of these wars produced territorial and strategic gains for France, they turned out to cost much more than they brought in which eventually severely damaged the French government's finances. Without a modern financial system, France had more difficulty funding its government through debt than Britain did so it had to rely more on burdensome taxes, which were unpopular. One example of France's inferior financial position affecting its geopolitical position is the differences in experiences of the British and the French during the American Revolution. The French paid for the war effort entirely by floating loans at interest rates at least double those the British government faced. This caused France's debt service payments to rise to over £14 million compared to Britain's £7 million (both had national debts of around £220 million). Because the nobility, clergy, and even certain privileged towns often paid lower taxes, high levels of taxation on the rest of society were imposed. That exacerbated France's already high income inequality. Many French laborers struggled to meet their basic needs. That caused more class warfare.

Along with extreme income inequality, there was corruption

and extravagance at the top. The court of King Louis XVI was infamous for its frivolous spending—for instance, Marie Antoinette's Hamlet, an ornamental farm near the gardens of Versailles built at great expense to replicate a rustic village. **Two major wars—the Seven Years' War and the American Revolution—led to massive deficits.** During the American Revolution the deficits were around 2–3 percent of GDP and about a third of France's annual tax revenue. Meanwhile, the American Revolution further popularized Enlightenment ideas of liberty and equality, while **bad harvests in 1788 and 1789 led to soaring bread prices and famines**. It was a recipe for revolution.

Due to France's inefficient and unrepresentative political decision-making system, the government was unable to raise needed revenues or enact needed changes. Decisions from the ancien régime could be and often were undermined at virtually every lower level. The nobility and clergy resisted decisions that hurt them and were able to carve out broad privileges for themselves. Local authorities (called *parlements*) were needed to enact tax policy, but often resisted doing so. The closest thing France had to a legislative body was the Estates General, where representatives of France's three estates (the clergy, the nobility, and the commoners) met to approve certain legislation when summoned by the king. Its consent was seen as necessary to levy new national taxes; however, its powers and procedures were unclear, and basic questions—like how representatives were chosen and how many votes each estate got—were unsettled. In 1789, the Third Estate—representing the commoners, who made up 98 percent of the population—formed its own assembly, inviting members of the First and Second Estates to join it. To stop this National Assembly from meeting, the king closed their meeting hall.

Protests, riots, and insurrection arose. **In 1791, a newly elected National Convention declared France a republic**, and in January

1793 Louis XVI (by then officially called "Citizen Louis") was sentenced to death. As is classic in revolutions, violence began soon after, in which those who were deemed insufficiently zealous were purged. It is estimated that between 20,000 and 30,000 people were executed during the French Reign of Terror. By 1795, France was broke, and the assignat—the currency it printed to finance government spending—was experiencing hyperinflation.

FRENCH INFLATION (5-YEAR AVG)

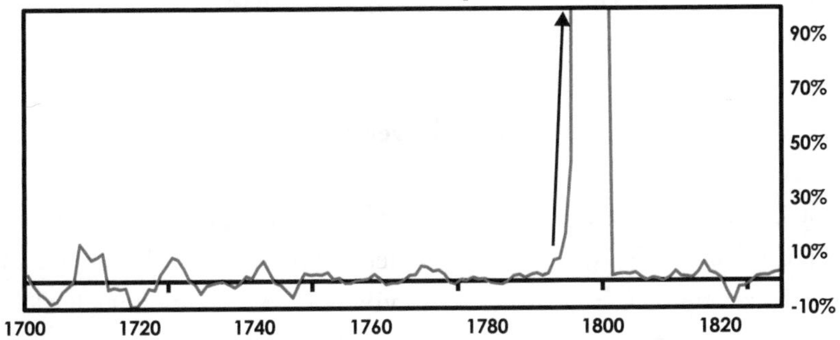

As is also classic, the revolution led to a counterreaction in which the revolution's leaders were themselves arrested and a new constitution written and approved. The new system (the Directorate) proved to be ineffective and was immediately crippled by financial problems. Still, **the government continued to print money and forced wealthy citizens to loan it funds.** Ultimately, the inflationary spiral was halted by the introduction of the hard currency that was acquired through Napoleon's successful military conquests in Italy and the decision to declare bankruptcy on two-thirds of the government's debt. Additional measures such as increased taxes further strengthened the government's fiscal condition. In 1796, the government held a ceremony in which it destroyed the presses it had been using to print money.

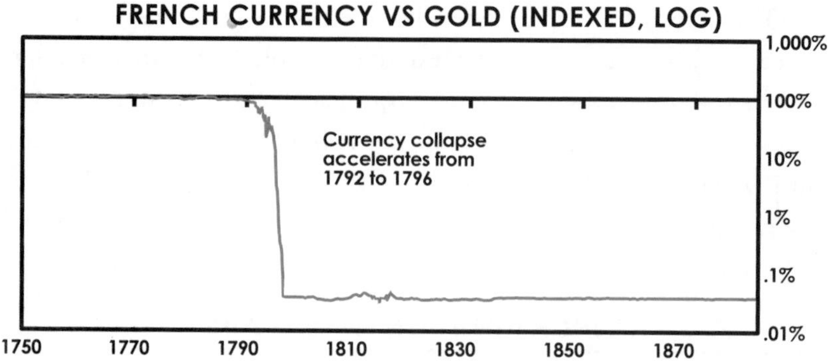

Enter Napoleon

The bubble, the big wealth gaps, and the costly expense of war led to the bust and then to revolution, which threw out the old order and put in a new one. That new order consisted of revolutionary leaders who fought with each other, producing 10 years of painful chaos that required a strong leader to get control of the mess. It was all consistent with the classic, melodramatic script that has played innumerable times in the past. **As if on cue, Napoleon entered the picture. Napoleon was the classic hero rising to the occasion.** He had gained a sterling reputation as a military commander as France attempted to spread its republican system across Europe, and he was very popular. So, in 1799, he led a coup to install himself as first consul and eventually emperor, and held dictatorial powers until 1814. **Armed with centralized power and widespread support, he stabilized the economy and professionalized the government**; France was widely seen as an empire on the rise and a formidable rival to other European powers.

When Austria and Russia declared war on France, Napoleon scored sizable early military victories. Before long, he controlled Spain, Portugal, Italy, and much of Germany. I won't go through the history of the Napoleonic Wars, except to say that like other such leaders he overreached. Napoleon's invasion of Russia swung the tide of war against him. **In the end, France was defeated. Great Britain**

and Russia were the primary victors.

It should be noted that a significant factor in the war was the UK's much greater financial strength. Because of their financial strength, **the UK was able to lend a lot of money to the European coalition forces against France.** It was both its financial resources and its naval power that allowed Britain to stay in the fight even as it and its allies suffered repeated defeats.

A New World Order: The Congress of Vienna

By now you know how these things go. After a war the victors come together and create a new world order. That happened at the Congress of Vienna. Just as the victors of the Thirty Years' War had done at Westphalia, **the quadruple alliance of Great Britain, Austria, Prussia, and Russia reorganized the world order in their favor at the Congress of Vienna (1814–15), creating a system of checks and balances among the European powers that would more or less hold for the next century.** The geopolitical importance of these developments is well-described by Henry Kissinger:

> It may not have fulfilled all the hopes of an idealistic generation, but it gave this generation something perhaps more precious: a period of stability which permitted their hopes to be realized without a major war or a permanent revolution . . . The period of stability which ensued was the best proof that a "legitimate" order had been constructed, an order accepted by all the major powers, so that henceforth they sought adjustment within its framework rather than in its overthrow.

All the major powers were represented in Vienna, though the most important decisions were negotiated by the core group and France itself. Like the US at the Paris Peace Conference after World War I and in the negotiations after World War II, the UK didn't seek to gain significant new territories. **Its primary goal was to address the power**

imbalances in Europe that had led to wars. Areas that had previously consisted of weak and divided states, such as Italy, Germany, and the Low Countries, saw significant territorial consolidation to counterbalance more centralized states like France, while agreements on the navigation of international rivers supported the expansion of trade. Tactically, the Treaties of Paris aimed to contain but not destroy France, which suffered only a minimal loss of territory.[2]

The victorious powers were all monarchies, and many of the policies they enacted were aimed at restoring the old status quo (for example, returning the Bourbon dynasty to power in France). Even so, the new ideas of the Enlightenment continued to have influence. **Governments shifted to more representative and rule-of-law-based systems, though to varying degrees (Tsarist Russia remained largely autocratic).** In England the liberalization came about as a result of gradual reforms, while on the continent a series of revolutions (most famously the liberal Revolutions of 1848) spurred the changes. **In time, nationalist movements led to the unification of Germany and Italy, as well as the destabilization of the multiethnic Austrian and Ottoman empires.**

British Power Approaches Its Peak

No power benefited more from the new stability than the British Empire. **Not only were Britain's main economic and military rivals weakened, but the power equilibrium allowed the UK to avoid expensive military conflicts close to home and focus on trade and its colonies, a policy known as "splendid isolation," which set the stage for its "Imperial Century."** Of course there were some bad economic periods during those years (e.g., the Panic of 1825 in the UK, and the panics of 1837 and 1873 in the US), and there were military

[2] The Treaty of Paris in 1814 saw France restore its borders to what they were in 1792, which meant France actually got back some of the colonial territories that the UK had taken during the wars. The Treaty of Paris in 1815, after Napoleon returned from exile and was defeated a second and final time, was less favorable, requiring France to pay a large indemnity, accept an army of occupation, and cede some additional territory, but still left France with the vast majority of the land it had controlled at the time of the French Revolution.

conflicts (e.g., the Crimean War between Russia on one side and the Ottoman Empire and a coalition of Western European powers on the other). But these were not significant enough to change the big picture, which was of a very prosperous period with the British on top. As mentioned, at their peak in the late 19th century around 1870, the British produced 20 percent of the world's income and controlled 40 percent of global exports, 20 percent of the world's land mass, and 25 percent of the world's population. And the pound, of course, became the world's undisputed reserve currency. The charts on the following pages help paint the picture of Britain's dominant strength.

Geopolitically, the UK continued to expand abroad throughout the 19th century, eventually encompassing Canada, Australia, India, and large portions of Africa.[3] And even where the British Empire didn't explicitly take control, it was increasingly able to intervene abroad in order to gain trade access on uneven terms (e.g., the Opium Wars against China ending with a treaty ensuring the UK's ability to export opium to China despite local Chinese laws against it). Maintaining these colonies gave the UK an assured source of commodities, wealth, and income, and preferential trade arrangements. This chart clearly paints the picture.

GBR EMPIRE SIZE (% WORLD, EST)

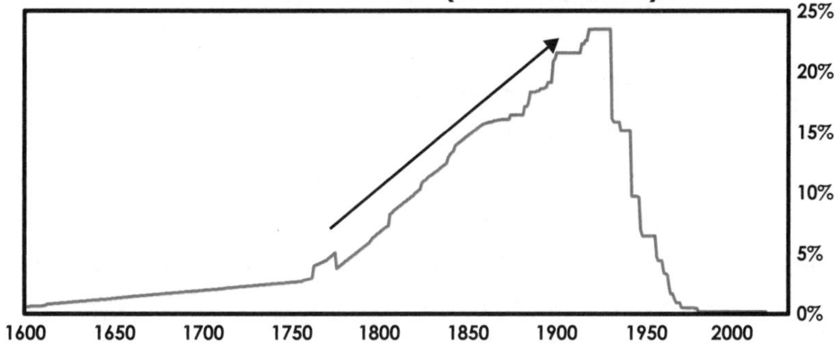

[3] A crucial dimension of the UK's early expansion was the role played by the British East India Company, which starting in the late 18th century and continuing into the 19th century consolidated its political and economic control of modern-day India, Pakistan, and Bangladesh. This vast area remained under the private control of the company until a major rebellion in 1857 led the British state to step in and take over India as a British territory.

THE TOP

The pound's status as a reserve currency complemented its dominance in colonial expansion, military reach, global trade, and investment flows. **The UK's share of global exports rose with the Industrial Revolution and the spread of the empire, peaking around 1850 at about 40 percent of global exports.** And the share of trade denominated in sterling was greater than the UK's trade share alone. From 1850 to 1914, around 60 percent of global trade was denominated in pounds. This set of conditions sowed the seeds of the decline that typify the top phase of the Big Cycle.

GBR SHARE OF WORLD EXPORTS (% TOTAL)

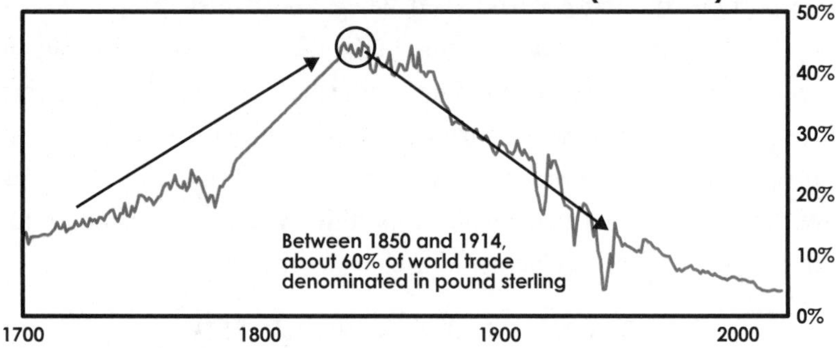

Even as the UK's share of world exports declined, the UK ran a persistent current account surplus throughout this period. After 1870, this was comprised of a persistent trade deficit funded by returns on overseas investments. The income from the current account surpluses funded an increasing share of global cross-border investment as other countries become more attractive to invest in.

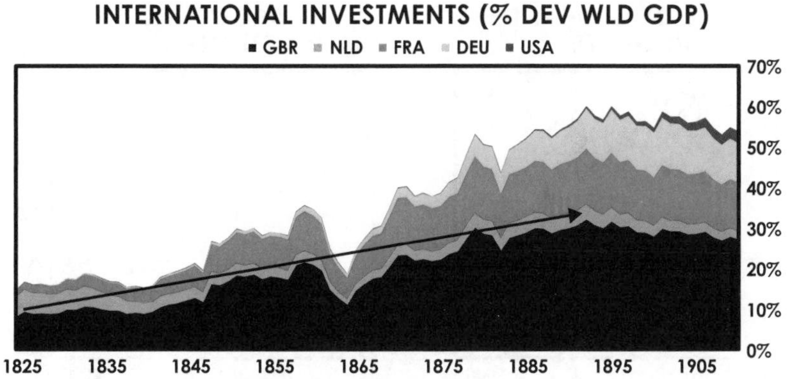

In 1818, the English Rothschild bank made its first major government loan, to Prussia. As the pound became increasingly liquid, a wave of other sovereign borrowers followed, and global debt, global trade, and global capital flows all came to be increasingly denominated in sterling.[4] Trust in the pound was bolstered by the economic management of the Bank of England, which increasingly operated as a "lender of last resort" to mitigate the effects of banking panics.[5]

[4] While there were widespread private holdings of pounds internationally, it's worth noting that for most of the 1800s there wasn't much in the way of central bank holdings, particularly relative to the role that the dollar plays in central bank portfolios today. Through World War I, central bank assets outside their own currency were generally held in precious metals.

[5] The Panic of 1866 demonstrates this well. To simplify the events, the London money markets were the most liquid markets for trade finance, but after a decade of boom lots of lenders were overextended and a big one (Overend, Gurney & Co.) went bust. It was the 19th century equivalent of Lehman Brothers. However, the crisis resolved within days as the Bank of England's demonstrated willingness to serve as the "lender of last resort" stemmed the loss of confidence in the system.

SHARE OF GLOBAL DEBT IN GBP (EST)

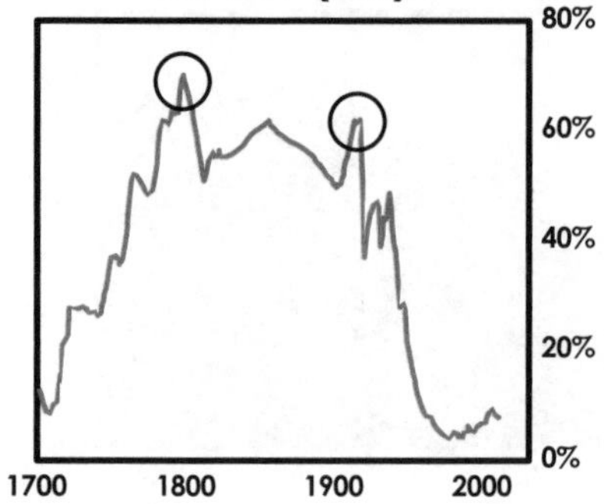

SHARE OF GLOBAL TRANSACTIONS IN GBP (EST)

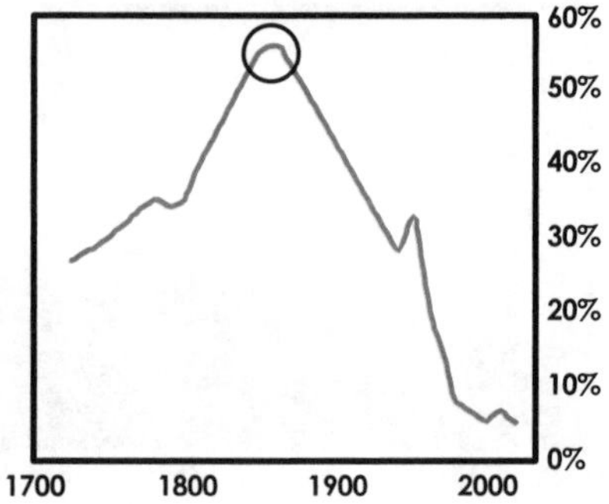

Even as the British Empire continued to expand its territorial and financial reach over the final decades of the 19th century, the seeds of its fall were evident, driven by the classic factors of 1) declining competitiveness, 2) rising inequality and conflict, and 3) the rise of new rivals, particularly Germany and the US.

Declining Competitiveness

Stepping back, the broader story of economic growth in the mid-to-late 1800s was the Second Industrial Revolution, a sustained period of innovation in which science as well as engineering played a major role, as synthetics and new alloys were produced and the use of new energy sources like petroleum and electricity exploded. This was when the telephone and the incandescent light bulb were developed and automobiles soon followed. **Transportation, communications, and infrastructure improved**, and the rise of corporate capitalism enhanced productivity. **The result was a sizable increase in output per worker in the countries able to make the switch efficiently—primarily the US and Germany.** The UK didn't keep up, even though British inventions were key to many of these new developments. The UK's failure to reorganize its industries led to marked declines in output per worker relative to the other leading industrial powers. You can see the secular shift in innovation and economic power in these charts.

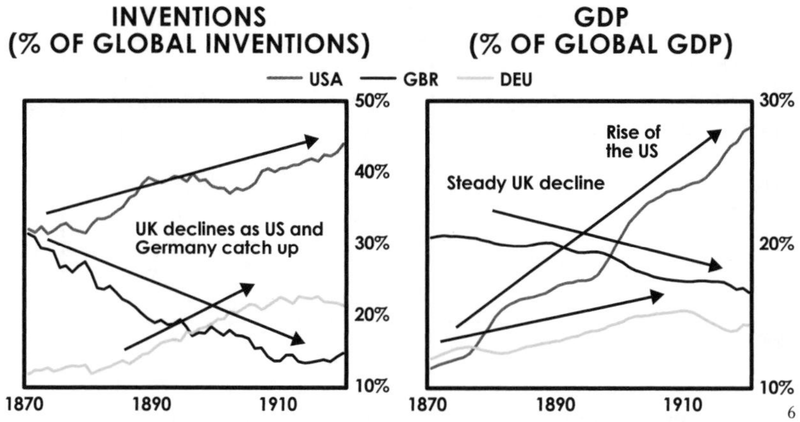

[6]

Rising Inequality

The gains from industrialization were distributed very unevenly in the UK, producing extreme levels of inequality. By the late 1800s, the top 1 percent of the population owned over 70 percent of all wealth, more than in peer countries. The UK's top 10 percent owned an astounding 93 percent of its wealth.[7] As shown in the next chart, the peak in the wealth gap coincided with the peak in the British Empire around 1900, which was the beginning of the next wave of conflict over wealth and power due to large wealth gaps and the classic late Big Cycle conditions described in Part I.

[6] GBR GDP share includes income of countries controlled by the British Empire.

[7] For comparison, the top 1 percent's share of wealth in the UK today is about 20 percent and the top 10 percent's share is about 50 percent.

UK WEALTH GAP (TOP 1% WEALTH SHARE)

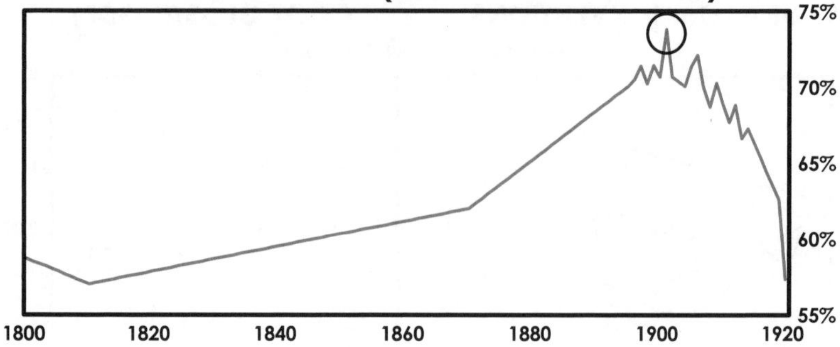

The combination of social change and rising inequality sparked significant tensions. England's policy response in the mid-1800s focused largely on reform bills that expanded voting rights and reduced the corrupt practices that had made elections less democratic. By the early 1900s, those political reforms were followed by social reforms, which included the introduction of a public pension system, medical and unemployment insurance, and the provision of free lunches for school children. Organized labor was also on the rise, strengthening workers' bargaining power. By 1911, around 25 percent of eligible men were union members, and the Labour Party became a significant force in politics. This greater power took the form of increasingly large strikes—for example, the first national strike by coal miners in 1912, which led to a minimum wage for miners.

Geopolitical Rivals Emerge

In addition to its domestic issues, the UK faced challengers to its empire abroad, competing for influence with France in Africa, Russia in the Middle East and Central Asia, and the US in the Americas. **Its most significant rivalry, however, was with Germany.** The United States, the other great rising power, remained blissfully isolationist with a big ocean allowing it to largely ignore the conflicts in Europe.

When the new world order began at the Congress of Vienna, Germany was still divided into a number of smaller states. While the Austrian Empire, ruled by the Habsburgs, had a lot of influence, Prussia was swiftly rising and had one of the strongest armies in Europe. **Over the next century, it successfully unified the other German states, becoming a first-rate power. It achieved this thanks in large part to Otto von Bismarck's brilliant strategic and diplomatic leadership**[8] **and the other classic ingredients for success: strong education and competitiveness.**

Once unified, Germany experienced the classic virtuous cycle of a power on the rise. Viewing an effective education system as a crucial step in its quest to raise its economy to the level of Great Britain's, the new Germany—and its predecessor states—built one from the ground up, focusing on teaching both practical trade skills and high-level scientific knowledge, theoretical and applied. Starting in the 1860s, primary education was mandatory for all and enforced by law. Germany also established three new research universities.

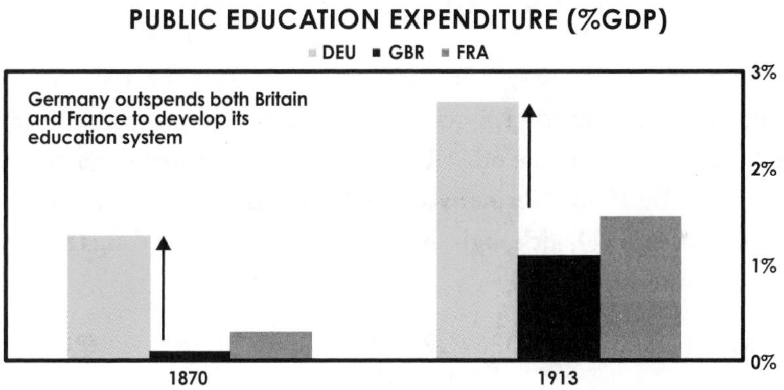

In order to create a culture of innovation, the German government provided credit to corporations, along with technical advice

[8] While Prussia, and later the German Empire, were monarchies ruled by the Hohenzollern family, Bismarck had immensely effective powers, having been appointed by the monarch first as minister president of Prussia, and then as chancellor of Germany from unification in 1871 until 1890. According to historian Eric Hobsbawm, "[Bismarck] remained undisputed world champion at the game of multilateral diplomatic chess for almost twenty years after 1871."

and assistance; awarded grants to inventors and immigrant entrepreneurs; bestowed gifts of machinery; and allowed rebates and exemptions of duties on imports of industrial equipment. Germany also maintained a strong rule of law, which was explicitly aimed at economic development.

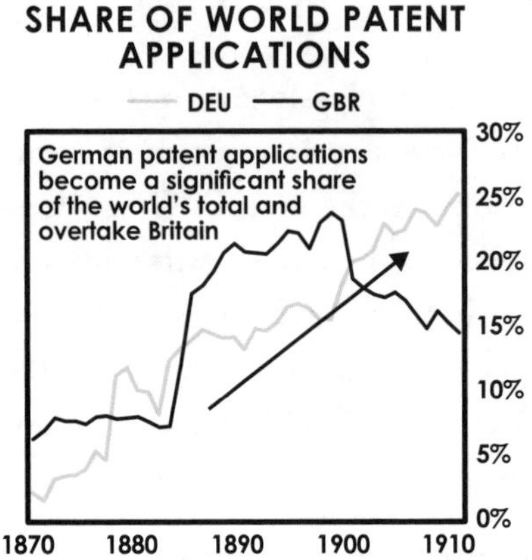

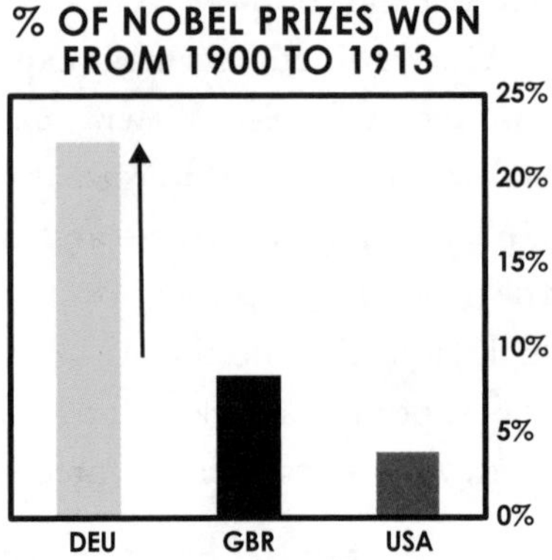

As a result of these efforts, Germany's share of the world's manufacturing output increased from about 5 to 13 percent between 1860 and 1900 while the other European powers' shares stagnated or decreased. **By 1900, Germany's GDP had surpassed Britain's (excluding its empire), although the latter was still the leading trading nation in the world.**

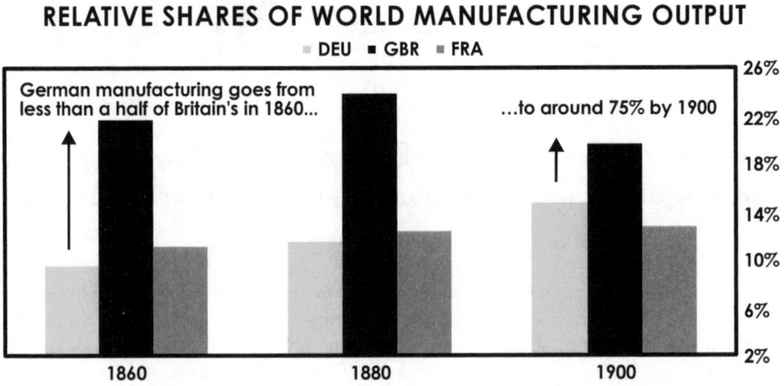

While Bismarck was a skilled diplomat who prioritized economic development and diplomacy with international competitors, his successors were less skilled and more aggressive. **When Wilhelm II became emperor in 1888, he forced Bismarck to resign and adopted a policy of turning Germany into a world power.** This led other powers, primarily Russia and the UK, to increasingly align with France (a bitter rival of Germany since the Franco-Prussian War in 1871) in an effort to contain Germany. **Wilhelm moved to build up Germany's military, particularly its navy, setting off an arms race with the UK.** This began the next rivalry between great powers.

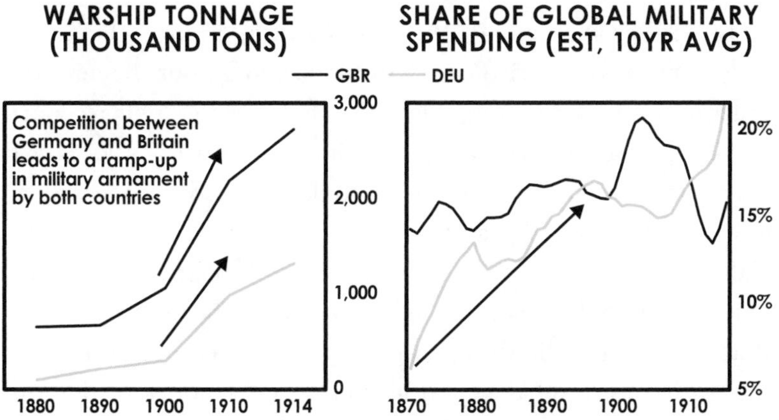

The UK retained its naval advantage, but the arms race strained the finances of the major powers and further destabilized the geopolitical order. **The rivalry between the UK and Germany was just one of many building across Europe—France and Germany were at odds, Germany was increasingly concerned about Russian industrialization, and Austria and Russia were struggling for influence in the Balkans. Though these countries were intertwined through marriage and commerce more than ever before, and despite most people believing it wouldn't happen, in 1914 the powder keg exploded into all-out war. This was the first world war because this was the first time the world had become so small and so interconnected that most**

of the major parts of the world were involved in one way or another.

Given the complexity and scale of World War I, and how extensively it has been written about, I will just attempt to convey the big picture: it was terrible. **The war killed about 8.5 million soldiers and 13 million civilians, leaving all of Europe exhausted, weakened, and indebted.** Russia devolved into revolution in 1917; in 1918, the Spanish flu arrived, killing an estimated 20–50 million people around the world over the next two years. As a percentage of the European population, more people died during this period than in either the Napoleonic Wars or Thirty Years' War. But the war ended and the next new world order was created.

In 1919, the victors—the US, Britain, France, Japan, and Italy—met at the Paris Peace Conference to lay out the new world order in the Treaty of Versailles. The United States, now recognized as a leading power, played a big role in the negotiations. In fact, the term "new world order" was coined to describe US President Woodrow Wilson's vision for a global governance system (the League of Nations, though this quickly failed). If the Congress of Vienna in 1815 had created a relatively sustainable order, the terms of the Paris Peace Conference did the opposite— it made a second war inevitable though it wasn't apparent at the time. The territories of the losing powers (Germany, Austria-Hungary, the Ottoman Empire, and Bulgaria) were carved up, and they were forced to pay reparations to the victors. **Those debt burdens contributed to an inflationary depression in Germany from 1920 to 1923. Elsewhere, much of the world entered a decade of peace and prosperity, the Roaring '20s. As is typical, the debts and the wealth gaps that were built up burst in 1929, causing the Great Depression. These two big boom and bust cycles came unusually close together, though they followed the classic stages. I won't digress into the 1920s boom to bust sequence here as it was covered elsewhere in this book. But I will pick up the story in the Great Depression.**

The Great Depression coupled with the large wealth gaps led to a rise in populism and extremism in nearly every major country. In some countries—e.g., the US and the UK—this led to big redistributions of wealth and political power while capitalism and democracy were maintained. In others, particularly those with weaker economies (Germany, Japan, Italy, Spain), populist dictators seized control and sought to expand their empires.

Classically, before all-out wars begin, there is typically about a decade of economic, technological, geopolitical, and capital skirmishing. The time between the depression and World War II was consistent with this rule. As Germany and Japan became more expansionist, they increasingly competed with the UK, the US, and France for resources and influence over territories. Ultimately, those tensions boiled over into war.

World War II, just two decades after World War I, was even more costly in lives and money. Germany and Japan lost and the US, the UK, and the Soviet Union won, though economically the UK and the Soviet Union lost too and the US gained enormously in relative wealth. GDP per capita in Germany and Japan fell by at least half, and their currencies collapsed in the aftermath of the war, as these charts show. **As is typical, the winners of the war got together and determined a new world order in 1945.**

DEU REAL GDP PER CAPITA

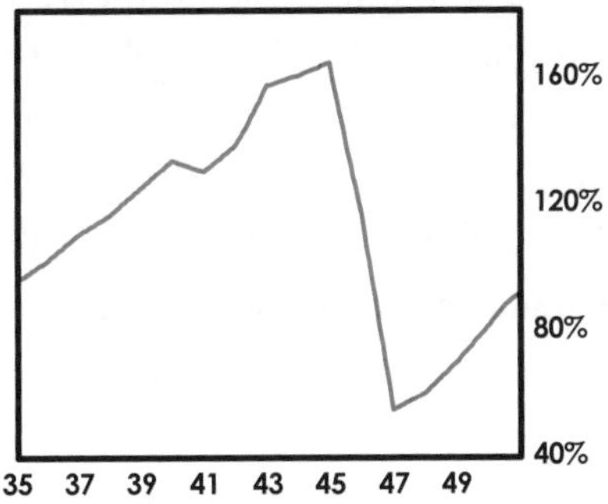

JPN REAL GDP PER CAPITA

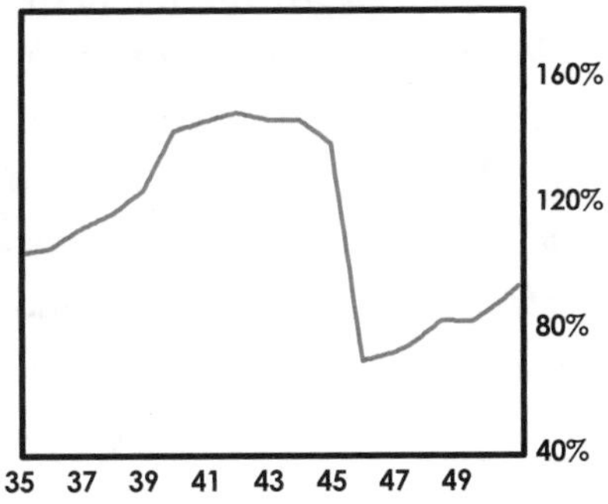

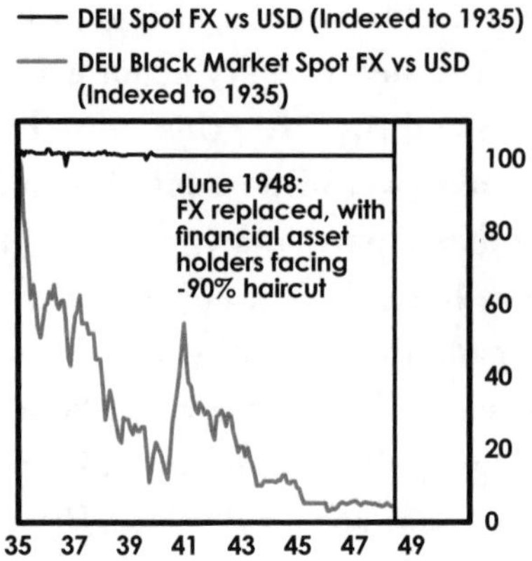

[9]

THE DECLINE

The Allied victory in 1945 produced a tremendous shift of wealth and power, with the US emerging as the world's dominant empire just as the British had after the Napoleonic Wars. The British were left with large debts, a huge empire that was more expensive to maintain than it was profitable, numerous rivals that were more competitive, and a population that had big wealth gaps that led to big political gaps.

It took another 20 years for the British pound to fully lose its status as an international reserve currency. Just as the English language is so deeply woven into the fabric of international business and diplomatic communications that it would be difficult to replace, the same is true of reserve currencies. Other countries' central banks continued to hold sizable shares of their reserves in pounds through the 1950s, and a third of all international trade was still denominated in sterling in 1960. **But the pound had been losing status since the end of the war** because smart investors recognized the great contrast

[9] This chart shows the official exchange rate between dollars and deutschemarks as well as an unofficial (black market) rate that was based on actual transactions between New York and Germany during that time period. The unofficial rate shows that the true value of the deutschemark was collapsing during the period.

between the UK's and the US's financial conditions, the UK's increased debt load, and the UK's low net reserves, which would make holding pound sterling debt a bad deal.

The decline in the British pound was a protracted affair that involved several significant devaluations. After attempts to make the pound convertible failed in 1946–47, it was devalued by 30 percent against the dollar in 1949. Though this worked in the short term, over the next two decades Britain's declining competitiveness led to repeated balance of payments strains that culminated with the devaluation of 1967. Around this time the deutschemark took the pound's place as the world's second most widely held reserve currency. The following charts paint the picture.

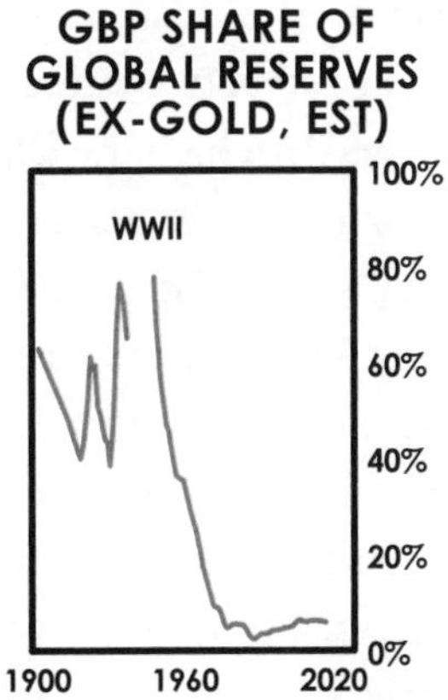

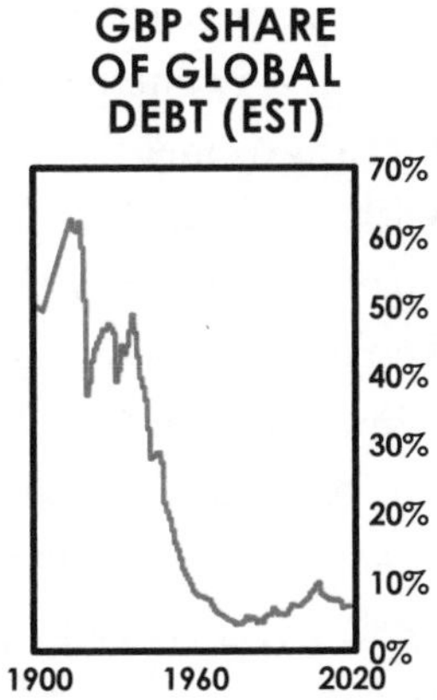

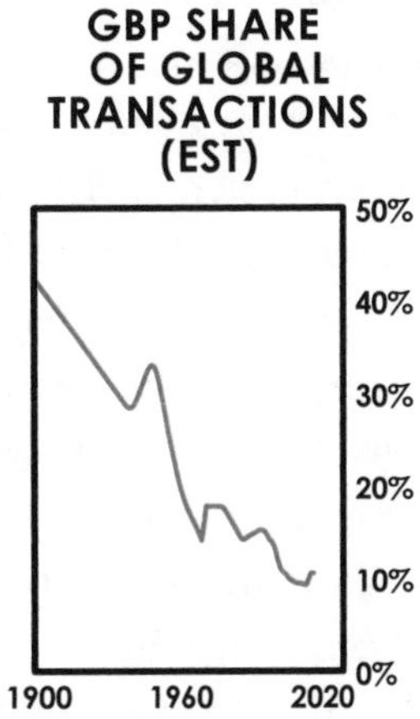

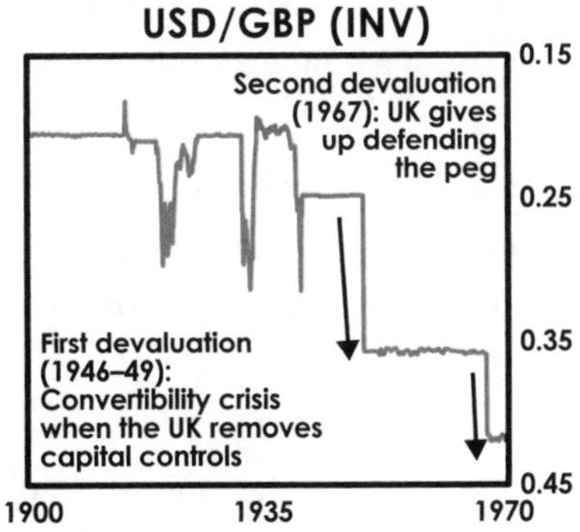

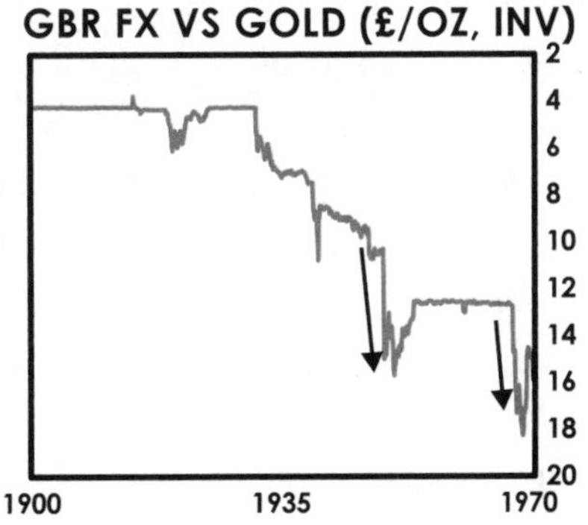

The Pound's Suspended Convertibility in 1947 and Its Devaluation in 1949

The 1940s are frequently referred to as "crisis years" for the pound. The war required the UK to borrow immensely from its allies and colonies, and those obligations were required to be held in sterling. When the war ended, the UK could not meet its debt obligations without either raising taxes or cutting government spending, so it necessarily mandated that its debt assets (i.e., its bonds) could not be proactively sold by its former colonies. The US was anxious for the UK to restore convertibility as soon as possible, as the restrictions were reducing liquidity in the global economy, affecting the US's export profits. The Bank of England was also eager to remove capital controls in order to restore the pound's role as a global trading currency, increase financial sector revenues in London, and encourage international investors to continue saving in sterling. **In 1946, an agreement was reached in which the US would provide the UK with a loan of $3.75 billion (about 10 percent of UK GDP)** to offer a buffer against a potential run on the pound. As expected, the pound came under considerable selling pressure when partial convertibility was introduced in July 1947, and the UK and the Sterling Area countries turned to austerity to maintain the pound's peg to the dollar. Restrictions were imposed on the import of luxury goods, defense expenditures were slashed, dollar and gold reserves were drawn down, and agreements were made among sterling economies to not diversify their reserve holdings to the dollar. Prime Minister Clement Attlee gave a dramatic speech calling for the spirit of wartime sacrifice:

> We are engaged in another battle for Britain. This battle cannot be won by the few. It demands a united effort by the whole nation. I am confident that this united effort will be forthcoming and that we shall again conquer.

Immediately following the speech, the run on the pound accelerated. **By the end of August, convertibility was suspended, much**

to the anger of the US and other international investors who had bought sterling assets in the lead-up to convertibility. The governor of the National Bank of Belgium threatened to stop transacting in sterling, requiring a diplomatic intervention. **The devaluation came two years later, as policy makers in both the UK and the US realized that the pound couldn't return to convertibility at the current rate.** Competitiveness returned, the current account improved, and by the mid-to-late 1950s full convertibility was restored. The following charts paint the picture.

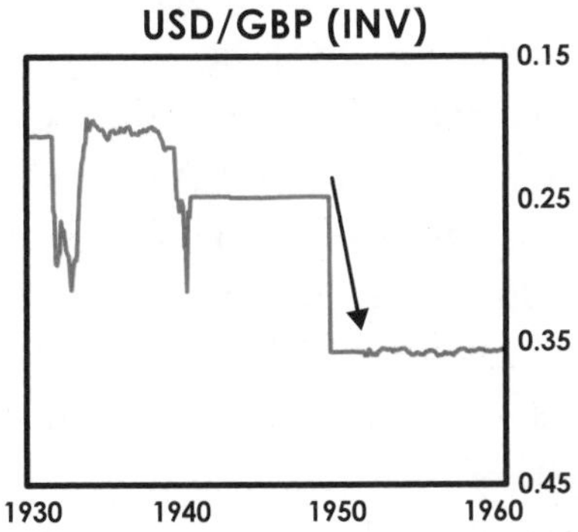

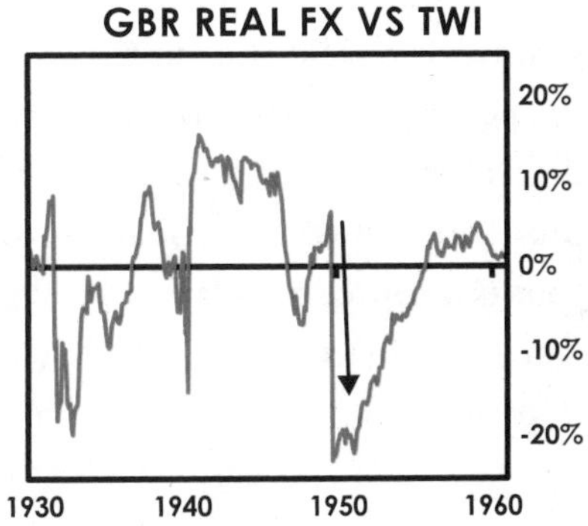

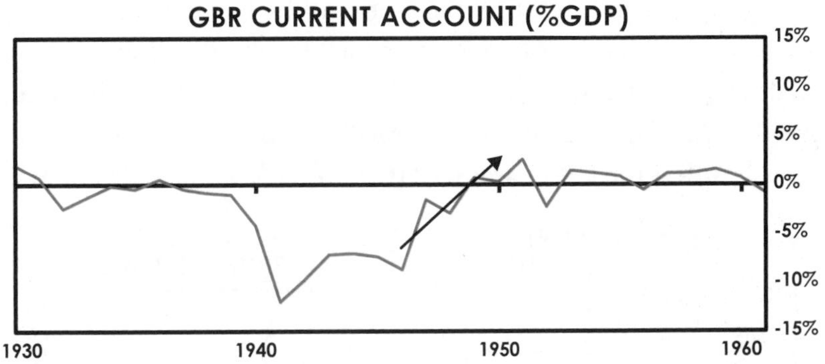

The devaluation did not lead to a panic out of sterling, even though the fundamentals remained poor, because a very large share of UK assets was held by the US government, which was willing to take the valuation hit in order to restore convertibility, and by Sterling Area economies, such as India and Australia, whose currencies were pegged to the pound for political reasons. Still, **the immediate post-war experience made it clear to knowledgeable observers that the pound would not enjoy the same international role it had prior to World War II**.

The Failed International Efforts to Support the Pound in the 1950s and 1960s and the Devaluation of 1967

Though the 1949 devaluation helped in the short term, the pound faced recurring balance of payments strains. These were very concerning to international policy makers, who feared that a collapse in the value of sterling or a rapid shift to the dollar could prove highly detrimental to the new Bretton Woods monetary system (particularly given the backdrop of the Cold War-and concerns around communism). **As a result, numerous efforts were made to shore up the pound and preserve its role as a source of international liquidity.** In addition, the UK mandated that all trade within the Common Market would be denominated in pounds and all its currencies pegged to sterling. The result was that for the 1950s and early 1960s, the UK was best understood as a regional economic power and sterling as a regional reserve currency. Yet those measures still didn't fix the problem: the UK was too indebted and too uncompetitive; it couldn't pay its debts and still buy what it needed to import. Sterling had to be devalued again in 1967. **After that, even Sterling Area countries were unwilling to hold their reserves in pounds unless the UK guaranteed their underlying value in dollars.**

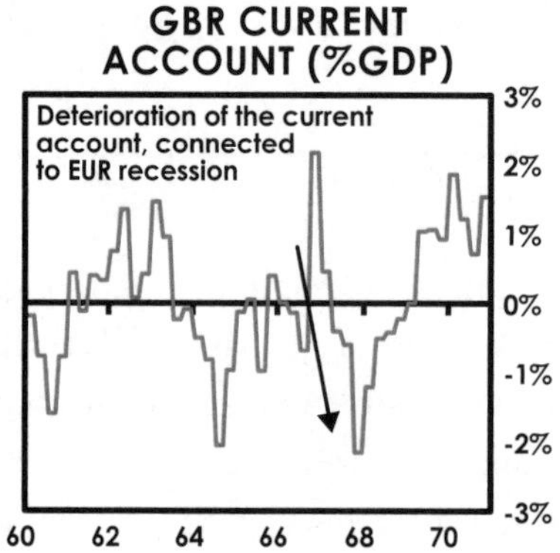

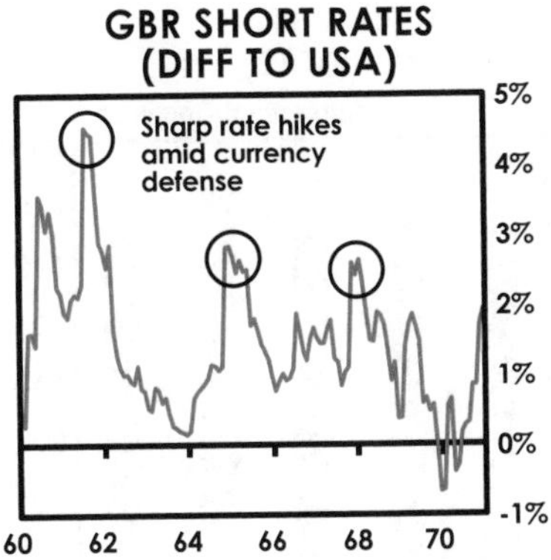

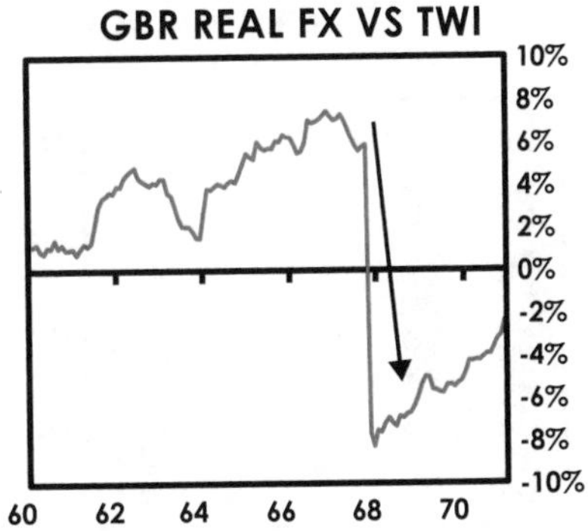

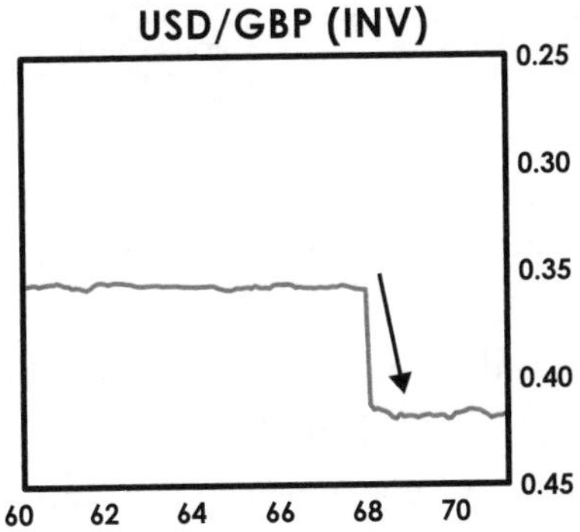

After the devaluation, little faith remained in the pound. Central banks began to sell their sterling reserves and buy dollars, deutschemarks, and yen, as opposed to simply accumulating fewer pounds in new reserve holdings. The average share of sterling in central bank reserve holdings collapsed within two years. **Countries that continued to hold a high share of their reserves in pounds after 1968 were holding de facto dollars because the Sterling Agreement of 1968 guaranteed 90 percent of their dollar value.**

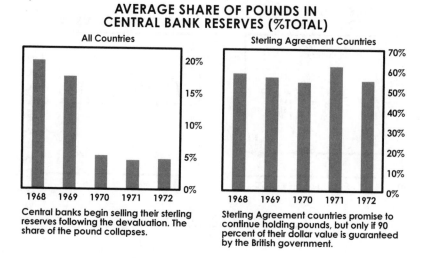

AVERAGE SHARE OF POUNDS IN CENTRAL BANK RESERVES (%TOTAL)

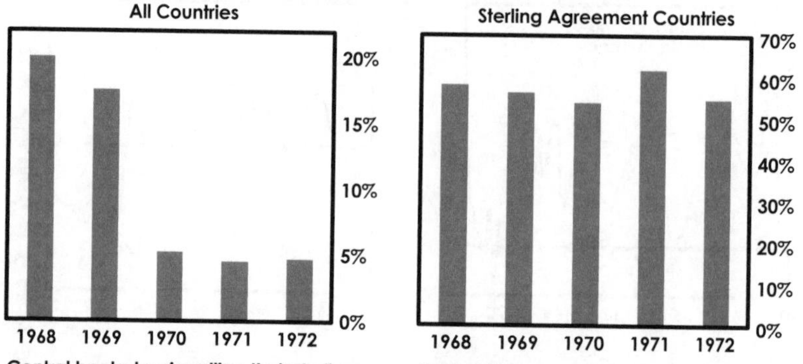

Central banks begin selling their sterling reserves following the devaluation. The share of the pound collapses.

Sterling Agreement countries promise to continue holding pounds, but only if 90 percent of their dollar value is guaranteed by the British government.

Europe after World War II

As we've seen again and again, the terrible costs of war push countries to create new world orders in their aftermaths in an attempt to ensure that such wars can never happen again. Naturally, new world orders revolve around the victor, which is often the newly ascendant empire. After World War II, that was clearly the US.

The most important geopolitical elements of the post-war order were:

- **The US was the dominant power, which made it the de facto global police force.** Naturally, tensions almost immediately arose between the US and the world's second leading power, the Soviet Union. The US and its allies formed a military alliance called NATO and the Soviet states formed the Warsaw Pact, and the two faced off in the Cold War.
- **The United Nations was established to resolve global disputes.** As is classic, it was headquartered in the heart of the ascendant empire (in this case, New York), with its main power organ, the Security Council, dominated by the war's victors, as is also classic.

The most important financial elements of the new world order consisted of:

- **The Bretton Woods monetary system, which established the dollar as the world's reserve currency.**
- **The IMF and the World Bank, designed to support the new global financial system.**
- **New York as the new global financial center.**

From the European perspective, the key aspect of the new world order was the shift from a balance of power in which the preeminent European powers were on top to a world in which they were exhausted and overshadowed by new superpowers that dwarfed any one European state (especially as their colonies gained independence). Given these pressures and the clear lesson of the costs of division that the World Wars had taught, the value of European unity was clear. That was the impetus for the new European order that gradually developed into the European Union.

The story of Robert Schuman, a key founder of the EU, helps explain why Europe came together. Schuman's father was a French citizen who became a German citizen when his home region of Alsace-Lorraine was annexed by the Germans in 1871. Schuman was born a German citizen, but became a French citizen when Alsace-Lorraine was returned to France after World War I. As a politician in World War II, he joined the Vichy government before abandoning it for the French Resistance. He ended the war in hiding, with a 100,000 Reichsmark bounty on his head. A key partner to Schuman was West Germany's first post-war chancellor, Konrad Adenauer. A centrist mayor, he had been driven from political life by the Nazis and sent to a concentration camp in 1944. Following his election as chancellor as a Christian Democrat in 1949, his policies focused on rebuilding the German economy, reconciling with other European powers, and opposing communism. Schuman and Adenauer's project, along with the rest of the EU's founders, was to make war "not merely unthinkable, but materially impossible."

Their first step was to create the European Coal and Steel Community. It sounds like a narrow economic pact, but its explicit goal was to create a European federation. From the Schuman Declaration:

> The pooling of coal and steel production should immediately provide for the setting up of common foundations for economic development as a first step in the federation of Europe, and will change the destinies of those regions which have long been devoted to the manufacture of munitions of war, of which they have been the most constant victims.

The agreement created supranational bodies—a High Authority, a Common Assembly, and a Court of Justice—that bound individual countries to its decisions and regulations, had the ability to levy taxes, could issue loans, and set up programs for worker welfare. Six nations signed on, and more joined over time. Eventually, it evolved into a customs union (in 1957, via the Treaty of Rome), opened up countries' borders (in 1985, via the Schengen Agreement), and eventually agreed on the framework for a political and economic union, including a shared European citizenship (in 1992, via the Maastricht Treaty).

As is classic, this new European geopolitical order came with a new financial/economic order. The Maastricht Treaty created the basis for a new common currency (the euro) and common economic rules, including rules around government deficits. The integration of its 27 member states (and their more than 400 million people), many of whom had been at war with one another in the past, is an impressive feat—one that puts the EU on a similar standing to the other great powers.

THE EUROZONE COMPARED TO THE US AND CHINA

	EUR	USA	CHN
Empire Score (0 to 1)*	0.55	0.87	0.75
GDP Per Capita (2017 USD, PPP Adj)	41,504	60,236	16,411
GDP (%WLD, PPP Adj)	13%	17%	23%
Population (%WLD)	4%	4%	18%
Exports (%WLD)	12%	11%	15%
Military Spending (%WLD)	9%	28%	19%
College Grads (%WLD)	13%	20%	22%
Patents (%WLD)	11%	17%	41%
Nobel Prizes (%WLD)	11%	32%	2%
Equity Mkt Cap (%WLD)	8%	55%	10%
Intl Transactions in Currency (%WLD)	28%	55%	2%
Official Reserves Held in Currency (%WLD)	21%	62%	2%

*Europe Empire Arc treats major Eurozone countries as single unit for purposes of comparison.

The European Union's relative declines and crises in the early 21st century occurred for the classic reasons Big Cycle declines occurred, which are reflected in the eight measures of power and other indicators described in Chapter 2. These are the same reasons that other empires have experienced crises. More specifically, Europe's debt is large, its economy is fundamentally weak, its internal conflicts are relatively large, its vitality and level of inventiveness are relatively weak, and its military is not strong. The wealth and income inequalities between and within its member countries have fueled the rise of populists, many of whom oppose the European Union, and who succeeded in causing the UK to leave it. In short, from its position of a leading empire not long ago, Europe as a whole (and the UK with it) has slipped to a position of secondary power.

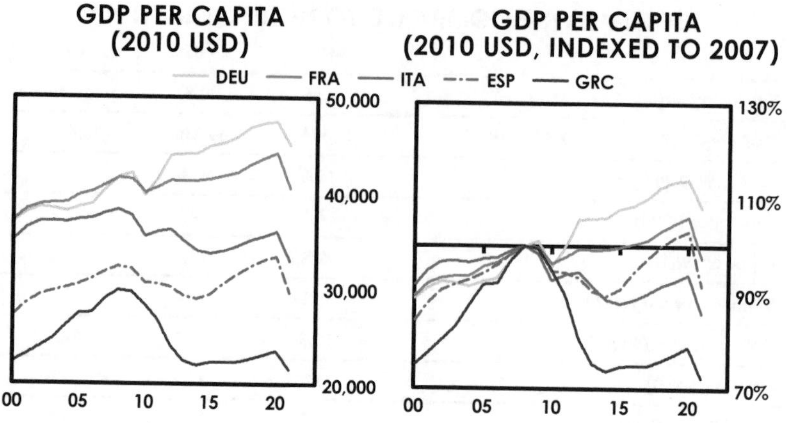

Let's now turn our attentions to the American and Chinese powers.

CHAPTER 11

THE BIG CYCLE RISE AND DECLINE OF THE UNITED STATES AND THE DOLLAR

This chapter covers the Big Cycle rise of the US beginning in the 19th century, its gradual surpassing of the UK as the world's most powerful empire, and its recent decline. As the story of the US as the world's leading empire is still unfolding and is highly relevant to the world today, I will be going through its Big Cycle in more detail than I did for the Dutch and British, especially as it relates to the dollar's status as a global reserve currency and the economic and monetary policy forces that have impacted it.

The chart on the next page shows the eight types of power that make up our overall US arc. **In them you can see the story behind the US's rise and decline since 1700.** The strong development and excellence in education led to advances in innovation and technology, competitiveness in world markets, and economic output, all of which fueled the development of financial markets and the US as a financial center, its leadership in military strength and world trade, and, with a significant lag, the emergence of the dollar as a reserve currency. The relative advantages in education, competitiveness, and trade have fallen, while those in innovation and technology, reserve currency status, and financial markets and financial center status remain strong. **What this chart doesn't show are the deviations in the**

US income and balance sheet conditions and its internal conflicts, both of which are more concerning. (For a more complete current picture, see the final chapter of this book.)

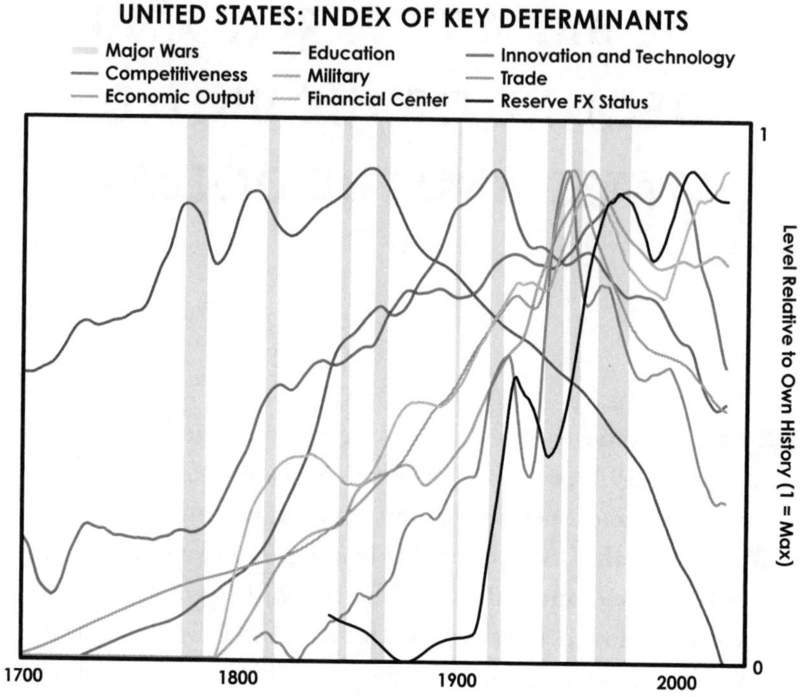

This next chart combines all the factors to show the overall arc of the US from before the Revolutionary War, marking the key events along the way. The numbers mark the approximate times of the six stages of the internal order cycle.

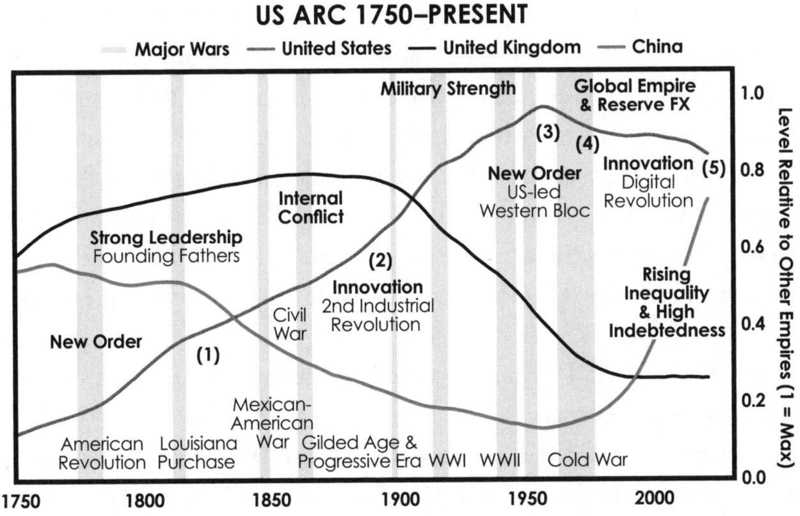

Now we will go through the US's story from the beginning until the time of my writing.

THE RISE

As with all new countries and dynasties, **the US went through the usual revolution and post-revolution process in which it created a new domestic order as 1) a coordinated group of strong leaders fought to gain control, 2) that group won and consolidated control, 3) the new leadership had a vision supported by the population, but 4) it split into factions that had conflicts over how the government should work to implement that vision. Eventually, these factions 5) figured out the system for control and laid it out in agreements (in the US case, at first in the Articles of Confederation and then in the Constitution), 6) set up the parts of government (e.g., the money and credit system, the legal system, the legislative systems, the military, etc.), and 7) put people in jobs and made it work well.** The US did these things in a uniquely peaceful way through negotiations, near-total respect for agreements, and good designs for governance that gave it a great start.

In the chart showing the eight types of power, you can see that rapidly improving levels of education preceded the big rises in innovation, technology, and competitiveness, which lasted until the World Wars, with an interruption during the US Civil War. There were many ups and downs in both domestic and external money/debt, economic, and military circumstances. I won't take you through them in detail, though I will note that all of them followed the archetypical patterns driven by the same basic cause/effect relationships previously described here. While the ascent of the US was most pronounced after World War II, it really started in the late 1800s. That's where we'll pick up the story.

After the US Civil War came the Second Industrial Revolution, which was one of those classic times in which the peaceful pursuit of wealth and prosperity created great gains in incomes, technologies, and wealth in England, continental Europe, and the United States.

In the US, these gains were financed through a system of free-market capitalism that, as is classic, produced both lots of wealth and big wealth gaps. These gaps led to discontent and Progressive Era policies that broke up rich and powerful monopolies ("trust busting") and raised taxes on the rich, starting with the passage of a constitutional amendment to allow federal income taxes in 1913. The US's increased strengths were reflected in its rising shares of global economic output and world trade, as well as its growing financial strength (exemplified by New York becoming the world's leading financial center), continuing leadership in innovation, and great usage of its financial products.

The Long Ascent of the Dollar and US Capital Markets

The dollar's path to being the world's dominant reserve currency was far from straightforward. In the US's first century of existence its financial system was completely underdeveloped. Banking worked in the United States in the classic ways it did in most countries, as I described in Chapters 3 and 4. In other words, hard money was put into banks that together lent out much more than they had. That Ponzi scheme unraveled, so banks failed to meet their commitments and devalued the money. The US had no central bank to control financial markets or act as a lender of last resort. **The US went through many boom/bust cycles, in which classically a flurry of debt-financed investments (into land, railroads, etc.) became overextended, leading to credit losses and a credit crunch. As a result, banking system panics were extremely common.** In New York alone, eight significant banking panics occurred between 1836 and 1913, and regional banking panics were also common. This was because the highly fragmented banking system had a rigid amount of currency, no deposit insurance, and a pyramidal reserve system (with a small number of large banks in New York serving as "correspondents" or holding reserves for a high percentage of the nation's banks) that heightened the risk of contagion from one bank going under.

Like London, New York was well-established as a trading center long before it became a global financial center, a development that didn't occur until after the turn of the 20th century. Only two US banks made the list of the top 20 largest global banks in 1913, at numbers 13 and 17. In comparison, British banks occupied nine slots, including three of the top five. For perspective, at this point the US was far larger than the UK in economic output, and they were neck and neck in export market share.

Many of the most important financial innovations in the emerging New York financial center came out of its needs as a large trading center. Investment banking took off in the US and emerged in the 1800s as a clearinghouse for capital—much of it flowing from Europe—to finance the US boom over the period. Like in London earlier, insurance companies developed more rapidly than banking; in the prewar period the large insurance trusts were bigger than the large banks.

The fact that the US economy was more dynamic and rapidly changing compared to European and British markets was also reflected in the US stock market, which boomed starting right after the US Civil War. As previously explained, **the second half of the 19th century**

was a boom period of peace and prosperity that has been called "the Second Industrial Revolution," "the Gilded Age," and "the Robber Barron Era" because it was the period in which capitalism and innovation flourished, wealth gaps widened enormously, decadence was apparent, and resentment built. The backlash started around 1900, and there was a classic debt bust in 1907. This turbulence led to the creation of the Federal Reserve central banking system in 1913. By 1910, US stock market capitalization had surpassed that of Great Britain. New sectors and companies rose to prominence quickly, such as US Steel, which was founded in 1901 and became the most valuable US company only 15 years later.

Then World War I, the war few people expected to happen and nobody expected to last so long, began in 1914 and ended in 1918. The US was not in World War I for most of it and was the only major country to maintain convertibility to gold during the war. Not only were the economies and markets of Europe badly hurt from the wartime efforts, but the policies undertaken by European governments also further undermined the faith in their currencies. In contrast, the United States' relative financial and economic position benefited from the war. That the Allies' wartime debts were largely owed to the US boosted the use of the dollar for denominating global government debt.

Following the standard script, the winning powers—in this case the US, Britain, France, Japan, and Italy—met after the war to set out the new world order. That meeting, called the Paris Peace Conference, took place in early 1919, lasted for six months, and led to the Treaty of Versailles. In that treaty, the territories of the losing powers (Germany, Austria-Hungary, the Ottoman Empire, and Bulgaria) were carved up and put under the control of the winning empires. The losing powers were put into deep debt to the winning powers to repay the winning countries' war costs. These debts were payable in gold.

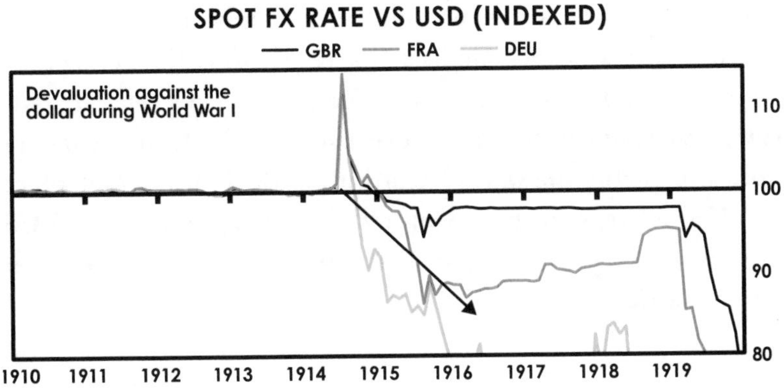

Geopolitically, the United States also benefited because it played a key role in shaping the new world order, though it remained more isolationist while Britain continued to expand and oversee its global colonial empire. The monetary system in the immediate post-war period was in flux. While most countries endeavored to restore gold convertibility, currency stability against gold came only after a period of sharp devaluations and inflation.

As is typical, after the war years and with the new world order came a period of peace and prosperity fueled by great innovations and productivity and a capital markets boom that produced big debts and big wealth gaps late in the upswing. In the Roaring '20s a lot of debt (promises to deliver paper money that was convertible to gold) was created to buy speculative assets (particularly stocks). To curtail that, the Federal Reserve tightened monetary policy in 1929, which caused the bubble to burst and the global Great Depression to begin. It brought economic suffering to virtually all nations, which led to fighting over wealth within and between countries, which led to the hot wars that began a decade later.

I covered the events leading up to and during World War II in depth in Chapter 6 as an example of the war period of the big external order/disorder cycle. The important thing to remember here is that the Allied victory in 1945 produced the next shift in the world order. It was a tremendous shift of wealth and power. **On a relative basis the US came out the big winner because the US sold and lent a lot before and during the war, basically all of the fighting took place off of US territory so the US wasn't physically damaged, and US deaths were comparatively low in relation to those of most other major countries.**

THE TOP

The Post-War Geopolitical and Military System

Following the standard script, the victorious powers met to determine the new world order and its new money and credit systems.

The US, Russia (then the USSR), and Great Britain emerged from the fighting as the world's great powers with the US clearly the richest and most powerful militarily. Germany, Japan, and Italy were largely destroyed; Great Britain was essentially bankrupt, and France was devastated by the war and contributed little to the victory. China was in civil war, which resumed right after Japan's surrender. **While there was relatively good cooperation between the US and Russia immediately after the war, it didn't take long for the two greatest powers with opposing ideologies to enter a "cold" war.** The next chart shows the aggregate power indices for the US, the UK, Russia, and China since the end of World War II. As you can see, Russia rose relative to the US until 1980 but it was never nearly as powerful, though it was much more powerful than China. After 1980, Russia began its decline while China then began its rapid ascent and the US continued its gradual decline.

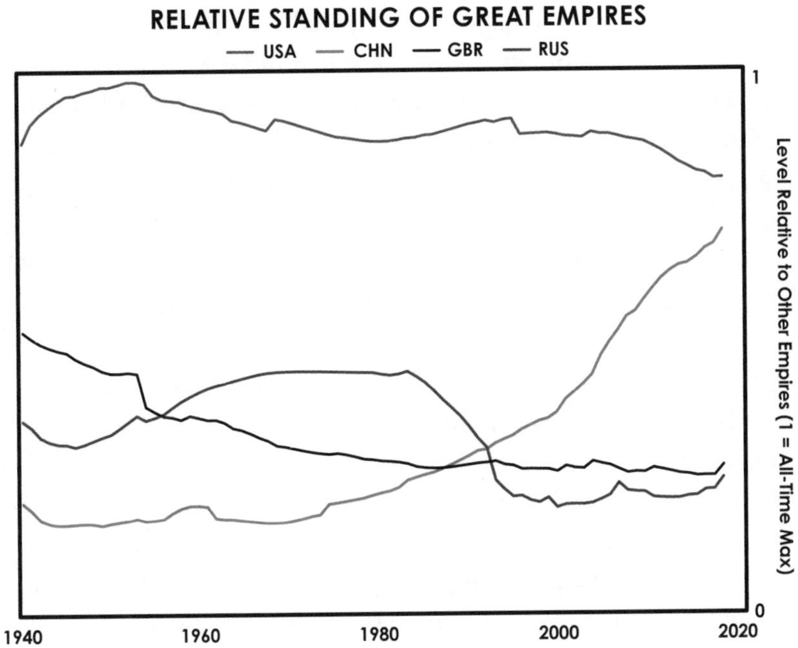

The split between the US- and Russian-controlled blocs had been clear from the outset. President Harry Truman outlined what is now referred to as the Truman Doctrine in a March 1947 speech:

> Every nation must choose between alternative ways of life. The choice is too often not a free one. One way of life is based upon the will of the majority, and is distinguished by free institutions, representative government, free elections, guarantees of individual liberty, freedom of speech and religion, and freedom from political oppression. The second way of life is based upon the will of a minority forcibly imposed upon the majority. It relies upon terror and oppression, a controlled press and radio, fixed elections, and the suppression of personal freedoms. I believe that it must be the policy of the United States to support free peoples who are resisting attempted subjugation by armed minorities or by outside pressures.

As I explained in Chapter 6, compared to domestic governance, ● ***international relations are driven much more by raw power dynamics.*** **That is because there are laws and standards of behavior within countries, whereas between them raw power matters most, and laws, rules, and even mutually agreed-upon treaties and organizations for arbitration (such as the League of Nations, the United Nations, and the World Trade Organization) don't matter much. That is what makes having a strong military and strong military alliances so important.** In 1949, 12 countries in the US camp (with more joining later) formed the North Atlantic Treaty Organization (NATO) military alliance, and in 1954 the Southeast Asia Treaty Organization (SEATO) was established among the US, the UK, Australia, France, New Zealand, the Philippines, Thailand, and Pakistan. Eight countries in the Soviet camp formed the Warsaw Pact in 1955.

As shown in the following chart, the Americans and Soviets invested massively in building up their nuclear weapons and a number of other countries followed. Today, 11 countries have nuclear weapons or are on the brink of having them, in varying amounts and degrees of capability. Having nuclear weapons obviously gives one a big negotiating chip in the world power game, so it's understandable why some countries would want to have them and other countries would not want other countries to have them. While there have been no nuclear wars, the US has fought a number of conventional wars since World War II, most notably the Korean War in the 1950s, the Vietnam War in the 1960s and 1970s, the two Gulf Wars in 1990 and 2003, and the War in Afghanistan from 2001 to 2021. These were costly in terms of money, lives, and public support for the United States. Were they worth it? That's for others to decide. For the Soviet Union, which had a much smaller and weaker economy than the US, spending enough to compete with the US militarily and maintain its empire pushed it into bankruptcy.

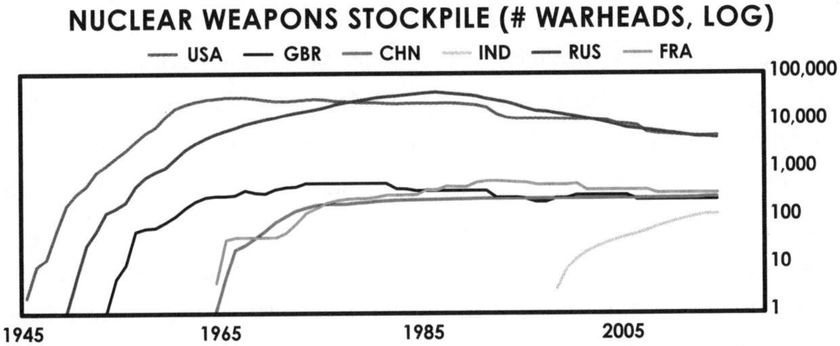

Of course, military power consists of a lot more than nuclear weapons and a lot has changed since the Cold War. While I'm no military expert, I get to speak to some who have led me to believe that, while the US remains the strongest military power overall, it is not dominant in all parts of the world in all ways, and military challenges to it are rising. There is a significant chance that the US would lose wars against China and Russia in their geographic areas of strength—or at least would be unacceptably harmed—and it could also be unacceptably harmed by some second-tier powers too. This is not the good ol' days of right after 1945 when the US was the sole dominant power. While there are a number of high-risk scenarios, in my opinion, the most worrying is a forceful move by China to bring Taiwan under its control.

What will the next high-stakes military conflict look like? Because of new technologies, it will be very different from previous ones. Classically the country that wins wars spends more, invests more, and outlasts the opposition. But it is a delicate balance.

● ***Because spending on the military takes government money away from spending on social programs, and because military technologies go hand in hand with private sector technologies, the biggest military risk for the leading powers is that they lose the economic and technology wars.***

In dealings between countries the transactions are more at arm's length. That means it is less easy to make the currency artificially cheap, harming the holders of it, so internationally traded currencies are more likely to be better value currencies. This is relevant when currencies are a storehold of wealth in the form of debt denominated in them. Sometimes there is too much debt around the world and it is in all governments' interests to devalue their currencies. At such times gold (and recently digital currencies) can be preferable. Also at such times governments are more likely to outlaw these alternative currencies, though they can't fully outlaw them. When the money and credit systems based on fiat currencies break down, it eventually leads to hard money monetary systems.

The Post-War Monetary and Economic Systems

As for the new post-war monetary and economic systems, there was one for the US-led camp and one for the Soviet-led camp, though there were also some nonaligned countries that had their own non-aligned currencies that were not widely accepted. Representatives of 44 countries gathered in Bretton Woods, New Hampshire, in 1944 to make a monetary system that linked the dollar to gold and other country's currencies to the dollar. The Soviet Union's system was built around the ruble, which nobody wanted. ● ***Transactions between countries are very different from transactions within countries.*** Governments want to control the money that is used within their borders because by increasing and decreasing its supply, its cost of borrowing, and its value the government has enormous power.

Because money and economics are so important I want to return to the subject, revisiting how the system works and is working. In the post-war monetary system, within countries, people and companies used the government-controlled paper money. **When they wanted to buy something from another country, they typically exchanged their own country's paper currency for the other country's paper currency with the help of their central bank that settled with the other country's central bank in gold.** If they were American, they paid in dollars and the seller from another country either exchanged them at their central bank for the local currency or held on to them believing that they were better storeholds of wealth than their own money. The results were that gold left the US central bank's reserve account and went into the accounts of other country's central bank and dollars accumulated abroad.

As a result of the Bretton Woods Agreement, the dollar became the world's leading reserve currency. This was natural because the two World Wars had made the US the richest and most powerful country by far. By the end of World War II the US had amassed its greatest gold/money savings ever—about two-thirds of all the government-held gold/money in the world, the equivalent to eight years of import purchases. Even after the war, it continued to earn a lot of money by exporting.

The economies of Europe and Japan had been destroyed by the war. As a solution, and to fight the spread of communism, the US supplied them with massive aid packages (known as the Marshall and Dodge plans), which were a) good for these devastated nations, b) good for the US economically because these countries used the money to buy US goods, c) good for the US's geopolitical influence, and d) good for reinforcing the dollar's position as the world's dominant reserve currency.

As for monetary policy, from 1933 until 1951, the amount of money, the cost of money (i.e., interest rates), and where that money went was controlled by the Federal Reserve to serve the greater objectives of the country rather than the free market.[1] More specifically, the Fed printed a lot of money to buy debt, capped interest rates that lenders could charge, and controlled what money was allowed to go into, so high inflation did not drive interest rates to unacceptable heights and government regulations prevented other investment options from becoming

[1] While 1933 to 1951 was the period from the Roosevelt peg break to the Monetary Accord between the Federal Reserve and Treasury, the policy of explicit yield curve control, in which the Federal Reserve controlled the spread between short-term and long-term interest rates, lasted from 1942 to 1947.

much more attractive than the debt the government wanted people to save in. **Following a brief post-war recession that was due to the decline of military spending, the US entered a prolonged period of peace and prosperity as is typical when a new Big Cycle begins.**

The post-war recession saw the unemployment rate double (to around 4 percent), as around 20 million people needed to find employment outside of the military and other adjacent jobs. But at the same time, the removal of rationing laws, which had limited people's ability to buy consumer goods, fueled a consumer spending surge. Cheap mortgages were also available for veterans, which led to a housing boom. The return to profit-making activities raised the demand for labor, so employment rebounded very quickly. Exports were strong because the Marshall and Dodge plans fueled foreign appetite for US goods; also the US private sector went global and invested abroad from 1945 through the 1970s. Stocks were cheap and dividend yields were high; the result was a multidecade bull market that reinforced New York's dominance as the world's financial center, bringing in still more investment and further strengthening the dollar as a reserve currency. All of this was classic; it was a mutually self-reinforcing Big Cycle upswing.

There was enough money for the US to improve education, invent fabulous technologies (e.g., those that allowed it to go to the moon), and a lot more. The stock market hit its high in 1966, which marked the end of the good times for 16 years, though nobody knew it then. That was around the time that my own direct contact with events began. I started investing in 1961 at age 12. Of course, I didn't know what I was doing and had no appreciation for how lucky my contemporaries and I were. I was born at the right time and in the right place. The United States was the leading manufacturing country, so labor was valuable. Most adults could get a good job, and their kids could get a college education and rise without limitation. Since the majority of people were middle class, the majority of people were happy.

The US did all the classic things that helped the world become more dollarized. Its banks increased their operations and lending in foreign markets. In 1965, only 13 US banks had foreign branches. By

1970, 79 banks had them, and by 1980 nearly every major US bank had at least one foreign branch, and the total number of branches had grown to 787. Global lending boomed. However, as is also typical, a) those who prospered overdid things by operating financially imprudently while b) global competition, especially from Germany and Japan, increased. As a result, American lending and America's finances began to deteriorate as its trade surpluses disappeared.

Americans never thought about how much the space program, the War on Poverty, and the Vietnam War would cost. Because they felt so rich and the dollar seemed secure as a reserve currency Americans assumed they could afford a "guns and butter" fiscal policy indefinitely. As the 1960s came to a close, real GDP growth was near 0 percent, inflation was around 6 percent, the short-term government interest rate was around 8 percent, and unemployment was around 4 percent. During this decade, US stocks returned 8 percent on an annual basis while bonds trailed, with equity-volatility-matched bonds returning -3 percent annually. The official gold price remained fixed in dollar terms, with some modest market price appreciation later in the decade, and commodities continued to be weak, returning 1 percent annually.

The 1970s: The Balance of Payments Problem Unfolds—Low Growth, High Inflation

As explained in Chapter 3, when claims on hard money (i.e., notes or paper money) are introduced, at first there is the same number of claims on the hard money as there is hard money in the bank. However, the holders of the paper claims and the banks soon discover the wonders of credit and debt. Debt holders like it because they can lend these paper claims to the bank in exchange for an interest payment so they get interest. The banks that borrow it from them like it because they can lend the money to others, who pay a higher interest rate so the banks make a profit. Those who borrow the money from the bank like it because it gives them buying power that they didn't have. And the whole society likes it because asset prices and productivity rise.

After 1945, foreign central banks had the option of holding interest-rate-paying debt or holding non-interest-rate-earning gold. Because dollar-denominated debt was considered as good as gold, was convertible to gold, and was higher-earning because it provided interest, central banks shrank their gold holdings relative to their dollar-denominated debt holdings from 1945 until 1971. **As explained in Chapter 4, investors making such a move is a classic behavior and ends when a) the claims on the real money (i.e., gold) substantially exceed the amount of real money in the bank and b) one can see that the amount of real money in the bank (i.e., gold reserves) is going down. That is when no interest rate can be high enough for it to make sense to hold the debt (i.e., claims on the hard money) rather than to turn one's paper money in for gold. At that time a run on the bank occurs and a default and debt restructuring have to happen. That is what led to the breakdown of the gold-linked Bretton Woods monetary system.**

As inflation accelerated and the economy weakened in 1969–70, the Fed could not afford to maintain a tight monetary policy, so the US's balance of payments worsened and the dollar took a nosedive. Rather than running surpluses, the US ran unsustainably huge balance of payments deficits (i.e., the US bought more from the rest of the world than it sold to the rest of the world). In the summer of 1971, Americans traveling in Europe had difficulty exchanging their dollars for German marks, French francs, and British pounds. **The Nixon administration vowed not to "devalue" the dollar, but in August 1971, the US defaulted on its commitments to pay in gold, offering paper money instead.** Money and credit growth were no longer constrained, and the decade of stagflation had begun. At the same time, other industrialized countries had regained their economic strength, becoming very competitive in the world markets.

Rather than seeing these problems as signs of things to come, Americans viewed them as nothing more than a temporary setback. Yet as the decade progressed, economic problems contributed

to political problems and vice versa. The Vietnam War and the Watergate affair dragged on, and there were OPEC-induced oil price increases and drought-induced food price hikes. As costs rose, Americans borrowed more in order to maintain their lifestyles, and the Fed allowed accelerated money supply growth to accommodate the high borrowing and prevent unacceptably high interest rates.

The dollars these deficits produced went to countries that were running budget surpluses, which deposited them in American banks, which lent them to Latin American and other emerging, commodity-producing countries. Savings and loan associations borrowed short to make longer-term mortgages and other loans, using the positive spread between short rates (which they borrowed at) and long rates (which they lent at) as a source of profits. Inflation and its effects on markets came in two big waves that were bracketed by periods of extreme monetary tightness, steep stock market declines, and deep recessions. **Early in the 1970s, most Americans had never experienced inflation, so they weren't wary of it and allowed it to blossom. By the end of the decade, they were traumatized by it and assumed that it would never go away.**

By the end of the 1970s real GDP growth was around 2 percent, inflation was around 14 percent, short-term interest rates were around 13 percent, and unemployment was around 6 percent. Over the decade, gold surged and commodities kept up with rising inflation, returning around 30 percent and 15 percent on an annualized basis, respectively. But the high rate of inflation wiped out the modest 5 percent annual nominal return for stocks and 4 percent return for treasuries matched to equity volatility.

The Post-Bretton Woods System

After the 1971 delinking of the dollar and other currencies from gold, the world moved to an unanchored fiat monetary system (or, Type 3, as I explained in Chapter 3) and the dollar fell in value against gold, other currencies, stocks, and eventually just about everything. The new monetary system was negotiated by the leading economic policy makers of the United States, Germany, and Japan.[2] Paul Volcker was Nixon's undersecretary of international monetary affairs when Nixon severed the link with gold, and he was head of the Federal Reserve from 1979 until 1987. He did more to shape and guide the dollar-based monetary system before, during, and after these years than anyone. I was lucky enough to know him well so I can personally attest that he was a person of great character, capabilities, influence, and humility—a classic hero/role model in a world that lacks hero/role models, especially in economic public service. I believe that he and his thinking deserve to be studied more.

I remember the inflation psychology of that time very well; it led Americans to borrow money and immediately take their paychecks to buy things to "get ahead of inflation." They also bought things that you couldn't make more of, like gold and waterfront properties. The panic out of dollar debt also led interest rates to rise and drove the gold price from the $35 that it was fixed at in 1944 and officially stayed at until 1971 to $850 in 1980.

While most people didn't understand how the money and credit dynamic worked, they felt the pain of it in the form of high inflation and high interest rates, so it was a chronic political issue. At the same time, there was a lot of conflict and rebellion due to the war in Vietnam, oil embargoes that led to high gas prices and gas rationing, labor union fights with companies over wages and benefits, Watergate and the Nixon impeachment, etc. These problems peaked in the late 1970s when 52 Americans were held hostage for 444 days at the US Embassy in Tehran. Americans felt that the country was falling apart. But what most Americans didn't understand was that economic conditions in communist countries were even worse.

As we'll see in the next chapter, Mao Zedong's death in 1976 brought Deng Xiaoping to power in a China that was stumbling economically and facing internal conflict. Deng's market reforms

[2] If you want to read a great description of this process of figuring out how to go from the old monetary system to the new fiat one, I recommend *Changing Fortunes* by Paul Volcker and Toyoo Gyohten.

led to a shift in economic policies that included capitalist elements like private ownership of businesses, the development of debt and equities markets, entrepreneurial technological and commercial innovations, and even the flourishing of billionaire capitalists—all under the strict control of the Chinese Communist Party. This shift in leadership and approaches, while seemingly insignificant at the time, would germinate into the biggest single force to shape the 21st century.

The 1979–1982 Move to Tight Money and Conservatism

President Jimmy Carter, who like most political leaders didn't understand the monetary mechanics very well, knew that something had to be done to stop inflation and appointed a strong monetary policy maker (Volcker) as head of the Federal Reserve in August 1979. In October 1979, **Volcker announced that he would constrain money (M1) growth at 5.5 percent.** I ran the numbers, which led me to figure that, if he really did what he said he was going to do, there would be a great shortage of money that would send interest rates through the roof, bankrupting debtors who could not get the credit they needed to cover their debt-service expenses. Volcker stuck to the plan despite great political backlash, driving interest rates to the highest levels seen "since Jesus Christ," according to German Chancellor Helmut Schmidt.

In the 1980 presidential election Carter was voted out and Ronald Reagan, who was perceived as a conservative who would impose discipline where it was needed, was elected. Leading countries at the time (reflected in the G7, which consisted of the US, the UK, Germany, Japan, France, Italy, and Canada—which shows how different the world power balance was 40 years ago versus today) made analogous moves in electing conservatives to bring discipline to their inflationary chaos. Early in their terms, both Reagan in the US and Margaret Thatcher in the UK had landmark fights with labor unions.

● ***Economics and politics have swings between the left and the right in varying extremes as the excesses of each become intolerable and the memories of the problems of the other fade.*** **It's like fashion—the widths of ties and the lengths of skirts change through time. When there is great popularity of one extreme, one should expect that it won't be too long before there will be a comparable move in the opposite direction.** The move to monetary tightness broke the backs of debtors and curtailed borrowing, which drove the world economy into its worst downturn since the Great Depression. The Federal Reserve slowly started to cut interest rates, but the markets continued to decline. Then Mexico defaulted on its debt in August 1982. Interestingly, the US stock market rallied in response.

What happened next created a jarringly painful learning experience for me. While I was able to anticipate the debt crisis, which was profitable for me, it also led me a) to anticipate a debt-default-triggered depression that never came and b) to lose a lot of money betting on it. As a result of my personal losses and the losses of clients, I had to let everyone in my fledgling company, Bridgewater Associates, go and was so broke I had to borrow $4,000 from my dad to help pay my family's bills. At the same time this was one of the best things that ever happened to me because it changed my whole approach to decision making. What I had missed was that when debts are in the currencies that central banks have the ability to print and restructure, debt crises can be well-managed so they are not systemically threatening. Because the Federal Reserve could provide money to the banks that made the loans that weren't being paid back, they didn't have a cash flow problem, and because the American accounting system didn't require the banks to account for these bad debts as losses, there was no big problem that couldn't be worked out. I learned that **the value of assets is the reciprocal of the value of money and credit (i.e., the cheaper money and credit are, the more expensive asset prices are) and the value of**

money is the reciprocal of the quantity of it in existence, so when central banks are producing a lot of money and credit and making it cheaper, it is wise to be more aggressive in owning assets.

The Disinflationary and Booming 1980s

In the 1980s there was a stock market and economic boom that was accompanied by falling inflation and falling interest rates in the United States at the same time as there were inflationary depressions in the debt-burdened emerging economies that didn't have central banks to bail them out. The debt-restructuring process progressed slowly from 1982 until 1989 when an agreement called the Brady Plan, named after Nicholas Brady, who was the US Treasury secretary at the time, was created and started to bring an end to the "lost decade" in these countries (as agreements were reached with different countries through the early '90s). **This whole 1971–91 up-and-down debt cycle, which profoundly affected just about everyone in the world, was the result of the US going off the gold standard, the inflation that followed it, and having to break the back of the inflation through tight monetary policies that led to the strength in the dollar and the dramatic fall in inflation.** In the markets that big cycle showed up via a) the soaring of inflation and inflation-hedge assets and bear markets in bonds in the 1970s, b) the 1979–81 bone-crushing monetary tightening that made cash the best investment and led to a lot of deflationary debt restructuring by non-American debtors, and then c) falling inflation rates and excellent performance of bonds, stocks, and other disinflationary assets in the 1980s. The following charts convey this very well, as they show the swings up and down in dollar-denominated inflation rates and interest rates from 1945 to the present. One needs to keep these moves and the mechanics behind them in mind when thinking about the future.

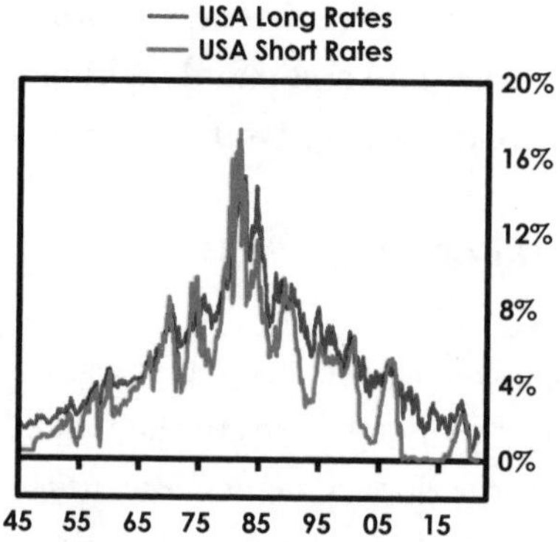

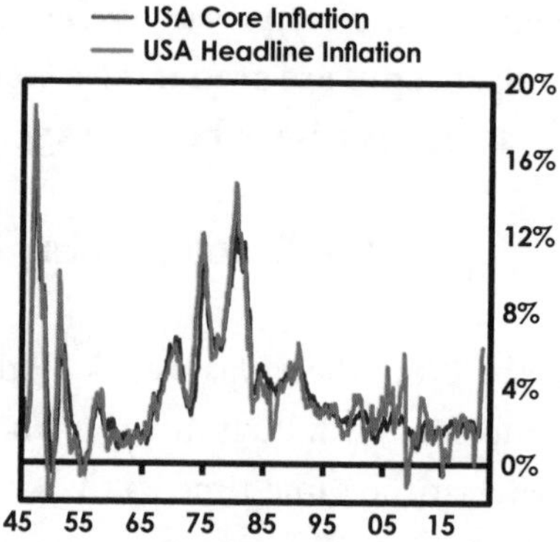

Through it all, the dollar remained the world's leading reserve currency. The entire period was a forceful demonstration of the benefits to the US of having the currency that most of the world's debts are denominated in.

1990–2008: Globalizing, Digitalizing, and Booming Financed by Debt

Because of its economic failures, the Soviet Union could not afford to support a) its empire, b) its economy, and c) its military in the face of Reagan's arms-race spending. As a result, the Soviet Union broke down in 1991. It was apparent that communism had failed or was failing everywhere, so many countries moved away from it and the world entered a very prosperous period of globalization and free-market capitalism.

Since then, three economic cycles have brought us to where we are at the time of my writing—one that peaked in the 2000 dot-com bubble that led to the recession that followed, one that peaked in the 2007 bubble that led to the 2008 global financial crisis, and one that peaked in 2019, just before the 2020 coronavirus-triggered downturn. In addition to the decline of the Soviet Union,

this period also saw the rise of China, globalization, and advances in technologies that replaced people, which was good for corporate profits but widened wealth and opportunity gaps.

Countries and their borders faded in importance; goods and the incomes they produced were generally made wherever they could be most cost-effectively produced, which led to production and development in emerging countries, accelerating mobility of people between countries, narrowing wealth gaps between countries, and ballooning wealth gaps within them. Lower- and middle-income workers in developed countries suffered, while workers in productive emerging countries saw big relative gains. Though a bit of an oversimplification, it's accurate to say that **this was a period in which workers in other countries, especially those in China, and machines replaced middle-class workers in the United States.**

The following chart shows the balances of goods and services[3] for the United States and China since 1990 in real (i.e., inflation-adjusted) dollars. As you will see when we look at China in the next chapter, China's economic reforms and open-door policies after Deng Xiaoping came to power in 1978 and China's being welcomed into the World Trade Organization in 2001 led to an explosion of Chinese competitiveness and exports. Note the accelerations in Chinese surpluses and the US deficits from around 2000 to around 2010 and then some narrowing of these differences (which have recently ticked up during the pandemic), with China still tending to run surpluses and the US still running deficits. These surpluses have given China big savings that are a great financial power.

[3] This measures whether the country as a whole is spending more than it's earning.

EXPORTS OF GOODS AND SERVICES MINUS IMPORTS OF GOODS AND SERVICES (REAL, USD BLN, 12MMA)

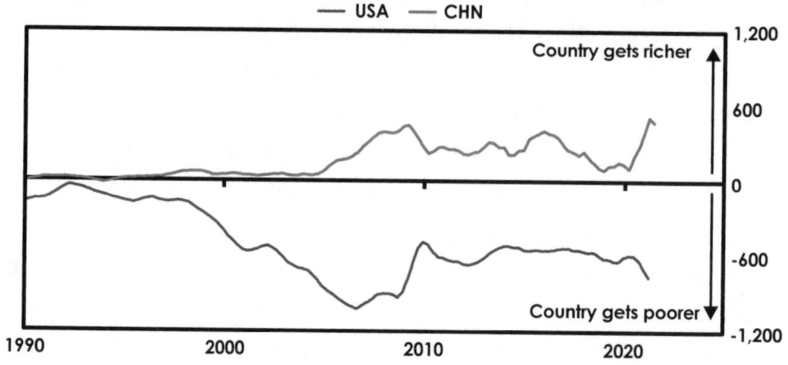

● ***Most people pay attention to what they get and not where the money comes from to pay for it, so there are strong motivations for elected officials to spend a lot of borrowed money and make a lot of promises to give voters what they want and to take on debt and non-debt liabilities that cause problems down the road.*** That was certainly the case in the 1990–2008 period.

Throughout the long-term debt cycle, from 1945 until 2008, whenever the Federal Reserve wanted the economy to pick up it would lower interest rates and make money and credit more available, which would increase stock and bond prices and increase demand. That was how it was done until 2008—i.e., interest rates were cut, and debts were increased faster than incomes to create unsustainable bubbles. That changed when the bubble burst in 2008 and interest rates hit 0 percent for the first time since the Great Depression. As explained more comprehensively in my book *Principles for Navigating Big Debt Crises* there are three types of monetary policy: 1) interest-rate-driven monetary policy (which I call Monetary Policy 1 because it is the first to be used and is the preferable way to run monetary policy), 2) printing money and buying financial assets, most importantly bonds (which I call Monetary Policy 2 and is now popularly called "quantitative easing"), and 3) coordination between fiscal policy and monetary policy in which the central government does a lot of debt-financed spending and the central bank buys that debt (which I call Monetary Policy 3 because it is the third and last approach to be used when the first two cease to be effective). The next charts show how the debt crises of 1933 and 2008 both led to interest rates hitting 0 percent and were followed by big money printing by the Federal Reserve.

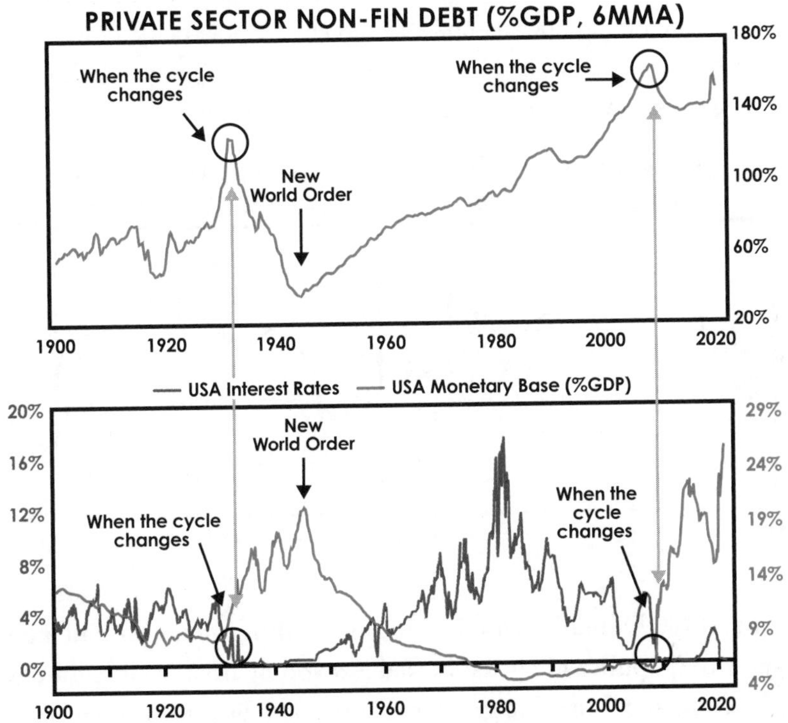

This change in monetary policy had big effects and implications.

The 2008–2020 Money-Financed Capitalist Boom

In 2008 the debt crisis led to interest rates being lowered until they hit 0 percent, which led the three main reserve currency central banks (led by the Fed) to move from an interest-rate-driven monetary policy to a monetary policy of printing money and buying financial assets. Central banks printed money and bought financial assets, which put money in the hands of investors who bought other financial assets, which caused financial asset prices to rise, which was helpful for the economy and particularly beneficial to those who were rich enough to own financial assets, so it increased the wealth gap. Basically, borrowed money was essentially free, so investment borrowers and corporate borrowers took advantage of this to get it and used it to make purchases that drove stock prices and corporate profits up. This money did not trickle down proportionately, so wealth and income gaps continued to grow. Wealth and income gaps grew to the largest since the 1930–45 period.

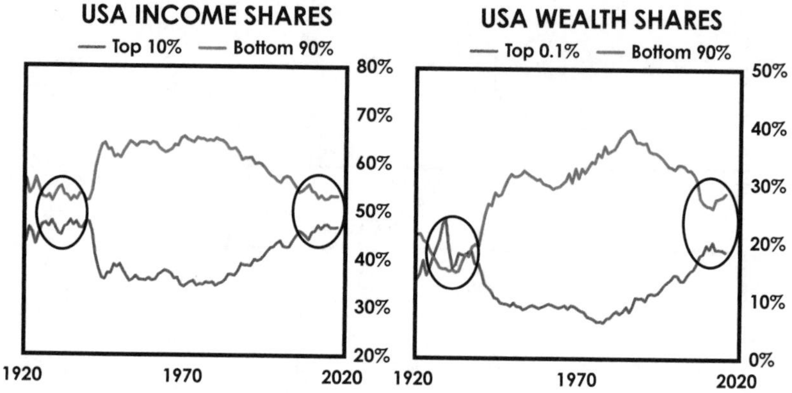

In 2016, Donald Trump, a blunt-speaking businessman and capitalist/populist of the right, led a revolt against establishment politicians and "elites" to get elected president by promising to support people with conservative values who had lost jobs and were struggling. He went on to cut corporate taxes and run big budget deficits that the Fed accommodated. While this debt growth financed relatively strong market-economy growth and created some improvements for lower-income earners, it was accompanied by a further widening of the wealth and values gap, leading the "have-nots" to become increasingly resentful of the "haves." **At the same time, the political gap grew with increasingly extreme Republicans on the one side and increasingly extreme Democrats on the other.** This is reflected in the next two charts. The first one shows how conservative

Republicans in the Senate and House and how liberal Democrats in the Senate and House have become relative to the past. Based on this measure they have become more extreme, and their divergence has become larger than ever before. While I'm not sure that's exactly right, I think it's by and large right.

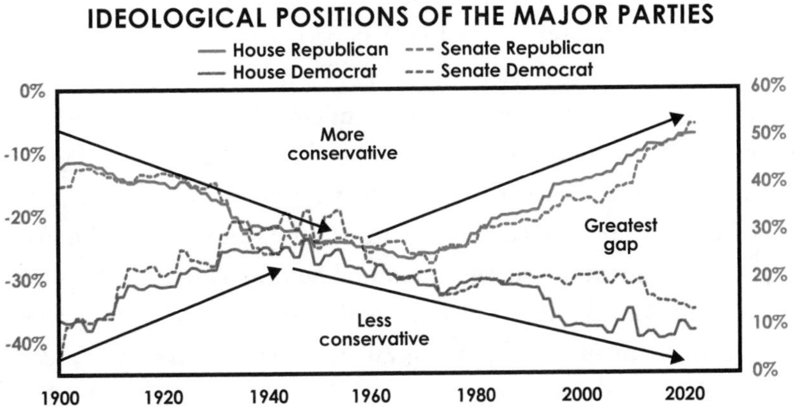

The next chart shows the percentage of votes along party lines for the average representative, which is the highest ever. This continues to be reflected in the reduced willingness to cross party lines to compromise and reach agreements. In other words, the political splits in the country have become deep and intransigent.

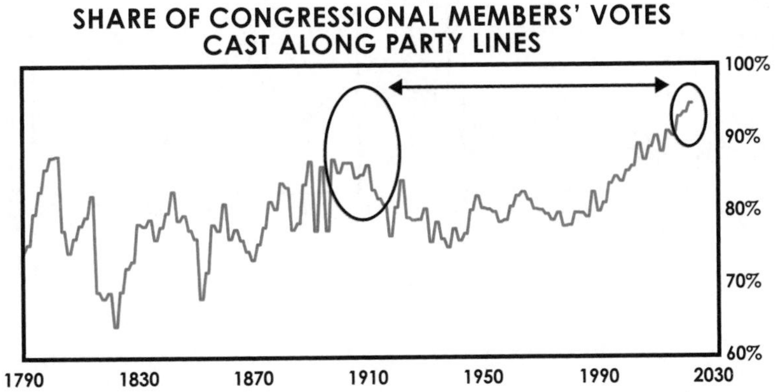

This chart shows the average predictiveness of a given member's left/right ideology in determining their vote across chambers for each congressional session as measured by NOMINATE, an academic model of ideological preference.

Trump took a more aggressive negotiating posture concerning economic and geopolitical disagreements with international rivals, particularly China and Iran, and allies such as Europe and Japan regarding trade and paying for military expenditures. The conflicts with China over trade, technology, geopolitics, and capital were intensifying as his term ended in 2021; economic sanctions such as those that were used in the 1930–45 period were being used or put on the table for possible use.

In March 2020 the coronavirus pandemic hit, and incomes, employment, and economic activity plunged as the country (and much of the world) went into lockdown. The US government took on a lot of debt to give people and companies a lot of money, and the Federal Reserve printed a lot of money and bought a lot of debt. So did other central banks. As a reflection of this, the following charts show the unemployment rates and central bank balance sheets of major countries for as far back as data is available. As shown, all the levels of central banks' printing of money and buying of financial assets rose to near or beyond the previous record amounts in the war years.

UNITED STATES

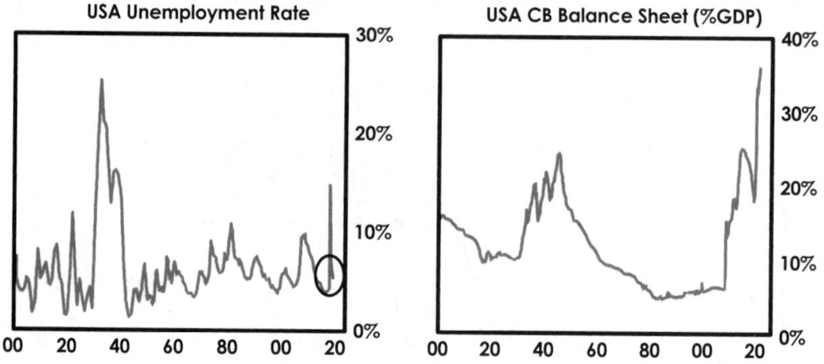

EUROPE

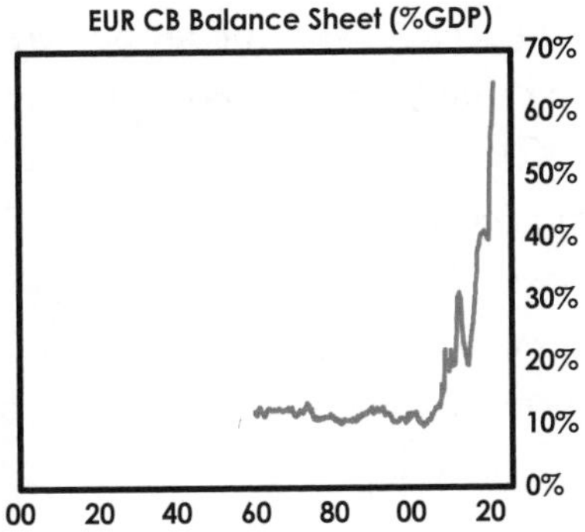

UNITED KINGDOM

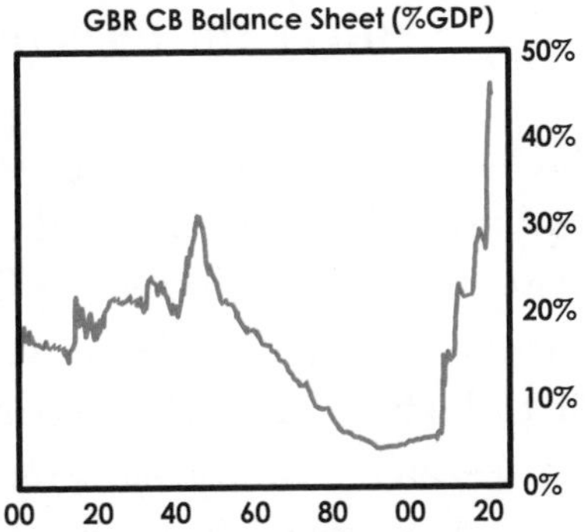

JAPAN

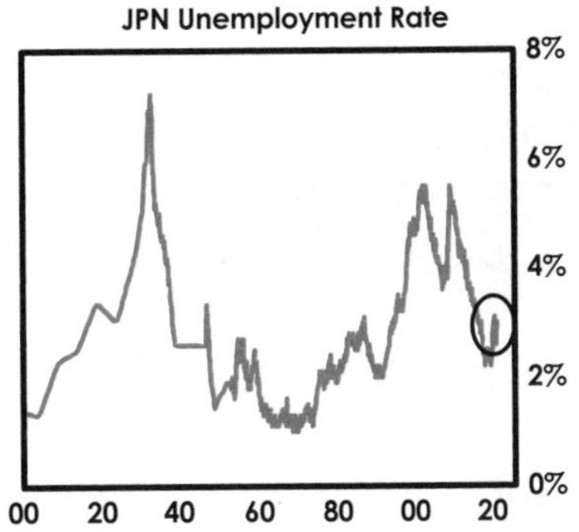

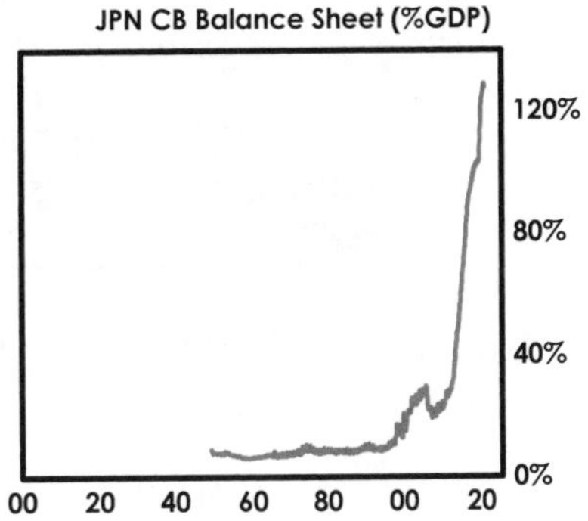

As history has shown and as explained in Chapter 4, ● *when there is a great increase in money and credit, it drives down the value of money and credit, which drives up the value of other investment assets.*

The printing and buying of debt that the Fed undertook in 2020 was much like Roosevelt's March 1933 move, Nixon's August 1971 move, Volcker's August 1982 move, Ben Bernanke's November 2008 move, and Mario Draghi's July 2012 move. It has become standard operating procedure for central banks, and it will persist until it no longer works.

WHERE THE US IS NOW IN ITS BIG CYCLE

The stats in my model suggest that the US is roughly 70 percent through its Big Cycle, plus or minus 10 percent. The United States has not yet crossed the line into the sixth phase of a civil war/revolution, when the active fighting begins, but internal conflict is high and rising. The recent elections show how split the country is—almost 50/50, along seemingly irreconcilable lines.

The next graphic represents what the population looked like 50 years ago—i.e., the majority of each party were moderates and the extremists were less extreme.

POLITICAL SPECTRUM 50 YEARS AGO

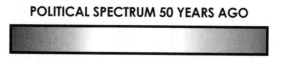

Now it looks like this—i.e., with a greater concentration and number of people at the extremes.

POLITICAL SPECTRUM 2021

4

[4] Shading indicates degree of polarization.

History has shown us that ● ***greater polarization equals either a) greater risk of political gridlock, which reduces the chances of revolutionary changes that rectify the problems or b) some form of civil war/revolution.***

In Chapter 5, I described the classic markers signaling the probabilities of escalation from Stage 5 to Stage 6. **The three most important markers I am watching now are: 1) the rules being disregarded, 2) both sides emotionally attacking each other, and 3) blood being spilled.**

In the final chapter of this book, I will share the quantitative measures that I use to track how things are going. I will continue to watch these and share what I'm seeing with you at economicprinciples.org. But first, we will look at a rising world power, China, and the ways in which it is coming into conflict with the US.

CHAPTER 12

THE BIG CYCLE RISE OF CHINA AND THE RENMINBI

Emotions have been running so high between the US and China that many people have urged me not to publish this chapter. We are in a kind of war, they say; any complimentary things you write about China will alienate US readers, while criticism of China will infuriate the Chinese—and the media will make things worse by distorting everything you say. That's probably true, but I can't not speak openly because the US-China relationship is too important to be left unmentioned by anyone who knows both countries as well as I do. To not speak honestly would cost me my self-respect.

I'm not afraid of criticism; I welcome it. What I am passing along here is just the latest iteration of my learning process, which is to develop my perspectives through direct experiences and research, to write up what I learn, to stress test it by showing it to smart people, to explore our differences if and when we have them, to evolve my thinking some more, and do that over and over again until I die. While this study reflects nearly 40 years of doing just that with China, it is still incomplete; it is right and wrong in ways that have yet to be discovered, and it is provided to you to use or criticize in the spirit of finding out what's true.

This chapter is focused on China and Chinese history; the

following chapter is on US-China relations. What I hope to provide in this chapter is a better understanding of where the Chinese are coming from—of how they see us and themselves as a result of having lived through their history. While I'm not a scholar of Chinese culture and the Chinese way of operating, I believe that my numerous direct encounters with China, my historical and economic research, and my US and global perspective give me a unique sense of its past and present. After you read this, you can decide for yourself whether or not that's true.

China's culture, by which I mean its people's innate expectations about how families and communities should behave with each other and how leaders should lead and followers should follow, evolved over thousands of years through the rises and falls of its many ruling dynasties and the development of Confucian and Neo-Confucian philosophy as well as other beliefs. I have seen these typical Chinese values and ways of operating manifested over and over again; for example, in the economic and leadership approaches of two men: Lee Kuan Yew, the former long-time prime minister of Singapore, and Deng Xiaoping, who initiated China's reform and opening up. Both combined Confucian values with capitalist practices, in Deng's case creating a "socialist market economy with Chinese characteristics."

Over the last couple of years, as part of my study of the rises and declines of empires and their currencies, I have also undertaken a study of Chinese history to help me understand how the Chinese think—especially their leaders, who are greatly influenced by history. I began my research with the year 600, just before the Tang Dynasty.[1] While I can be pretty certain about my impressions of the people and things that I have had direct contact with, I of course can't be as certain about those I haven't. My thoughts about historical figures such as Mao Zedong are based on facts gathered, experts'

[1] The entire report on China's dynasties is available at economicprinciples.org.

thinking gathered from conversations and books, and conjecture. What I can say is that between my own experience, the efforts of my research team, and my extensive triangulation with some of the most knowledgeable China scholars and practitioners on the planet, I have a high degree of confidence in my conclusions.

Since my first trip to China in 1984, I have come to know many Chinese, from the lowest to the highest in rank, in an up-close, personal way, and I have experienced their recent history as directly as I have experienced America's. As a result, I believe that I understand both the American and Chinese perspectives pretty well. I urge those of you who haven't spent considerable time in China to look past the caricatured pictures that are often painted by biased parties and rid yourself of any stereotypes you might have that are based on what you thought you knew about the old "communist China"—because they're wrong. Triangulate whatever you are hearing or reading with people who have spent a lot of time in China working with the Chinese people. As an aside, I think the widespread media distortions and the blind and near-violent loyalties that stand in the way of the thoughtful exploration of our different perspectives are a frightening sign of our times.

To be clear, I'm not ideological. I don't choose a side on an issue based on whether it aligns with American, Chinese, or my own personal beliefs. I'm practical; I approach things like a doctor who relies on logic and cause/effect relationships and believes in what works well through time. The only thing I can do is beg for your patience and open-mindedness as I share what I've learned with you.

I laid out the factors that I believe are most important to a country's health when I discussed the 18 determinants at the beginning of this book. Of those, I highlighted eight measures of power: education, competitiveness, innovation/technology, trade, economic output, military, financial center status, and reserve currency status. When I judge China's strengths and weaknesses, it is through the lens of those factors. I also try to understand China's circumstances as the Chinese themselves do, through their eyes.

To refresh your memory, this chart shows the relative standing of the world's leading countries as measured in indices that measure eight different types of power. In examining the rises and declines of the great empires since 1500, I looked at each of these measures. I will now do the same for China, briefly conveying the long arc of its history while diving into its highlights in a more granular way.

RELATIVE STANDING OF GREAT EMPIRES

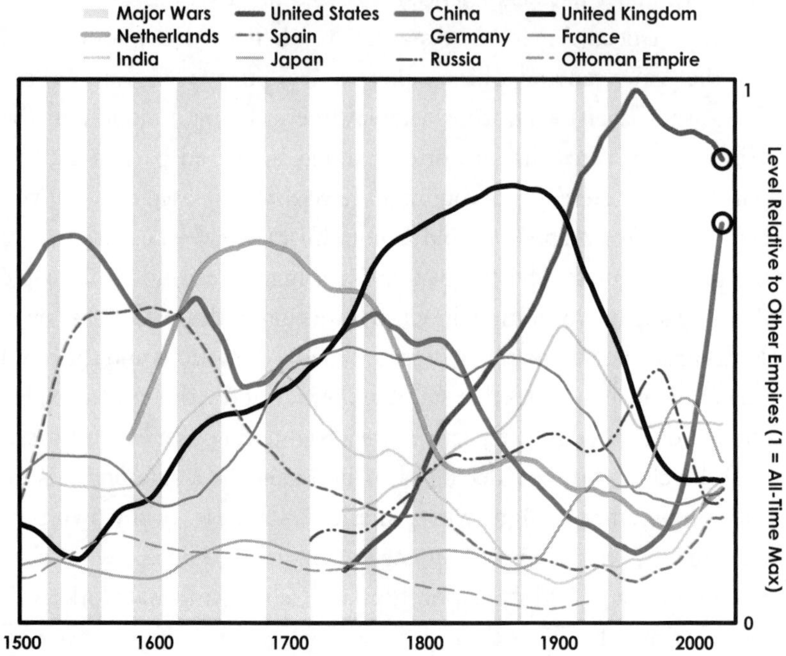

Breaking this rise down further, the following chart shows the eight measures of power for China between 1800 and the present.

CHINA: INDEX OF KEY DETERMINANTS

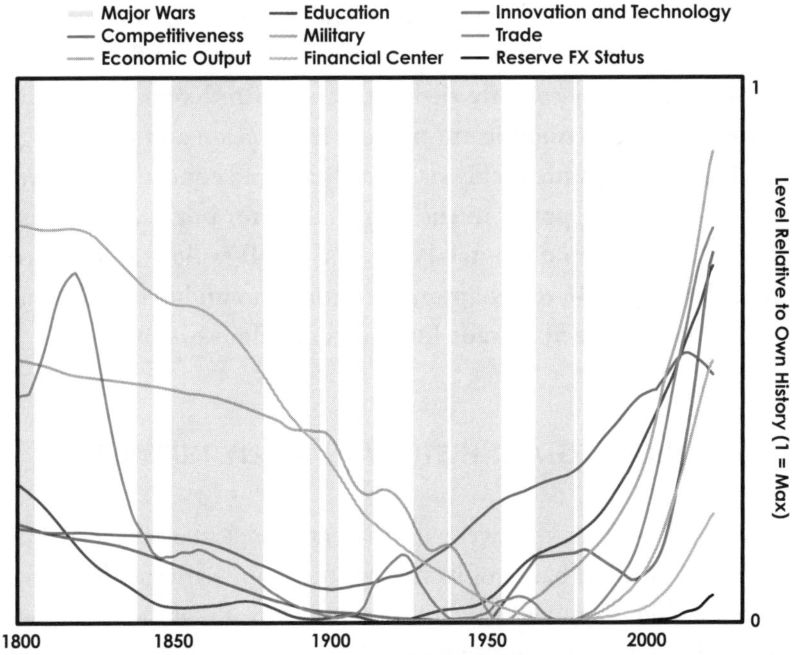

Unlike the cycles for the Dutch, British, and American empires, which began with their rises and were followed by their protracted declines, China's cycle over the past 200 years was a long decline followed by a rapid rise. Though the order is reversed, the same forces drove the cycle. Seven of the eight powers hit their lowest points in the 1940–50 period. Since then, most of them—notably, economic competitiveness, education, and military power—improved gradually until around 1980, when China's economic competitiveness and trade took off. That was right after Deng Xiaoping's open-door and reform policies began. That is no coincidence. From my first visit to China in 1984 until about 2008, debt growth was in line with economic growth, which was very strong. In other words, extremely rapid improvements were made without loading the economy up with debt. Then the 2008 financial crisis came along and China, like the rest of the world, used a lot of debt to stimulate its economy, so debts rose relative to incomes. When Xi Jinping came to power in

2012, he improved China's debt and economic management dramatically, continued growth in innovation and technologies, strengthened education and the military, and encountered greater conflict with the US. **China is now roughly tied with the US in being the leading power in trade, economic output, and innovation and technology, and it is a strong and quickly rising military and educational power. It is an emerging power in the financial sector but is lagging as a reserve currency and financial center. We will explore all of this in more detail later in the chapter, but in order to understand China's present we first need to wade into its tremendous history.**

CHINA'S GIANT HISTORY IN A TINY NUTSHELL

Anyone who wants to have a fundamental understanding of China needs to know the basics of its history, the many patterns that repeat within it, and the timeless and universal principles that its leaders have gained from studying those patterns. Getting even a basic understanding of Chinese history is a considerable undertaking. Spanning some 4,000 years, it is so vast and complicated, and has inspired so many different and sometimes contradictory interpretations, that I am confident that there is no single source of truth—and I am especially confident that I'm not it. Still, there is a lot that knowledgeable people agree on, and many scholars and practitioners, both Chinese and non-Chinese, have shared valuable insights with me. Trying to piece together all that I have learned has not only been a valuable experience for me but also a fascinating one. While I can't guarantee that my perspectives are the best, I can guarantee that they have been well-triangulated with some of the most informed people in the world.

China's civilization began around 2000 BCE with the Xia Dynasty, which lasted about 400 years and is credited with bringing the Bronze Age to Asia. Confucius, who developed the philosophy that most influences how the Chinese behave with each other to this day, lived from 551 to 479 BCE. The Qin Dynasty united most of the geographic area that we now call China around 221 BCE and was followed by the 400-year Han Dynasty, which pioneered governance systems that are still in use. The Tang Dynasty came to the fore in 618 CE.

This chart applies to China the same overall power gauge that I showed you in the chart of great empires, covering the more than 1,400 years between 600 and today. With the notable exception of the period from around 1840 to 1950, when it experienced a steep decline, China has historically stood among the most powerful empires in the world. As it emerged from civil war, it began to rise again, at first slowly and then very rapidly. Today it is second only to the US and is poised to surpass it.

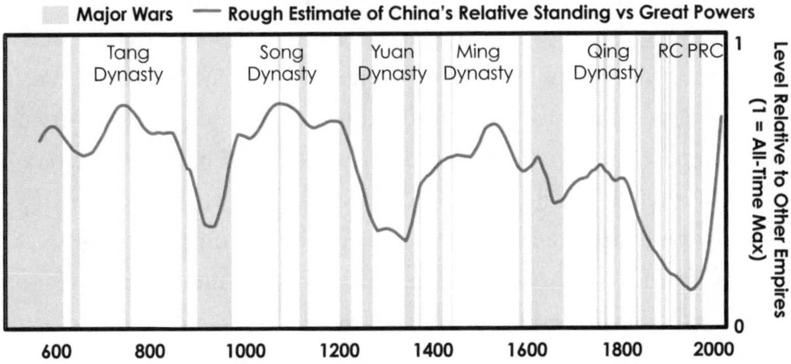

Most of the dynasties that ruled China over the course of this time span were as cultured as they were powerful. (I only name the most prominent in the chart; there were many others.) Each of these dynasties has its own fascinating story, but to do those stories justice would take far more space than can fit in this chapter.

- **The Tang Dynasty (618–907) is considered by many Chinese to be a high point of Imperial China.** The Tang came to power after a prolonged period of disunion and civil war, which had culminated in China being reunified by the short-lived Sui Dynasty, which immediately preceded the Tang. The dynasty was established by a father-son pair of strong leaders—with the son, the Tang's second Emperor Taizong, being especially notable. They not only militarily unified China, but also established a stable government system and policies that were highly effective, producing quality education, excellent development of technologies, international trade, and diverse ideas. Taizong was a great revolutionary leader who was able to consolidate power, build a great dynasty, and transition well so that the dynasty remained strong without him. A period of great prosperity lasted about 150 years, with a particularly strong military that helped the Tang control valuable trade routes in Central Asia. By the late 700s, however, the Tang slipped into decline for the classic reasons: the quality of governance fell, fragmentation over economic and values gaps led to a weakened and corrupt central government (which, combined with internal conflict, led to a series of rebellions), its finances deteriorated, and natural disasters increased in impact.

- **Then came the Northern and Southern Song dynasties (960–1279), during which China was the most innovative and dynamic economy in the world.** The deterioration of the Tang Dynasty led to its own period of civil war and disunion in the 900s. Out of this conflict the Song Dynasty came to power under the rule of Emperor Taizu in 960. Taizu was one of those classic strong revolutionary leaders who needed to and could bring order to chaos. He successfully rose to power as a military leader and, when in power, implemented widespread reforms to a) bring together the different factions that had previously fought for power, b) create a centralized, top-down system of military and civilian governance, and c) expand education and the quality of governance (particularly through reforming the imperial examination system). These investments in education and meritocracy under Taizu and his successors set the Song Dynasty on the classic good path that led to immense scientific and technological advancement.[2] However, after a few generations, around the year 1100, the dynasty declined due to a combination of weak leadership, financial problems, and other classic factors. In its weakened state, it became vulnerable to external powers. During the 1100s and 1200s, the Song first lost control of the northern half of China, then, after a revival period known as the Southern Song Dynasty, were conquered by Mongol leader Kublai Khan.

- **Kublai Khan founded the comparatively short-lived Yuan Dynasty (1279–1368).** For much of his rule, Kublai Khan governed well and behaved like a classic dynastic founder: he encouraged education, unified the state, and, relative to many other Mongol leaders, stood out for his meritocratic and open-minded style of governing. Under Kublai Khan, China's economy and trade strengthened after a long period of conflict. At the same time, the Yuan pursued expensive wars of conquest. Corruption grew later in his rule, and the failure to establish a stable succession structure led to frequent civil wars and crises after his death. This corruption and instability helped produce rebellions that ended the dynasty after less than a century.
- **The Ming Dynasty (1368–1644) presided over an empire that was largely prosperous and peaceful. It was founded by the Hongwu Emperor, who was born into poverty and rose to be a great general who captured Beijing and threw out the Mongol rulers. He consolidated power in a 14-year purge that led to about 30,000 executions.** After winning power through a successful rebellion against the unpopular Yuan Dynasty, early Ming leaders built a meritocratic society with excellent education and civil behavior that fostered innovation. Over time the Ming Dynasty expanded trade with Europe

[2] Among the many inventions of the Song Dynasty were the moveable-type printing press, a compass for navigation, and paper currency.

(as Chinese goods were of superior quality), which brought in enormous amounts of silver and redirected the nation's energies from subsistence agriculture to industry. However, the Ming's failure to manage monetary and fiscal policy well, to consistently support China's influence over international trade, and to adequately respond to a series of crises left China exposed and vulnerable. To make matters worse, the Little Ice Age led to agricultural disaster and famine. In the end, war, famine, and ecological disaster—combined with a rigid and ineffectual state—created an unrecoverable catastrophe that led to the collapse of the nearly three-centuries-old Ming Dynasty by 1644.

- **The Qing Dynasty (1644–1912) came to power when the neighboring Manchu people capitalized on instability and rebellions in Ming China to challenge it.** This culminated in the sacking of Beijing by rebels during which the last Ming emperor committed suicide. **Then the cycle began again under the Qing Dynasty. China achieved its maximum territorial expansion, governing over a third of the world's population while reforms under the reigns of three long-ruling emperors led to an extended period of economic prosperity.**[3] Then the European powers arrived. Earlier in this book we saw how the European powers, in the Age of Exploration, used their military strength to trade with and exploit resource-rich but militarily weaker foreigners. That's what happened starting in the early 1800s, which began what is called the Century of Humiliation in China. The Europeans came offering to trade but the Chinese didn't want anything they had to offer. This led to the British bringing opium into China to get the Chinese addicted, so that they would trade for it. A series of military confrontations followed during the 1800s (most notably

[3] China's share of world GDP rose to 30 percent and the population more than doubled during the 1700s.

> the Opium Wars), which sped China's decline. Chinese moves to stem their decline failed and there was great internal conflict and uprisings (most notably the Taiping Rebellion), which continued until the collapse of the Qing Dynasty in 1912.

The lessons this history provides remain very much in the forefront of the minds of China's current leaders and are fascinating to me, especially in the context of the patterns of history.

How the Typical Dynastic Cycle Transpires

The typical major Chinese dynasty, like the typical empire, lasted about 250 years, give or take 150 years, and by and large followed the same pattern of rises and declines.[4] You can especially see the internal order cycle, described in Chapter 5, at play time and time again. As a reminder of that cycle:

- **Stage 1, when the new order begins and the new leadership consolidates power**, which leads to . . .
- . . . **Stage 2, when the resource-allocation systems and government bureaucracies are built and refined**, which if done well leads to . . .
- . . . **Stage 3, when there is peace and prosperity**, which leads to . . .
- . . . **Stage 4, when there are great excesses in spending and debt and the widening of wealth and political gaps**, which leads to . . .
- . . . **Stage 5, when there are very bad financial conditions**

[4] To clarify, most dynasties were minor, short-lived dynasties or regional dynasties that swiftly rose and fell during periods of instability in China. Different sources give different numbers for the total number of dynasties because it's not even clear what constituted a minor or regional dynasty versus some other form of administration. Concerning the major dynasties, there were roughly nine that unified China and often ruled for extended periods. This group includes the five our case study focuses on from 600 to the present (the Tang, Song, Yuan, Ming, and Qing), and four from the 800 years prior (the Qin, Han, Jin, and Sui).

and intense conflict, which leads to . . .

- . . . **Stage 6, when there are civil wars/revolutions**, which leads to . . .
- . . . Stage 1, which leads to Stage 2, etc., with the whole cycle happening over again.

Let's review this cycle quickly. **The typical cycle begins with strong leaders who win control and implement improvements needed to build a great empire**. As with most other empires, the initial winning of the war for control is typically followed by **struggling to get most of the population in line and united** (often through conflict to establish the leadership's power). That is typically followed by a peace that is due to no entities wanting to challenge the dominant power (Stage 1).

Then the new ruler turns to building up the empire. To be successful an empire needs **a smart and determined population that works well with each other**. It also needs to be **strong financially**. These things are obtained by systems that train and produce people who have **strong education and self-discipline. Getting the most capable people into the most important roles requires the meritocratic selection of people. In Chinese dynasties, the imperial exams often played that role, and it was common for new dynasties to implement educational reforms.** It also requires **an effective resource-allocation system** (Stage 2).

During that period of peace and rising power, the empire typically works well economically and improves its financial condition. While the empire typically starts with limited financial resources and low debts because the previous empire's debts have been wiped out, in some cases it has assets that were acquired as an outcome of the prior war that it won. In the case of Chinese history, key variables were the distribution of land ownership and taxation of it—often the arrival of a new dynasty weakened or overturned the "corrupt elites" of the prior system, vastly improving the resources available to the state. With these resources, the dynasty profits and expands. It builds commercial, technological, and military strengths that reinforce each other. For example, having strong technologies helps the dynasty economically and militarily because they can be used for both purposes and because being strong militarily protects the country's commercial interests (e.g., protects trade routes), which also strengthens the dynasty financially. At its peak, the dynasty's government is functioning well, its resources and people are employed productively, and prior investments are yielding new gains. The economy is strong and self-sustaining, and the people are prosperous and produce great achievements in scholarship, the arts, trade, architecture, and other elements of great civilizations (Stage 3).

The decline of the empire typically happens because the forces that strengthened it fade and a rival power emerges. Leadership weakens, often becomes corrupt, and/or allows corruption in others.[5] Also, the dynasty typically becomes overextended and quite often becomes heavily indebted, which causes it to have debt problems that are typically dealt with by printing lots of money, which in turn devalues the money. The dynasty's population also becomes increasingly fragmented and loses its unity of purpose and ability to work well together. The wealth gap increases, which undermines productivity and leads to political conflict. Often there is some form of natural disaster, frequently a drought or a flood that exacerbates the dynasty's problems. The more of these that happen at the same time, the greater the chance that the dynasty will fall.

The fall itself comes with escalating rebellions and then a bloody civil war (Stage 5 and Stage 6). Eventually a strong new leader emerges, wins the conflict, and begins the cycle again with a new dynasty (Stage 1 again).

There are **common themes in the decline of the different dynasties—themes also visible in the decline of some of the other powers mentioned in this book**:

[5] Typically, the "bad" emperors were distant from managing the affairs of the empire and tolerated—or even participated in—corruption while ignoring public investment needs. Several were known for greater ideological rigidity, for their poor judgement and the poor judgment of their top advisors, and for being preoccupied with the luxuries that their positions afforded them. The last emperors of most dynasties often came after the dynasty was already weakened and often had limited control or even involvement in political events (e.g., child emperors).

1. **Growing inequality and fiscal problems over the course of the dynasty are critical drivers of the decline.** Dynasties often started with more equal land and wealth holdings, as the concentrated holdings of the old dynasty's elites were redistributed—which helped with preventing social conflict and helped the fiscal position (because elites often were more able to shelter themselves from taxes than the broader base of small landholders). But over the years, land became concentrated in fewer and fewer families, who could evade taxes (via bribery, using official influence, and finding other ways to hide/shelter their wealth from taxation)—which in turn allowed them to build their wealth further. The inequality this produced helped directly spawn conflict, and the weakening tax base of the state made the state weaker and more vulnerable to crisis.
2. **Monetary problems were common contributors to the decline of the empires.** In the Song, Yuan, and Ming dynasties, the government struggled to maintain a large enough money supply in metal coins and resorted to money printing, especially in times of war and natural or human-caused disaster. The problems with collecting taxes made the incentive to print even stronger. This caused high inflation or hyperinflation, making matters worse.
3. **The quality of governance and infrastructure tended to rise early in each dynasty and then fall over the course of the dynasty.** Later in the Song, Ming, and Qing dynasties, years of underinvestment in public works built up, leaving China vulnerable to famines and floods. And while it's hard to generalize over dozens of emperors, the visionary founder of the dynasty (e.g., the founders of the Song and Yuan dynasties who embraced technology and science) was typically succeeded by rulers who were more rigid and conservative (e.g., in the Qing Dynasty), too focused on imperial riches and luxuries (e.g., the last rulers of the Northern Song Dynasty), and/or less supportive of foreign trade (in the Ming Dynasty).

4. **Internal conflict usually arose from economic differences combined with bad times (most typically caused by agricultural problems, high debts, poor governance, and natural disasters, and sometimes by conflicts with outside forces).** Significant natural disasters and periods of quick climate change that were painfully disruptive often coincided with the fall of dynasties. The classic downward spiral has been that 1) inadequate technology and investment (both new projects and maintenance) leaves infrastructure susceptible to natural disasters; 2) a disaster hits (in China's case this was typically via droughts and flooding from the major rivers), which damages crop yields and, in some cases, destroys communities, as lower crop yields lead to food scarcity and famine; and 3) domestic populist uprisings result from the disasters. This process played a significant role in the declines of the Song, Yuan, Ming, and Qing dynasties.
5. **Bad conditions and large wealth gaps led to the most significant uprisings**, which were due to the common man rebelling against the excesses of the elite (e.g., the Fang La Rebellion in the Song Dynasty, the Red Turban Rebellion in the Yuan Dynasty, and the White Lotus Rebellion in the Qing Dynasty). Conversely, domestic stability arising from good conditions for most people was a key characteristic of the more prosperous periods.
6. **Isolation and Confucian cultural influences that favored scholarship over commerce, technology, and military strength led to China's weaker competitiveness in business, technology, and the military, which led it to be beaten by or fall behind stronger "barbarians"—e.g., the Mongols, the foreign powers in the Opium Wars, and the rest of the world in the Mao isolation period.**

China's physical geography and geology have also had a big impact on the rise and fall of dynasties. The main thing to know is that China's terrain is varied and often volatile. For example, the north is colder, flatter, and drier, and the south is more mountainous, much warmer, and wetter, which leads to China's different areas having often inconsistent crop production. However, a united China is largely self-contained because the diversification and coordination of the parts make it that way. Still, these conditions plus shortages of clean water, cropland, and coastal marine fisheries have historically made China vulnerable to food shortages. For that reason, **China has often been food-insecure** and even today imports a lot of food. **China also has shortages of important natural resources**, such as oil, some minerals, and some foodstuffs. **It also has bad air pollution that adversely affects the health of its people and its agriculture, though it is quickly improving these conditions.**

Such events led **past and current leaders of China to learn lessons and establish protections against these natural and political disasters** being repeated or leading to unacceptable consequences. In other words, there are many lessons embedded in these histories, and—believe me—all of them influence the decision making of China's leaders today, whether they are planning for the long term or dealing with cases at hand.

What is especially interesting to me is seeing how far back in history the patterns of the archetypical Big Cycle go, since China's history is both so ancient and so well-documented. I was also fascinated to see what happened when the Eastern and Western worlds interacted more significantly from the 17th through the 19th centuries, and how, as the world became much smaller and more interconnected, the Chinese and Western Big Cycles affected each other.

Probably the most important thing I gained from studying the history of so many countries is the ability to see the big patterns of causes and effects. Shifting my perspective to the very long term felt like zooming out in Google Maps because it allowed me to see contours that I couldn't see before and how the same stories play out over and over again for basically the same reasons. I also came to understand how having so much history to study has affected the Chinese way of thinking, which is very different from the American way of thinking, which is much more focused on what is happening now. Most Americans believe their own history is just 300 or 400 years old (since they believe the country began with European settlement), and they aren't terribly interested in learning from it.

Whether they are interested or not, 300 years seems like a very long time ago to Americans, but for the Chinese, it isn't long at all. While the prospect of a revolution or a war that will overturn the US system is unimaginable to most Americans, both seem inevitable to the Chinese because they have seen those things happen again and again and have studied the patterns that inevitably precede them. While most Americans focus on particular events, especially those that are happening now, most Chinese leaders view current events in the context of larger, more evolutionary patterns.

Americans are impulsive and tactical; they fight for what they want in the present. Most Chinese are strategic; they plan for how they can get what they want in the future. I have also found Chinese leaders to be much more philosophical (literally, readers of philosophy) than American leaders. For example, I had a meeting with a Chinese leader who had just met President Donald Trump and had concerns about the possibility of a US-China conflict. He explained how he approached the meeting, which struck me as starkly different from how President Trump likely had. This leader and I have known each other for many years, during which time we have talked mostly about the Chinese and world economies and markets. Over those years we have developed a friendship. He is a very skilled, wise, humble, and likable man. He explained that going into his meeting with Trump, he was concerned about the worst-case scenario where tit-for-tat escalations could get out of control and lead to war. He referred to history and gave a personal story of his father to convey his perspective that wars were so unimaginably harmful and the damage of the next war could be worse than the last war, which had killed more people than any other. He focused on World War I as an example. He said that to calm himself down and gain equanimity he read *Critique of Pure*

Reason by Immanuel Kant, and he realized that he could only do his best and then the outcomes would take their course. I told him about the Serenity Prayer[6] and suggested meditation to him. I went home and read *Critique of Pure Reason* again, which I found challenging. I did, and still do, admire him and value his perspective greatly.

I tell this story to share with you one Chinese leader's perspective on the risk of wars and to also give one example of the many interactions I've had with this leader and of the many interactions I've had with many Chinese leaders and Chinese people in order to help you see them through my eyes and through their eyes.

Chinese history and philosophy, most importantly Confucian/Taoist/legalist/Marxist philosophies, have a much bigger influence on Chinese thinking than American history and its Judeo-Christian/European philosophical roots have on American thinking. An esteemed Chinese historian told me that Mao read the mammoth 20-volume chronicle *Comprehensive Mirror for Aid in Government*, which covers the 16 dynasties and 1,400 years of Chinese history from around 400 BCE to 960 CE, and the even more mammoth *Twenty-Four Histories* several times, as well as numerous volumes about Chinese history and the writings of non-Chinese philosophers, most importantly Marx. He also wrote and spoke philosophically, wrote poetry, and practiced calligraphy. If you are interested in what Mao thought or, more importantly, how he thought, I suggest you read *On Practice, On Contradiction*, and of course *The Little Red Book*, which is a compendium of his quotations on a number of subjects.[7]

The planning horizon that Chinese leaders concern themselves with is well over a century because that's at least how long a good dynasty lasts. They understand that the typical arc of development has different multidecade phases in it, which they plan for.

---

[6] "God, grant me the serenity to accept the things I cannot change, the courage to change the things I can, and the wisdom to know the difference."

[7] I'd like to thank Kevin Rudd, former prime minister of Australia and current president and CEO of the Asia Society Policy Institute, for pointing me to these books and helping me understand Chinese politics.

The first phase of the current Chinese Empire occurred under Mao when the revolution took place, control of the country was won, and power and institutions were solidified. The second phase of building wealth, power, and cohesiveness without threatening the leading world power (i.e., the United States) occurred under Deng and his successors up to Xi. The third phase of building on these accomplishments and moving China toward where it has set out to be on the 100th anniversary of the People's Republic of China in 2049—which is to be a "modern socialist country that is prosperous, strong, democratic, culturally advanced, and harmonious"—is occurring under Xi and his successors. **Its ultimate goal is to make the Chinese economy about twice the size of the US's and to have the benefits of its growth broadly shared.**[8] Nearer-term goals and ways to achieve them were set out in the Made in China 2025 plan,[9] Xi's new China Standards Plan 2035, and the usual five-year plans.[10]

Chinese leaders don't just try to implement their plans; they set out clear metrics by which to judge their performance, and they achieve most of their goals. I'm not saying that this process is perfect because it isn't, and I'm not saying that they don't have political and other challenges that lead to disagreements, including some brutal fights over what should be done, because they do (in private). What I am saying is that the Chinese have much longer-term and historically based perspectives and planning horizons, which they break down into shorter-term plans and ways of operating, and they have done an excellent job of achieving what they have set out to do by following this approach. Coincidentally, my own search for patterns in history and my way of dealing with tactical decisions has had a similar effect

[8] Because China's population is about four times as large as the US's, it only takes an income that is half as much per capita to have twice as much in total. There is nothing that I can see that stands in the way of China and the US having comparable per capita incomes over time, which would make China four times bigger.

[9] The Made in China 2025 plan is for China to be largely self-sufficient in most areas and to be world leaders in high-tech fields, including artificial intelligence, robotics, semiconductors, pharmaceuticals, and aerospace.

[10] In March 2021 China released their 14th Five-Year Plan and targets for 2035.

on how I see and do things—e.g., I now view the last 500 years as recent history, the most relevant historical arcs seem about 100-plus years long, and the patterns I've gleaned from this perspective help me anticipate how events are likely to transpire, and how I should be positioned for them over the coming weeks, months, and years.

CHINA'S LESSONS AND ITS WAYS OF OPERATING

Chinese culture developed as an extension of the experiences the Chinese had and the lessons they learned from them over the course of millennia. These were set out in philosophies about how things work and what ways work best in dealing with those realities, which made clear how people should be with each other, how political decision making should be done, and how economic systems should work. In the Western world, the dominant philosophies are Judeo-Christian, democratic, and capitalist/socialist, and each individual pretty much chooses from them to come up with a mix that suits them. In China, the main philosophies were Confucian, Taoist, and legalist until the early 20th century, when Marxism and capitalism entered the mix. Emperors typically choose their own preferences, put them into practice, learn, and adapt. If the mix works, the dynasty survives and prospers (in their parlance, it has the "mandate of heaven"). If it doesn't, it fails and is replaced by another. This process has gone on from before history was recorded and will go on for as long as there are people who have to decide how to do things collectively.

While I can't do these philosophies justice in a couple of sentences, here are my attempts:

- **Confucianism seeks to bring about harmony by ensuring that people know their roles in the hierarchy and how to play them well**, starting from within the family (between the husband and the wife, the father and the son, the older sibling and the younger sibling, etc.) and extending up to the ruler and their subjects. Each person respects and obeys those above them, who are benevolent and at the same time impose strict standards of behavior. All people are expected to be kind, honest, and fair. Confucianism values harmony, broad-based education, and meritocracy.

- **Legalism favors the rapid conquest and unification of "everything under heaven" by an autocratic leader.** It argues that the world is a kill-or-be-killed jungle in which strict obedience to the emperor's central government is required, without much benevolence given in return. The Western equivalent of legalism is fascism.
- **Taoism teaches that it is of paramount importance to live in harmony with the laws of nature**. Taoists believe that nature is composed of opposites—yin and yang—and that harmony is achieved when they are balanced well.

Until the early 20th century, when Marxism gained favor with Mao and his successors, Confucianism and Neo-Confucianism were the most influential philosophies, usually with some legalism thrown in. I will briefly explain Marxism when we get into the 20th century.

All of these Chinese systems are hierarchical and nonegalitarian. Wang Qishan, the vice president of China and a remarkable historian and explorer of different cultures, told me that the core difference between Americans and the Chinese is that Americans hold the individual above all else while the Chinese put the family and the collective above everything. **America is run from the bottom up (e.g., democracy) and optimized for the individual; China is run from the top down and optimized for the collective.** The Chinese word "country" consists of the two characters for "state" and "family," he explained, so Chinese leaders seek to run their state the way they think parents should run their families, with each person knowing their place and having filial respect for those above them. As a result, the Chinese are more humble, respectful, and rules-bound, while Americans are more arrogant, egalitarian, and rules-averse. I've observed that while the Chinese are more interested in asking questions and learning, Americans are more interested in telling you what they think.

As for governance structure (i.e., who reports to whom within the hierarchy of the central government and how that extends down to interactions with regional and local governments), the Chinese have evolved well-developed approaches over many dynasties and thousands of years; to go into them in depth would require too great a digression.

Unlike other great empires that have conquered and occupied other countries, it was relatively uncommon for China to occupy distant states. **China is basically a giant plain surrounded by big natural borders (mountains and seas), with the bulk of its population spread across the plain. Most of China's world was confined within those borders, and most of its wars were fought for control of it, mostly among the Chinese, though sometimes between foreign invaders and the Chinese.**

Traditional Chinese military philosophy teaches that the ideal way to win a war is not by fighting but by quietly developing one's power to the point that simply displaying it will cause an opponent to capitulate. It also calls for the extensive use of psychology to influence opponents' behaviors.[11] **Still, there have been numerous violent dynastic wars inside China. The few wars that were fought outside China were for the purpose of establishing China's relative power and opening trade.**

Scholars believe that China was loathe to expand its empire because its land mass was already so large and difficult to control and because they have preferred to maintain a cultural purity that is best achieved through isolation. **Traditionally the Chinese have preferred to enter into relations with empires outside their borders in a manner that is similar to what one might expect from the previously mentioned philosophies—i.e., with the parties knowing their**

---

[11] If you haven't read Sun Tzu's *The Art of War*, I suggest you do to get the flavor of what I am referring to.

places and acting accordingly. If China was more powerful, which was typically the case, the less powerful states paid "tribute" with gifts and favors and typically received guarantees of peace, recognition of their authorities, and trading opportunities in return. These subordinate countries typically maintained their customs and experienced no interference in how their countries were run.[12]

CHINA'S MONETARY AND ECONOMIC HISTORY

As for money, credit, and the economy, the history is very long and complicated. That said, China has gone through the full range of money/credit/economic systems and cycles that I described earlier when discussing the big cycle of money and credit. The currency the Chinese used the most was metal (mostly copper coins, and some silver, domestically), which continued long after China invented paper money in the 9th century, until the introduction of the yuan in the late 19th century. Silver was the main currency used internationally, though gold was also sometimes used.

Understanding the different systems is especially important for China, as they shifted frequently between them and it helped produce prosperity or ruin in different periods, depending on how the system was managed. China experienced several cycles of 1) transitioning from hard currency to paper backed by hard currency (Type 1 to Type 2), then 2) seeing trust in the currency increase until the paper

[12] In his excellent book *The Chinese World Order: Traditional China's Foreign Relations*, the historian John Fairbank described China's relations with non-Chinese states as follows: "The graded and concentric hierarchy of China's foreign relations included other peoples and countries which we may group into three main zones—first, the Sinic Zone, consisting of the most nearby and culturally similar tributaries, Korea and Vietnam, parts of which had anciently been ruled within the Chinese empire, and also Liu-ch'iu (Ryuku) Islands and, at brief times, Japan. Secondly, the Inner Asian Zone, consisting of tributary tribes and states of the nomadic or seminomadic peoples of Inner Asia who were not only ethnically and culturally non-Chinese but were also outside or on the fringes of the Chinese cultural area, even though sometimes pressing upon the Great Wall frontier. Third, the Outer Zone, consisting of the 'outer barbarians' (wai-i) generally, at further distance overland or sea, including eventually Japan and other states of Southeast and South Asia and Europe that were supposed to send tribute when trading."

currency was circulated with no backing, (Type 2 to Type 3), then 3) having the paper currency collapse due to overprinting and loss of faith, leading to the return to a hard currency (Type 3 to Type 1).

As I explained in Chapter 3 there are three basic types of monetary systems. In the first, which I call a Type 1 monetary system, money has intrinsic value (because the coins are made from gold, silver, and copper). In the second, which I call a Type 2 monetary system, money is linked to assets that have intrinsic value (typically in the form of paper notes that can be exchanged for gold or silver at a fixed price). In a Type 3 (or fiat) monetary system, money is not linked to anything objective. The following diagram conveys an ultra-simplified picture of how these currency systems rotated throughout China's history since the Tang Dynasty. In fact, different parts of China had different currencies and at times used coins and ingots from other countries (e.g., Spanish silver dollars in the late 16th century). Still **the diagram is broadly indicative and meant to show that China had the same range of monetary systems as the rest of the world, and they worked in essentially the same ways, most importantly, with cycles in which hard money was abandoned due to debt problems, leading to inflation, hyperinflation, and finally a return to hard money.**

TRANSITIONS ACROSS DIFFERENT TYPES OF MONEY IN CHINESE HISTORY

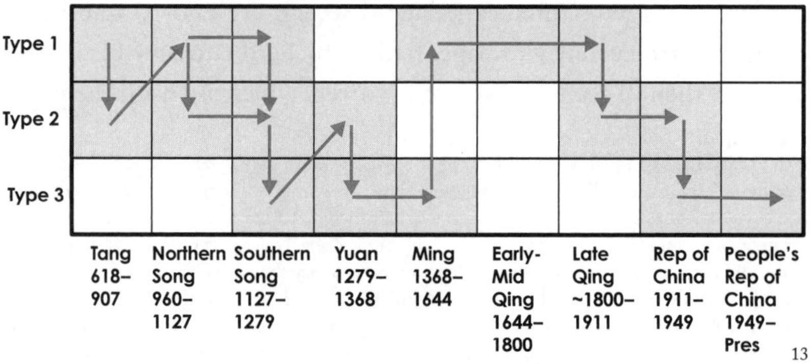

[13]

[13] I produced this diagram working with Professor Jiaming Zhu.

At the start of the Tang Dynasty, money primarily consisted of copper coins (i.e., hard currency). But as is classic, the supply of hard currency proved to be constraining—China was growing quickly, and the supply of copper wasn't keeping up to provide enough money. Additionally, each copper coin was of low value, and so to trade, merchants had to physically carry perhaps hundreds of thousands of copper coins, which was impractical. These pressures led to the invention of the earliest forms of non-hard, money-like instruments. "Flying cash" started out as essentially drafts from a bank (like checks), but merchants would circulate them like money. Eventually, the Tang government started to supervise their issuance and use.[14] That said, day-to-day monetary transactions continued to be mainly in copper coinage.

True paper money (i.e., designed to be in widespread use as legal tender) came a bit later in Chinese history. In the early 1100s during the Song Dynasty, the government took over the money-making industry and created the first commodity-backed paper money. The paper money soon was accepted and what it was backed by took on a subordinate importance. Thus began an early version of a fiat monetary system. However, similar to bonds, the paper money had a maturity date, after which it was retired.

The Song Dynasty not only invented fiat money, they also were the first to overprint and devalue paper money. By the mid-1100s the financial demands on the Song treasury were extremely high, due to foreign wars and domestic revolts. As is quite typical of the declines of empires, rather than increasing taxes or cutting spending, which they didn't want to do because it would have increased discontent, they printed fiat currency to fund their deficits. Initially, the monetization of deficits was manageable—the first fiat currency, known as huizi notes, was issued in modest quantities starting in 1160 and traded at near face value for more than 30 years. But the Song government soon

[14] These promissory notes were similar to what today would be called a bill of exchange. Earlier promissory notes were denominated in variable units, but eventually government-issued notes were in fixed denominations. The government office issued these notes (known as jiaozi and huizi) in exchange for cash coins.

printed more freely, more than tripling the amount of huizi in circulation. As internal and external conflicts continued to strain the imperial treasury, the money supply nearly tripled again between 1209 and 1231. As a result, the market value of that paper money (measured in specie coins) fell by over 90 percent between 1195 and the 1230s.

The same patterns repeated several more times. The Yuan Dynasty, feeling constrained by metal currency, created a new paper currency (which Marco Polo marveled at), but then overprinted it, causing the currency to eventually collapse. The early Ming Dynasty, also feeling constrained by metal currency, created paper money to provide funds to establish a new state, but then overprinted it, eventually causing the currency to collapse. These are fascinating stories I won't delve into now.

Following the failure of fiat money at the start of the Ming Dynasty, China gave up experimentation with paper currencies until the 20th century. Instead, from the mid-14th century to around 1933, China had different types of metal coins, primarily silver. The intrinsic value of that silver constituted the significant majority of their value, though there was some premium placed on the coins themselves. For a major portion of that time, largely up until 1933, China didn't mint, and the coins came first from Spain, then Mexico, then North America. In 1933, the Chinese chose to create their own national coinage, which began to circulate. Two years later, the Chinese government decided to replace the yuan with the fabi (which means "legal tender"), in order to move from a currency they couldn't print to one they could. The fabi in turn experienced increasingly rampant hyperinflation due to overprinting by the Republic of China government in World War II and the final phases of the Chinese Civil War that followed. Following the foundation of the People's Republic of China (PRC), the renminbi was introduced and remains in use to this day.

As for China's broader economy, it went from being primarily agricultural and feudal through a variety of manufacturing incarnations, such as the Bronze Age and the Iron Age, and developed various approaches to trading with foreigners (most importantly through the Silk Road). This gave rise to a rich merchant class, producing cycles in which big wealth gaps developed followed by uprisings in which their wealth was seized. Since China has always been an intelligent and industrious society, numerous technological inventions moved its economy forward. Private entrepreneurial businesses also arose at different times in China's history, producing cycles in which wealth disparities grew, until governments expropriated and redistributed wealth in countless ways. China experienced debt cycles like those described in Chapter 3 as well, which took place for the same reasons. There were stable periods within these big debt cycles when debt growth wasn't excessive; bubble periods when it was; crisis periods when there wasn't enough money to service debt; and inflationary (and sometimes hyperinflationary) periods when money was printed to alleviate the debt crises.

It's interesting to note that while the most powerful empires had global reserve currencies, this has not been true for China's most powerful dynasties.

That is because:

- In the years prior to frequent oceanic travel, there was no such thing as a global reserve currency (trade was limited and generally conducted in precious metals), and throughout its history, China never became such an extensive empire (i.e., a "world power") that a large portion of the world wanted to transact with and hold its promissory notes as storeholds of wealth. China never established a financial center rivaling those in Europe, and it was much less commercial. While China was ahead in financial market development in the Song Dynasty (establishing the first stock companies and using paper currency), by the 1600s financial/capital market developments in China were far behind those in Europe. Culturally, being commercial was not held in high regard by China's leaders so there was less development of the commercial legal system and the financial markets. Because of that lesser commercial development and its more isolationist policies, China generally fell behind Europe in terms of innovation, which we will discuss later.

- Further, China's support for private commerce and financial markets was inconsistent—stronger in the Song and Tang periods and then more hostile in the Ming and Qing, when global trade empires were first being established. As a result, the social and legal structures were less conducive to capital accumulation/investment (e.g., corporate law was much less developed than in Europe and Chinese businesses tended to be family-owned). Also, the state overall was less willing and able to invest in strategic industries or push innovation. Confucian ideology probably played a role in this, as merchants/businesspeople were of lower status compared to scholars, a viewpoint that strengthened as more conservative strains of Confucianism gained sway in the Ming and Qing dynasties.

Debt grew dramatically during the civil unrest and wars of the 1920s and '30s, which led to the classic cycle in which promises to deliver money far exceed capacities to do so. This caused widespread defaults, which classically led to the abandonment of the metal standard and the outlawing of metal coins and private ownership of silver. As previously explained, **currencies are used for 1) domestic transactions, which the government has a monopoly in controlling (and hence can be carried out with fiat or even flimflam currencies) and 2) international transactions, in which case the currencies must be of real value or they won't be accepted. The test of the real value of a currency is whether it is actively used and traded at the same exchange rate internationally as domestically. When there are capital controls that prevent the free exchange of a domestic currency internationally, that currency is more susceptible to being devalued. By definition reserve currencies have no such controls. So, as a principle:** ● ***when you see capital controls being put on a currency, especially when there is a big domestic debt problem, run from that currency.***

China had two currencies in the 1930s—a fiat paper one for domestic transactions, and a gold one for international payments. The fiat paper one was printed abundantly and frequently devalued. After the turbulence of World War II and the Chinese Civil War, in December 1948, the first renminbi was issued as a fiat currency and it was kept in limited supply to end the hyperinflation. In 1955, a second issuance of renminbi was made, and in 1962 a third. From 1955 to 1971 the exchange rate was fixed at 2.46 to the US dollar. Then there was another round of high inflation in the 1970s and '80s, which was caused by the global devaluation of money against gold in 1971, global inflationary pressures, China phasing out its price controls, easy credit, and a lack of spending controls among state-owned enterprises. In 2005, the peg to the dollar was ended.

The next chart shows Chinese inflation rates going back to 1750, including the periods of hyperinflation. The era of relatively stable inflation early on was largely the result of China using metals (silver and copper) as money, which were valued by weight. When the Qing Dynasty broke down, provinces declared independence and issued their own silver and copper coins, which were also valued by their weights. This is why there were not exceptionally high levels of inflation, even during this terrible period.

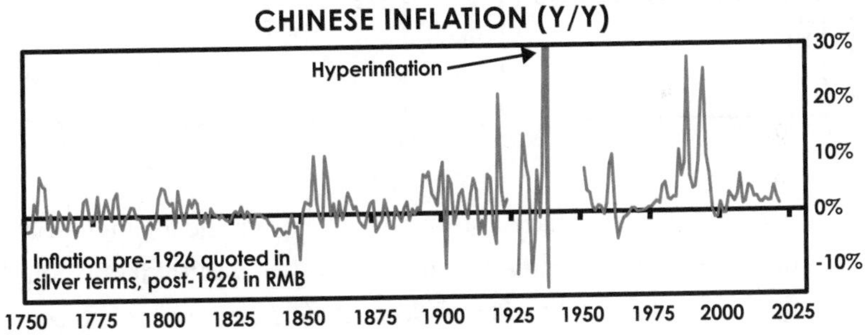

The following charts show the value of Chinese currency in dollar and gold terms since 1920, plus the inflation and growth rates over that period. As you can see, there were two major periods of devaluation: the first when the new exchange rate was set up in 1948, and between 1980 and the 1990s when there was a series of devaluations aimed to support exporters and manage current account deficits,[15] which caused very high inflation. As shown, growth was relatively fast and erratic until around 1978, then fast and much less erratic until the recent brief plunge due to the COVID-19 pandemic.

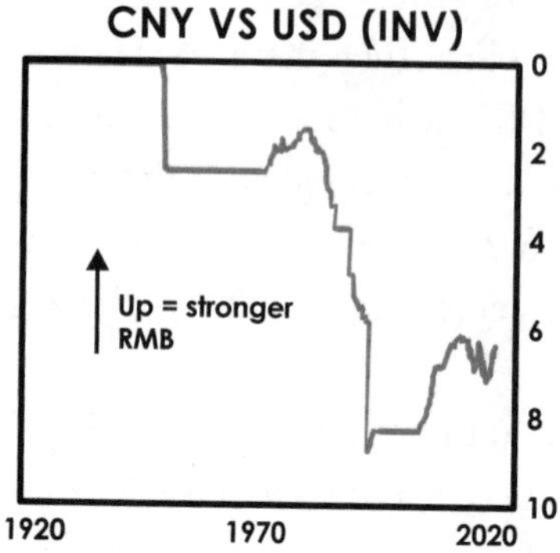

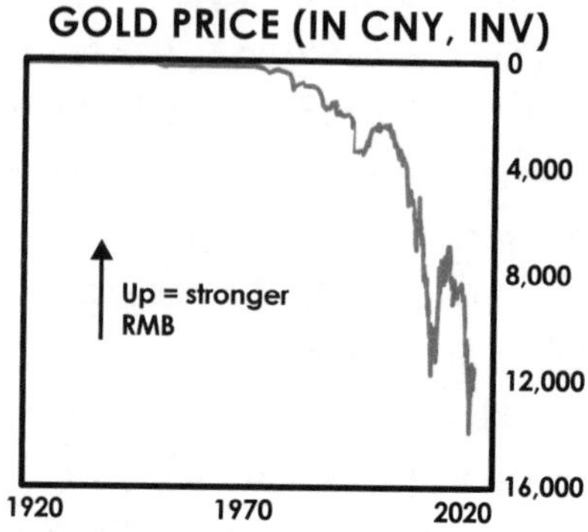

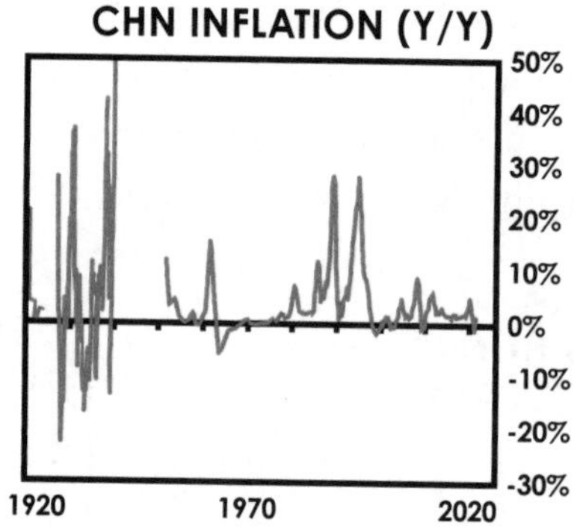

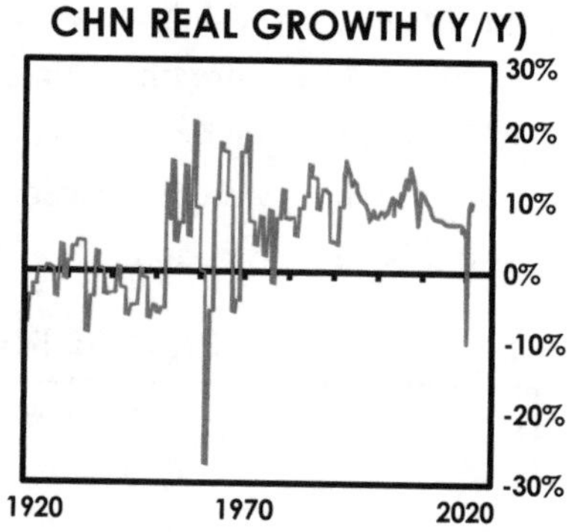

While most Chinese have a strong desire to save and an appropriate sense of risk that innately drives them to store their wealth in safe liquid assets (e.g., cash deposits) and tangible assets (e.g., real estate and some gold), some investors have limited experiences with riskier assets such as equities and risky debt and so can be naïve, though they are learning

[15] The devaluations in 1985–86 and 1993 came after a period of opening up trade and an expansion in Special Economic Zones. These openings created immense demand for foreign currency and imports to build production capacity—but it would still be a couple more years before those zones yielded much higher exports. That mismatch contributed to China's growing current account deficit.

very fast. But when it comes to Chinese policy makers' understanding of money, credit, monetary policy, fiscal policy, and how to restructure bad debts, I have found them to have the same kinds of deep and timeless perspectives that they have for the rest of their history.

FROM 1800 UNTIL NOW

I'll begin with a brief overview of the period between 1800 and the foundation of the People's Republic of China in 1949, examine the Mao period a bit more closely, then take a deeper look at the period spanning the rise of Deng Xiaoping (from 1978 to 1997) and the advent of Xi Jinping (in 2012) until now. Then, in the next chapter, we will look at US-China relations.

The Decline from 1800 until 1949

China's post-1800 decline began when a) the last Chinese royal dynasty (the Qing Dynasty) became decadent and weak at the same time that b) the British and some other Western countries became strong, which led British and other capitalist/colonialists to increasingly take control of China economically. Meanwhile, c) China's financial and monetary system broke down under the burden of debts that couldn't be paid and the printing of money that caused a collapse in its value, while d) there were massive domestic rebellions and civil wars.[16] That severe Big Cycle decline, in which all the major strengths were in mutually reinforcing free falls, continued from around 1840 until 1949. The end of World War II in 1945 led to the repatriation of most foreigners in China (except for Hong Kong and Taiwan) and a civil war to determine how the wealth and power would be divided—i.e., a war between the communists and the

[16] The massive Taiping Rebellion—one of the bloodiest wars in human history, which led to an estimated 20–30 million killed—caused a giant fiscal crisis that led to an issuance of debt that got monetized and led to high inflation.

capitalists—on the Chinese mainland. **This long period of decline was a classic case of the archetypical Big Cycle, and it was followed by an equally classic case of a Big Cycle upswing, in which a new leader wins control, consolidates power, and begins building the basic structures that are passed on to succeeding generations, who build on each other's accomplishments.**

As discussed in previous chapters, the early 1800s was the time of Britain's rise and expansion across the globe—which brought the rising British Empire into greater contact with China. The British East India Company wanted tea, silk, and porcelain from China because it was extremely lucrative to sell back home. However, the British didn't have anything that the Chinese wanted to trade for so they had to pay for these goods in silver, which was a global money at the time. When the British began to run out of silver, they smuggled opium into China from India, which they sold for silver, which they then used to pay for Chinese goods. The Chinese fought to stop those sales, which led to the First Opium War, in which **the technologically superior British Navy defeated the Chinese in 1839–42, leading Britain to impose a treaty that gave the British Hong Kong and opened up a number of Chinese ports, most notably Shanghai, to traders from Britain (as well as other powers in subsequent treaties), which eventually led to the loss of large parts of northern China to Russia and Japan and the loss of what we now call Taiwan to Japan**.

The Qing government borrowed heavily from foreigners to fight internal rebellions. Reparations, especially after the Boxer Rebellion (a Chinese rebellion against foreigners in 1901), also created huge liabilities. When the rebellion failed, the victorious foreign powers demanded the equivalent of about 18,000 tons of silver, which was structured around a 40-year debt that was guaranteed by the tariff income on the ports they controlled. The Qing government, starved of financial resources, faced many uprisings over the couple decades following the Opium Wars and spent down their savings to finance fighting them. **The combination of 1) not having strong leadership, 2) not having sound finances, 3) having internal rebellions that undermined productivity and were**

costly in money and lives, 4) fighting foreigners, which was costly financially and in lives, and 5) experiencing some big disruptive acts of nature produced the mutually and self-reinforcing decline known as the Century of Humiliation.

It is easy to see the important role that period has played in shaping Chinese leaders' perspectives—e.g., why Mao saw capitalism as a system in which companies pursued profits through imperialism (i.e., through the control and exploitation of countries, just as the British and other capitalist powers did to China), enriching the greedy elites while exploiting workers. Mao's view of capitalism differs from my own because his experience with it was so different, though both of our views of it are true. Capitalism has provided me and most others I know, including immigrants from all over the world, with enormous opportunities. The America I came of age in was the land of opportunity, in which one could learn, contribute, and be rewarded fairly and without boundaries. This experience of seeing through another's eyes was another reminder for me of how important radical open-mindedness and thoughtful disagreement are to finding out what is true. It led me to study Marxism a bit, so I could understand why it made sense to Mao and others as a philosophy. My inclination up until then was to think of it as at best impractical and at worst a potentially evil threat, yet I was ignorant about what Marx had actually said.

Enter Marxism-Leninism

Before I examined it for myself, I'd assumed that Marxism-Leninism was a dysfunctional system in which resources were theoretically distributed "from each according to his abilities, to each according his needs" that failed to produce much because of its lack of incentives to be inventive and efficient. I didn't appreciate that Marx was a brilliant man who came up with some good theories and some seemingly bad ones that he would probably agree were not adequately tested and refined by the evolutionary system he espoused. Now I wonder how

Marx, a very practical man who believed that philosophies should only be judged by the successes and failures they produce, would have diagnosed communism's near total and universal failure and changed his thinking as a result.

Marx's most important theory/system is called "dialectical materialism." "Dialectical" refers to how opposites interact to produce change, and "materialism" means that everything has a material (i.e., physical) existence that interacts with other things in a mechanical way. **In a nutshell, dialectical materialism is a system for producing change by observing and influencing the "contradictions" of "opposites" that produce "struggles" that, when resolved, produce progress. Marx meant it to apply to everything. The conflict and struggle between the classes that is manifest in the conflict between capitalism and communism is just one of many such examples.**

Much of that sounds right to me.

Though I'm no expert on Marxism, the process of dialectical materialism is similar to the process that I discovered for myself and explained in my book *Principles: Life and Work*, in which I struggle with conflicts, reflect on them, write down the principles I derive from them, and then improve them—and do that over and over again, in a never-ending, evolutionary way that I describe as "looping." In other words, I believe, and it sounds like Marx believed, that learning and evolving from conflicts and mistakes is the best approach.

It is also my opinion that capitalism—an incentive system that rewards the people who are most inventive and productive, and that has capital markets that reward good capital allocation decisions and penalizes bad ones—will lead to a) more productivity over the long run (and hence a bigger total pie), b) big wealth differences, and c) capital markets (especially debt markets) that become overextended and then break down. When there is a capital market/economic breakdown at the same time that there are big wealth and values disparities, that is likely to lead to some form of revolution. Such revolutions can end harmoniously and productively, but most are preceded by great conflict and destruction. So, thus far the way Marx appeared to see things and the way I see things aren't radically different, though what we would choose and what we would think should be done are probably radically different. If you asked me a) whether I'd rather have what capitalism has delivered or what communism delivered and b) if I think the capitalist path we have now is more logical than the communist path we have seen, I'd choose capitalism as my answer to both. On the other hand, if you asked me a) if both the capitalist and the communist systems need to be reformed to make the pie grow more effectively and to be distributed more fairly and b) if Marx's dialectical materialism approach to evolving and my 5-Step Process to evolving are broadly similar and the best ways of evolving well, I would say yes to both questions (without getting hung up on how, exactly, our two approaches are different). Also, as far as the wealth gap goes, I share the view that it has been a big issue throughout history that can threaten all systems. I too believe that conflicts produce struggle and that working through struggle produces progress. I consider the conflicts between the classes (i.e., the "haves" and the "have-nots") to be among the main drivers of the rise and decline of empires, and hence the progress of history, with those drivers being the three big cycles—money and credit, internal order/disorder, and external order/disorder—discussed earlier in this book.

All of those cycles across the leading countries were in their decline/conflict phases between 1930 and 1945, which led to revolutions and wars in China and all over the world. But as always happens, the forces of decline ran their course and new domestic and world orders began. More specifically, the external war ended in 1945 and foreign forces left most of mainland China. China's communists and capitalists then fought an internal war that ended in 1949, which led to a new domestic order, which was communism under Mao. Put yourself in Mao's position during the 1900–49 period. Imagine him reading what Marx wrote, and think about his actions during that period and in the post-1949 period. It makes sense that Mao was a Marxist and held the established Confucian approach to harmony in disdain. Democracy as we know it doesn't have any roots in China. Legalism, with its autocratic approach, does. Capitalism, on the other hand, is

growing and becoming much more deeply rooted today.

Lenin built on what Marx said to create a two-step process for building the state, in which there is at first a vanguard of workers though "democratic centralism" (in which only members of the party vote), which eventually leads to a higher communist state in which there is common ownership of the means of production, social and economic equality, and general prosperity. **Mao liked the Marxist-Leninist approach, in which the achievement of the communist ideal came at the end of a very long evolutionary process. Deng Xiaoping reiterated this view in an interview with "60 Minutes" in 1986, in which he said that the capitalism he was adopting and communism were not incompatible. "According to Marxism," he said, "communist society is based on material abundance . . . Only when there is material abundance can the principle of a communist society—'from each according to his ability, to each according to his needs'—be applied. Socialism is the first stage of communism . . . " Maybe that's true and maybe it's not. Time will tell.** To me, thus far capitalism—in China or anywhere else—is winning the competition. However, there can be no question that the Chinese mix of communism and capitalism has produced remarkable economic results over the last 40 years.

In the next section I will very briefly summarize what happened between 1949 and now. Then I will delve into each of its phases in greater detail.

The Rise from 1949 until Now

Though it's a bit of an oversimplification, we can think of China's evolution from 1949 until now as occurring in three phases:

1. **The Mao phase, from 1949 to 1976.**
2. **The Deng and Deng's successors phase, from 1978 to 2012 when Xi Jinping came to power.**
3. **The Xi Jinping phase from 2012 until now.**

Each phase moved China along the arc of its long-term development, building on its earlier accomplishments. In brief, events transpired as follows:

- **From 1949 until he died in 1976, Mao (with his various ministers, most importantly Zhou Enlai) consolidated power; built China's foundation of institutions, governance, and infrastructure; and ruled China as a communist emperor.** Isolated from the rest of the world, China followed a strict communist system in which the government owned everything and maintained tight bureaucratic controls. Immediately following the deaths of Mao and Zhou Enlai, there was a power struggle in 1976–78 between the Gang of Four hardliners and the reformists. Deng Xiaoping and the reformists emerged victorious in 1978, leading to the second phase.
- **Deng and his ministers ran China directly or indirectly until his death in 1997.** During this phase China moved to a more collective leadership model, opened up to the outside world, introduced and developed market/capitalist practices, and became much stronger financially and more powerful in other ways that didn't appear threatening to the United States or to other countries. To finance what was then viewed as a symbiotic relationship in which the US bought items that were attractively priced from China, China lent Americans money. As a result, the US acquired US dollar-denominated debt liabilities and the Chinese acquired dollar-denominated assets. After Deng's death his successors Jiang Zemin and Hu Jintao (and those who led China with them) continued in the same direction so China's wealth and power grew in fundamentally sound ways that did not appear threatening to the US. In 2008, the global financial crisis came along, which led to greater tensions over wealth in the United States and other developed countries, increased resentment at the flight of manufacturing jobs to China, and increased debt-financed growth in all countries, including China.

- **Xi Jinping came to power in 2012, presiding over a richer, more powerful China that was becoming overly indebted, too corrupt, and increasingly at odds with the United States.** He accelerated economic reforms, took on the challenge of trying to contain debt growth while aggressively reforming the economy, supported the building of leading technologies, and took an increasingly global stance. He also became more proactive in reducing China's gaps in education and its income inequality, in protecting the environment, and in consolidating political control. As China's powers grew and Xi's bold objectives (e.g., the Belt and Road Initiative and the Made in China 2025 plan) became more apparent, tensions with the US rose, especially after Donald Trump was elected president (a populist/nationalist who campaigned on stanching the US's loss of manufacturing jobs to China). China's position vis-à-vis the US became one of a rapidly strengthening power challenging the dominant one.

Now let's take a closer look.

Phase One: Building the Foundation (1949–1976)

Mao and the communists won the civil war and started the People's Republic of China in 1949 and quickly consolidated power. Mao became the de facto emperor (titled "chairman of the People's Republic of China") and Zhou Enlai his prime minister (titled "premier"). Domestically, the new government quickly repaired transportation and communications infrastructure and nationalized the banking system under the aegis of the new central bank, the People's Bank of China. To bring down inflation it tightened credit and stabilized the value of the currency. The government also nationalized most businesses and redistributed agricultural land from large landowners to the peasants who farmed the land. Whether one worked or not, one received basic pay. There was no merit-based pay. The protections that these guaranteed basic incomes and benefits provided everyone were collectively called "the iron rice bowl." These changes created a stable economy but little motivation.

Internationally, China was isolationist, though it wasn't long before the new government found itself in a war. As explained in the last chapter, in 1945 the new world order divided the world into two main ideological camps—the democratic capitalists led by the United States and the autocratic communists led by the Soviet Union—with a third group of countries that were not committed to either side. Many of these nonaligned countries had until recently been colonies, most notably under the declining British Empire. China was clearly in the Soviet-led camp. On February 14, 1950, Mao and Stalin signed the Treaty of Friendship, Alliance, and Mutual Assistance to cooperate and come to each other's aid militarily.

At the end of World War II, Korea was divided at the 38th parallel, with the Russians controlling the north and the Americans the south. In June 1950, North Korea invaded South Korea. The Chinese stayed out of the fighting initially, as they were preoccupied with their own challenges and didn't want to be drawn into a war. In conjunction with the United Nations, the United States responded by bringing its forces into the fighting, taking the war into North Korea, which borders China. The Chinese viewed this as a threat, especially since US General Douglas MacArthur made it clear that he would attack China. Though the Soviets and the Chinese had a pact to support each other, Stalin didn't want to go war with the United States so he didn't provide China with the military support it expected. Though the Chinese were ill-prepared for war against the much greater (and nuclear-armed) American power, the Chinese entered the war, pushing the American and UN troops back to the previously established border. This was Mao's first great challenge, and it is considered a great victory by the Chinese.

Between the PRC's founding in 1949 and Mao's death in 1976, the Chinese economy grew rather quickly, at an average annual rate of about 6 percent, with an average annual inflation rate of

around 1–2 percent, accumulating around $4 billion dollars in foreign exchange reserves. This represented a modest improvement, but China remained poor. And there was a lot of volatility along the way. Specifically:

- Between 1952 and 1957, with the help of the Soviets, industrial production grew at 19 percent a year, national income grew at 9 percent a year, and agricultural production grew by 4 percent a year. The Chinese government built industrial facilities and imported lots of equipment from the Soviets. It also reformed its agricultural practices and methods by creating cooperatives to achieve economies of scale by having farmers work together. These were highly productive years. However, after Stalin's death in 1953, Nikita Khrushchev came to power, criticized Stalin and his policies, and alienated Mao, which led to these Chinese and Soviet leaders openly criticizing each other, which began a period of reduced Soviet support.
- Around 1960 the Soviet Union shifted from being an ally to being an enemy and withdrew economic support.
- From 1958 through 1962, due to a drought, economic mismanagement from the top-down mandated attempt to become an industrial power called the Great Leap Forward, and reduced Soviet economic support, the economy contracted by 25 percent and an estimated 16–40 million people died of famine. Estimates suggest that over that period industrial output fell by 19 percent in aggregate, with a fall of around 36 percent from the 1959 peak. Historians agree that it was a terrible period, though there is some disagreement about how much it was terrible because of terrible management by Mao versus other causes.
- Between 1963 and 1966, the economy recovered and went to new highs. But then came the Cultural Revolution.

As is classic in all cycles, challenges to Mao's leadership and ideology arose. Since most Chinese emperors were taken down by insiders, this risk had to be on Mao's mind (and everyone else's). So from 1966 until 1976, he fostered a political revolution, called the Cultural Revolution, to "purify class ranks" and reinforce "Mao Zedong Thought." Mao won the political/ideological battle, purging his rival Lin Biao, who died in a plane crash during a botched coup he was accused of organizing, and "Mao Zedong Thought" was written into the constitution. The cost of Mao's triumph was appalling. The Cultural Revolution curtailed education and damaged or cost countless lives (estimates range from hundreds of thousands to as many as 20 million dead) and dealt a huge blow to the Chinese economy. By the early 1970s the situation had begun to stabilize under the operational leadership of Premier Zhou Enlai. In 1969, there were clashes between Chinese and Russian troops along the border.

1971 was a year of great change in China. The Cultural Revolution was producing turmoil and Mao's health was declining. That contributed to Zhou Enlai playing an increasing leadership role from the background, which led to him being elected "vice chairman of the Communist Party" in 1973, putting him in the position of appearing to be Mao's successor. Also in 1971 China was threatened by the Soviet Union, which was militarily much more powerful and shared a 2,500-mile border with China, leading to increasing border threats. In 1975, after the US withdrew from Vietnam, which shares a 900-mile border with southern China, Russia built an alliance with Vietnam and moved in troops and arms. Mao had a geopolitical principle to identify the main enemy, neutralize the enemy's allies, and draw them away from the enemy. Mao identified the Soviet Union as China's main enemy and recognized that the Soviets were in a war with the United States that hadn't yet turned hot but could. That led him to make the strategic move of approaching the US. Henry Kissinger quoted Chinese officials as saying, "The last thing the US imperialists are willing to see is a victory by Soviet revisionists in a Sino-Soviet war, as this would [allow the Soviets] to build up a big empire more powerful than the American empire in resources and manpower."

I also know that Zhou Enlai, a reformist, had wanted to build a strategic relationship with the United States for decades because a close Chinese friend of mine, Ji Chaozhu, who was Zhou Enlai's interpreter for 17 years and interpreted in the first Kissinger-Zhou Enlai talks, told me that that was the case.[17] China wanted to open a relationship with the United States to neutralize the Russian threat and to enhance its geopolitical and economic position. **Because in 1971 it was especially clear that it was in the interests of China and the United States to build a relationship, they both made overtures to establish relations.** In July 1971 Kissinger—and then in February 1972 President Richard Nixon—went to China and in October 1971 the United Nations recognized the Mao-led communist Chinese government and gave China a seat on the Security Council. **During Nixon's visit, Nixon and Zhou Enlai signed an agreement—the Shanghai Communique—in which the US stated that it "acknowledges that all Chinese on either side of the Taiwan Strait maintain that there is but one China and that Taiwan is part of China.** The United States government does not challenge that position. It reaffirms its interest in a peaceful settlement of the Taiwan question by the Chinese themselves." **Despite those assurances, reunification with Taiwan still remains the most consistently contentious issue between China and the US.**

Following those moves of rapprochement, US relations with China and trade and other exchanges began.

Then, in January and September 1976, first Zhou Enlai and then Mao died and communist China faced its first succession crisis. From 1976 to 1978, there was a fight for power between the Gang of Four (hardline conservatives who fostered the Cultural Revolution) and the reformists (who wanted economic modernization and

[17] Ji Chaozhu was raised in the United States until he was a junior at Harvard. His brother was close to Zhou Enlai, who sent the brother and Ji Chaozhu to the United States to try to build good relations with Americans. When the Korean War broke out he returned to China, became Zhou's interpreter, and later served in the first Chinese delegation to the UN and as China's ambassador to England. While he told me a lot that I won't discuss to respect his privacy, I don't believe that this is sensitive information.

an opening up to the outside world). The reformists won, and Deng Xiaoping became the paramount leader in 1978.

Phase Two: Deng and His Successors Gain Strengths Through Economic Reforms and Opening Up Without Creating Threats to Other Countries (1978–2012)

Deng Xiaoping was 74, with a wealth of experience under his belt. From 1978 until he died in 1997 his most important policies were conveyed in a single phrase: reform and opening up. "Reform" meant market reforms, using markets to help allocate resources and incentivize people, and "opening up" meant interacting with the outside world to learn, improve, and trade. Capitalism became a part of the communist mix. China was still extremely poor—its per capita income was less than $200 a year. Deng knew these moves would make China financially stronger if they were not disrupted by the far stronger foreign powers who wanted China to remain weak; the key was to pursue them in ways that benefited and didn't threaten them. **In 1979, he established full diplomatic relations with the US.**

Early on, Deng set out a 70-year plan to a) double incomes and ensure that the population would have enough food and clothing by the end of the 1980s, b) quadruple GDP per capita by the end of the 20th century (which was achieved in 1995, five years ahead of schedule), and c) increase per capita GDP to the levels of medium-level developed countries by 2050 (on the 100th anniversary of the PRC). He made it clear that China would achieve those goals by having a "socialist market economy," which he also referred to as "socialism with Chinese characteristics." He made that radical shift without criticizing Marxism-Leninism; indeed, as noted earlier, he did not see the two systems as fundamentally at odds, but rather viewed them through the lens of dialectical materialism, as opposites that could be resolved, leading to progress along the long arc toward communism's ideal state.

During his term, Deng also reformed the decision-making

structure of government. More specifically, he moved its decision-making process from one that was dominated by a single leader (previously Mao) to one in which the Politburo Standing Committee took votes when a consensus couldn't be reached. He also changed the system of choosing the standing members of the Politburo from one in which the supreme leader personally selected them to one in which candidates—generally qualified government officials—were chosen via consultation and negotiation with experienced party elders. To institutionalize his governing philosophy, Deng shaped the new Chinese constitution, which was adopted in 1982. This new constitution also made a number of changes to facilitate the economic reforms and open-door policies that Deng wanted. It established term limits for leaders (two five-year terms) and discouraged autocratic decision making by formalizing his "collective leadership/democratic centralist" policies. The new constitution also provided for greater freedom of religion, opinion, speech, and the press, to encourage the Chinese to "seek truth from facts." **These reforms enabled the first orderly transition of power to the next-generation Politburo Standing Committee, led by Jiang Zemin, and then on to Hu Jintao, with their transitions following the prescribed two five-year terms. Each successive leadership team kept to Deng's basic path of making China richer and more powerful by making its economy more market-driven/capitalist and by increasing China's trade with and learning from other countries, with those in other countries feeling more excited than threatened by their interactions and trade with China.**

Regaining territories it lost during its Century of Humiliation was also a very important long-term goal. In 1984, after a lot of haggling with the UK, it was agreed that Hong Kong would return to Chinese sovereignty in 1997, with a "one country, two systems" approach. Then in 1986, China reached an agreement with Portugal to obtain Macau's return to Chinese sovereignty in 1999.

In 1984, I had my first direct contact with China. I visited China at the invitation of the China International Trust Investment

Corporation (CITIC), China's only "window company" (which meant that it was allowed to deal freely with the outside world), whose leaders had asked me to help them understand how world financial markets work. The company had been set up as an extension of Deng's reform and opening-up policies and was run by Rong Yiren, an old Chinese capitalist who had chosen to stay in China even after his family's business was nationalized.

China was very poor and backward then. However, it was immediately clear to me that its people were smart and civilized and its poverty was widely shared. In this regard, it wasn't like most other undeveloped countries I'd been to, where the poor seemed to live in a different century. China's backwardness stemmed from a general lack of access to what was available in the outside world and from its demotivating system. For example, I gave out $10 calculators as gifts, and even the highest-ranking people thought they were miraculous devices. At the time, all businesses (including small restaurants) were government-owned and bureaucratic. The Chinese couldn't choose their jobs, never mind their careers, and received no financial incentives for working well. There was no private ownership of property, such as one's home, and there was no contact with what the world had to offer in terms of best practices and products.

Because it was clear to me that the closed door was the reason for China's poverty, I believed that its removal would naturally equalize its standards of living with the developed world, just as unconstrained water naturally seeks the same level. It was easy to visualize that happening. I remember being on the 10th floor of CITIC's "Chocolate Building" to give a lecture. I pointed out the window at the two-story *hutongs* (poor neighborhoods) below us and told my audience that it would not be long before they would be gone and skyscrapers would stand in their place. "You don't know China," they said in disbelief. I told them that they did not know the power of the economic arbitrages that would occur as a result of opening up.

While the opening up created a great natural opportunity, the Chinese made the most of it and performed even beyond my highest expectations. They did that by making and implementing Deng's reforms, supported by uniquely Chinese cultural influences. The expressed goal that I heard a lot of in those early days of reform was to "break the iron rice bowl," which was to no longer provide demotivating guaranteed employment and ensured basic benefits and replace them with more incentive-based compensation. Globalization also helped a lot; the world wanted to include China.

Deng was an eager learner and he directed his policy makers to learn from outsiders in the same way that he did. He especially relied on Lee Kuan Yew of Singapore and other leaders of the culturally aligned "Asian Tiger" economies for advice. I remember a dinner with the head of China's MOFTEC (which was their ministry of commerce), in which he rattled off details about the operations of Singapore's airport (including how long a passenger had to wait to get their bags at the baggage claim), how Singapore achieved such great results, and how China was going to implement those practices itself. Many years later I had the opportunity to host Lee Kuan Yew at my house, along with some other esteemed guests. We asked him to share his thoughts about leaders of the present and past. We were eager to get his perspective because he had known most of them over the last 50 years and was one of the greats himself. Without hesitating, he said that Deng was the greatest leader of the 20th century. Why? Because he was smart and wise and open-minded, he was extremely practical, and he delivered great results for his country of a billion people.

While Deng formally stepped down from the Politburo's Standing Committee in 1987, he remained the de facto leader of China, which continued to open up and become more capitalist at a breakneck pace. I played a small part in its evolution over the years. In 1989, my CITIC friend Wang Li (who was responsible for bond trading) introduced me to the group of people who, along with her, had been designated to create the organization that would set up the first stock markets in the new China (the Stock Exchange Executive Council, known as SEEC). They had been appointed by seven companies at the request of the visionary economic reformer and historian Wang Qishan.

China was still very poor, and SEEC's office was in a dingy hotel because the group lacked adequate funding. Still, they had what mattered most—a clear mission to create big changes, smart people of good character, open-mindedness to allow rapid learning, and determination to achieve their goals. This was not a job to them; it was a noble mission to improve their country. I was thrilled to help them. And over the decades that followed, I saw how they and many others built the Chinese financial markets to become among the largest in the world.

Then, a shock happened that led everyone to question just about everything. In 1989, a movement to democratize China grew into the demonstrations that led to the crackdown known as the Tiananmen Square incident. The leadership was split on how to handle the movement. Deng made the defining choice, which was to sideline the liberal forces and go ahead with the conservatives' crackdown. Most Chinese people I spoke with at the time were worried that China would slip back into its old Mao/Gang-of-Four-type ways. A very close friend from CITIC, Madame Gu, whose brother was China's minister of defense, happened to be staying with my family at the time, so I saw events unfold through her eyes as well as through the eyes of other Chinese friends. Madame Gu had been an idealistic follower of Mao in the early years after "liberation." When the Cultural Revolution came along she lost her husband to persecution and was shunned by friends. She got past that terrible experience to work on behalf of the country she loved and rose to a senior job at CITIC. She cried at the prospect of a return to those terrible old days. Tiananmen Square significantly set back most countries' relationships with China, but it didn't keep Deng and his government from continuing their reforms. Over time, most of my Chinese friends who were heartbroken about the crackdown came to believe that the government had made the right move because their greatest fear was revolutionary disorder.

Over the next decade, the economy continued its strong growth, and relations and trade with the West became better than ever. Globalization, which helped China immensely, can be said to have begun in 1995 with the formation of the World Trade Organization (the epoch effectively ended with the election of Donald Trump in 2016). China joined the WTO in 2001 and its position in world trade soared. That year, the United States had more trade than China with 80 percent of WTO member countries. Now China is a larger trading partner than the United States for about 70 percent of those countries.

During this period of globalization, a symbiotic relationship developed between China and the US in which the Chinese manufactured consumer goods in an extremely cost-effective way and loaned the US money to buy them. It was a hell of a "buy now, pay later" deal for the Americans, and the Chinese liked it because they built their savings in the world's reserve currency. It struck me as odd that the Chinese, who were earning about a 40th of Americans on average, would be lending money to Americans, since rich people are in a better position to lend than poor ones. To me, it was a shocking reflection of how deeply Americans were willing to get into debt to finance their overconsumption and how much more the Chinese valued saving. It was also a reflection of how emerging countries that want to save in the bonds/debt of the leading reserve currency countries can lead those countries to become overindebted.

In 1992, China's "triangular" debt crisis came to a head. These were debt and economic problems that arose from China's five major government-owned banks lending to large, inefficient, and unprofitable state-owned enterprises with the implicit guarantee of the central government. Zhu Rongji, a bold reformer at the top of the party, led the efforts to restructure the economy to become more efficient. This process was extremely controversial and hurt a lot of people who had benefited from the old system, so it took a lot of courage and intelligence, as well as support from the top, to execute. Best practices (e.g., using "bad banks" to take, sell off, and wind down the bad debts) were used and modified for the Chinese environment. Zhu became premier in 1998 and in that capacity continued to aggressively pursue reforms to modernize and make the Chinese economy more efficient, until he retired in 2003. Many of his former aides are among China's senior economic policy makers today.

In 1995, I sent my 11-year-old son Matt to China, where he lived with Madame Gu and her husband and attended what was then a poor local school (*Shi Jia Hu Tong Xiao Xue*). Matt had been to China with me many times since he was 3 years old and had gotten to know Madame Gu well. He didn't speak the language, so he would have to learn through immersion, which he did. Though his school was poor (for example, there wasn't heat until late November, so students wore their coats in class), it had smart and caring teachers who provided the children with an excellent, complete education that included character development. Though Matt was deprived of some comforts he was used to (he couldn't take hot showers because the old apartment building he lived in only had hot water two days a week, for example), he was superbly educated, loved, and better developed than he would have been in our rich community. He built deep attachments with his teachers and friends that still exist. The experience led him to set up a foundation to help Chinese orphans that he ran for 12 years. Around that time I also **hired a Chinese team to invest American institutional money in Chinese businesses. I pursued the effort for a couple of years but had to discontinue it because I found it too difficult to run it and Bridgewater at the same time.**

In 1995–96 it became widely known that Deng's health was failing. Chinese leaders worried that his death would be viewed as an opportunity to challenge Chinese authority. They were especially worried that the Taiwanese would hold a referendum in favor of independence. President Lee Teng-hui, whom China regarded as a pro-independence leader, had just made a controversial visit to the US, shortly in advance of his nomination for Taiwan's 1996 presidential election. Madame Gu knew the Chinese official in charge of relations with Taiwan and arranged for me to meet with him. He told me that China would do anything, including going to war, to prevent Taiwanese independence. Should a new Chinese leader permit a referendum, he explained, the Chinese people would regard him as too weak to lead. China had seen how Russia's brutal suppression of rebels in the Chechen Republic had led to reduced support for independence; the

Chinese hoped that a series of missile tests in the Taiwan Strait would similarly dampen Taiwan's enthusiasm. In March 1996, President Bill Clinton, who was facing re-election, sent two aircraft carriers into the Taiwan Strait. Further military movements and threats on both sides followed. At the end of the day, the Taiwanese never held the referendum, so my Chinese friends thought their moves had been successful, while the Americans believed that they had humiliated the Chinese (which I only recently found out from an American friend who was involved in the decision to send in the American warships). As a result of the "Third Taiwan Strait Crisis," the Chinese significantly built up their military capabilities in the region. I point this out to convey a) how important Taiwan's reunification with China is and b) how risky the situation was 25 years ago, when China was not nearly as strong militarily as it is now. In short, **I would worry a lot if we were to see a "Fourth Taiwan Strait Crisis."**

Deng died on February 19, 1997, having transformed China almost beyond recognition. When he came to power, 90 percent of the population lived in extreme poverty; at the time of his death that number had fallen by more than half, and as of the most recent data is below 1 percent. From the start of his reforms in 1978 until his death in 1997, the Chinese economy grew at an average rate of 10 percent a year, sextupling in size while experiencing an average inflation rate of just 8 percent. Its reserves grew from $4 billion to nearly $150 billion (inflation-adjusted to today's dollars, its reserves grew by over $250 billion). Those reserves covered 60 percent of annual imports in 1978. By 1998, they covered more than 125 percent of imports (and nearly 800 percent of foreign debt service).

Deng's successors Jiang Zemin and Hu Jintao and their teams continued the reforms and the advances through many ups and downs (though more ups than downs). In 1997, the Asian financial crisis came along. With Zhu Rongji assigned to run the effort, China did a very successful debt and corporate restructuring, which included sales of unprofitable state-owned enterprises, the building up of exports and foreign exchange reserves, a crackdown on corruption, and the further development and improvement of markets and market functioning. These and other changes were all important evolutionary steps. I felt lucky to be intimately involved at the grassroots level with some of them—e.g., the debt restructuring and asset sales. Though these events seemed bigger at the time than they appear in retrospect, they were all significant achievements. I also ran into cases of corruption and bad behavior, and witnessed close-up the ongoing struggle between the good and the bad that led to further reforms.

As is typical of post-war periods of peace and prosperity, when the leading power isn't threatened and emerging countries aren't yet threatening, emerging countries can learn a lot from the leading powers as they work together in a symbiotic way, until the emerging power becomes powerful enough to threaten the leading power. In addition to benefiting from the learning, they benefit from trading with each other (until that becomes disadvantageous), and they benefit from using the capital markets to their mutual benefit (until that becomes disadvantageous).

More specifically, the 1978–2008 period of fast growth in China came about because 1) the world was still in the peace and prosperity phase of the Big Cycle in which globalization and capitalism—i.e., the belief that goods and services should be produced wherever is most cost-effective, there should be free flows of talented people without prejudice toward their nationalities, nationalism is bad, and global equal opportunity and profit-seeking capitalism are good—were understood to be the widely accepted paths to a better world, while at the same time 2) Deng Xiaoping swung the pendulum from communist and isolationist policies that worked terribly to market/state-capitalist and open-door policies that worked terrifically. That led China to learn a lot, attract a lot of foreign capital, and become a giant exporter and big saver.

As the Chinese became more capable of producing cost-effectively, they provided the world with inexpensive goods at first and more advanced goods later, becoming much richer in the process. Other emerging countries did so as well, the world expanded, and the wealth gaps between the richest countries and the poorest countries narrowed as the poorest countries rose the most while the richest countries grew at slower rates. These circumstances lifted most boats, especially the boats of the global elites. China rose to be a nearly comparable power to the United States, and together they created most of the world's new wealth and new technologies. Europe, which had been the source of the greatest global powers from the 15th to the 20th centuries, became relatively weak, and Japan and Russia became secondary powers. All other countries were peripheral. While emerging countries like India improved their conditions, none of them achieved world power status.

Phase Three: The Emergence of US-China Conflicts and the End of Globalization (2008–Present)

As is classic, periods of prosperity financed by debt growth lead to debt bubbles and large wealth gaps. In the US, the bubble burst in 2008 (as it did in 1929), and the world economy contracted and middle-class Americans and those in other countries were hurt (as in 1929–32). Interest rates were pushed down to 0 percent (as in 1931), which still wasn't enough easing, so central banks printed a lot of money and bought a lot of financial assets after 2008 (like in 1934), which drove up their prices in most countries starting in 2009 (as happened in 1933–36). This benefited the "haves" (people who had financial assets) more than the "have-nots" (those without them) so the wealth gaps grew wider still (as they did in the 1933–38 period). The "have-nots," especially those whose jobs were being taken by the Chinese and immigrants, began to rise up against the elites who were benefiting from globalization. As is typically the case when economic bad times coincide with large wealth gaps, populism and nationalism grew around the world (as they also did in the 1930s). That is when the threat the rising powers pose becomes more apparent to the leading powers. **The era of peace, prosperity, and globalization began to wane, giving way to an era of conflicts between the rich and the poor within countries and between the rising country (China) and the dominant world power (the US).**

The Chinese were holding a lot of US dollar-denominated debt—especially from US government agency lenders Fannie Mae and Freddie Mac. For quite a while, the US government didn't let the Chinese holders of this debt know whether it would stand behind it. I had conversations with top Chinese holders of this debt, as did David McCormick (who is now CEO of Bridgewater and was the US Treasury's undersecretary for international affairs at the time) and Hank Paulson (who was the US Treasury secretary). We were all impressed with the consideration and cooperation with which the Chinese approached the dilemma that the US had caused them. They were calm, empathetic, and cooperative.

In November 2008, leaders of the G20 countries gathered in Washington, DC, and agreed to jointly stimulate their economies through aggressive fiscal and monetary policies. These required a substantial increase of government debt, which was financed by having central banks create more money and credit. **Debt growth in China was significantly faster than economic growth between 2009 and 2012 as a result of those policies.**

Becoming a World Power

In 2012, Xi Jinping came to power and a new administration was chosen. Following the well-established sequence, first Politburo members were chosen, then ministers, vice ministers, and their senior subordinates. Then the first rounds of plans were made. As when most new leaders take power, there was a lot of excitement and an eagerness to strengthen both the rule of law by purging corruption and China's economy by strengthening and adding to its market-based reforms. There were a number of brainstorming sessions, and I was lucky enough to participate in a few. They were wonderful collaborations of people with different perspectives who wanted to help; the frankness, open-mindedness, friendliness, and intelligence that they brought to the table was remarkable.

Since then, I have closely followed China's financial and economic circumstances and have had numerous conversations with its top economic policy makers about such matters as excessive debt growth, the development and management of their shadow banking system, the vulnerabilities in their financial systems, their trade disputes with the US, and more. I always tried to see things from their perspective and think about what I would do if I were in their shoes. I shared what I saw with them as frankly as a doctor discussing a medical case with colleagues, in much the same way as I am sharing it with you in this book.[18] As you probably know by now, I believe that everything works like a machine, with timeless and universal cause/effect relationships. Chinese leaders do too, so we almost always came to similar conclusions.

Over the years, the Xi administration has aggressively pursued policies to reform and open up its markets and its economy; manage its debt growth; more flexibly manage its currency; support entrepreneurship and market-oriented decision making, especially in industries that China wants to be world leaders in; establish sensible regulations run by well-developed regulatory organizations; build its capabilities in the technologies and industries of the future; broaden the economic benefits extended to the people and regions that were lagging the most; and control pollution and environmental degradation. Yet many people don't see it that way, which I suspect is because a) the reforms are coming at the same time as other controls are tightening up, b) some of the supports (like credit availability) for small- and medium-size organizations are not as good as they are for larger state-owned enterprises (which has more to do with technical challenges than any reduced desire to foster the development of small- and medium-size organizations), c) the government directs the economy from the top down, sometimes expecting banks and companies to make uneconomic loans (because it wants to do what is best for the country as a whole), d) China coordinates with its businesses in pursuit of national goals, e) it doesn't let some foreign companies operate on the same terms as Chinese

[18] I never ask questions that put them in the awkward position of having to choose between conveying confidential information and having to decline my request. I make it clear at all times that my sole desire is to understand and help.

companies, and f) it coordinates fiscal and monetary policy to regulate the economy much more than is done in the major reserve currency countries—all of which are typically unpopular with capitalist outsiders.

Certainly many Americans are critical of these policies. While I won't delve into the merits of them, I will say that **we should expect all countries' leaders to try to get the best balance between "state" (government influence and control of the economy) and "capitalism" (free-market control of the economy and capital markets) through the proper management and coordination of monetary and fiscal policies, and we should try to understand the thinking behind their approaches.** For example, President Xi has said he wants to a) reduce the government's role in pricing and allocating resources, develop the capital markets, and stimulate entrepreneurship while also b) strongly directing the macro economy and regulating markets and other aspects of life to be what he and the party believe are best for most Chinese. In other words, he wants a mix of capitalism and Marxist communism. This is understandably confusing to those who aren't used to seeing capitalism and communism go together, aren't watching closely, and haven't spoken with the policy makers to understand their circumstances and perspectives, **so they can't see the consistencies that exist amid the seemingly great inconsistencies (i.e., "the dialectics" as Marx and the Chinese leaders would call them).**

To understand their circumstances and perspectives, I suggest that you not view what they are doing through stereotypes (e.g., of "what communists do") and accept that they are trying, and will continue to try, to juggle these two seemingly inconsistent things. In their view capitalism is a way of raising the living standards of most people and is not meant to serve capitalists. Whether one thinks this approach is good or bad, their results have been extremely impressive so we should not expect the Chinese to abandon it for an American or Western approach. Rather, we should study it to see what we can learn from it, the same way that the Chinese have studied and learned from the West. After all, what we have is a competition of approaches that we need to understand in order to play this competitive game well.

As far as foreign policy is concerned, China has become stronger and more forceful while the United States has become more confrontational. More specifically, from 2012 until the time of my writing China's strengths have grown, which has become increasingly apparent and more openly shown (e.g., the Made in China 2025 plan trumpets its plans to dominate certain industries that the United States currently controls). This has sparked a strong reaction in the US, which became most evident after the election of Donald Trump in 2016.

Trump tapped into the resentments of those left behind by globalization, who believed that China was unfairly competing and stealing their jobs, and nurtured a new spirit of protectionism and nationalism. **It wasn't just Trump. China's strength had become a provocation for more moderate policy makers as well. Where there had been synergy there was now raw competition.**

Basically China does not want to be contained and the United States (and some other countries) want to contain it. What does that mean geopolitically? As you know by now, countries' boundaries have constantly changed over time, they are often in dispute, and international law isn't worth a hill of beans relative to power in resolving these disputes. In 2009 China declared to the United Nations that it has "indisputable sovereignty over" an area in the East and South China Seas. The area is marked by a "nine-dash line" on a World War II era map presented by China; it covers offshore waters east of Vietnam, north of Malaysia, and west of the Philippines, which include a bunch of islands, are important for shipping that China needs, and are believed to have undiscovered oil reserves, which I imagine China would love to have given its huge imported oil needs and the risk of oil imports from the Middle East being cut off. If you read the World War II case study in Chapter 6 and saw how the US cut off resources to Japan, you know the issue: China has a great need for oil and other imports that currently come through a choke point at the Strait of Malacca.

As a result of all of this and other assertions, the perception of

China as a threat/enemy has emerged, globalization has reversed, and "wars" have intensified, starting with the trade and economic wars, expanding to the technology and the geopolitical wars and, most recently, to the capital war. All remain relatively mild in relation to what they could be, but they should be watched closely. Eventually the actual powers of a country that are recognized become consistent with the actual powers that exist. The actual powers that exist are reflected in the gauges and other facts that I'm watching for guidance.

China has continued to grow internally and to expand its investment and business activities outside its borders. **It has invested heavily in the developing world, most notably through the Belt and Road Initiative, which extends through Central Asia, starting with the countries on its border (Kazakhstan, Pakistan, Tajikistan, and Afghanistan) to Europe, and through the Arabian Peninsula and South Asia into the Mediterranean and Africa. The amounts invested and earmarked for investment are enormous—the largest such program since the Marshall Plan. It is a good demonstration that wealth = power.** While these moves have been appreciated by the countries that received the benefits from roads and other infrastructure, resources, and trade, they have also sparked resentments from recipient countries who are having problems paying back their loans and find that China is too controlling, and from the United States because China's assertions of soft power have lessened American influence in those countries.

As far as China's internal politics are concerned, in 2018 Xi a) consolidated power around himself and his supporters (called "the core" leadership), b) amended the Chinese constitution to make it clear that the Chinese Communist Party has control over everything, c) eliminated term limits for the president and vice president, d) created supervisory commissions to ensure that government officials are operating consistently with the party's wishes, and e) enshrined Xi's perspective, called "Xi Jinping Thought," into the constitution. As of this writing, big political changes, increased

controls, and wider distribution of wealth are all underway. Some people are concerned that Xi is becoming more autocratic than Mao. I'm no expert on Chinese politics so I don't have much to offer when it comes to China's internal political matters, but I will pass along what I am told, which is that Xi's controversial moves to tighten his control came about because of the belief that China is entering a more difficult phase in a more challenging world, and that at such times, unity and continuity of leadership are especially important, and that will be the case even more over the next few years. As mentioned earlier, ● ***during periods of great crisis, more autocratic and less democratic leadership tends to be preferred.***

Then, in late 2019, the COVID-19 pandemic began in China, sparking a worldwide economic downturn in 2020 and the massive printing and creation of money and credit, which coincided with various types of conflicts in the US (most obviously, protests related to racial injustice, and a very contentious presidential campaign). That brings us up to today.

Looking back over the last four decades, China's shift from isolation to opening up and from hard-core communism to "market reforms" and capitalism have had a greater impact on the economies of China, the US, and the rest of the world than anything else. China transitioned from one of the most backward countries in the world to one of the two most powerful economically, technologically, militarily, and geopolitically. Most of that progress occurred during an era of peace and prosperity, when the leading empire wasn't threatened and globalization and cooperation flourished. The period lasted until the bursting of the debt bubble in 2008, when the United States and much of the rest of the world became more nationalistic, protectionist, and confrontational, following the archetypical Big Cycle progression.

The results of China's reform and opening up are reflected in the following table, which shows just a few representative statistics. Output per person has increased 25 times, the percentage of people living below the poverty line has fallen from 96 percent to less than 1 percent, life expectancy has increased by an average of about 10 years, and the average number of years of education has increased by 80 percent. I could go on and on, rattling off equally impressive statistics in virtually every area.

CHINA'S DEVELOPMENT SINCE 1949 AND 1978

	1949	1978	2018	Δ Since 1949	Δ Since 1978
RGDP Per Capita*	348	609	15,243	44x	25x
Share of World GDP	2%	2%	22%	12x	11x
Population Below the Poverty Line ($1.90/Day)**	—	96%	1%	at least -96%	-96%
Life Expectancy	41	66	77	+36 Yrs	+11 Yrs
Infant Mortality Rate (per 1,000 Births)	200	53	7	-96%	-86%
Urbanization	18%	18%	59%	+41%	+41%
Literacy	47%	66%	97%	+50%	+31%
Avg Yrs of Education	1.7	4.4	7.9	+6.2 Yrs	+3.5 Yrs

*USD 2017, PPP-adjusted
**The World Bank only has poverty data back to 1981

While the indicators of China's rise are broadly representative, they aren't precise because the powers can't be precisely measured. Take education, for example. While our index for education rises at a fairly brisk pace, it fails to fully capture the relative improvements in China because it is made up of average as well as total levels of education. This distortion is best conveyed in the next table. As you can see, while the average education level in China is considerably below the average education level in the US, China's total number of people who have attained higher-level education is significantly greater than the United States'. Its total number of STEM (science, technology, engineering, and math) graduates is about three times the United States'. At the same time, there are reasons to believe that the average quality of Chinese education isn't as high, especially at the college level. For example, in a recent ranking, only two Chinese universities appeared among the top 50 universities in the world (Tsinghua University at number 29 and Peking University at number 49) while 30 American universities did. This picture, in which the average of something in China is below the average of the same thing in the United States but the total in China is greater than the total in the US, is because the average level of development in China is lower while the Chinese population is more than four times as large as the American population. That comes across in a number of stats. For example, while the United States is militarily stronger in total all over the world, the Chinese appear to be militarily stronger in the East and South China Seas area, and there is a lot that is unknown about both countries' military powers because they are kept secret.

	UNITED STATES				CHINA			
	1980	Today	Change	Change (%)	1980	Today	Change	Change (%)
Average Years of Schooling	11.9	13.6	+1.7	+14%	4.6	7.9	+3.3	+72%
Govt Spending on Education (% of GDP)	5.30%	5.50%	0.20%	+4%	1.90%	5.20%	3.30%	+174%
Est Population w/ Tertiary Education (Mln)	25	60	+35	+140%	3	120	+117	+3,900%
Population w/ Tertiary Education (% Working-Age Pop)	17%	28%	11%	+68%	1%	12%	11%	+2,272%
Population w/ Tertiary Education (% World)	35%	15%	-20%	-57%	4%	31%	+27%	+590%
STEM Majors (Mln)	3	8	+5	+141%	1	21	+21	+4,120%
STEM Majors (% World)	29%	11%	-18%	-62%	5%	31%	+26%	+535%

In conclusion, this modern era for China has led to some of the most rapid improvements in basic living conditions in history as well as an obvious climb in the factors that create powerful empires. In all respects, China is now a major and expanding power. Next we will turn to the US-China relationship in light of where it is now and what matters most to Americans and the Chinese.

CHAPTER 13

US-CHINA RELATIONS AND WARS

In this chapter I will be looking at the positions that the US and China now find themselves in and what being in these positions means for US-China relations. Because the US and China are now rival powers in a number of domains, they are in "conflicts" or "wars" in these domains, so I will be looking at where these stand. Because for the most part these are just new versions of old and classic conflicts (e.g., new technologies in a classic technology war, new weapons in a classic military war, etc.), I will be putting them in the context of what has happened repeatedly in history and with the timeless and universal principles we have learned from studying these cases. While I will explore the range of possibilities that one might consider, I will be doing that without getting into what the future might look like. I will do that in the concluding chapter of this book. In this chapter I will also be moving a bit more from just conveying facts to sharing opinions (i.e., sharing my uncertain conjectures).

I am primarily focusing on US-China relations in this chapter, but in truth the game macro investors and global policy makers are playing is like multidimensional chess that requires each player to consider the many positions and possible moves of a number of key players (i.e., countries) that are also playing the game, with each of these players having a wide range of considerations (economic, political, military, etc.) that they have to weigh to make their moves well. The relevant other players that are now in this multidimensional game include Russia, Japan, India, other Asian countries, Australia, and European countries, and all of them have many considerations and constituents that will determine their moves. From playing the game I play—global macro investing—I know how complicated it is to simultaneously consider all that is relevant in order to make winning decisions. I also know that what I do is not as complicated as what those in the seats of power do and I know that I don't have access to information that is as good as what they have, so it would be arrogant for me to think I know better than they do about what's going on and how to best handle it. For those reasons I am offering my views with humility. With that equivocation I will tell you how I see the US-China relationship and the world setting in light of these wars, and I will be brutally honest.

THE POSITIONS THE AMERICANS AND CHINESE ARE IN

As I see it, destiny and the Big Cycle manifestations of it have put these two countries and their leaders in the positions they are now in. They led the United States to go through its mutually reinforcing Big Cycle successes, which led to excesses that led to weakening in a number of areas. Similarly they led China to go through its Big Cycle declines, which led to intolerably bad conditions that led to revolutionary changes and to the mutually reinforcing upswings that China is now in. So, the United States appears to be in decline and China appears to be on the rise for the all the classic reasons.

Destiny and the big debt cycle led the US to find itself now in the late-cycle phase of the long-term debt cycle in which it has too much debt and needs to rapidly produce much more debt, which it can't service with hard currency. So it has to monetize its debt in the classic late-cycle way of printing money to fund the government's deficits.

Ironically, and classically, being in this bad position is the consequence of the United States' successes leading to these excesses. For example, **it is because of the United States' great global successes that the US dollar became the world's dominant reserve currency, which allowed Americans to borrow excessively from the rest of the world (including from China), which put the US in the tenuous position of owing other countries (including China) a lot of money which has put those other countries in the tenuous position of holding the debt of an overly indebted country that is rapidly increasing and monetizing its debt and that pays significantly negative real interest rates to those holding its debt.** In other words, it is because of the classic reserve currency cycle that China wanted to save a lot in the world's reserve currency, which led it to lend so much to Americans who wanted to borrow so much, which has put the Chinese and the Americans in this awkward big debtor-creditor relationship when these wars are going on between them.

Destiny and the way the wealth cycle works, especially under capitalism, led to incentives and resources being put into place that allowed Americans to make great advances and produce great wealth—and eventually created the large wealth gaps that are now causing conflicts and threatening the domestic order and productivity that is required for the US to stay strong. **In China it was the classic collapse of its finances due to debt and money weaknesses, internal conflicts, and conflicts with foreign powers that led to its Big Cycle financial declines at the same time that the US was ascending**, and it was the extremity of these terrible conditions that produced the revolutionary changes that eventually led to the creation of incentives and market/capitalist approaches that produced China's great advances, great wealth, and the large wealth gaps that it is understandably increasingly concerned about.

Similarly, destiny and the way the global power cycle works have now put the United States in the unfortunate position of having to choose between fighting to defend its position and its existing world order or retreating. For example, it is because the United States won the war in the Pacific in World War II that it, rather than any other country, will have to choose between defending Taiwan—most Americans don't know where in the world it is or how to spell it—or retreating. It is because of that destiny and that global power cycle that the United States now has military bases in more than 70 countries in order to defend its world order even though it is uneconomical to do so.

● ***History has shown that all countries' success depends on sustaining the strengthening forces without producing the excesses that lead to countries' declines. The really successful countries have been able to do that in a big way for 200–300 years. No country has been able to do it forever.***

Thus far we've looked at the history of the last 500 years focusing especially on the rise and decline cycles of the Dutch, British, and American reserve currency empires and briefly at the last 1,400 years of China's dynasties, which has brought us up to the present. The goal has been to put where we are in the context of the big-picture stories that got us here and to see the cause/effect patterns of how things work so that we can put where we are into better perspective. Now we need to drop down and look at where we are in more detail, hopefully without losing sight of that big picture. As we drop down, things that seem imperceptibly small in retrospect—Huawei, Hong Kong sanctions, closing consulates, moving battleships, unprecedented monetary policies, political fights, social conflicts, and many others—will at the time appear much larger, and we will find ourselves in the blizzard of them that comes at us every day. Each warrants more than a chapter-long examination, which I don't intend to do here, but I will touch on the major issues.

History has taught us that there are five major types of wars: 1) trade/economic wars, 2) technology wars, 3) geopolitical wars, 4) capital wars, and 5) military wars. To these I would add 6) culture wars and 7) the war with ourselves. While all sensible people wish that these "wars" weren't occurring and instead that cooperation was happening, we must be practical in recognizing that they exist. We should use past cases in history and our understandings of actual developments as they are taking place to think about what is most likely to happen next and how to deal with it well.

We see these wars transpiring in varying degrees now. They should not be mistaken for individual conflicts but rather recognized as interrelated conflicts that are extensions of one bigger evolving conflict. In watching them transpire we need to observe and try to understand each side's strategic goals—e.g., are they trying to hasten a conflict (which some Americans think is best for the US because time is on China's side because China is growing its strengths at a faster pace) or are they trying to ease the conflicts (because they believe that they would be better off if there is no war)? In order to prevent these conflicts from escalating out of control, it will be important for leaders of both countries to be clear about what the "red lines" and "trip wires" are that signal changes in the seriousness of the conflict.

Let's now take a look at these wars with the lessons from history and the principles they provide in mind.

THE TRADE/ECONOMIC WAR

Like all wars, the trade war can go from being a polite dispute to being life-threatening, depending on how far the combatants want to take it.

Thus far we haven't seen the US-China trade war taken very far. It features classic tariffs and import restrictions that are reminiscent of those we have repeatedly seen in other similar periods of conflict (e.g., the Smoot-Hawley Tariff Act of 1930). We have seen the trade negotiations and what they achieved reflected in a very limited "phase one" trade agreement from 2019 that was tentatively implemented. As we have seen, this "negotiation" was about testing each other's powers rather than looking to global laws and judges (like the World Trade Organization) to achieve fair resolution. Tests of power are how all these wars will be fought. The big question is how far these tests of power will go and what form will they take.

Beyond the trade dispute there are three major economic criticisms the US has about China's handling of its economy:

1. **The Chinese government pursues a wide range of evolving interventionist policies and practices** aimed at limiting market access for imported goods, services, and businesses, thus protecting its domestic industries by creating unfair practices.
2. **The Chinese offer significant government guidance, resources, and regulatory support to Chinese industries,** most notably including policies designed to extract advanced technologies from foreign companies, particularly in sensitive sectors.
3. **The Chinese are stealing intellectual property,** with some of this stealing believed to be state-sponsored and some of it believed to be outside the government's direct control.

Generally speaking, the United States has responded both by trying to alter what the Chinese are doing (e.g., to get them to open their markets to Americans) and by doing its own versions of these things (closing American markets to the Chinese). Americans won't admit to doing some of the things they are doing (e.g., taking intellectual property) any more than the Chinese will admit to doing them because the public relations costs of admitting to doing them are too great. When they are looking for supporters of their causes, all leaders want to appear to be the leaders of the army that is fighting for good against the evil army that is doing bad things. That is why we hear accusations from both sides that the other is doing evil things and no disclosures of the similar things that they are doing.

● ***When things are going well it is easy to keep the moral high ground. However, when the fighting gets tough, it becomes easier to justify doing that which was previously considered immoral (though rather than calling it immoral it is called moral).*** As the fighting becomes tougher a dichotomy emerges between the idealistic descriptions of what is being done (which is good for public relations within the country) and the practical things that are being done to win. That is because in wars leaders want to convince their constituents that "we are good and they are evil" because that is the most effective way to rally people's support, in some cases to the point that they are willing to kill or die for the cause. Though true, it is not easy to inspire people if a practical leader explains that "there are no laws in war" other than the ethical laws people impose on themselves and "we have to play by the same rules they play by or we will stupidly fight by self-imposing that we do it with one hand behind our backs."

I believe that we have pretty much seen the best trade agreement that we are going to see and that the risks of this war worsening are greater than the likelihood that they will lessen, and that we won't see any treaty or tariff changes anytime soon from the Biden administration. Whatever approach they eventually take will be a big influence on how Americans and the Chinese approach the Big Cycle destinies that are in the process of unfolding. As it now stands, the one thing—maybe the only thing—that both US political parties agree on is being hawkish on China. How hawkish and how exactly that hawkishness is expressed and reacted to by the Chinese are now unknown.

How could this war worsen?

Classically, the most dangerous part of the trade/economic war comes when countries cut others off from essential imports. The case study of the US and Japan leading up to World War II (found in Chapter 6) is a useful analogue to US-China circumstances because the geographies and the issues are analogous. For example, the US cutting off China's imports of oil, other needed commodities, technologies, and/or other essential imports from the US or other countries would be clear and obvious signs of the war escalating. Likewise, China could escalate by cutting off companies like General Motors (which sells more cars in China than in the US) and Apple, or cutting off US imports of rare earth elements that are needed for the production of lots of high-tech items, automobile engines, and defense systems. I'm not saying such moves are likely, but I do want to be clear that **moves to cut off essential imports from either side would signal a major escalation that could lead to a much worse conflict**. If that doesn't happen, evolution will take its normal course so international balances of payments will evolve primarily based on each country's evolving competitiveness.

For these reasons **both countries, especially China, are shifting to more domestic production and "decoupling."**[1] As President Xi has said, the world is "undergoing changes not seen in a century" and "[i]n the face of an external environment characterized by rising protectionism, global economic downturn, and a shrinking international market . . . [China must] give full play to the advantage of a huge domestic market." Over the last 40 years it has acquired the abilities to do this. Over the next five years we should see both countries become more independent from each other. The rate of reducing one's dependencies that can be cut off will be much greater for China over the next five to 10 years than for the United States.

THE TECHNOLOGY WAR

The technology war is much more serious than the trade/economic war because whoever wins the technology war will probably also win the military wars and all the other wars.

The US and China are now the dominant players in the world's big tech sectors and these big tech sectors are the industries of the future. **The Chinese tech sector has rapidly developed domestically to serve the Chinese in China and to become a competitor in world markets. At the same time China remains highly dependent on technologies from the United States and other countries.** That makes the United States vulnerable to the increased development and competition of Chinese technologies and makes the Chinese vulnerable to being cut off from essential technologies.

The United States appears now to have greater technology

[1] Decoupling, while required given the circumstances, will be difficult and will lead to significantly reduced efficiency. China's main program for building self-sufficiency goes under the name of "dual circulation." One knowledgeable party described it as a compartmented rather than a broad-based decoupling, which makes sense to me.

abilities overall, though it varies by type of technology and the US is losing its lead. For example, while the US is ahead in advanced AI chip development, it is behind in 5G. As an imperfect reflection of the present stage of the US's advantage, the market capitalizations of US tech companies in total are about four times the size of China's. This calculation understates China's relative strength because it doesn't include some of the big private companies (like Huawei and Ant Group) and the non-company (i.e., government) technology developments, which are larger in China than they are in the United States. The largest public Chinese tech companies (Tencent and Alibaba) are already the seventh and eighth largest technology companies in the world, right behind some of the largest US "FAAMG" stocks. Some of the most important technology areas are being led by the Chinese. Consider that 40 percent of the world's largest civilian supercomputers are now in China, and it is leading in some dimensions of the AI/big data race and some dimensions of the quantum computing/encryption/communications race. Similar leads in other technologies exist, such as in fintech where the volume of e-commerce transactions and mobile-based payments in China is the highest in the world and well ahead of that in the US. There are likely technologies that even the US's most informed intelligence services don't know about that are being developed in secret.

China will probably advance its technologies, and the quality of decision making that is enabled by them, faster than the US will because big data + big AI + big computing = superior decision making. The Chinese are collecting vastly more data per person than is collected in the US (and they have more than four times as many people), and they are investing heavily in AI and big computing to make the most of it. The amount of resources that are being poured into these and other technology areas is far greater than those in the US. As for providing money, both venture capitalists and the government are providing virtually unlimited amounts to Chinese developers. As for providing people, the number of science, technology, engineering, and math (STEM) graduates that are coming out of college and pursuing tech careers in

China is about eight times that in the US. The United States has an overall technology lead (though it is behind in some areas) and of course has some big hubs for new innovations, especially in its top universities and its big tech companies. While the US isn't out of the game, its relative position is declining because China's technological innovation abilities are improving at a faster pace. Remember that China is a country whose leaders 37 years ago marveled at the handheld calculators I gave them. Imagine where they might be 37 years from now.

To fight the technology threats, the United States has responded at times by preventing Chinese companies (like Huawei) from operating in the United States, trying to undermine their usage internationally, and possibly hurting their viability through sanctions that prevent them from getting items needed for production. Is the United States doing that because China is using these companies to spy in the United States and elsewhere, because the United States is worried about them and other Chinese technology companies being more competitive, and/or because they are retaliating for the Chinese not allowing American tech companies to have free access to the Chinese market? While that is debatable, there is no doubt that these and other Chinese companies are becoming more competitive at a fast pace. In response to this competitive threat the United States is moving to contain or kill threatening tech companies. Interestingly, while the United States is cutting off access to intellectual property now, it would have had a much greater power to do so not long ago because the United States had so much more intellectual property relative to others. China has started to do the same to the United States, which will increasingly hurt because Chinese IP is becoming better in many ways.

Regarding the stealing of technologies, while it is generally agreed to be a big threat,[2] it does not fully explain actions taken against Chinese tech companies. If a company is breaking a law within a country (e.g., Huawei in the US) one would expect to see that

[2] One in five North America-based companies in a 2019 CNBC Global CFO Council survey claimed to have had intellectual property stolen by Chinese companies.

crime prosecuted legally so one could see the evidence that shows the spying devices embedded within the technologies. We aren't seeing this. Fear of growing competitiveness is as large, or larger, a motivator of the attacks on Chinese technology companies, but one can't expect policy makers to say that. American leaders can't admit that the competitiveness of US technology is slipping and can't argue against allowing free competition to the American people, who for ages have been taught to believe that competition is both fair and the best process for producing the best results.

Stealing intellectual property has been going on for as long as there has been recorded history and has always been difficult to prevent. As we saw in earlier chapters, the British did it to the Dutch and the Americans did it to the British. "Stealing" implies breaking a law. When the war is between countries there are no laws, judges, or juries to resolve disputes and the real reasons decisions are made aren't always disclosed by those who are making them. I don't mean to imply that the reasons behind the United States' aggressive actions are not good ones; I don't know if they are. I'm just saying that they might not be exactly as stated. Protectionist policies have long existed to insulate companies from foreign competition. Huawei's technology is certainly threatening because it's better in some ways than American technology. Look at Alibaba and Tencent and compare them with American equivalents. Americans might ask why these companies are not competing in the US. It is mostly for the same reasons that Amazon and a number of other American tech companies aren't freely competing in China. In any case, **there is a tech decoupling going on that is part of the greater decoupling of China and the US, which will have a huge impact on what the world will look like in five years**.

What would a worsening of the tech war look like?

The United States has a technology lead (though it's shrinking fast). As a result, the Chinese currently have great dependencies on imported technologies from both US and non-US sources that the US can influence. This creates a great vulnerability for China, which in turn creates a great weapon for the United States. It most obviously exists in advanced semiconductors, though it exists in other technologies as well. The dynamic with the world's leading chip maker—Taiwan Semiconductor Manufacturing Company, which provides the Chinese and the world with needed chips, and which can be influenced by the United States—is one of many interesting dynamics to watch, especially since it is located in Taiwan. There are many such Chinese technology imports that are essential to China's well-being and many fewer American imports from China that are essential to the United States' well-being. **If the United States shuts off Chinese access to essential technologies, that would signal a major step up in the risk of a shooting war.** On the other hand, if events continue to transpire as they have been transpiring, China is poised to be much more independent and in a much stronger position than the United States technologically in five to 10 years, at which time we will likely see these technologies much more decoupled. This picture changes by the day, and it is important to stay on top of it.

THE GEOPOLITICAL WAR

Sovereignty, especially as it relates to the Chinese mainland, Taiwan, Hong Kong, and the East and South China Seas, is probably China's biggest issue. Beyond these are several other areas of strategic economic importance, such as those countries involved in China's Belt and Road Initiative.

As you might imagine, the Century of Humiliation in the 19th century and the invasions by foreign "barbarians" during it gave Mao and the Chinese leaders to this day compelling motivations to have complete sovereignty within their borders, get back the parts of China that were taken away from them (e.g., Taiwan and Hong Kong), and never again be so weak that they can be pushed around by foreign powers. China's desire for sovereignty and for maintaining its distinct ways of doing things (i.e., its culture) are why the Chinese reject American demands for them to change Chinese internal policies (e.g., to be more democratic, to handle the Tibetans and Uighurs differently, to change its approach to Hong Kong and Taiwan, etc.). In private some Chinese point out that they don't dictate how the United States should treat people within its borders. They also believe that the United States and European countries are culturally prone to proselytizing—i.e., to imposing on others their values, Judeo-Christian beliefs, morals, and ways of operating—and that this inclination has developed through the millennia, since before the Crusades.

To the Chinese the sovereignty risk and the proselytizing risk make a dangerous combination that could threaten China's ability to be all it can be by following the approaches that it believes are best. The Chinese believe that their having sovereignty and the ability to approach things the way that they believe is best as determined by their hierarchical governance structure is sacrosanct. Regarding the sovereignty issue, they also point out that there are reasons for them to believe that the United States would topple their government—the Chinese Communist Party—if it could, which is also intolerable.[3] These are the biggest existential threats that I believe the Chinese would fight to the death to defend and the United States must be careful in dealing with China if it wants to prevent a hot war. For issues not involving sovereignty, I believe the Chinese expect to look to influence them nonviolently and avoid a hot war.

Probably the most dangerous sovereignty issue is Taiwan. Many Chinese people believe that the United States will never follow through with its implied promise to allow Taiwan and China to unite, unless the US is forced to do so. They point out that when the US sells the Taiwanese F-16 fighter jets and other weapons systems it sure doesn't look like the United States is facilitating the peaceful reunification of China. As a result, they believe that the only way to ensure that China is safe and united is to have the power to oppose the US in the hope that the US will sensibly acquiesce when faced with a greater Chinese

[3] It is widely recognized that "regime change" has been commonly employed by the United States for managing its world order.

power. My understanding is that China is now stronger militarily in that region of the world. Also, the Chinese military is likely to get stronger at a faster pace, though deterrence through mutually assured destruction is most likely the case. So, as I mentioned earlier, **I would worry a lot if we were to see an emerging fight over sovereignty, especially if we were to see a "Fourth Taiwan Strait Crisis."** Would the US fight to defend Taiwan? Uncertain. The US not fighting would be a great geopolitical win for China and a great humiliation for the US. It would signal the decline of the US Empire in the Pacific and beyond in much the same way as the British loss of the Suez Canal signaled the end of the British Empire in the Middle East and beyond. The implications of that would extend well beyond that loss. For example, in the British case it signaled the end of the pound as a reserve currency. The more of a show the US makes of defending Taiwan the greater the humiliation of a lost war or a retreat would be. That is concerning because the United States has been making quite a show of defending Taiwan while destiny appears to be bringing a direct conflict to a head before long. If the US does fight, I believe that a war with China over Taiwan that costs American lives would be very unpopular in the US and the US would probably lose that fight, so the big question is whether that would lead to a broader war. That scares everyone. Hopefully the fear of that great war and the destruction it would produce, like the fear of mutually assured destruction, will prevent it.

At the same time, from my discussions **it is my belief that China has a strong desire not to have a hot war with the US or to forcibly control other countries (as distinct from having the desire to be all it can be and to influence countries within its region)**. I know that the Chinese leadership understands how terrible a hot war would be and worries about unintentionally slipping into one, à la World War I. They would much prefer a cooperative relationship if such a relationship is possible, and, I suspect, they would happily divide the world into different spheres of influence. Still they have their "red lines" (i.e., limits to what can be compromised on that if crossed would lead to a hot war) and they expect more challenging times ahead. For example, as President Xi said in his 2019 New Year's address, "Looking at the world at large, we are facing a period of major change never seen in a century. No matter what these changes bring, China will remain resolute and confident in its defense of national sovereignty and security."[4]

Regarding influence around the world, for both the United States and China there are certain areas that each finds most important, primarily on the bases of proximity (they care most about countries and areas closest to them) and/or of obtaining essentials (they care most about not being cut off from essential minerals and technologies), and to a lesser extent of their export markets. The areas that are most important to the Chinese are first those that they consider to be part of China, second those on their borders (in the China seas) and those in key supply lanes (Belt and Road countries) or those that are suppliers of key imports, and third other countries of economic or strategic importance for partnerships.

Over the past few years China has significantly expanded its activities in these strategically important countries, especially Belt and Road countries, resource-rich developing countries, and some developed countries. This is greatly affecting geopolitical relations. These activities are economic and are occurring via increasing investments in targeted countries (e.g., loans, purchases of assets, building infrastructure facilities such as roads and stadiums, and providing military and other support to countries' leaders) while the US is receding from providing aid to these places. This economic globalization has been so extensive that most countries have had to think hard about their policies regarding allowing the Chinese to buy assets within their borders.

Generally speaking, the Chinese appear to want tributary-like relationships with most non-rival countries, though the closer their proximity to China, the greater the influence China wants over them. In reaction to these changing circumstances most countries, in varying degrees, are wrestling with the question of whether it is better to be aligned with the United States or with China, with

---

[4] This statement was made in connection with the Taiwan reunification issue.

those in closest proximity needing to give the most consideration to this question. In discussions with leaders from different parts of the world I have repeatedly heard it said that there are two overriding considerations—economic and military. They almost all say that if they were to choose on the basis of economics, they would choose China because China is more important to them economically (in trade and capital flows), while if they were to choose on the basis of military support, the United States has the edge but the big question is whether the United States will be there to protect them militarily when they need it. Most doubt that the US will fight for them, and some in the Asia-Pacific region question whether the US has the power to win.

The economic benefits that China is providing these countries is significant and is working in a way that is broadly similar to the way the United States provided economic benefits to key countries after World War II to help secure the desired relationships. It was not many years ago that there were no significant rivals to the United States, so it was quite easy for the United States to simply express its wishes and find that most countries would comply; the only rival powers were the Soviet Union (which in hindsight wasn't much of a rival) and its allies and a few of the developing countries that were not economic rivals. **Over the last few years Chinese influence over other countries has been expanding while US influence has been receding.** That is also true in multilateral organizations—e.g., the United Nations, the IMF, the World Bank, the World Trade Organization, the World Health Organization, and the International Court of Justice—most of which were set up by the United States at the beginning of the American world order. As the United States has been pulling back from them, these organizations are weakening and China is playing a greater role in them.

Over the next five to 10 years, in addition to there being decoupling in other areas, we will be seeing which countries align themselves with each of these leading powers. Beyond money and military power, how China and the US interact with other countries (how they use their soft powers) will influence how these alliances will be made. Style and values will matter. For example, during the Trump years I heard leaders around the world describe both countries' leaders as "brutal." While you don't hear that as much with President Biden, other countries broadly fear that they will be punished if they don't do exactly what these two countries' leaders want, and they don't like it to the point of being driven into the other's arms. **It will be important to see what these alliances will look like because throughout history, as we've seen, the most powerful country is typically taken down by alliances of countries that are less powerful but collectively stronger.**

Perhaps the most interesting relationship to watch is between China and Russia. Since the new world order began in 1945, among China, Russia, and the United States, two out of the three have become allied to attempt to neutralize or overpower the third. Russia and China each has a lot of what the other needs (natural resources and military equipment for China from Russia and financing for Russia from China). Also, because Russia is militarily strong it would be a good military ally. We can start to see this happening by watching where the countries line up on the issues; for example, whether to allow Huawei in, with the United States or China.

In addition to the international political risks and opportunities, there are of course big domestic political risks and opportunities in both countries. That is because there are different factions who are fighting for control of both governments and there will inevitably be changes in leadership that will produce changes in policies. While nearly impossible to anticipate, whoever is in charge will be faced with the challenges that now exist and that are unfolding in the Big Cycle ways we have been discussing. Since all leaders (and all other participants in these evolutionary cycles, including all of us) step on and get off at different parts of these cycles, they (and we) face a certain set of likely situations to be encountered. Since other people in history have stepped on and off at the same parts of past cycles, by studying what these others encountered and how they handled their encounters at the analogous stages, and by using some logic, we can imperfectly imagine the range of possibilities.

THE CAPITAL WAR

As history has shown, one of the biggest risks in a conflict is that access to one's money/capital can be shut off. This can happen by a) the moves of one's opponents and/or b) self-inflicted harmful actions (e.g., getting into too much debt and devaluing one's money) that lead those who provide capital to not want to provide it. In Chapter 6, I reviewed classic capital war moves. Some of these are now being used and could be used in a more forceful way, so they have to be watched closely.

The goal in a capital war is to cut the enemy off from capital because no money = no power.

The degrees to which these things occur correspond to the severity of the conflict. "Sanctions" as they are now called and employed come in many forms, with the broad categories being financial, economic, diplomatic, and military. Within each of these categories there are many versions and applications. I'm not going to delve into the various versions and targets because that would be too much of a digression.

The main things to know are:

- **The United States' greatest power comes from having the world's leading reserve currency, which gives the US enormous buying power because it gives it the ability a) to print the world's money and have it widely accepted abroad and b) to control who gets it.**
- **The United States is at risk of losing its reserve currency status.**

The US dollar remains the dominant world reserve currency because it is used for trade, global capital transactions, and reserves much more than any other currency. History and logic show that the leading reserve currency is slow to be replaced for the same reasons that the leading world language is slow to be replaced—because so many people have adopted it and because it is entwined within the system. The existing positions of reserve currencies as reflected by the amounts held by central banks are shown here:

SHARE OF CENTRAL BANK RESERVES BY CURRENCY

USD	51%
EUR	20%
Gold	12%
JPY	6%
GBP	5%
CNY	2%

Based on data through 2019

Because the dollar is the dominant currency in world trade, capital flows, and reserves, it is the world's leading reserve currency, which puts the US in the enviable position of being able to print the world's money and to inflict sanctions on its enemies. The US now has an arsenal of sanctions, which is its most used arsenal of weapons. As of 2019, there were approximately 8,000 US sanctions in place targeted at individuals, companies, and governments. Through these powers the US can get the money it needs and it can cut off opposing countries from getting money and credit by preventing financial institutions and others from dealing with them. These sanctions are by no means perfect or all-encompassing, but they are generally effective.

The United States is at risk of losing its dominant position as a reserve currency because:

- **The amounts of dollar-denominated debt in foreigners' portfolios, such as central bank reserves and sovereign wealth funds, are disproportionately large based on a number of measures of what the size of reserve currency holdings should be.**[5]
- **The US government and the US central bank are increasing the amounts of dollar-denominated debt and money at an extraordinarily fast pace, so it will likely be hard to find adequate demand for US debt without the Federal Reserve having to monetize a lot of it, while at the same time the financial incentives to hold this debt are unattractive because the US government is paying a negligible nominal yield and a negative real yield on it.**
- **Holding debt as a medium of exchange or as a storehold of wealth during wartime is less desirable than during peacetime, so if there were movements toward war, the value of debt (which is a promise to receive fiat currency) and fiat currency would likely go down relative to other things.** This is not currently an issue but would become one if wars intensify.
- **The roughly $1 trillion of US debt that China holds is a risk but not an unmanageable one as that equals only around 4 percent of the roughly $28 trillion outstanding (as of May**

[5] The shares of dollar-denominated debt are large in relation to a) the percentage of asset allocations that international investors would hold to balance their portfolios well, b) the sizes of reserve currency holdings that are appropriate to meet trade and capital flow funding needs, and c) the size and importance of the US economy relative to other economies. Dollar-denominated debt is now disproportionately large because the dollar is the world's leading reserve currency, which means it is perceived as a safer asset than it really is, and because dollar borrowings have been disproportionately large. Now most of those who are responsible for determining what the shares of their holdings should be in different markets are not inclined to increase the shares in line with the greater amounts of US bonds to be sold and are in fact considering reducing their shares held in US debt, which, if it happens, will require larger purchases by the Federal Reserve.

2021). However, because other countries realize that actions taken against China could be taken against them, any actions taken against Chinese holdings of dollar assets would likely increase the perceived risks of holding dollar-debt assets by other holders of these assets, which would reduce the demand for such assets. This is not currently an issue though it appears to be close to becoming an issue.

- **The dollar's role as a reserve currency largely depends on its being freely exchanged between countries, so to the extent that the US might in the future put controls on its flows and/or run monetary policy in ways that are contrary to the world's interests in pursuit of its own interests, that would make the dollar less desirable as the world's leading reserve currency.** This is not currently an issue but will become one if foreign exchange controls are raised as a possibility, which is typical at the next stage of the cycle.
- **Countries being hurt by US sanctions are developing ways to get around them or undermining the United States' power to impose them.** For example, Russia and China, which both are encountering these sanctions and are at great risk of encountering more of them in the future, are each now developing and cooperating with the other to develop an alternative payment system. China's central bank has created a digital currency, which will make China less exposed to US sanctions.

There are no good currency alternatives because:

- **The dollar (51 percent of central bank reserves)** has weakening fundamentals in the way described in Chapter 11, which I won't repeat here.
- **The euro (20 percent)** is a weakly structured fiat currency made by smaller, uncoordinated countries with weak finances that are tenuously held together by a highly fragmented currency union. Because the European Union is financially,

economically, and militarily at best a secondary power, buying its currency and debt denominated in its currency, which its central bank is free to print, is not an enticing thing to do.

- **Gold (12 percent)** is a hard currency that is held because it has worked the best over the ages and because it is an effective diversifier to other assets held, particularly fiat currencies. While before 1971 gold was at the foundation of the world's currency system, at this time it is a relatively dead asset since there are no significant international trade and capital transactions in it and it isn't used to balance external accounts. It is also a market that is too small to become a high share of wealth at current prices. A move to gold from fiat-currency-based assets (i.e., credit assets), which would only come in the event of an abandonment of that system (which history shows could come), would lead to an explosion in gold's price.
- **The yen (6 percent)** is a fiat currency that is also not widely used internationally by non-Japanese people and suffers from a lot of the same problems that the dollar has including having too much debt that is increasing quickly and being monetized so that it is paying unattractive interest rates. Also Japan is only a moderate global economic power and is a weak military power.
- **The pound (5 percent)** is an anachronistically held fiat currency that has relatively weak fundamentals, and the UK is relatively weak in almost all of our measures of a country's economic/geopolitical power.
- **The renminbi (2 percent)** is the only fiat currency to be chosen as a reserve currency because of its fundamentals. China's potential is sizable. Its shares of world trade, world capital flows, and world GDP are roughly equal to the United States'.[6] China has managed its currency to be relatively stable against other currencies and against goods and services prices, it has large foreign exchange reserves, it doesn't have a 0 percent

[6] This data is adjusted for purchasing power parity.

interest rate and a negative real interest rate, and it isn't printing and monetizing a lot of debt. Increasing investments in China strengthens the currency because those purchases have to be made in its currency. Those are the positives. The negatives are that China has a relatively large amount of domestic debt that has to be restructured, the renminbi is not a currency that is widely used for global trade and financial transactions, China's clearing system is undeveloped, and money is not allowed to freely flow in and out of the currency.

So there are no attractive world reserve currencies to compete with the dollar.

● ***History has shown that whenever a) currencies are not desired and b) there are no other currencies that are attractive to go into, the currencies are still devalued and the capital finds its way into other investments (e.g., gold, commodities, stocks, property, etc.). As a result, there is no need to have a strong alternative currency for a devaluation of a currency to take place.***

Things will change. To the extent that the United States and China are in a capital war, the development of Chinese currency and capital markets would be detrimental for the United States and beneficial for China. Without the US attacking China's currency and capital markets in an attempt to weaken them, and/or the Chinese hurting their own currency and capital markets (by making policy shifts that make these markets less attractive), China's currency and capital markets will probably develop quickly to increasingly compete with US markets. It is up to American policy makers to decide whether or not they will try to disrupt this evolutionary path by becoming more aggressive or accept that evolution, which will likely lead to China becoming relatively stronger, more self-sufficient, and less vulnerable to being squeezed by the US. Though the Chinese have less power to hurt the US dollar and its capital markets, and its best moves would be to strengthen its own currency, there are some possibilities that it will attempt to harm the dollar.

As explained in my study of past cycles, the war typically intensifies as the cycle progresses. Comparing historical cases with their modern-day equivalents—e.g., moves by the US and Japan prior to World War II with moves by the US and China now—should be helpful as the cycle progresses.

THE MILITARY WAR

I am not a military expert but I get to speak with military experts and I do research on the subject, so I will pass along what has been shared with me. Take it or leave it as you wish.

● ***It is impossible to visualize what the next major military war will be like, though it probably will be much worse than most people imagine.*** That is because a lot of weaponry has been developed in secret and because the creativity and capabilities to inflict pain have grown enormously in all forms of warfare since the last time the most powerful weapons were used and seen in action. There are now more types of warfare than one can imagine and, within each, more weapons systems than anyone knows. While of course nuclear warfare is a scary prospect, I have heard equally scary prospects of biological, cyber, chemical, space, and other types of warfare. Many of these are untested so there is a lot of uncertainty about how they would go.

Based on what we do know **the headline is that the United States and China's geopolitical war in the East and South China Seas is escalating militarily because both sides are testing the other's limits. China is now militarily stronger than the United States in the East and South China Seas so the US would probably lose a war in that region, while the United States is stronger around the world and overall and would probably "win" a bigger war.** But a bigger war is too complicated to imagine well because of the large number of unknowns, including how other countries would behave in it and what technologies secretly exist. The only thing that most informed people agree on is that such a war would be unimaginably horrible.

Also notable, China's rate of improvement in its military power, like its other rates of improvement, has been extremely fast, especially over the last 10 years, and the future rate is expected to be even faster, even more so if China's economic and technological improvements continue to outpace those of the United States. **Some people imagine that China could achieve broad military superiority in five to 10 years. I don't know if that is true.**

As for potential locations of military conflict, Taiwan, the East and South China Seas, and North Korea are the hottest spots, and India and Vietnam are the next (for reasons I won't digress into).

As far as a big hot war between the United States and China is concerned, it would include all the previously mentioned types of wars plus more pursued at their maximums because, in a fight for survival, each would throw all it has at the other, the way other countries throughout history have. It would be World War III, and World War III would likely be much deadlier than World War II, which was much deadlier than World War I because of the technological advances in the ways we can hurt each other.

Proxy wars are also part of the picture and should be watched as they are very effective in chipping away at a leading world power's strength and global influence.

In thinking about the timing of a war, I keep in mind the principles that: ● ***when countries have big internal disorder, it is an opportune moment for opposing countries to aggressively exploit their vulnerabilities.*** For example, the Japanese made their moves to invade China in the 1930s when China was divided and exhausted by its ongoing civil war.

● ***History has taught us that when there are leadership transitions and/or weak leadership at the same time that there is big internal conflict, the risk of the enemy making an offensive move should be considered elevated.*** Because time is on China's side, if there is to be a war, it is in the interest of the Chinese to have it later (e.g., five to 10 years from now when it will likely be stronger and more self-sufficient) and in the interest of the US to have it sooner.

I'm now going to add two other types of war—the culture war, which will drive how each side will approach these circumstances, including what they would rather die for than give up, and the war with ourselves, which will determine how effective we are and which will lead us to be strong or weak in the critical ways we explored in Chapter 1.

THE CULTURE WAR

● ***How people are with each other is of paramount importance in determining how they will handle the circumstances that they jointly face, and the cultures that they have will be the biggest determinants of how they are with each other.*** What Americans and the Chinese value most and how they think people should be with each other determine how they will deal with each other in addressing the conflicts that we just explored. Because Americans and the Chinese have different values and cultural norms that they will fight and die for, if we are going to get through our differences peacefully it is important that both sides understand what these are and how to deal with them well.

As described earlier, **Chinese culture compels its leaders and society to make most decisions from the top down, demanding high standards of civility, putting the collective interest ahead of individual interests, requiring each person to know their role and how to play it well, and having filial respect for those superior in the hierarchy. They also seek "rule by the proletariat," which in common parlance means that opportunities and rewards are broadly distributed. In contrast, American culture compels its leaders to run the country from the bottom up, demanding high levels of personal freedom, favoring individualism over collectivism, admiring revolutionary thinking and behavior, and not respecting people for their positions as much as for the quality of their thinking. These core cultural values drove the types of economic and political systems each country chose.**

To be clear, most of these differences aren't obvious in day-to-day life; they generally aren't very important relative to the shared beliefs that Americans and the Chinese have, which are numerous, and they aren't held by all Chinese or all Americans, which is why many Americans are comfortable living in China and vice versa. Also, they are not pervasive. For example, the Chinese in other domains, such as Singapore, Taiwan, and Hong Kong, have had governance systems that are similar to Western democratic systems. Still these cultural differences subtly affect most everything, and in times of great conflict, they are the defining differences that determine whether the parties fight or peacefully resolve their disputes. **The main challenge the Chinese and Americans have with each other arises from some of them failing to understand and empathize with the other's values and ways of doing things, and not allowing each other to do what they think is best.**

While the opening up of both countries has increased their interactions and their increasingly shared practices (e.g., their similar economic freedoms that produce similar desires, products, and outcomes) have made both environments and their people much more similar than they ever were before, the differences in approaches are still notable. They are reflected in how each country's government and its people interact with each other and how Americans and the Chinese interact especially at the leader-to-policy-maker level. **Some of these cultural differences are minor and some of them are so major that many people would fight to the death over them**—e.g., most Americans believe in "give me liberty or give me death" while to the Chinese individual liberty isn't nearly as important as collective stability is.

These differences are also reflected in everyday life. For example, the Chinese government, being more paternal, regulates what types of video games children play and how many hours a day they can play them, whereas in the United States video games aren't government-regulated because such things are considered an individual parent's decision to make. One could argue the merits of either approach.

The Chinese hierarchical culture makes it natural for the Chinese to simply accept the government's direction, while the American nonhierarchical culture makes it acceptable for Americans to fight with their government over what to do. Similarly, different cultural inclinations influenced how Americans and the Chinese reacted to being told that they had to wear masks in response to COVID-19, which led to second-order consequences because the Chinese followed the instructions and Americans often didn't, affecting the numbers of cases and deaths and the economic impact. These culturally determined differences in how things are handled affect how the Chinese and Americans react differently to many things— information privacy, free speech, free media, etc.—which add up to lots of ways that the countries operate differently.

While there are pros and cons to these different cultural approaches, and I'm not going to explore them here, I do want to get across that **the cultural differences that make Americans American and the Chinese Chinese are deeply embedded**. Given China's impressive track record and how deeply imbued the culture behind it is, there is no more chance of the Chinese giving up their values and their system than there is of Americans giving up theirs. Trying to force the Chinese and their systems to be more American would, to them, mean subjugation of their most fundamental beliefs, which they would fight to the death to protect. To have peaceful coexistence Americans must understand that the Chinese believe that their values and their approaches to living out these values are best, as much as Americans believe their American values and their ways of living them out are best.

For example, one should accept the fact that when choosing leaders most Chinese believe that having capable, wise leaders make the choices is preferable to having the general population make the choice on a "one person, one vote" basis because they believe that the general population is less informed and less capable. Most believe that the general population will choose the leaders on whims and based on what those seeking to be elected will give them in order to buy their support rather than what's best for them. Also, they believe—like Plato believed and as has happened in a number of countries—that democracies are prone to slip into dysfunctional anarchies during very bad times when people fight over what should be done rather than support a strong, capable leader.

They also believe that their system of choosing leaders lends itself to better multigenerational strategic decision making because any one leader's term is only a small percentage of the time that is required to progress along its long-term developmental arc.[7] They believe that what is best for the collective is most important and best for the country and is best determined by those at the top. Their system of governance is more like what is typical in big companies, especially multigenerational companies, so they wonder why it is hard for Americans and other Westerners to understand the rationale for the Chinese system following this approach and to see the challenges of the democratic decision-making process as the Chinese see them.

To be clear, I'm not seeking to explore the relative merits of these decision-making systems. **I am simply trying to make clear that there are arguments on both sides and to help Americans and the Chinese see things through each other's eyes and, most importantly, to understand that the choice is between accepting, tolerating, and even respecting each other's right to do what each thinks is best or having the Chinese and Americans fight to the death over what they believe is uncompromisable.**

The American and Chinese economic and political systems are different because of the differences in their histories and the differences in their cultures that have resulted from these histories. As far as economics is concerned the two different viewpoints—the classic left (favoring government ownership of the means of production, the poor, the redistribution of wealth, etc., which the Chinese call communism) and the classic right (favoring private ownership of the means of production, whoever succeeds in the system, and much more limited redistributions of wealth)—exist in China as in the rest of the world, and there have been swings from one to the other in all societies,

[7] In fact, it is a challenge for the Chinese to deal with the lack of continuity of policies and directions in the US arising from seemingly whimsical shifts in what matters to the American public as expressed in whom they choose to represent them.

especially in China, so it would not be correct to say that the Chinese are culturally left or right. Similar swings in American preferences have existed throughout its much more limited history. I suspect that if the United States had a longer history we would have seen wider swings, as we have in Europe through its longer history.

For these reasons these "left" versus "right" inclinations appear to be more big cycle swings around revolutionary trends than evolving core values. In fact, we are seeing these swings now taking place in both countries, so it's not a big stretch to say that policies of the "right," such as capitalism, are close to being more favored in China than in the United States and vice versa. In any case, when it comes to economic systems, there don't appear to be a lot of clear distinctions rooted in deep cultural preferences. In contrast to economic systems, the inclination of the Chinese to be top-down/hierarchical versus bottom-up/nonhierarchical appears to be deeply embedded in their culture and in their political systems while Americans are strongly inclined to be bottom-up/nonhierarchical. As for which approach will work best and win out in the end, I will leave that for others to debate, hopefully without bias, though I will note that most knowledgeable observers of history have concluded that neither of these systems is always good or bad. ● ***What works best varies according to a) the circumstances and b) how people using these systems are with each other. No system will sustainably work well—in fact all will break down—if the individuals in it don't respect it more than what they individually want and if the system is not flexible enough to bend with the times without breaking.***

As we imagine how Americans and the Chinese will handle their shared challenge to evolve in the best possible way on this shared planet, I try to imagine where their strong cultural inclinations, most importantly where the irreconcilable differences that they would rather die for than give up, will lead them. For example, most Americans and most Westerners would fight to the death for the ability to have and express their opinions, including their political opinions. In contrast, the Chinese value the respect for authority more, which is reflected in and demonstrated by the relative powers of individuals and the organizations they belong to and the responsibility to hold the collective organization responsible for the actions of individuals in the collective.

Such a culture clash took place in October 2019 when the then-general manager of the Houston Rockets (Daryl Morey) tweeted an image expressing support for Hong Kong's pro-democracy protest movement. He quickly pulled down his tweet and explained that his views weren't representative of his team's views or the NBA's views. Morey was then attacked by the American side (i.e., the press, politicians, and the public) for not standing up for free speech, and the Chinese side held the whole league responsible and punished it by dropping all NBA games from China's state television, pulling NBA merchandise from online stores, and reportedly demanding that the league fire Morey.

This clash arose because of how important free speech is to Americans and because Americans believe that the organization should not be punished for the actions of the individual. The Chinese, on the other hand, believe that the harmful attack needed to be punished and that the group should be held accountable for the actions of the individuals in it. One can imagine much bigger cases in which much bigger conflicts arise due to such differences in deep-seated beliefs about how people should be with each other.

When they are in a superior position, the Chinese tend to want a) the relative positions to be clear (i.e., the party in a subordinate position knows that it is in a subordinate position), b) the subordinate party to obey, and c) the subordinate party to know that, if it doesn't do so, it will be punished. That is the cultural inclination/style of Chinese leadership. They can also be wonderful friends who will provide support when needed. For example, when the governor of Connecticut was desperate to get personal protective equipment in the first big wave of COVID-19 illnesses and deaths and couldn't get it from the US government or other American sources, I turned to my Chinese friends for help and they provided what was needed, which was a lot. As China goes global a number of countries' leaders (and their populations) have been both grateful for and put off by China's acts of generosity and strict punishments. Some of these cultural differences can be negotiated to the parties' mutual satisfaction, but some of the most important ones will be very difficult to negotiate away.

I think the main thing to realize and accept is that the Chinese and Americans have different values and will make different choices for themselves than the other would like. For example, Americans might not like how the Chinese handle their human rights issues and the Chinese might not like how Americans handle their human rights issues. The question is: what should be done about that—should Americans fight with the Chinese to impose what they think the Chinese should do on them and vice versa, or should they agree not to intervene into what each other does? In my opinion it is too difficult, inappropriate, and probably impossible to force others in other countries to do what they strongly believe is not good for them. **The United States' ability to impose things on the Chinese and China's ability to impose things on the United States will be a function of their relative powers.**

While I just explored the US-China war issues conveying the little that I know about them relative to what I need to know, I want to remind you that these wars are far more complex than one-to-one conflicts. They are like multidimensional chess games because many countries are involved with many other countries in many dimensions. For example, when I think of US-China relations I have to think way beyond their bilateral relations to think about their multilateral relationships in all important dimensions—e.g., with all notable Asian, European, and Middle Eastern governments and private sectors, and with all of those countries' important relationships with the other countries, etc. In other words, in order to think about the US-China relationship I have to think about the Saudi Arabia-US and the Saudi Arabia-China relationship and to that I have to think about the Saudi Arabia-Iran relationship, the Saudi Arabia-Israel, the Saudi Arabia-Egypt, and many other relationships in all of their important dimensions, plus the other analogous relationships. Without the aid of a good computer and a whole lot of data, it is impossible to follow, let alone understand, what's going on. It is way beyond me, and frankly when I speak with world leaders I find it shocking how little they really understand what the others in this multidimensional chess game are really thinking.

THE RISK OF UNNECESSARY WAR

As I explained in Chapter 6, stupid wars often happen as a result of a tit-for-tat escalation process in which responding to even small actions of an adversary is more important than being perceived as weak, especially when those on both sides don't really understand the motivations of those on the other side. History shows us that this is especially a problem for declining empires, which tend to fight more than is logical because any retreat is seen as a defeat.

Take the issue of Taiwan. Even though the US fighting to defend Taiwan would seem to be illogical, not fighting a Chinese attack on Taiwan might be perceived as being a big loss of stature and power over other countries that won't support the US if it doesn't fight and win for its allies. Additionally, such defeats can make leaders look weak to their own people, which can cost them the political support they need to remain in power. And, of course, miscalculations due to misunderstandings when conflicts are transpiring quickly are dangerous. All these dynamics create strong pulls toward wars accelerating even though such mutually destructive wars are so much worse than cooperating and competing in more peaceful ways.

There is also risk of untruthful, emotional rhetoric taking hold in both the US and China, creating an atmosphere for escalation. For example, in a recent Pew survey a record 73 percent of Americans had an unfavorable opinion of China, 73 percent believed the United States should promote human rights in China, and 50 percent believed the US should "hold China responsible" for the role it played in COVID-19. Though I don't have surveys of Chinese public opinion of the United States, I am told by many people that it has deteriorated. It wouldn't take much to have these people demand accelerations of the conflicts.

Ultimately, it would be wise for leaders and citizens of both countries to recognize that the US and China are in a competition of systems and abilities. Each will inevitably follow the system that they believe works best for them, Americans have a slight lead in power but it is shrinking and they're outnumbered, and history has shown that while numbers of people can matter a lot, other factors (e.g., the 18 determinants listed in Chapter 2) matter more, so even small-population empires become leading world powers if they manage themselves well. That all implies that what's most important to being strong is how we act with ourselves.

THE WAR WITH OURSELVES: THE ENEMY IS US

Our greatest war is with ourselves because we have the most control over how strong or weak we are. Because it is pretty clear what makes countries strong and weak, and because these strengths and weaknesses are measurable, it is easy to see how each country is doing. These factors were laid out in the first and second chapters and measured by 18 determinants. I will briefly review them here, and in the next and final part, I will show these determinants for most countries and will explore the leading indicators of them so that we can make projections of what's to come.

Before we do that, let's review the specific items that help make a great empire. They are . . .

. . . **leadership that is strong enough and capable enough to provide the essential ingredients for success**, which include . . .

. . . **strong education.** By strong education I don't just mean teaching knowledge and skills; I also mean teaching . . .

. . . **strong character, civility, and a strong work ethic**, which are typically taught in the family as well as in school. These lead to improved civility that is reflected in factors such as . . .

. . . **low corruption and high respect for rules, such as the rule of law.**

. . . **People being able to work well together, united behind a common view of how they should be together**, is also important. When people have knowledge, skills, good character, and the civility to behave and work well together, and there is . . .

. . . **a good system for allocating resources**, which is significantly improved by . . .

. . . **being open to the best global thinking**, the country has the most important ingredients in order to succeed. That leads to it gaining . . .

. . . **greater competitiveness in global markets**, which brings in revenues that are greater than expenses, which leads the country to have . . .

. . . **strong income growth**, which allows it to make . . .

. . . **increased investments to improve infrastructure, education, and research and development**, which lead it to have . . .

. . . **rapidly increasing productivity** (more valuable output per hour worked). Increasing productivity is what increases wealth and productive capabilities. When the country achieves higher productivity levels, it can become productive inventors in . . .

. . . **new technologies.** These new technologies are valuable for both commerce and the military. As the country becomes more competitive in these ways, naturally it gains . . .

. . . **a rising and significant share of world trade**, which requires it to have . . .

. . . **a strong military** to protect its trade routes and to influence those who are important to them outside their borders. In becoming economically preeminent the country develops . . .

. . . **strong and widely used currency, equity, and credit markets.** Naturally those dominant in trade and capital flows have their currency used much more as the preferred global medium of exchange and the preferred storehold of wealth, which leads to **their currency becoming a reserve currency** and the building of . . .

. . . **at least one of the world's leading financial centers** for attracting and distributing capital and expanding their trade globally.

Whatever makes these measures go up is good and whatever makes them go down is bad. For this reason it is wise for citizens of all countries to ask themselves how well they collectively and their leaders are doing at making the lines in these measures go up. I also hope that they will remember the cause/effect relationships, avoiding the excesses and divisions that lead to declines.

As for the case at hand, the internal wars and challenges in both China and the US are more important and bigger than external wars and challenges. These include political wars within the leadership of the country and at all levels of government, wars between different factions (e.g., the rich and the poor, the rural and the urban, conservatives and progressives, ethnic groups, etc.), demographic changes, climate change, etc. Fortunately, the most important of these forces are within our control and are measurable, which allows us to see how we are doing and, if we're not doing well, to make changes so these things move in the right directions. **By and large we will get what we deserve. As Churchill said to the British people, "Deserve Victory!"**

PART III

THE FUTURE

CHAPTER 14

THE FUTURE

"He who lives by the crystal ball is destined to eat ground glass" is a market adage I learned when I was about 14. Since I've personally experienced it to be true, it has affected how I look at both the future and the past. I have learned to look at the past 1) to determine what's likely to happen and 2) to protect myself and others I am responsible for against the possibility I am wrong or missing something important. While you and I and others can argue about the patterns and cause/effect relationships described in this book, if you are reading this for practical purposes rather than just casual interest, then you, like me, need to do those two things well.

The purpose of this chapter is to share my thoughts about how I approach the future. While what I don't know about the future is probably much more than what I do know, what I do know is also a lot. Dealing with the future is all about 1) perceiving and adapting to what is happening, even if it can't be anticipated; 2) coming up with probabilities for what might happen; and 3) knowing enough about what might happen to protect oneself against the unacceptable, even if one can't do that perfectly.

Knowing how things have changed in the past leads me to consider the possibility that something similar might happen in the future. That is a big advantage relative to being unaware. For example, there are numerous examples in history of revolutions, wars, and acts of nature leading to violent events in which virtually all wealth is wiped out or confiscated. Knowing this, I am constantly looking for leading indicators of the same things happening again, and having leading indicators of these things, even if they aren't perfect, puts me in a better position to protect myself than remaining blissfully unaware and unprepared for what might happen.

While that example is of a worst-case scenario, being unaware of best-case scenarios can be equally bad. I remember very well how my dad and his friends failed to take advantage of the boom that followed the Great Depression and World War II, as their mindsets had been formed by those awful eras. In playing the game of life it pays to do one's best to understand how the world works, imagine the full range of possibilities (including their risks and rewards), and know how to spread one's bets around well.

While I will pass along my thinking, please remember that everything I say is debatable; the purpose of this whole project is to improve my assessed probabilities of being right. As such, it is a work in progress, and I hope you will join me in evolving it. To that end, I plan to continually update my understandings of these patterns and lessons at economicprinciples.org, where we can interact to refine the picture.

MY APPROACH

To quickly review, **my approach is based on my ideas about a) evolution, which causes changes over time, generally toward improvement, such as increasing productivity, b) cycles, which cause rhythmic ups and downs in the economy (like debt bubbles and busts) and bumps along the way (non-rhythmic ups and downs, like acts of nature), and c) indicators that can help us see where we are in the cycles and what might come next**. I will briefly recap my thoughts on each.

EVOLUTION

The most important things evolve in ways that are easy to see and extrapolate forward, so it's not difficult to get a pretty good sense of roughly where they are likely to be in the future, so long as a once-in-500-years-type game changer doesn't come along. The following charts tell the story about population, life expectancy, and prosperity.

Let's start with world population. The chart on the left starts at 1500 and the one on the right starts at 1900. I show them both because I want you to see how different one's perspective would be if one were looking back 100 years from 1900 versus 100 years from today. Note how dramatically the population grew in the 20th century. Also note that the major historical events mentioned in this book—including the Great Depression, the two World Wars, and any number of natural catastrophes—had no visible effect on the larger evolutionary trend.

GLOBAL POPULATION (MLN)

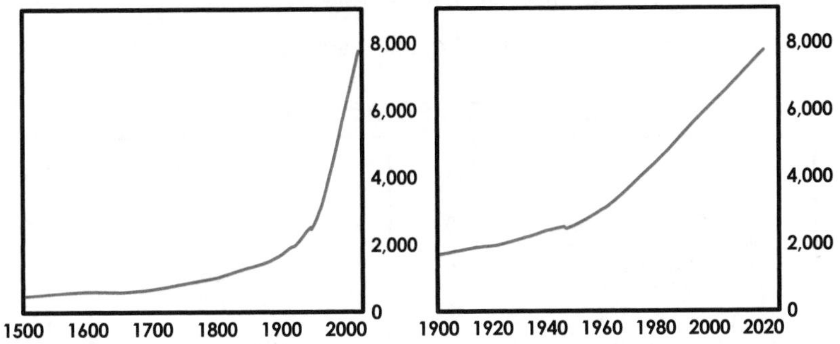

The next two charts show the population growth rate. Notice the big ups and downs that don't show up in the prior charts because they are so minor in comparison to the long-term trend. If we had personally experienced any of this volatility, it would have felt like a life or death experience (which it very much was).

GLOBAL POPULATION GROWTH (10YR CHG, EST)

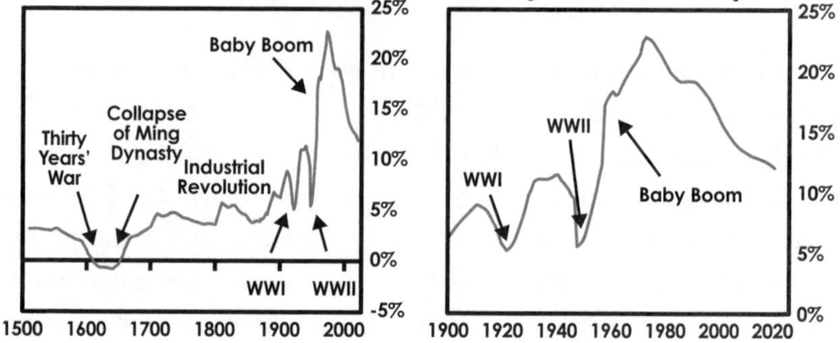

The next two charts show a similar picture for life expectancy. There are a lot more wiggles in these charts than in the previous ones because average life expectancy changes more when there are big events like wars and pandemics (I will show you what those big killers were and where they occurred at economicprinciples.org). Note how life expectancy stayed roughly the same (about 25–30 years) for about 350 years and then accelerated starting around 1900, when there were big improvements in infant mortality rates and several medical advances, like antibiotics.

GLOBAL LIFE EXPECTANCY AT BIRTH

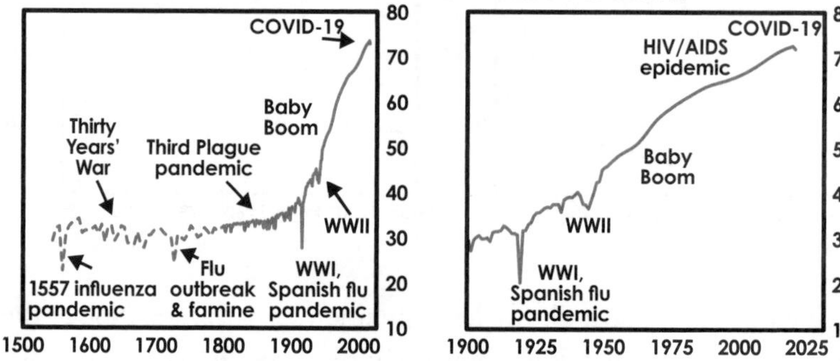

[1]

---

[1] Importantly, a number of the charts shown on these pages rely on the record from fewer countries further in the past, due to limited reliable data history. Life expectancy prior to the 1800s is solely based on Great Britain (marked by the dotted line). Global RGDP is primarily a mix of European countries before 1870. And there are not good records of total wealth prior to the 1900s, so I can't show you the picture before then.

Now let's look at economic prosperity as measured by real (i.e., inflation-adjusted) GDP. The first chart shows a similarly, sweeping picture: the real value of what was produced per person grew slowly until the 19th century and then accelerated, with that broad evolutionary trend dominant relative to the wobbles within it.

GLOBAL RGDP PER CAPITA (LOG)

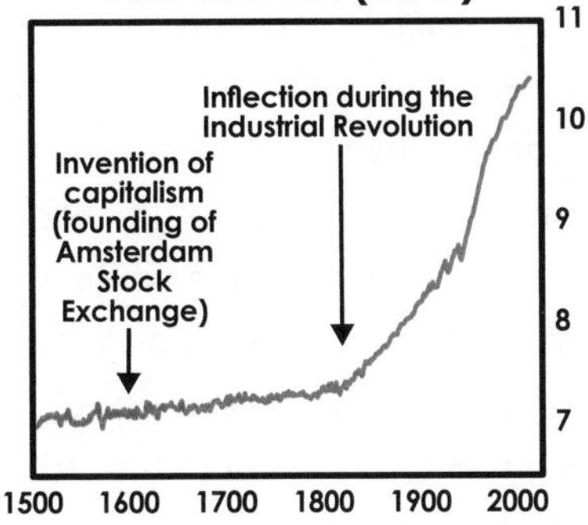

GLOBAL RGDP PER CAPITA (2017 USD)

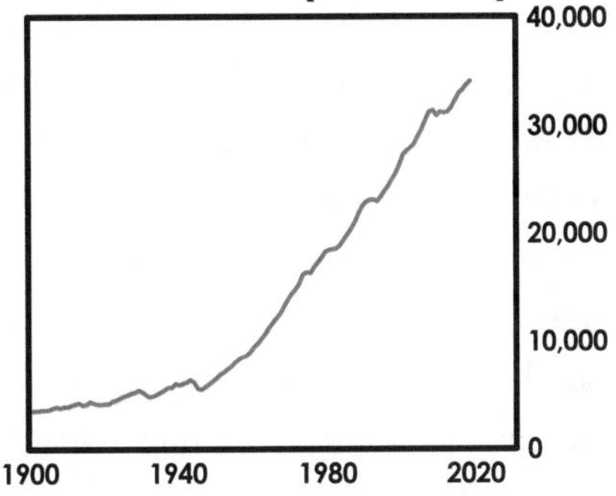

The next chart shows real wealth per capita since 1900. From 1900 until 1945, there was no increase to speak of as that was the late-cycle transition phase from the 19th century boom to the new world order in 1945. Peace and prosperity followed the creation of the new world order, and the uptrend was strong and pretty steady (averaging 4 percent per year), even though the movements around it felt big when we went through them.

GLOBAL REAL WEALTH PER CAPITA (ROUGH ESTIMATE, 2017 USD, LOG)

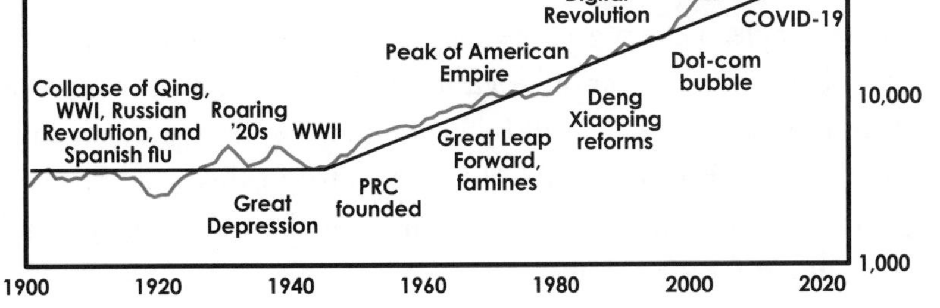

With these evolutions in mind, let's start looking toward the future.

If we look back carefully to see how the present was created, we can see that these evolutionary advances didn't just happen on their own: every day, there were events that affected the present while people's actions shaped them. At the same time, we know that we never could have anticipated them individually—if we had tried to predict each of the specific wars, droughts, pandemics, inventions, prosperous periods, declines, etc., we would have failed. But even without knowing about any of those specific developments, we could have pretty confidently said that advances would occur that would enable significantly larger populations to live significantly longer while enjoying significantly higher standards of living because of the evolution that has already occurred, and that we have every reason to expect to continue to occur, from humanity's inventiveness. We could have also confidently asserted that there would be booms and busts, feasts and famines, and periods of great health and disease along the way.

Based just on what happened in the past 100 years, one might conclude that one can get pretty good estimates just by extrapolating the past forward. As an example, by simply extrapolating the past 100 years, it would be reasonable to expect that in the next 10 years the world's population will be around 10–15 percent higher than it is today, the output per person will be about 20 percent higher, the wealth per person will be 30 percent higher, and the average life expectancy will be 7.5 percent higher, give or take a bit. It would be reasonable to expect that in the next 20 years they will be up 25–30 percent, 45 percent, 70 percent, and around 15 percent, respectively, without knowing specifically how that will happen.

That simple, not-especially-thoughtful analysis paints a picture that probably won't be far off—but it could be. It is easy to paint this picture in much greater detail by looking at the same stats for each country and each sub-group within a country in this way. Processing all of this information is pretty complicated for the human mind alone, but not for a good human mind working with a computer.

But we can see that a picture drawn from pure extrapolation is not good enough. For example, standing in 1750, it would have been reasonable to believe that it was a timeless and universal truth that monarchies and landowning nobles overseeing peasants with the help of soldiers would be the governance system in the future, that agricultural land would continue to be the most important money-earning asset, that per capita incomes would grow at only around half a percent per year, and that life expectancy would remain steady at about 30 years. That was how it had always been. You would not have imagined capitalism and democracy as we now know it, let alone that there would be a United States and that it would be the leading world power.

The big curveballs come when a few really big things cause a paradigm shift that alters the evolutionary rates of change. The paradigm shifts that came in the early 19th century arose from the confluence of the invention of modern tools of finance, machines that could do the work of people, the development of more inclusive societies that broadened opportunities to be inventive and productive, the increased use of books and libraries so knowledge could be more broadly shared, and the application of the scientific method. While these things couldn't be anticipated, they could have been perceived, understood, and adapted to. That's why ● ***while extrapolating the past is generally a reasonable thing to do, also be prepared to be surprised because the future will be much different than you expect it to be.***

Throughout my roughly 50 years of investing, I have seen a number of well-established beliefs based on both what happened before and what seemed logical at the time be proven wrong (to choose a recent example, the belief that bond yields can't go negative). The greatest recent disruptor of well-established beliefs was the Digital Revolution. Through these experiences and observations I learned that ● ***identifying, understanding, and adapting to paradigm shifts is essential, even if one can't anticipate them—though trying to anticipate them with good indicators that help is important too.*** Having good indicators can also help you tell when what looks like a paradigm shift is only a passing fad, which is just as important.

CYCLES AND BUMPS ALONG THE WAY

Cycles and bumps were covered comprehensively in prior chapters, but they warrant reflection now that we are shifting our attention from the past to the future.

Though they barely register when compared to the mega-macro picture, they can damage and kill large numbers of people. Just look at the following charts that show depressions, declines in wealth, deaths in wars, and deaths via pandemics over the past 500 years to gain some perspective about them. Those bad times were even worse than they look because the charts capture them in terms of averages; as such they understate the severity of the experience for the people who were most directly affected. Most people don't think about this darker picture. They look at the positive post-1945 trends and extrapolate them forward. It's up to you to decide if you're in that camp too. As for me, seeing that these big, deadly things have happened in the past leads me to distrust the belief that they won't happen again. Unless and until someone shows me better evidence that they won't happen again than the simple fact that they haven't happened yet, I am going to assume they will and try to protect myself from their consequences.

GLOBAL RGDP PER CAPITA DRAWDOWNS

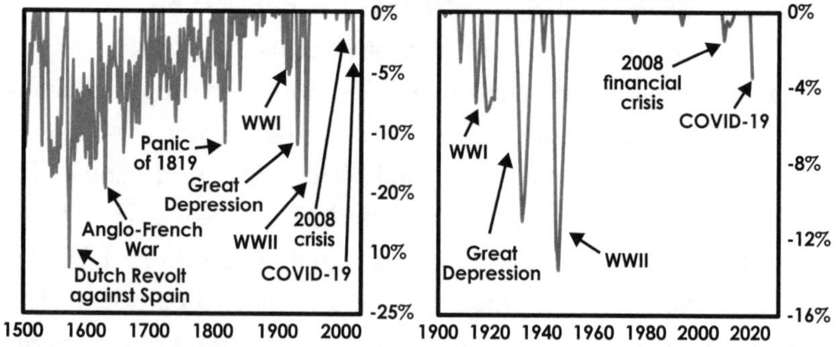

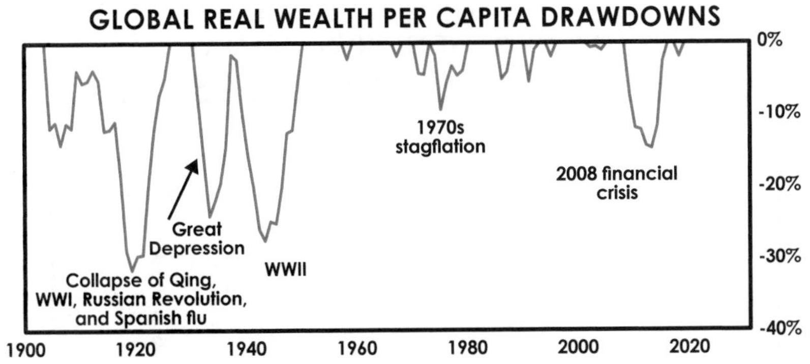
GLOBAL REAL WEALTH PER CAPITA DRAWDOWNS
0%
-10%
-20%
-30%
-40%
1970s stagflation
2008 financial crisis
Great Depression
WWII
Collapse of Qing, WWI, Russian Revolution, and Spanish flu
1900
1920
1940
1960
1980
2000
2020

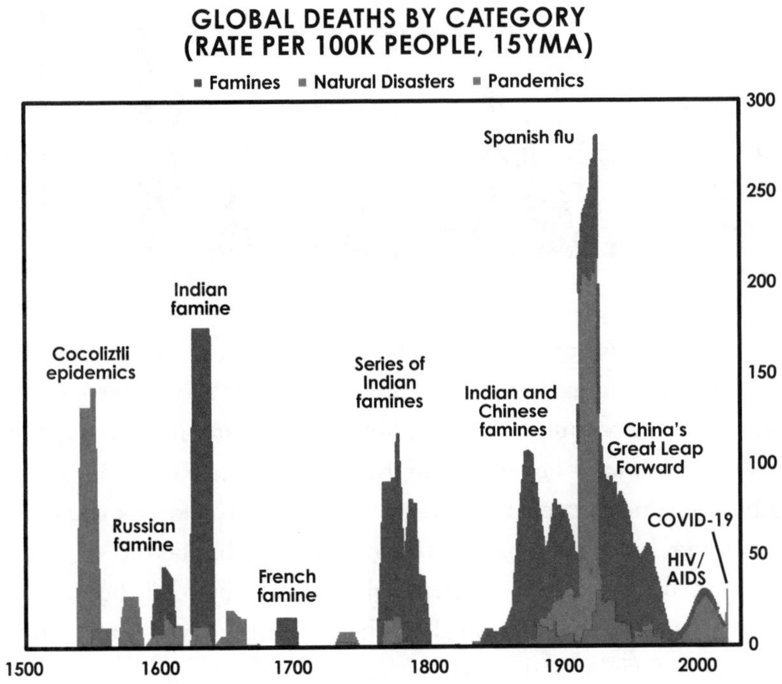
GLOBAL DEATHS BY CATEGORY (RATE PER 100K PEOPLE, 15YMA)
Famines
Natural Disasters
Pandemics
300
250
200
150
100
50
0
Spanish flu
Indian famine
Cocoliztli epidemics
Series of Indian famines
Indian and Chinese famines
China's Great Leap Forward
COVID-19
Russian famine
French famine
HIV/ AIDS
1500
1600
1700
1800
1900
2000

ESTIMATED DEATHS FROM CONFLICT (MAJOR POWERS, %POP, 15YMA)

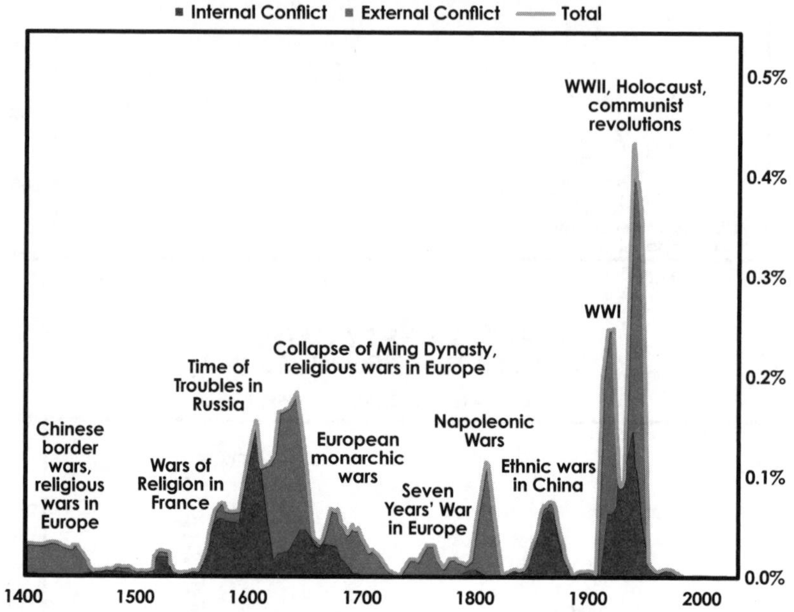

One of the overarching principles I derived from my research and my 50-plus years of investing experience is ● ***in the markets and in life, to be successful one should bet on the upside that comes from a) evolution that leads to productivity improvements, but not so aggressively that b) cycles and bumps along the way knock you out of the game.*** In other words, betting on things being better—e.g., real earnings being greater—is pretty much a sure bet. But betting too much on that so that a bump along the way can ruin you is bad. That's why having quality indicators helps a lot.

QUALITY INDICATORS

Because everything that happens is the result of events that have happened before, I have some pretty good and logical, though imperfect, leading and coincident indicators of important changes.

Some can be quantified, while others can't be.

As previously explained, I found 18 determinants that explain most of the conditions and changes in wealth and power both within and between nations. I will soon show you the readout of all of these 18 determinants for each of the 11 major powers I'm following in this book (more detail on the top 20 countries is shown at economicprinciples.org). But first I want to share some big-picture thoughts about the five determinants that have had the biggest impacts in the past and that I believe will have the biggest impacts on what happens in the years ahead: innovation, the debt/money/capital market cycle, the internal order and disorder cycle, the external order and disorder cycle, and acts of nature. When looking at the charts, remember that in some cases the determinants rise and fall together because they are mutually reinforcing, while in others one country's gains are at the expense of another's. For example, inventing new technologies raises all of humanity's living standards, but it puts the countries that are better at inventing in a superior position. Rising levels of military strength are clearly less beneficial for humanity, as they benefit some countries at the expense of others.

HUMANITY'S INVENTIVENESS

As previously discussed, innovation and inventiveness are clearly the most powerful determinant of a country's conditions.

Think about all the things that we can't imagine not having that were invented or discovered in just the last 150 years. Before we had them, nobody could have imagined them—e.g., the telephone (1876), the electric light bulb (1879), the internal combustion powered vehicle (1885), the radio (1895), movies (1895), the airplane (1903), television (1926), antibiotics (1928), the computer (1939), nuclear weapons (1945), nuclear power plants (1951), GPS (1973), digital cameras (1975), online shopping (1979), the internet (1983), online search (1990), online banking (1995), social media (1997), Wi-Fi (1998), the iPhone (2007), CRISPR gene editing (2012), etc., etc., etc. Progress unfolds in big and steady ways to shape the future but does so through specific breakthroughs that we can't imagine. That is what evolution in technologies and techniques looks like. Evolution in most everything else—approaches to life, domestic and international politics, etc.—happens in a similar way.

I believe that humanity's evolution through its inventiveness is accelerating and that most people will benefit from it. That is because the most significant inventions we are now seeing, and that we know we will see many more of, improve the quality and quantity of all thinking. These inventions are coming in the forms of advances in computers, AI, and other thinking-related technologies. Because they can be applied to many domains of human activity and decision making, it seems obvious to me that the rate of invention and improvement in most areas will accelerate at an even faster pace, rapidly raising productivity and living standards.

Humans now have computers to help them think in ways in which they are comparatively handicapped (e.g., computers have far more memory than the human brain and it is readily accessible, they can process more data at a fantastically faster rate, and they do not make emotional mistakes); at the same time, humans can help computers get past their inherent limitations (e.g., their complete absence of imagination, intuition, common sense, value judgements, and emotional intelligence). This collaboration between humans and computers will increase both the quantity and quality of thinking,[2] portending radical improvements in almost every area of life. I know this because I have experienced it, and I can already see some of these improvements on the horizon.

In other words, **the abilities of both computers and humans will improve at an increasing pace. Perhaps most importantly, advances in and the wider use of quantum computing with AI will lead to**

[2] Soon not being able to read and write computer code will be like not being able to read and write words.

unimaginable advances in rates of learning and improvement and changes in global wealth and power. These changes will occur in varying degrees in the next five to 20 years, but I believe they will add up to the greatest shift in wealth and power that the world has ever seen. Quantum computing with AI will be to traditional computing what the computer was to the abacus, providing humanity with vastly more power to see, understand, and shape things. That makes me long-term very optimistic and eager to bet on great new discoveries.

Even without the boosts from quantum computing, I'd expect the human lifespan to increase by a lot over the next two decades (by 20–25 percent or more), for reasons we can see and for many more reasons that we can't yet see. A few inventions that are already on the horizon are AI and robotics in healthcare, health monitoring, and advice-providing wearables; advances in and the practical use of genome sequencing and gene editing; mRNA improvements in vaccines; and breakthroughs in nutrition and drugs. And if the past is any guide (and it is) there will be many more inventions that we can't yet fathom.

Naturally I can't help but imagine the implications for investing. All else being equal, equities in the companies making new inventions and the companies that benefit from them are the right ones to own if you want to bet on evolution happening, but whether the returns to investors match the performance of the innovations depends on how governments decide to divide the profits of productivity. If the world is financially overextended and has large wealth gaps, this creates headwinds. Also, price matters. It's possible to invest in great companies and lose money because they are so expensive and invest in bad companies and make money because they are so cheap. Finally, and as with everything else, there are downsides. Humanity's inventiveness and the new technologies it produces can have bad as well as good effects. Advances in technologies for inflicting harm will certainly occur alongside advances in medical care. So my view is that **inventiveness and increases in living standards will probably get a**

lot better a lot faster—if humanity doesn't kill itself first.

The next chart shows our latest reading on the inventiveness, technological advancement, and entrepreneurship we see in major countries. The arrows on the top of the bars show whether the trend in each country's standing has been up, sideways, or down. This gauge gives about half its weight to 1) a combination of external rankings and measures of innovation per capita (to help capture how widespread innovation is in the economy) and half to 2) the country's absolute share of key innovation metrics (e.g., researchers, R&D spending, patents, Nobel Prizes, and venture capital funding). Like all my gauges, it is approximately right but not perfectly right, so it's meant to be broadly indicative. **As shown, the US is at the top of these measures with a marginal lead over China, which ranks second (primarily due to the US's share of global research spending, researchers, and its lead in other areas such as venture capital funding). But the US's position is steady, while China's position in the standings is rising fast. Remember that whoever wins the technology war usually wins the economic and military wars.** For more detail on all the gauges shown in this chapter, please refer to the end of this chapter, where you can read a short description of each.

CURRENT INNOVATION AND TECHNOLOGY SCORE

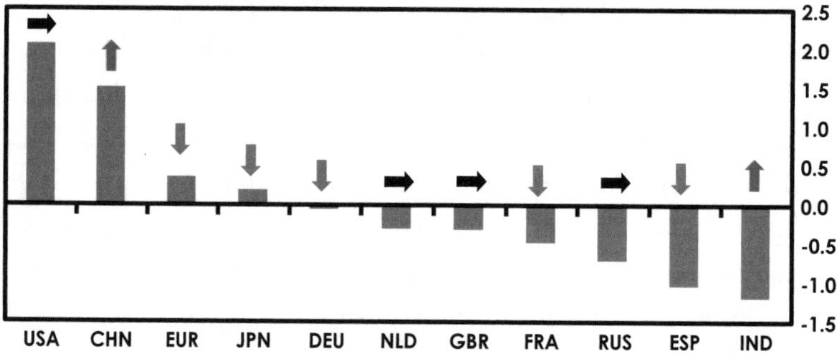

[3]

[3] Arrows denote the 20-year change in the gauge.

THE DEBT/MONEY/CAPITAL MARKET/ECONOMIC CYCLE

As I explained earlier, this cycle is the biggest driver of the ups and downs in economies that have big implications for internal and external politics and wars, so knowing where countries are in this cycle is essential to anticipating what's likely to come next.

Based on my readings of history, my readings of existing conditions, and my understanding of how the economic machine works, the promises that are denominated in the world's reserve currencies, most importantly the dollar, are too large and growing too fast to be paid in hard money. In other words, the debt that is denominated in these currencies is an overhang, so money will probably be printed to service debts and debt growth[4] and interest rates will probably be held below inflation and economic/income growth rates. This reflects the fact that the major reserve currency countries are late in their debt/money/capital market/economic cycles and that wealth will probably be increasingly redistributed from those who have a lot of it to those who don't have enough of it in one way or another. The extent to which these things will be true will vary from country to country, though it will likely be worldwide.

For that reason, **the biggest risk in the long run is the "currency value of money" risk, which most people don't pay enough attention to. I hope Chapter 4 helps people understand and deal with it better.**

To be clear, because the reserve currency countries that are running big deficits have their deficits and debts denominated in their own currencies, their ability to print the money to service the debts transfers the risks from them as debtors to those who are holding the debt as creditors. **So, the big risk is not that those big debtors will default; it is that creditors will hold assets that will be devalued—i.e., that the returns from holding debt assets will be less than the inflation rate.** I believe a great transfer of wealth from creditors to debtors (as

[4] As a result, debt assets (especially cash) will probably perform poorly and debt liabilities will probably be good to have, especially if invested in profitable, disruptive technologies and solid investments that have higher returns than the cost of funding them.

happened in the biblical years of Jubilee, as explained in Chapter 3) is coming for the same reasons it has always come in the past.

What does that mean for the dollar (most importantly) and the other more minor reserve currencies? Will they decline and others replace them? **Most probably they will decline analogously to past reserve currency declines: slowly for a long time and then very quickly.** As we saw in those cases, the pace of reserve currency decline significantly lags the pace of the declines in other measures of strength. Reserve currencies tend to live on long after their fundamentals cease to justify their prominence because they become deeply entrenched in the ways things are done and there is a strong inclination to keep them. Then they abruptly plunge when it becomes clear that the fundamentals behind the currency make holding debt in it a bad deal.

The fall happens fast because the currency's rate of decline outpaces the interest rate paid to the holders of the debt; the net losses lead to selling, which causes more losses, so the spiral becomes self-reinforcing. The Dutch guilder and the British pound both plunged in this way due to geopolitical crises/defeats happening when they had large debts. Those events made it clear to creditors that their fundamentals were weaker than they had assumed and the interest rate couldn't compensate for the decline.

While I have very good indicators to identify this kind of decline happening as it happens, and some pretty good leading indicators that indicate when it will happen in the short term, my long-term leading indicators are only so-so for timing purposes. That is because they are financial and based on supply and demand. It is pretty easy to assess the financial conditions of countries in the same ways that one assesses the financial conditions of people and companies (by checking whether they are running surpluses or deficits and have more assets than liabilities, and finding out if their debts are in their own or foreign currencies and who is funding them and why). Because these are all long-term drivers, it is also pretty easy to see which countries and currencies are vulnerable. But anticipating exactly when the big fall will happen is difficult.

The debt burden gauge shown next is based on a combination of a) debt levels relative to asset levels, b) the sizes of external and internal surpluses and deficits, c) the sizes of debt service costs relative to GDP, d) the amount of debt in a country's own currency versus foreign currency, e) the amount of debt held by its own citizens versus foreigners, and f) its credit rating. I composed it this way because this way has proven to be the most reliable way we have of foreshadowing declines in the real value of money and the debt assets that are promises to receive money, whether they come in the form of debt defaults that result from not creating enough money and credit to satisfy excessive debt needs or devaluations that come from creating more than enough money and credit to satisfy excessive debt needs. I constructed this index to exclude reserve currency status so that I can see the exposure a country would have if it lost its reserve currency status. Reserve currency status is shown in the chart that follows.

Together these charts paint a pretty clear picture. For example, while the **US's debt burdens are high, its debt is denominated in dollars, the world's leading reserve currency, so it has the ability to print money to service its debts. This reduces its risk of default but increases its devaluation risk. As you can see, if the US lost its reserve currency status, it would be in serious financial trouble.** Russia and Germany rank strongest on the debt burden gauge because they are the least indebted. Russia has no reserve currency status, and Germany has a fair amount because it uses the euro, now the second most important reserve currency. China is in the middle of the rankings on the debt burden gauge because its debts are moderately high, mostly in its own currency, and mostly held by the Chinese. Its reserve currency status is emerging.

DEBT BURDEN (UP = WORSE FINANCIAL POSITION)

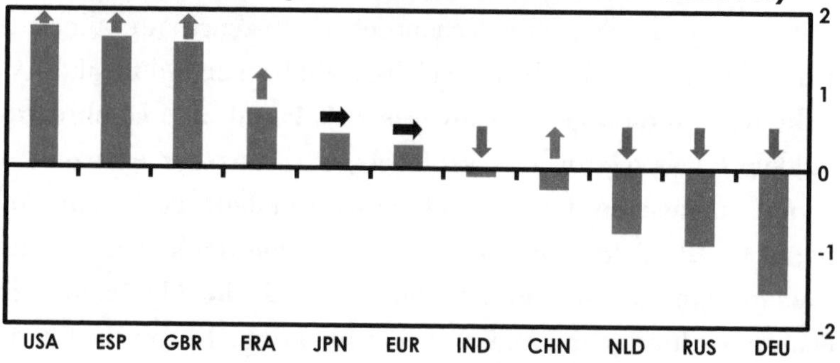

RESERVE CURRENCY STATUS

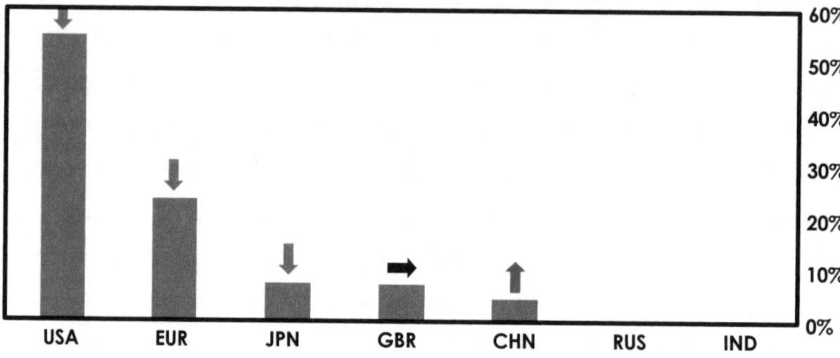

[5]

THE INTERNAL ORDER AND DISORDER CYCLE

Luo Guanzhong's classic book *Romance of the Three Kingdoms* begins: ***"The empire long divided must unite and long united must divide. Thus it has ever been."*** That has been true of China and most other places, and it is likely to continue, so it's a good principle. I explained the big cycle of internal order and disorder in Chapter 5, so I won't reiterate it here other than to remind you of a key principle: ● ***peace is profitable and war is costly.***

[5] Individual European countries are not shown on the reserve currency status gauge due to the European Monetary Union (all these countries use the euro)—so only the Europe aggregate is shown. The measure shows an average of what share of global transactions, debts, and official central bank reserve holdings are denominated in each country's currency.

That holds both within countries and between them. When parties cooperate and compete well, and don't waste resources on fighting, productivity and living standards rise. When they fight, they waste resources (sometimes including lives), they destroy more than they produce, and living standards fall. It is for this reason that the degree of conflict within a country is such an important indicator.

As of this writing there are varying amounts of conflict going on within different countries, as shown in the next chart. Internal conflict is especially high in the United States, which appears to be in Stage 5 of the cycle (when there are bad financial conditions and intense conflict), while China appears to be in Stage 3 (when there is peace and prosperity). Changes to this measure can happen quickly—e.g., the changes that produced the Arab Spring, the conflicts in Hong Kong, internal wars in Syria and Afghanistan, recent big protests in Peru and Chile, etc.—leading to revolutionary changes in their internal orders. **Because I expect that these readings will be out of date by the time this book is in your hands, I will update them regularly at economicprinciples.org.**

RELATIVE INTERNAL CONFLICT GAUGE Z-SCORE FOR MAJOR POWERS TODAY (UP = MORE CONFLICT)

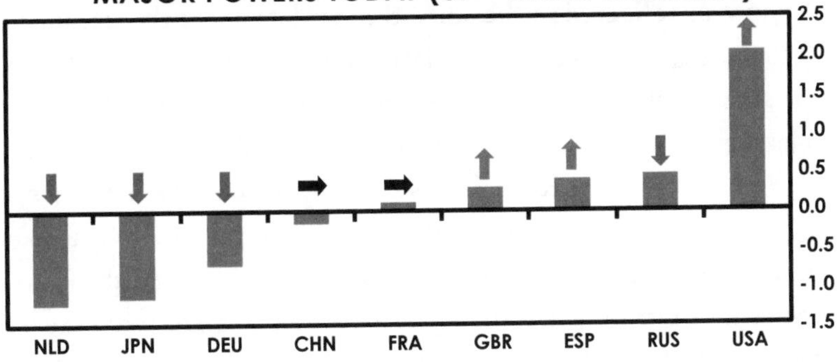

At the end of the day, ● ***power rules and tests of power are the ways one learns who rules.*** Sometimes that happens within a framework of rules that are respected. In those cases, fights for power occur in a mutually agreed-upon and productive way that supports the internal order. But they can also happen in unproductive, no-holds-barred ways that can lead to the violent disruption of both the leadership and the internal order. **While I think that the odds of the US devolving into a Stage 6 (civil-war-type) dynamic within the next 10 years are only around 30 percent, that is a dangerously high risk that must be protected against and watched closely via my coincident and leading indicators.**

All internal orders, even those that are not democratic, have rules about how decisions are made and how power is gained and shared. Because one can usually see how well these governance rules are respected or ignored, it is pretty easy to see when an internal order is being threatened by an emerging civil war. For example, when close elections are adjudicated and the losers respect the decisions, it is clear that the order is respected. When power is fought over and grabbed, that clearly signals the significant risk of a revolutionary change with all its attendant disorder.

There have been signs of that happening in the US, with some people contesting the validity of elections and expressing a willingness to fight for their aims. This bears watching.

There is also an exceptional amount of polarization in the US right now, as reflected in the stats. Survey data about the sentiments of the voters paints a picture of polarization and intransigence. For example, in a 2019 Pew survey 55 percent of Republicans and 47 percent of Democrats viewed the other as more immoral than other Americans, and 61 percent of Republicans and 54 percent of Democrats said that those of the other party don't share their values. When asked whether they had warm or cold feelings to those of the other party, 79 percent of Democrats and 83 percent of Republicans said they had "cold" or "very cold" feelings for members of the other party (of that, 57 percent of Democrats and 60 percent of Republicans selected "very cold"). Another study reported that 80 percent of Democrats think that the Republican Party has been taken over by racists and 82 percent of Republicans think that the Democratic Party has been taken over by socialists. A 2010 study showed that nearly half of Republican parents and a third of Democratic parents would be displeased if their child married someone from the other political party. That compares with about 5 percent for both parties in 1960. One recent survey showed that 15 percent of Republicans and 20 percent of Democrats thought the country would be better off if large numbers of the other side "just died."

Very important and very telling political conflicts and changes lie ahead in the next few years. They will be indicative of what the next stage in the increasingly disorderly internal orders will be like in the major countries, especially in the US. **While the United States looks like it is in the precarious Stage 5 of the cycle, it also has the longest-lasting and most widely admired internal order (its constitutional system).** As explained in Chapter 5, this makes it less likely that it will be abandoned, but more traumatic if it is. The most reliable signs of an escalation to civil war are 1) the rules being disregarded, 2) both sides emotionally attacking each other, and 3) blood being spilled. While Stage 6 is the most dysfunctional and harmful stage, increasing amounts of dysfunction happen in the stages leading up to it. These sorts of conflicts can exist throughout society, not just in government.

Shown next is how the conflict gauge has changed for the US since the late 1700s, including the breakdowns between the two sub-gauges. What these charts reflect is that the **overall level of conflict within the United States is now as high as it's been since the civil rights and Vietnam War protests of the late 1960s, but meaningfully less than it was then. The "internal strife" index (which mostly reflects demonstrations in the streets) is moderately high, and the "political conflict" index is the highest it's been since the early 1920s,** when a deep post-war recession and massive labor unrest[6] contributed to big electoral losses for the Democrats.

[6] In 1919, over 20 percent of the US labor force went on strike.

USA INTERNAL CONFLICT GAUGE Z-SCORE
(UP = MORE CONFLICT)

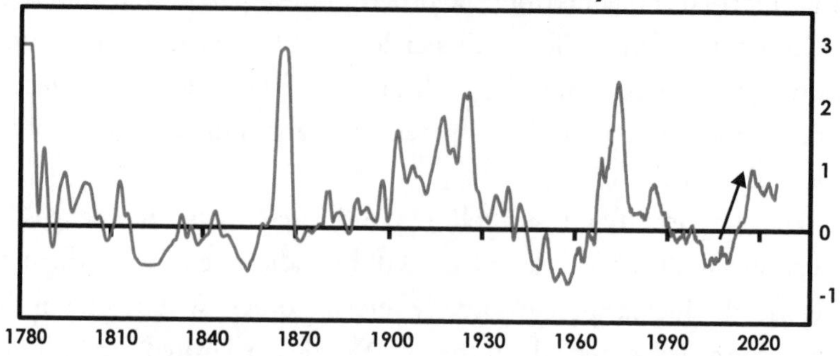

USA INTERNAL CONFLICT GAUGE BREAKDOWN

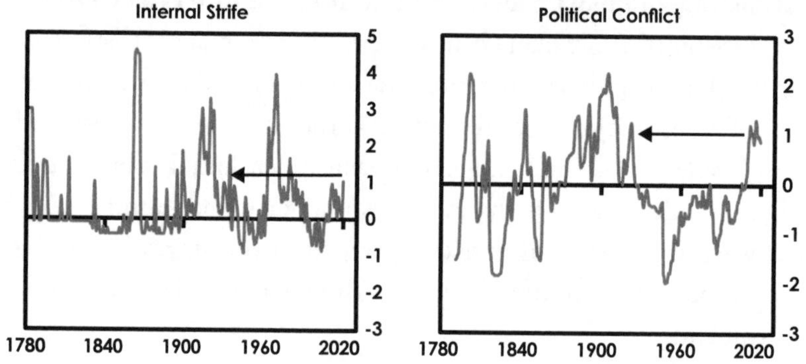

Note that the comparable periods before then were the 1900s–1910s (which saw a backlash against the "robber barons," the rise of the Progressive movement, and eventually World War I), and the 1860s, when economic and values conflicts led to civil war. **The risks are high, but not unprecedentedly so.** Still, the picture should be scary for Americans and scary for the world because the world's leading power is on the brink and could tip one way or the other. Fractured conditions within the US are now contributing to instability in other parts of the world. Any worsening would be at least as disruptive as those past periods.

So what does this all mean for the US? As I explained in Chapter 11, our measures suggest that it is very roughly 70 percent through its big cycle. Can it slow or reverse its relative decline? **History shows us**

that reversing a decline is very difficult because it requires undoing so many things that have already been done. For example, if one's spending is greater than one's earnings and one's liabilities are greater than one's assets, those circumstances can only be reversed by working harder or consuming less. The question is whether we Americans can face our challenges honestly and adapt and change to meet them. For example, while the capitalist profit-making system allocates resources relatively efficiently, Americans now need to ask themselves: "Who is it optimizing these efficiencies for?" "What should be done if the benefits are not broad-based?" "Will we modify capitalism so that it both increases the size of the pie (by increasing productivity) and divides it well?" These questions are especially important to answer in an era when, thanks to new technologies, employing people will increasingly become unprofitable, inefficient, and uncompetitive. "Should we, or should we not, invest in people to make them productive, even when it's uneconomic to do so?" "What if our international competitors choose robots over people?" These and so many more important, difficult questions come to mind. **But while we can't know for certain whether the splits and conflicts in the US will increase or reverse, we do know that the long-term momentum is toward increasing division and this is a serious risk. The fact that the US is simultaneously deeply indebted, its international standing is weakening, and it is experiencing serious conflict should be concerning both to Americans and to non-Americans who depend on them.** At the same time, in its 245-year history the US has shown a great capacity to bend without breaking. The greatest challenges it faces are internal ones: **can it remain strong and united, or will it continue to allow division and internal struggles to lead to decline?**

THE EXTERNAL ORDER AND DISORDER CYCLE

● ***All empires decline and new ones rise to replace them.*** Understanding when that change might happen requires watching all of the indicators and tracking the relative conditions of countries. Remember from earlier in the book that there are five major types of wars that have existed throughout history: 1) trade/economic wars, 2) technology wars, 3) capital wars, 4) geopolitical wars, and 5) military wars. The external conflict gauge shown here measures the levels of economic, political/cultural, and military conflict between pairs of major countries. As shown, the greatest conflict is between the US and China, the two greatest powers in the world that have comparable amounts of power—more than enough to make a war between them the most devastating in history.

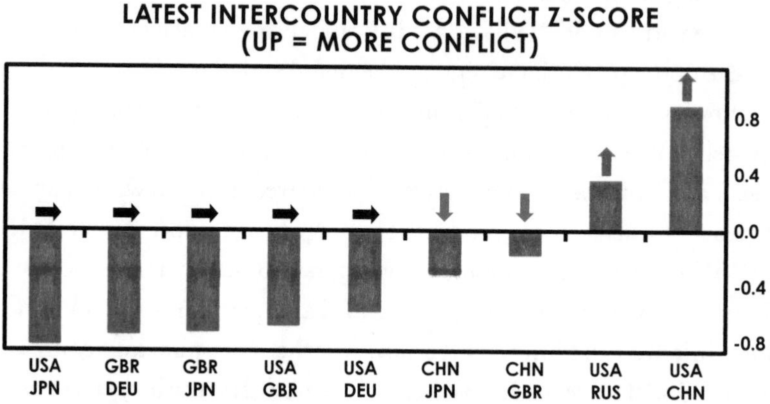

The amount of this conflict is 1 standard deviation above normal, which is pretty severe in relation to past conflicts between countries.

This next chart shows my index of conflict just between the US and China since 1970.

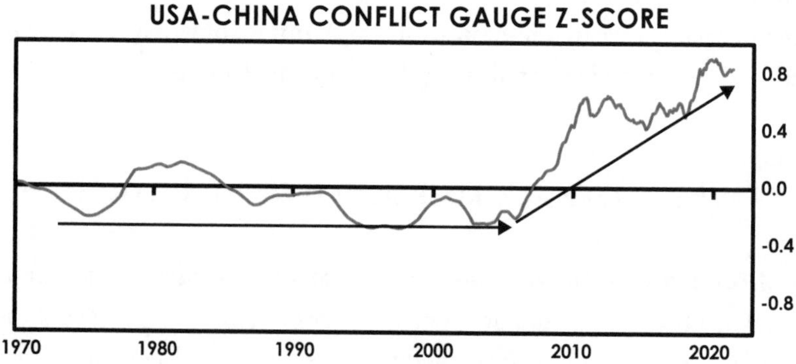

Based on what we have been seeing, the United States and China are clearly in four types of war (trade/economic war, technology war, capital war, and geopolitical war), though not intensely but they are intensifying. They are not yet in the fifth type of war (military war). As shown in the previous cases, in particular the 1930–1945 case, these four types of wars precede military wars by about five to 10 years. Though the risks of military war seem relatively low, they are increasing.

Looking back over the last 500 years, one can see that military wars between major empires started on average about once every 10 years, give or take a couple of years, and it has been about 75 years since the last really big one (World War II). Since 1500, major powers have been at war a little bit more than half the time.[7] From that perspective, the odds of a big military war in the next 10 years are about 50/50, but of course that's simple minded. Let's look at the picture a bit more carefully.

The following chart shows the current individual readings of my military strength gauge. While overall these readings make sense—the US is the most powerful by most measures, China is the next most powerful, Russia comes next, etc.—they don't capture the important realities beneath these summary numbers. For example, they don't show that some countries are as powerful as or more powerful than the United States in specific geographic areas (e.g., right around China) and in some types of warfare (e.g., space, cyber, etc.) Also, they don't consider the effects of military cooperation and alliances (e.g., China and Russia), and they can't account for what unknown military abilities countries may have. For me, the big headline is that there are lots of ways these countries can hurt or destroy each other in the most contested geographic areas.

[7] There have been just over 50 wars between great powers since 1500, per Steven Pinker's *The Better Angels of Our Nature* (2011). Eighty percent of the years before 1800 had wars; it's been 20 percent since.

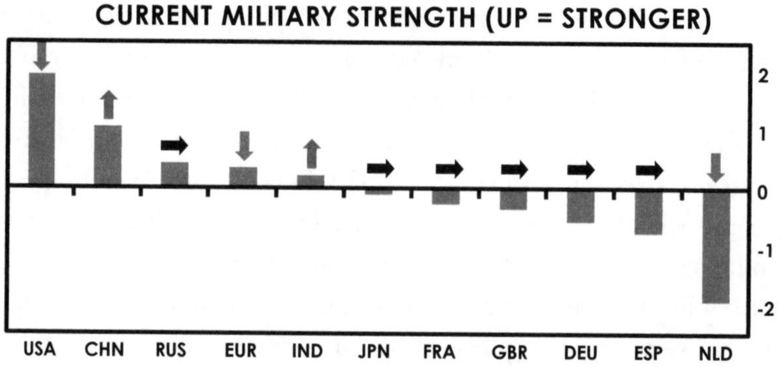

History shows that wars are terribly costly in lives and money, and the capacity to inflict harm has advanced exponentially since nuclear weapons were developed and used in World War II. I am unable to imagine what the next military war would look like. I have also seen that those who are most informed on both sides are not fully informed because a lot is unknown and because military wars always transpire in unexpected ways. For those reasons, **it is impossible to confidently say who the winners and losers in the next big war would be**. We also know from logic and from studying history that the losers of really big wars are completely wiped out and the winners lose too, as they suffer severe consequences and end up with big debts. What that means for economies and markets was explained earlier in the book, but in a word, it is devastating.

Students of history know that the doctrine of mutually assured destruction prevented the US and the USSR from entering a hot war before the Soviet Empire fell, mostly due to the failure to grow its other strengths in the face of big military spending. China is roughly comparable in power to the United States in the most important ways, and it is on its way to becoming more powerful in many ways. China won't be as easy to defeat in any of the five types of war as the USSR was, and the USSR wasn't easy to defeat. That means the wars are likely to intensify and increasingly favor China, especially if the US doesn't turn around the other fundamental underpinnings of strength that are highlighted in this chapter. However, it seems like it will be a long time before China can win a war without having the war lead to its own destruction as well.

So, in summary, my computer and I working together now believe that **because for the foreseeable future China and the US will be powerful enough to inflict unacceptable harm on each other the prospect of mutually assured destruction should prevent military war, though there almost certainly will be dangerous skirmishes. I expect this to be true unless some unexpected technological breakthrough, like dramatic advances in quantum computing, gives one of these powers such an asymmetrical advantage that mutually assured destruction would cease to exist.** Also, though of less importance, an impediment to fighting is the interlinked well-being of Americans and the Chinese in this highly interconnected world.

However, as time passes the risks increase. If the US continues to decline and China continues to rise, what matters most is whether or not each can do so gracefully. The big risk is that when existential irreconcilable differences exist and there is no mutually agreed-upon party or process to adjudicate the conflict, there is a good chance that there will be a fight. As explained in the last chapter, **the main seemingly irreconcilable difference between the US and China is over Taiwan, so I am watching developments there very closely.** Taiwan is a one-of-a-kind interest that China would fight for because of its belief that "there is but one China and Taiwan is part of China." It is doubtful that the US would consider it worth a major fight to defend, though it might. This seems to me to be the only possible trigger for a military war between the two greatest powers in the next 10 years.

The next locations to pay attention to are the areas immediately around China, like those countries surrounding the East and South China Seas, and other neighbors such as India, Russia, South Korea, North Korea, Japan, Afghanistan, Pakistan, etc. Considering what China's culture is like and what's most beneficial for China, I believe it will work to influence those countries through an exchange of benefits but won't fight to control them outright.

While the most important conflicts are between the United States and China, there are other important players operating in this classic drama of the balance of power and the prisoner's dilemma. It is important to watch the actions of China's and the United States' allies and friends. As previously discussed, the alignments are gradually changing, with China gaining allies and the United States losing them. Overextended and less willing to lose lives fighting for others, the US is now in the position of trying to cat herd its allies without catnip. In the past, the US merely needed to hint at what it wanted other countries to do for them to do it. Now they go their own ways.

In the end, which country wins the game of obtaining the most wealth and power depends most on their internal capacities, which is why I monitor those factors in my indices as I do for military strength. As the Chinese know very well (and it would be good for others to keep in mind), ● ***the best way to fight a war is to get strong and show one's opponent one's strength so they don't want to fight violently.*** This will most likely be the dynamic that we see in the years ahead.

All of this is to say that **I think the odds favor intensifying trade/economic wars, technology wars, capital wars, and geopolitical wars as China becomes even more competitive and increasingly goes global in these areas.** As Graham Allison explained in his excellent book, *Destined for War*, in the past 500 years, when two nearly equal powers experienced irreconcilable differences, there were military wars in 12 out of 16 cases, and big military buildups were associated with major wars in 80–90 percent of cases.[8] I balance those historical insights with the logic of mutually assured destruction, which lowers the odds of war. On net, I would conclude that the probability of a big war in the next 10 years is 35 percent, give or take, which is essentially a wild guess. In any case, it's a dangerously high risk.

---

[8] We *may* be seeing such a buildup now. China's military spending has risen sharply in dollar terms over the past decade, though as a share of GDP it remains relatively steady (at around 2 percent). At around 3 percent of GDP, military spending has fallen a bit for the US.

ACTS OF NATURE

Throughout history, droughts, floods, pandemics, and other severe natural and biological disasters have inflicted more harm on people than people have inflicted on themselves, killing millions, disrupting economies, and contributing to the falls of many empires and dynasties. This chart shows some of the major events.

GLOBAL DEATHS BY CATEGORY
(RATE PER 100K PEOPLE)

■ Famines ■ Natural Disasters ■ Pandemics

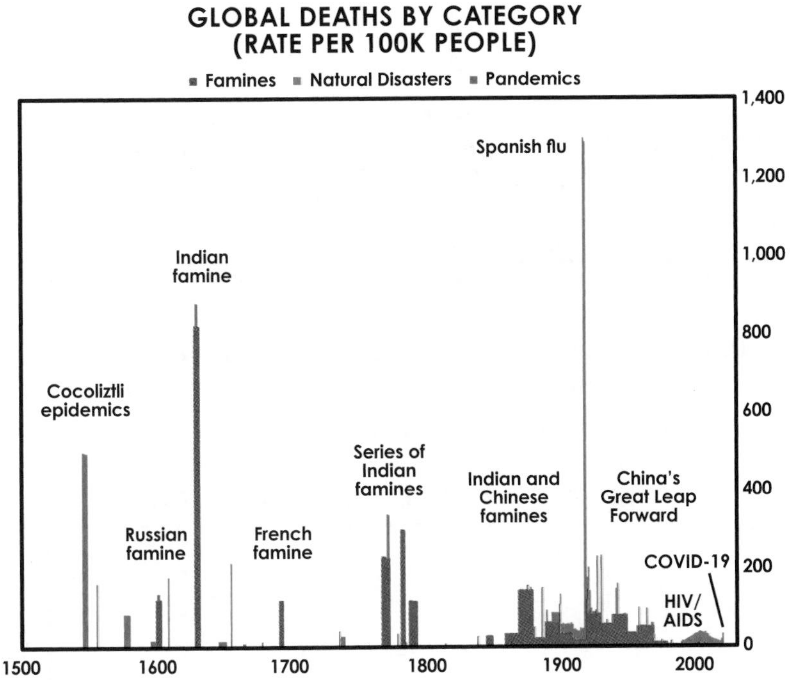

While we all know about climate change, no one knows precisely how much damage and how many deaths it will ultimately cause. But based on expert projections, there is reason to believe that all of these kinds of disasters will be bigger in the years ahead than they were before. While I'm no expert on the subject myself, I can show you some interesting stats and pass along what I've learned.

The next chart on the right shows the world's average temperature and the amount of CO2, indicating global warming. There is

little doubt this is happening, will pick up, and will have big and costly effects. What is notable is this is increasing at a faster rate. The chart on the left shows the very long-term perspective on temperature (since 0 CE).

GLOBAL TEMPERATURE VS 1961–1990 AVG (°C, SINCE 0 CE)

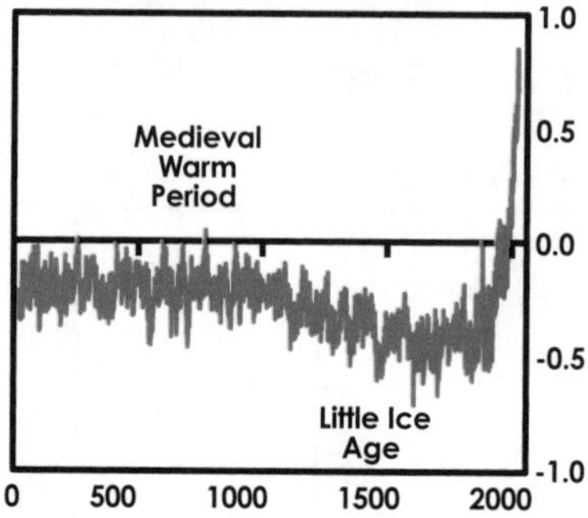

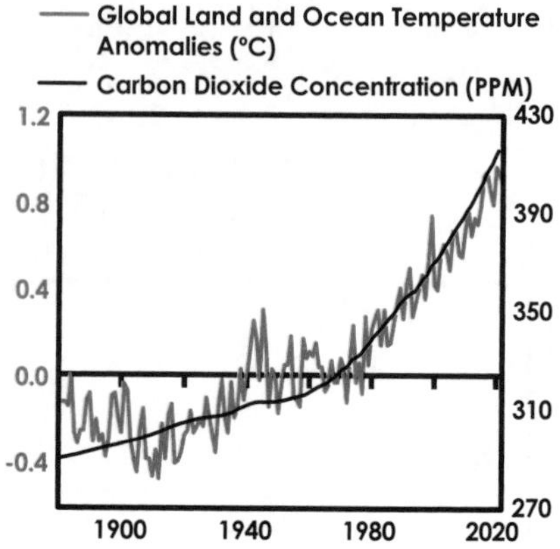

This chart captures extreme environmental events. The headline is that from 1970 to 2020 they increased from fewer than 50 per year to nearly 200 per year and are trending higher.

NUMBER OF NATURAL CATASTROPHIC EVENTS

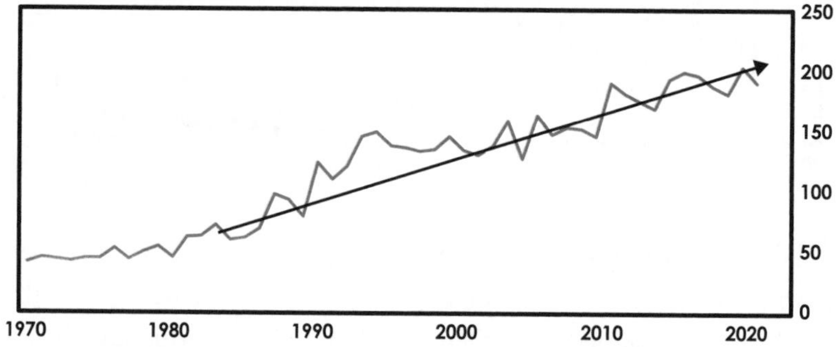

The next chart shows the estimated dollar cost of these events (adjusted for inflation). As shown, this is also trending higher, with extreme spikes.

TOTAL LOSSES FROM CATASTROPHES SINCE 1970 (2020 USD, BLN)

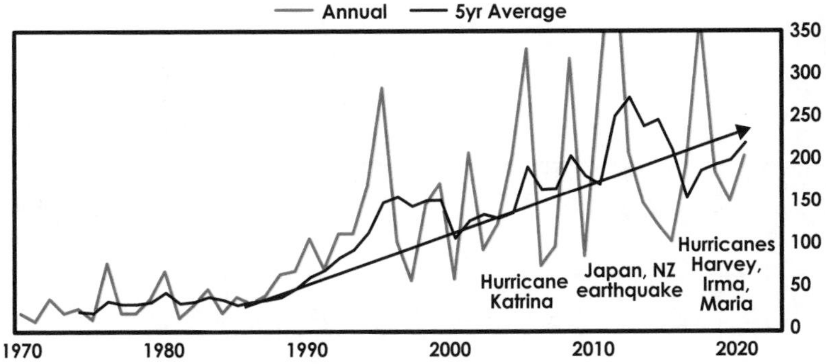

It is pretty clear to me that humanity and natural evolution together are doing great damage to the environment that will be very costly in both money and quality of life. This will affect countries very differently, in ways that we can broadly anticipate based on their locations, climates, and—most importantly—industries. At the same time, this is a slow, steady, and well-telegraphed change, which lends itself to the kind of adaptation and innovation humanity is uniquely able to do, though often too slowly and only in response to pain. I am inclined to believe that slowly and reactively is how it will happen. Having said that, I don't know enough about the subject to know what it means for every country and locality.

The next chart shows an index of climate change vulnerability across major countries based on an equal average of the Notre Dame-Global Adaptation Index (ND-GAIN) Country Index, which quantifies a country's vulnerability to climate change, and academic estimates of the future impact of climate change on GDP by country.

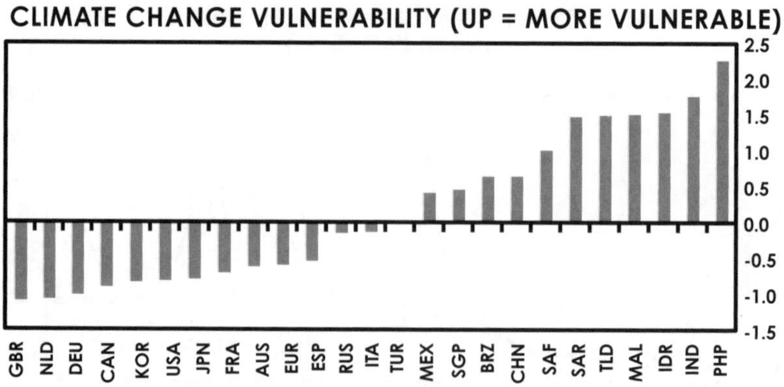

IN SUMMARY

Based on just these five indicators, it appears to me that:

- **Humanity's inventiveness will probably lead to great advances while the debt/economic cycle, the internal order cycle, the external order cycle, and worsening acts of nature will almost certainly pose problems. In other words, *there will be a battle between humanity's inventiveness and these other challenges.***
- **Very different conditions exist within and between countries, which will determine which countries will rise and decline and in what ways.**

All of this reflects my thinking about the future of the world's 11 major countries based on just five of the 18 determinants. Now let's look at all 18 indicators to see what they tell us.

ALL THE MAJOR DETERMINANTS ACROSS THE WORLD

The following table paints a much richer picture of what's happening and what is likely to happen across the 11 major countries. While I have many of these readings for the top 20 countries, I don't have the space to show them here; you can find the complete set at economicprinciples.org. While this table might look like a bunch of numbers and arrows at first glance, when you get into it a clearer picture will emerge.

But first, **here's how to read the table and how these gauges work. The first column shows the determinant being measured. The second rates the quality of the gauge.** It is provided because for some of these important determinants we have good, clear measurements (e.g., for education, innovation and technology, cost competitiveness, productivity and output growth) and for some we don't (e.g., acts of nature), and I want to show which is which. Additionally, there are other determinants that aren't shown because they are either too subjective or too difficult to quantify (e.g., leadership). The quality of leadership can't be measured as objectively as the amount of economic output (e.g., how can you measure whether Donald Trump was a good leader or a bad one?). Each is an aggregate of many indicators that I combined in the way that I felt best captured that particular determinant, giving consideration to both quantity and quality. For example, a country with a large population like China, India, and the United States when compared to a country with a small population like Singapore, the Netherlands, and Switzerland might have more of something but of lesser quality. I tried to structure these weightings so that I could imagine who would win if they had a competition like the Olympics or a war.

CURRENT READINGS ACROSS MAJOR POWERS
(Z-Score and 20-Year Change Denoted by Arrows)

	GAUGE QUALITY	USA	CHN	EUR	DEU
EMPIRE SCORE (0–1)		0.87 ◢	0.75 ▲	0.55 ▶	0.37 ▶
Debt Burden (Big Economic Cycle)	Good	-1.8 ▼	0.3 ▼	-0.3 ▶	1.6 ▲
Expected Growth (Big Economic Cycle)	Good	-0.7 ◢	0.4 ▼	-1.0 ▶	-1.0 ▶
Internal Conflict (Internal Order; low is bad)	Good	-2.0 ▼	0.2 ▶	0.4 ▶	0.7 ◥
Education	Good	2.0 ◢	1.6 ▲	0.3 ▶	-0.2 ▶
Innovation & Technology	Good	2.0 ▶	1.5 ▲	0.4 ◢	-0.1 ◢
Cost Competitiveness	Good	-0.4 ▶	1.2 ◢	-0.6 ▶	-0.6 ▶
Military Strength	Good	1.9 ◢	1.0 ▲	0.3 ◢	-0.6 ▶
Trade	Good	1.1 ◢	1.8 ▲	1.3 ▶	0.6 ▶
Economic Output	Good	1.7 ◢	1.8 ▲	0.6 ▼	-0.1 ◢
Markets & Financial Center	Good	2.6 ▶	0.5 ▲	0.4 ▶	-0.2 ◢
Reserve Currency Status (0–1)	Good	0.55 ◢	0.04 ▲	0.23 ◢	
Geology	Good	1.4 ▶	0.9 ◥	-0.4 ▶	-0.7 ▶
Resource-Allocation Efficiency	OK	1.3 ◢	0.0 ▶	-0.8	0.6 ▲
Acts of Nature	OK	-0.2	-0.1	0.0	1.1
Infrastructure & Investment	Good	0.7 ◢	2.7 ▲	0.2 ◢	-0.3 ▶
Character/Civility/Determination	OK	1.1 ▶	1.5 ▶	-1.0 ▶	-0.5 ▶
Governance/Rule of Law	Good	0.7 ◥	-0.7 ◥	-0.4	0.7 ▶
Gaps in Wealth, Opportunity & Values	OK	-1.6 ◢	-0.4 ▶	0.3 ▲	0.7 ▶

Scanning the table, you can quickly get a picture of each country's circumstances and the overall state of the world. For example, by looking at the empire scores and the arrows next to them you can see that the United States is the most powerful country but declining and China is close behind and rising quickly. You can see in what ways the United States is exceptionally strong—i.e., its reserve currency status, military strength, economic output, innovation and technology, and education—and you can see in what ways it is weak—i.e., its internal conflicts, wealth gaps, indebtedness, and expected economic growth.

You can also see that China is close behind the US in most other key areas and that it is relatively strong in its infrastructure and investment, innovation and technology, education, cost competitiveness, economic output, trade, military strength, and trade/capital flows, and relatively weak because of its reserve currency status, rule of law/corruption, and wealth gaps. I find this data invaluable. It's crucial to watch for changes in it when thinking about what's happening and what is likely to happen.

	GAUGE QUALITY	JPN	IND	GBR	FRA
EMPIRE SCORE (0–1)		0.30 ▼	0.27 ◥	0.27 ▶	0.25 ▶
Debt Burden (Big Economic Cycle)	Good	-0.4 ▶	0.1 ◥	-1.6 ▼	-0.8 ▼
Expected Growth (Big Economic Cycle)	Good	-1.1 ▶	1.1 ▼	-0.8 ◢	-0.9 ▶
Internal Conflict (Internal Order; low is bad)	Good	1.1 ▲		-0.3 ▼	-0.1 ▶
Education	Good	0.2 ▶	-1.2 ▶	-0.2 ◢	-0.5 ▶
Innovation & Technology	Good	0.2 ◢	-1.2 ◥	-0.3 ▶	-0.5 ◢
Cost Competitiveness	Good	-0.3 ▶	2.4 ◥	-0.3 ▶	-0.6 ▶
Military Strength	Good	-0.1 ▶	0.2 ▲	-0.3 ▶	-0.3 ▶
Trade	Good	-0.5 ▼	-0.8 ◥	-0.6 ▶	-0.5 ▶
Economic Output	Good	-0.3 ▼	-0.2 ▶	-0.3 ▶	-0.5 ▼
Markets & Financial Center	Good	0.1 ◢	-0.8 ▶	0.0 ◢	-0.3 ▶
Reserve Currency Status (0–1)	Good	0.07 ◢	0.0	0.07 ▶	
Geology	Good	-1.1 ▶	0.3 ▶	-0.9 ▶	-0.5 ▶
Resource-Allocation Efficiency	OK	0.1 ◢	0.2	0.3 ▶	-1.3 ▼
Acts of Nature	OK	1.5	-2.4	0.4	0.0
Infrastructure & Investment	Good	-0.2 ▼	-0.3 ▲	-0.6 ◢	-0.2 ◥
Character/Civility/Determination	OK	0.5 ◢	1.3 ▶	-0.4 ◢	-1.5 ▶
Governance/Rule of Law	Good	0.8 ▶	-1.1 ◥	1.2 ▶	0.3 ▶
Gaps in Wealth, Opportunity & Values	OK	0.9 ▲	-1.8 ▶	-0.2 ▼	1.1 ◥

	GAUGE QUALITY	NLD	RUS	ESP
EMPIRE SCORE (0–1)		**0.25**	**0.23**	**0.20**
Debt Burden (Big Economic Cycle)	Good	0.8 ▲	1.0 ▲	-1.7 ▼
Expected Growth (Big Economic Cycle)	Good	-0.8	**-0.2**	-1.1
Internal Conflict (Internal Order; low is bad)	Good	1.2	-0.5 ▲	**-0.4**
Education	Good	-0.7	-0.5	-0.9
Innovation & Technology	Good	**-0.3**	-0.7	-1.0 ▼
Cost Competitiveness	Good	-0.8	0.7	-0.6
Military Strength	Good	-1.9	**0.4**	-0.8
Trade	Good	-0.6	-0.9	-0.9
Economic Output	Good	**-0.3**	-1.4	-0.9 ▼
Markets & Financial Center	Good	-0.5	-1.1	-0.6
Reserve Currency Status (0–1)	Good		**0.0**	
Geology	Good	-0.5	1.9	-0.6
Resource-Allocation Efficiency	OK	**-0.1**	1.3	-1.6
Acts of Nature	OK	0.5	**-0.1**	-0.7
Infrastructure & Investment	Good	**-0.4**	-1.0 ▼	-0.6 ▼
Character/Civility/Determination	OK	**-0.3**	**0.1**	-1.0
Governance/Rule of Law	Good	1.0	-1.9	-0.7
Gaps in Wealth, Opportunity & Values	OK	0.6		**0.4**

For example, as shown before, **when 1) a country's finances are deteriorating at the same time as 2) the level of internal conflict is high (e.g., over wealth and/or values differences), while 3) the country is being challenged by one or more strong foreign rivals, that typically produces 4) a mutually and self-reinforcing decline. That's because the country's deteriorating finances make it impossible for it to satisfy domestic spending needs and finance the war, which causes worse outcomes.**

Now that these things are quantified, we can see them happening in the table and make projections. The greater the number of important determinants that are worsening and the more severely they are worsening, the surer and more severe the decline will be. For example, if a few other determinants are weak and weakening at the same time that others are faltering, the expected severity of the decline increases. Because I, with the help of my computer, can monitor such things, I can assess a country's relative health, vulnerabilities, and future prospects. For example, many of the most worrying conditions now exist in the United States, even though the United States is still the most powerful country in the world. That merits close attention.

As conveyed in some earlier charts, we saw that **1) these determinants tend to reinforce each other, whether in strength (e.g., stronger education tends to create stronger incomes) or weakness (e.g., weakening trade leads to higher indebtedness), so they tend to transpire in cycles that come together to create the Big Cycle, and 2) when the determinants are weak and weakening, the empires are weak and weakening.**[9] **Big swings up occur when lots of determinants are strengthening and big swings down occur when lots of determinants are weakening.**

Our computers use this data to generate written reports, which are available to read at economicprinciples.org. They project real GDP growth rates for the next 10 years, along with the gauge readings for each factor that leads to those estimates. The data, and hence the projections, is more reliable for some countries than others, which is conveyed in the readouts. Still, they do a good job of reflecting the current health of a country and serve as leading indicators of their future health. Based on backtesting, these estimates would have predicted a country's average growth rate over the next decade within 1 percent of the actual growth 59 percent of the time, and within 2 percent about 90 percent of the time, with a correlation to subsequent growth of 81 percent. I have found them to be invaluable.

[9] Determinants like geology (i.e., minerals in the ground) are relatively easy to measure, though the implications of having them might change. Determinants that evolve like humanity's innovations and technologies can typically be seen emerging by watching the trends. Those that transpire in cycles (like debt and capital markets) can be understood by understanding the cycles. The fact that acts of nature like pandemics, droughts, and floods come along shouldn't be a surprise, though their timing often is.

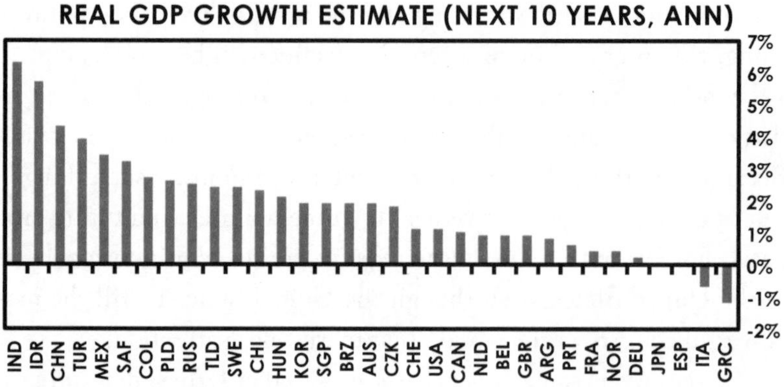

While these are good and useful indicators, they have to work hand in hand with my thinking. Consider the question, "What is the mix of powers that makes a country powerful?" While the total power index at the top of the current readings tables is intended to indicate that and is arrived at via a weighted average of the indices below it, the truth is that the type of power that is most important to have at any one time varies according to circumstances. For example, military power is expensive and it typically sits around doing nothing until it is the most important power to have. How do I properly weight that against economic output that consists of mostly nonessentials? The answer is not well. I don't have it modeled well, but I think about it a lot and apply my experience and intuition to it. In time I will have it modeled better, but I know that I will always need to have what is in my head work with what's in the computer, as the computer and I need each other to be at our best.

THE NEXT 10 YEARS

While this book is about the really big cycles, I'd like to focus now on the dynamics within these cycles that will be most important over the next 10 years. As I've explained, there are cycles within cycles within cycles, with the little ones adding up to the bigger ones, plus there are non-cyclical bumps that all together determine what happens. **Over the next 10 years, the most important dynamics are the short-term debt/money/economy cycle (also called the business cycle), the internal political cycle, and the escalating conflicts/reducing inter-dependencies between the US and China.** I find that keeping these cycles in mind, thinking about how they affect each other, and assessing where things stand within them are helpful for timing my decisions.

As discussed in Chapter 4, the short-term debt/money/economic cycle consists of alternating periods of central banks stimulating the economy by creating money and credit and then attempting to slowing it down by reducing the flow of them. They never get this precisely right, which is what produces the excesses that lead to bubbles, busts, and the cycle beginning again. Sometimes other negative events happen around the same time as a downturn—September 11, 2001 was such a case.

This cycle typically takes about eight years, give or take a few, though the timing is less the result of how long it's been since the last one and more the result of the underlying economic drivers themselves. Most importantly, the amount of slack in the economy, the amounts and types of financial bubbles, the amount of central bank tightening, and the markets' and economies' sensitivity to tightening all matter. The last cycle began in April 2020 with largest dose of fiscal and monetary stimulation ever. The one before that began in 2008, which was also a giant dose though much less big. The ones before that began in 2001, 1990, 1982, 1980, 1974, 1970, 1960, etc. With the amounts of stimulation injected into this recent downturn being so enormous (especially in the US), with the slack in the major economies being relatively limited (especially in the US), with the signs of bubbles now being moderate to strong, and with the interest rate sensitivity of markets and the economy being high, my guess is that the next downturn will come sooner than is typical. I'd estimate in about four years from the publication of this book, give or take a couple of years (which is about five-and-a-half years from the bottom).

Don't bet on what I just said happening because that configuration is not precise. I will need to monitor the factors I just mentioned, especially the rate of rebound in inflation and how quick and strong central bank tightening will be in order to home in on the precise timing. Also, I would expect any downturn to be promptly followed by a quick reversal of central bank policies toward the next big round of stimulation. That makes me less worried about the impact of the downturn and more worried about the excess money printing and the loss of value of money (particularly cash and debt in dollars, euros, and yen). Of course what happens in this economic cycle will be affected by what happens with the other cycles and the bumps along the way, just as this cycle will affect the other cycles.

As far as the internal order/disorder cycle is concerned, it typically lags the debt/economic cycle because people are less confrontational in good times than in bad ones. When these cycles interact strongly, it can lead to major changes. In the US the short-term political cycles of change come every two years with congressional elections and every four years with presidential elections, with an eight-year limit on the total presidential term. In China the changes come every five and 10 years with the next big one happening around the time of this book's publication (November 2021). There is no limit on the presidential term. While we can look at the calendars and know something about what's ahead, there will be lots of uncertainties, some of which can be really impactful. Based on my estimates, there is a significant chance the next downturn will come around the time of the next presidential election in the US.

The external order/disorder cycle has traditionally followed the path of accelerating conflicts that lead to wars. As mentioned earlier, the United States and China are now preparing themselves for increasing intensity in the five types of war. They are operating with roughly five-year plans to gain greater amounts of self-sufficiency and preparedness for each of these wars, which will give them greater ability to wage them, though it's doubtful that either will become dominant enough to ignore the deterrent of mutually assured destruction. Since China's strength is gaining relative to that of the US, it would seem to imply that important changes will come neither too soon nor too far ahead. As mentioned earlier, there is significant risk that we are approaching a conflict between an unstoppable force and an immovable object regarding Taiwan and the East and South China Seas—i.e., China is an unstoppable force for change to Taiwan's current status and the United States is an immovable object against it. Beyond the US and China, other nations—most notably Russia, India, Japan, Korea, and the key European and Middle Eastern powers—will play important roles in this global drama. Over the next five years or so, alliances are likely to harden.

These things point toward the next big risk point being around five years from this writing, give or take a couple of years.

To reiterate, there is nothing precise about the timing of these cycles. They're like hurricane/typhoon seasons; we know they are likely to happen at roughly certain times so we prepare for them, and when those times come, we watch for storms emerging, follow them closely, and do our best to get out of harm's way. While we can't say exactly when they will come and exactly how strong they will be, we do know that the trend and the fundamentals have been for them to get stronger, so we should be prepared for that possibility.

Despite all the analytical work I do, I know that the unknown is still much greater than the known. While history can be told pretty precisely, the future is exactly the opposite. I am not aware of a single case of the future being foretold accurately in any detail. For an investor, understanding history accurately is of no use relative to being a bit more right than wrong about the future. Since non-investors place bets in the form of their life decisions, that's true for them too. That brings me to the final point of this chapter, which is about knowing how to place one's bets based on the assumption that one is likely to be wrong a lot.

DEALING WITH WHAT YOU KNOW AND WHAT YOU DON'T KNOW

Whatever success I've had has been more due to my knowing how to deal with what I don't know than anything I know. Betting on the future is betting on probabilities and nothing is certain, not even the probabilities. That's just the way it is. While what I've given you up until this point is what I believe I know about the future based on my reasoning about the past, what I want to pass along that is probably more important is how I make decisions in life and in the markets based on what I don't know. In a nutshell, here's what I try to do:

- ***Know all the possibilities, think about the worst-case scenarios, and then find ways to eliminate the intolerable ones.*** Identifying and eliminating the intolerable worst-case scenarios comes first. That's because the most important thing in playing the game (of life or the markets) is to not get knocked out of it. I learned that from a big mistake I made in 1982, which nearly broke me. After that painful loss I calculated what my basic needs would cost and worked toward having enough money stashed away so my worst-case scenario would be tolerable. As I built up from nothing, I remember regularly calculating how many weeks, then months, and then years my family and I would be fine if not another dime came in. I now have an "end of the world" portfolio that I know will keep us fine in the worst-case scenarios, and I build from there. From reading this book, you can probably see that I imagine a lot of worst-case scenarios, including depressions, devaluations, revolutions, wars, pandemics, my big mistakes, health problems, and death from different causes. I start by trying to protect myself against all of them and more. While you might think that my paying so much attention to eliminating worst-case scenarios is depressing and prevents me from making the most of opportunities, the opposite is true. It's liberating and exciting to operate this way because knowing that the worst-case scenarios are covered gives me the safety, freedom, and ability to go for great results.
- ***Diversify.*** In addition to making sure I've covered all the worst-case scenarios I can think of, I try to cover those I can't think of by diversifying well. I learned the math of it and I'm drawn to it instinctively. Essentially, if I have a bunch of bets that are attractive but unrelated, I can reduce my risks by up to 80 percent without reducing my upside at all. While this sounds like an investment strategy it's actually an old and well-established good life strategy that I apply to

investments as well. There is a Chinese saying that "a smart rabbit has three burrows," meaning three places to go to in case any one of them becomes dangerous. This principle has saved many people's lives when things got bad, and it's one of my most important principles.

- ***Put deferred gratification ahead of immediate gratification so you will be better off in the future.***

- ***Triangulate among the smartest people possible.*** I tag along with the smartest people I can find, so I can stress test my thinking and learn from them.

It is through these principles that I got so much upside with relatively little downside and a steadily improving future, albeit with bumps along the way. That's why I recommend these principles to you, though as always, you should feel free to take them or leave them as you like.

One more thing for policy makers, those they report to, and others who are interested:

Use the gauges I gave you, or take the stats and make your own, to 1) measure the health of your country and other countries you're interested in, 2) see if it is improving or worsening and in what ways, and 3) make changes in the determinants of the future to get a better future.

That's it.

I now feel that doing all this has given me an adequate understanding of the possibilities, both worst-case scenarios and opportunities, and a time-tested plan for dealing with them well. I also believe that I have adequately conveyed to you in this book and on economicprinciples.org the most important things I know about how the lessons of the past can help you deal with the future. I hope you find them to be of some use. I plan to evolve all of this to make it better, which I hope we can do together.

May the Force of Evolution be with you,

Ray

MORE DETAIL ON EACH OF THE GAUGES

- **Education:** This gauge measures basic and higher education, split about evenly between the two. Half of the measure captures the absolute quantity of educated people at various levels and about half is placed on quality such as higher education rankings, test scores, and average years of education. The US ranks highest in this gauge (driven by strong absolute and relative measures of higher education), with China close behind (due to its large number of educated people).
- **Innovation & Technology:** This gauge measures inventiveness, technological advancement, and entrepreneurship. It gives about half its weight to the country's absolute share of key innovation metrics (e.g., patents, researchers, R&D spending, and venture capital funding) and half to a combination of external rankings and measures of innovation per capita (to help capture how widespread innovation is in the economy). The US is at the top of this measure due to its strength across a variety of metrics, while China ranks second due to its large share of global research spending, researchers, and patents. China is rising quickly in this area.
- **Cost Competitiveness:** This gauge measures what one gets for what one pays. We want to see this because countries that produce the best at costs that are too expensive aren't in good shape, even though they rank high in quality. We look at quality-adjusted and productivity-adjusted labor costs, along with other productivity measures. Major developing economies (particularly India) rank highest in this gauge, while the US ranks around the middle of the pack and European countries rank lowest (due to high labor costs).
- **Infrastructure & Investment:** This gauge measures the quantity of infrastructure and investment spending and the quality of it. It captures a country's absolute share of global investment,

as well as the extent to which a country prioritizes quality of infrastructure and productivity-enhancing investments. The gauge weighs measures of investment as a share of world investment, overall infrastructure quality, investment and savings as a share of GDP, and logistics performance. China is currently the strongest according to this gauge (having risen sharply over the past 20 years) because of its high rates of productive investment relative to both the world and the size of its own past investment; the US is second, due largely to its high share of global productive investment, though it is worsening.

- **Economic Output:** This gauge measures the strength of a country's economic resources. We measure output primarily through GDP levels as a share of world total (adjusted for price differences across countries). We allocate some weight to GDP per capita rather than total GDP to capture quality. China ranks first in this gauge, insignificantly ahead of the US but also rising fastest, due its large PPP-adjusted GDP share. Europe ranks third.
- **Expected Growth (Big Economic Cycle):** This gauge measures how well a country is positioned to grow its economy over the next 10 years. We look at a variety of metrics to estimate forward-looking 10-year economic growth, placing two-thirds weight on metrics that predict productivity and one-third on metrics that predict the impact of indebtedness on growth. Currently India is predicted to grow the fastest, followed by China, with the US predicted to grow a bit slower than average, and with Japan and a number of European countries predicted to grow least.
- **Trade:** This gauge measures how strong of an exporter a country is. It looks at the absolute level of a country's exports as a share of the world. China scores highest (being the largest exporter in the world), followed by Europe and the US.
- **Military Strength:** This gauge is driven mostly by the absolute share of military spending and strength measured by the number of personnel, the number of nuclear weapons, and external

indices of military capabilities. It does not look at military powers in varying regions or of various types, failing to capture some military superiorities Russia and China have in certain geographic areas, certain types of military technologies, or the role of alliances. The US is still the strongest overall military power based on these measures, with a strong lead in spending and a nuclear weapons program that is only rivaled by Russia. China is now ranked second and is rising quickly.

- **Financial Center:** This gauge measures the level of development and sizes of a country's financial markets and financial center. We look at absolute measures of transaction shares and market capitalizations, as well as external indices of financial center cities. The US remains the top-ranked power in this metric by a significant margin (driven primarily by its very large share of world equity and debt markets), with China and Europe ranking second and third, respectively.
- **Reserve Currency Status:** This gauge measures the extent to which a country's currency operates as a global reserve currency. We measure reserve currency status by the share of transactions, debts, and central bank reserves that are denominated or held in a country's currency. Similar to financial center status, the US remains the top-ranked power in this metric by a significant margin, with Europe and Japan ranking second and third, respectively.
- **Debt Burden (Big Economic Cycle):** This gauge is based on a combination of a) debt levels relative to asset levels, b) the sizes of external and internal surpluses and deficits, c) the sizes of debt service costs relative to GDP, d) the amount of debt in a country's own currency versus foreign currency, e) the amount of debt held by its own citizens versus foreigners, and f) its credit rating. We composed it this way because it has proven itself to be the most reliable way we have of foreshadowing declines in the value of real wealth, whether they come in the form of debt defaults that result from not creating enough

money and credit to satisfy excessive debt needs or devaluations that come from creating more than enough money and credit to satisfy excessive debt needs. I constructed this index to exclude reserve currency status so that I could see the exposure a country would have if it lost its reserve currency status.

- **Internal Conflict (Internal Order):** This gauge looks at how much domestic conflict and discontent there is. It measures actual conflict events (e.g., protests), political conflict (e.g., partisanship), and general discontent (based on surveys). The US ranks highest in this gauge among the major countries, driven by measures of partisanship and higher incidence of internal conflict events, and it has been rising fast.
- **Governance/Rule of Law:** This gauge measures the extent to which a country's legal system is consistent, predictable, and conducive to growth and advancement. It combines rule of law measures (based primarily on business surveys of doing business in the country) and corruption measures (via a combination of external corruption indices and surveys of businesses). Russia and India score lowest (worst) on the gauge, while the UK, the Netherlands, and Japan score highest (best), with Germany and the US close behind.
- **Geology:** This gauge measures each country's geographic endowment, including land size and the value of its natural resources. It includes the total production of energy, agriculture, and industrial metals in order to capture the absolute production capacity of each nation, as well as net exports to capture relative self-reliance for each of the categories (in addition to measuring some other natural resources like freshwater supply). Russia and the US score highest (followed by China, which relies more on the rest of the world to cover its natural resource needs), while Japan and the UK score lowest.
- **Gaps in Wealth, Opportunity & Values:** This gauge measures how big the gaps in wealth/income, opportunities, and values are. It combines measures of both a) wealth and income

inequality (e.g., how much does the top 1 percent have versus the rest) and b) political conflict (e.g., how split is the legislature on ideology). India, the US, and China score worst because of very large wealth and income gaps (and in the case of the US also significant political gaps). At the other end of the spectrum are the European nations and Japan, which generally speaking have lower income and wealth inequality.

- **Character/Civility/Determination:** This gauge attempts to measure to what extent the attitudes of each country's people create an environment that's supportive to civility and hard work, which supports growth and advancement. It uses a) surveys around attitudes toward working hard and success and b) other measures that proxy how much a society values self-sufficiency and work (e.g., government transfer payments size, effective retirement age) to quantify this. China and India score highest (the US is third), and the European countries (notably Spain and France) score lowest.
- **Resource-Allocation Efficiency:** This gauge attempts to measure how efficiently each country is using its labor and capital. It looks at whether the country has chronically high unemployment (i.e., not finding efficient ways to employ its people), if debt growth generates commensurate income growth over time, and external indices and surveys about the rigidity of the labor market and ease of getting loans. Much of Europe (particularly France and Spain) score lowest on these measures, while the US and Germany score near the top. Developing countries (particularly Russia, but also China and India) also score fairly well in this measure—as generally speaking they produce more income growth per unit of debt growth.
- **Acts of Nature:** This gauge measures how vulnerable to and impacted by acts of nature each country is. While it is difficult to quantify all the various acts of nature that might affect a country, we used expert assessments of future climate change impact on each country's GDP, external assessments of each

country's preparedness for natural disasters, and the outcomes from the COVID pandemic (as that was a real-time test against an act of nature). I consider this rating so-so and find that there is still a lot more we want to capture to make this gauge better, hence its low quality.

- **External Conflict:** While not a part of the model for individual countries, the external conflict gauge measures the levels of economic, political/cultural, and military conflict between pairs of major countries. Within each category, we tried to come up with a mix of structural indicators (to establish a baseline level of conflict between countries) and timely indicators (to flag major escalations above that baseline). For example, for economic conflict we track bilateral trade between countries, tariff rates, and timely news around sanctions, trade wars, etc.

APPENDIX

COMPUTER ANALYSIS OF THE CONDITIONS OF, AND PROSPECTS FOR, THE WORLD'S LEADING COUNTRIES

As I described earlier, I feed data into a computer that can create an output summarizing the conditions of, and long-term prospects for, the world's leading countries. These computer-generated summaries follow on the next few pages. I use these outputs to supplement my own thinking and other computer models I run to help me understand the world. This system is a never-ending work in progress. I will update these summaries on economicprinciples.org at least annually or more frequently if any big changes take place.

The text for each country highlights a few of the major gauges and a few of the stats within each gauge that reflect the broad trends we are seeing. The aggregate gauges and final country power score I am showing include hundreds of individual stats that we aggregate based on relevance, quality, and consistency across countries and time. To best capture the overall strength of a country, I gave considerations to both quantity and quality, but structured things to best capture who would win in a competition or war.

THE POWERS AND PROSPECTS OF THE UNITED STATES

This is our computer-generated reading for the United States as of August 2021.

Based on the latest readings of key indicators, **the United States appears to be a strong power (No. 1 among major countries today) in gradual decline. As shown in the table, the key strengths of the United States that put it in this position are its strong capital markets and financial center, its innovation/technology, its high level of education, its strong military, its reserve currency status, and its high economic output. Its weaknesses are its unfavorable economic/financial position and its large domestic conflicts.** The eight major measures of power are very strong today but are, in aggregate, trending downward. In particular, the United States' relative position in education, its importance to global trade, and its relative military strength are declining.

The table shows our aggregate country power gauge and the major drivers, as well as the rank of each measure of power across 11 major countries today and the trajectory over the past 20 years.

To understand a country, we start by looking at **the big cycles**, as well as **measures of power** that both reflect and drive the rise and fall of a country. While we refer to these factors individually, they are not separate; they interact with and reinforce one another to move a country along its cycle.

For the United States, **the big cycles look unfavorable**.

The United States is in an unfavorable position in its economic and financial cycles, with a high debt burden and relatively low expected real growth over the next 10 years (1.1 percent per year). The United

UNITED STATES—KEY DRIVERS OF OUR COUNTRY POWER SCORE

Overall Empire Score (0–1) **Level: 0.87** **Rank: 1** ↘

The Big Cycles	Level	Z-Score	Rank	Trajectory
Economic/Financial Position	Unfavorable	-1.7	10	↘
Debt Burden	High Debt	-1.8	11	↘
Expected Growth	1.1%	-0.7	4	↘
Internal Order	High Risk	-1.8	11	↘
Wealth/Opportunity/Values Gap	Large	-1.6	9	↘
Internal Conflict	Very High	-2.0	10	↘
External Order	At Risk			↘
Eight Key Measures of Power				
Markets & Financial Center	Very Strong	2.6	1	→
Innovation & Technology	Very Strong	2.0	1	→
Education	Very Strong	2.0	1	↘
Military Strength	Very Strong	1.9	1	↘
Reserve Currency Status	Very Strong	1.7	1	↘
Economic Output	Very Strong	1.7	2	↘
Trade	Strong	1.1	3	↘
Cost Competitiveness	Average	-0.4	6	→
Additional Measures of Power				
Geology	Strong	1.4	2	→
Resource-Allocation Efficiency	Strong	1.3	2	↘
Infrastructure & Investment	Strong	0.7	2	↘
Character/Determination/Civility	Strong	1.1	3	→
Governance/Rule of Law	Strong	0.7	5	↗
Acts of Nature	Average	-0.2	9	

↗ **Getting better** ↘ **Getting worse** → **Flat**

States has significantly more foreign debts than foreign assets (net IIP is -64 percent of GDP). Non-financial debt levels are high (277 percent of GDP), and government debt levels are high (128 percent of GDP). The bulk of these debts (99 percent) are in its own currency, which mitigates its debt risks. The ability to use interest rate cuts to stimulate the economy is low (short rates at 0.1 percent), and the country is already printing money to monetize debt. That said, being the world's leading reserve currency is extremely beneficial to the US. If this were to change, it would significantly weaken the US position.

Internal disorder is a high risk. Wealth, income, and values gaps are large. Regarding inequality, the top 1 percent and top 10 percent in the United States capture 19 percent and 45 percent of income (both the second highest shares across major countries). Our internal conflict gauge is very high. This gauge measures actual conflict events (e.g., protests), political conflict (e.g., partisanship), and general discontent (based on surveys).

External disorder is a risk. Most importantly, the United States and China, which is fast-rising and the No. 2 power (all things considered), are having significant conflict.

Looking in more detail at the eight key measures of power, the United States has the largest capital markets and the strongest financial center among major countries. Its equity markets are a majority of the world total (55 percent of total market cap and 64 percent of volume), and a majority of global transactions happen in dollars (55 percent). **In addition, the United States has the strongest reading on our measures of technology and innovation among major countries.** A large share of global patent applications (17 percent), global R&D spending (26 percent), and global researchers (26 percent) are in the United States. **The United States also has the strongest position in education among major countries.** The United States has a large share of the world's bachelor's degrees (20 percent). On years of education, the United States is good—students have on average 13.7 years of education versus 11.5 in the average major country. PISA scores, which measure the proficiency of 15-year-old students across countries, are around average—495 versus 483 in the average major country. The United States also has a mix of other strengths, as detailed in the table.

THE POWERS AND PROSPECTS OF CHINA

This is our computer-generated reading for China as of August 2021.

Based on the latest readings of key indicators, **China appears to be a strong power (No. 2 among major countries today) in rapid ascent. As shown in the table, the key strengths of China that put it in this position are its strong economic and financial position, its infrastructure and investment, its importance to global trade, its high economic output, its people's self-sufficiency and strong work ethic, its high level of education, and its strong military.** The eight major measures of power are somewhat strong today and are, in aggregate, trending sharply upward. In particular, China's importance to global trade, its innovation and technology, and its importance as a financial center are increasing.

The table shows our aggregate country power gauge and the major drivers, as well as the rank of each measure of power across 11 major countries today and the trajectory over the past 20 years.

To understand a country, we start by looking at the **big cycles**, as well as **measures of power** that both reflect and drive the rise and fall of a country. While we refer to these factors individually, they are not separate; they interact with and reinforce one another to move a country along its cycle.

For China, **the big cycles look somewhat favorable**.

China is in a somewhat favorable position in its economic and financial cycles, with a low debt burden and relatively high expected real growth over the next 10 years (4.3 percent per year). China has slightly more foreign assets than foreign debts (net IIP is 12 percent of GDP). Non-financial debt levels are high (263 percent of GDP), though government debt levels are low (48 percent of GDP). The bulk

CHINA—KEY DRIVERS OF OUR COUNTRY POWER SCORE

Overall Empire Score (0–1) **Level: 0.75** **Rank: 2** ↑

The Big Cycles	**Level**	**Z-Score**	**Rank**	**Trajectory**
Economic/Financial Position	Somewhat Favorable	0.4	3	↘
Debt Burden	Low Debt	0.3	4	↘
Expected Growth	4.3%	0.4	2	↘
Internal Order	Moderate Risk	-0.1	7	→
Wealth/Opportunity/Values Gap	Relatively Large	-0.4	8	→
Internal Conflict	Average	0.2	5	→
External Order	At Risk			↘
Eight Key Measures of Power				
Trade	Very Strong	1.8	1	↗
Economic Output	Very Strong	1.8	1	↗
Education	Strong	1.6	2	↗
Innovation & Technology	Strong	1.5	2	↗
Cost Competitiveness	Strong	1.2	2	↘
Military Strength	Strong	1.0	2	↗
Markets & Financial Center	Average	0.4	2	↗
Reserve Currency Status	Weak	-0.7	5	↗
Additional Measures of Power				
Infrastructure & Investment	Very Strong	2.7	1	↗
Character/Determination/Civility	Strong	1.5	1	→
Geology	Strong	0.9	3	↗
Resource-Allocation Efficiency	Average	0.0	7	→
Governance/Rule of Law	Weak	-0.7	8	↗
Acts of Nature	Average	-0.1	8	

↗ **Getting better** ↘ **Getting worse** → **Flat**

of these debts (96 percent) are in its own currency, which mitigates its debt risks. The ability to use interest rate cuts to stimulate the economy is modest (short rates at 1.9 percent).

Internal disorder is a moderate risk. Wealth, income, and values gaps are relatively large. Regarding inequality, the top 1 percent and top 10 percent in China capture 14 percent and 41 percent of income (respectively the third and fourth highest shares across major countries). Our internal conflict gauge is average. This gauge measures actual conflict events (e.g., protests), political conflict (e.g., partisanship), and general discontent (based on surveys).

External disorder is a risk. Most importantly, China and the United States, which is declining but remains the No. 1 power (all things considered), are having significant conflict.

Looking in more detail at the eight key measures of power, China is the largest exporter among major countries. It exports 14 percent of global exports. **In addition, China has the largest economy among major countries.** A large share of global economic activity (22 percent; adjusted for differences in prices across countries) is in China. **China also has the second strongest position in education among major countries.** China has a large share of the world's bachelor's degrees (22 percent). China also has a mix of other strengths, as detailed in the table.

THE POWERS AND PROSPECTS OF THE EUROZONE

This is our computer-generated reading for the Eurozone as of August 2021.

Based on the latest readings of key indicators, **the Eurozone appears to be a strong power (No. 3 among major countries today) on a flat trajectory. As shown in the table, the key strengths of the Eurozone are its importance to global trade and its reserve currency status. Its weaknesses are its people's lower-than-average work ethic and low self-sufficiency and its relatively poor allocation of labor and capital.** The eight major measures of power are somewhat strong today but are, in aggregate, moving sideways.

The table shows our aggregate country power gauge and the major drivers, as well as the rank of each measure of power across 11 major countries today and the trajectory over the past 20 years.

To understand a country, we start by looking at **the big cycles**, as well as **measures of power** that both reflect and drive the rise and fall of a country. While we refer to these factors individually, they are not separate; they interact with and reinforce one another to move a country along its cycle.

For the Eurozone, **the big cycles look mixed**.

The Eurozone is in a moderately unfavorable position in its economic and financial cycles, with a moderately high debt burden and relatively low expected real growth over the next 10 years (0.3 percent per year). The Eurozone has similar levels of foreign debts and foreign assets (net IIP is 0 percent of GDP). Non-financial debt levels are high (241 percent of GDP), though government debt levels are typical for major countries today (104 percent of GDP). The ability to use

EUROZONE—KEY DRIVERS OF OUR COUNTRY POWER SCORE

Overall Empire Score (0–1) **Level: 0.55** **Rank: 3** ➔

The Big Cycles	Level	Z-Score	Rank	Trajectory
Economic/Financial Position	Moderately Unfavorable	-0.9	6	↘
Debt Burden	Moderately High Debt	-0.3	6	➔
Expected Growth	0.3%	-1.0	8	➔
Internal Order	Low Risk	0.3	5	↗
Wealth/Opportunity/Values Gap	Typical	0.3	6	↗
Internal Conflict	Average	0.4	4	➔
External Order				
Eight Key Measures of Power				
Trade	Strong	1.3	2	➔
Reserve Currency Status	Average	0.1	2	↘
Economic Output	Strong	0.6	3	↘
Markets & Financial Center	Average	0.4	3	➔
Innovation & Technology	Average	0.4	3	↘
Education	Average	0.3	3	➔
Military Strength	Average	0.3	4	↘
Cost Competitiveness	Weak	-0.6	8	➔
Additional Measures of Power				
Infrastructure & Investment	Average	0.2	3	↘
Geology	Average	-0.4	5	➔
Governance/Rule of Law	Average	-0.4	7	
Resource-Allocation Efficiency	Weak	-0.8	9	
Character/Determination/Civility	Weak	-1.0	10	➔
Acts of Nature	Average	0.0	5	

↗ **Getting better** ↘ **Getting worse** ➔ **Flat**

interest rate cuts to stimulate the economy is very low (short rates at -0.5 percent), and Europe is already printing money to monetize debt.

Internal disorder is a low risk. Wealth, income, and values gaps are typical. Regarding inequality, the top 1 percent and top 10 percent in the Eurozone capture 11 percent and 35 percent of income (respectively the eighth and seventh highest shares across major countries). Our internal conflict gauge is average. This gauge measures actual conflict events (e.g., protests), political conflict (e.g., partisanship), and general discontent (based on surveys).

Looking in more detail at the eight key measures of power, the Eurozone is the second largest exporter among major countries. It exports 12 percent of global exports. **In addition, the Eurozone has the second strongest reserve currency among major countries.** A large share of global currency reserves are in euros (21 percent), and a large share of global debt is denominated in euros (22 percent).

This summary reflects our estimate of the power of the Eurozone in aggregate. For most stats, we're using an aggregate across the eight major countries in the Eurozone.

THE POWERS AND PROSPECTS OF GERMANY

This is our computer-generated reading for Germany as of August 2021.

Based on the latest readings of key indicators, **Germany appears to be a middle-of-the-pack power (No. 4 among major countries today) on a flat trajectory. As shown in the table, the key strengths of Germany are its strong economic and financial position and its high internal order.** The eight major measures of power are somewhat strong today but are, in aggregate, moving sideways.

The table shows our aggregate country power gauge and the major drivers, as well as the rank of each measure of power across 11 major countries today and the trajectory over the past 20 years.

To understand a country, we start by looking at **the big cycles**, as well as **measures of power** that both reflect and drive the rise and fall of a country. While we refer to these factors individually, they are not separate; they interact with and reinforce one another to move a country along its cycle.

For Germany, **the big cycles look mostly favorable**.

Germany is in a somewhat favorable position in its economic and financial cycles, with a low debt burden but very low expected real growth over the next 10 years (0.3 percent per year). Germany has significantly more foreign assets than foreign debts (net IIP is 71 percent of GDP). Non-financial debt levels are typical for major countries today (183 percent of GDP), as are government debt levels for major countries today (69 percent of GDP). Germany's debts are largely in euros, which increases Germany's debt risks, since this is not a currency that Germany directly controls. The ability to use interest rate cuts to stimulate

GERMANY—KEY DRIVERS OF OUR COUNTRY POWER SCORE

Overall Empire Score (0–1)	Level: 0.37		Rank: 4	→
The Big Cycles	**Level**	**Z-Score**	**Rank**	**Trajectory**
Economic/Financial Position	Somewhat Favorable	0.4	4	↗
Debt Burden	Low Debt	1.6	1	↗
Expected Growth	0.3%	-1.0	9	→
Internal Order	Low Risk	0.7	3	↗
Wealth/Opportunity/Values Gap	Narrow	0.7	3	→
Internal Conflict	Low	0.7	3	↗
External Order				
Eight Key Measures of Power				
Trade	Strong	0.6	4	→
Economic Output	Average	-0.1	4	↘
Innovation & Technology	Average	-0.1	5	↘
Education	Average	-0.2	5	→
Markets & Financial Center	Average	-0.2	6	↘
Military Strength	Weak	-0.6	9	→
Cost Competitiveness	Weak	-0.6	10	→
Reserve Currency Status				
Additional Measures of Power				
Resource-Allocation Efficiency	Strong	0.6	3	↗
Governance/Rule of Law	Strong	0.7	4	→
Infrastructure & Investment	Average	-0.3	7	→
Character/Determination/Civility	Average	-0.5	8	→
Geology	Weak	-0.7	9	→
Acts of Nature	Strong	1.1	2	

↗ **Getting better** ↘ **Getting worse** → **Flat**

the economy is low for the Eurozone (short rates are at -0.5 percent), and Europe is already printing money to monetize debt.

Internal disorder is a low risk. Wealth, income, and values gaps are narrow. Regarding inequality, the top 1 percent and top 10 percent in Germany capture 13 percent and 38 percent of income (respectively the fourth and fifth highest shares across major countries). Our internal conflict gauge is low. This gauge measures actual conflict events (e.g., protests), political conflict (e.g., partisanship), and general discontent (based on surveys).

On the eight key measures of power, Germany looks somewhat strong in aggregate. It has no particularly prominent strengths or weaknesses that I will call out.

THE POWERS AND PROSPECTS OF JAPAN

This is our computer-generated reading for Japan as of August 2021.

Based on the latest readings of key indicators, **Japan appears to be a modest power (No. 5 among major countries today) in gradual decline. As shown in the table, the key strength of Japan is its high internal order. Its weaknesses are its unfavorable economic/financial position and its relative lack of natural resources.** The eight major measures of power are somewhat strong today but are, in aggregate, trending downward. In particular, Japan's share of global output, its importance to global trade, and its innovation and technology are declining.

The table shows our aggregate country power gauge and the major drivers, as well as the rank of each measure of power across 11 major countries today and the trajectory over the past 20 years.

To understand a country, we start by looking at **the big cycles**, as well as **measures of power** that both reflect and drive the rise and fall of a country. While we refer to these factors individually, they are not separate; they interact with and reinforce one another to move a country along its cycle.

For Japan, **the big cycles look mixed**.

Japan is in an unfavorable position in its economic and financial cycles, with a moderately high debt burden and very low expected real growth over the next 10 years (0 percent per year). Japan has significantly more foreign assets than foreign debts (net IIP is 68 percent of GDP). Non-financial debt levels are very high (400 percent of GDP), as are government debt levels (241 percent of GDP). The bulk of these debts (99 percent) are in its own currency, which mitigates its debt risks. The ability to use interest rate cuts to stimulate the economy is

JAPAN—KEY DRIVERS OF OUR COUNTRY POWER SCORE

Overall Empire Score (0–1) **Level: 0.30** **Rank: 5** ↘

The Big Cycles	Level	Z-Score	Rank	Trajectory
Economic/Financial Position	Unfavorable	-1.1	7	→
Debt Burden	Moderately High Debt	-0.4	7	→
Expected Growth	0.0%	-1.1	11	→
Internal Order	Low Risk	1.0	1	↗
Wealth/Opportunity/Values Gap	Narrow	0.9	2	↗
Internal Conflict	Low	1.1	2	↗
External Order				
Eight Key Measures of Power				
Reserve Currency Status	Weak	-0.5	3	↘
Education	Average	0.2	4	→
Innovation & Technology	Average	0.2	4	↘
Markets & Financial Center	Average	0.1	4	↘
Cost Competitiveness	Average	-0.3	4	→
Trade	Average	-0.5	5	↘
Military Strength	Average	-0.1	6	→
Economic Output	Average	-0.3	7	↘
Additional Measures of Power				
Governance/Rule of Law	Strong	0.8	3	→
Character/Determination/Civility	Average	0.5	4	↘
Infrastructure & Investment	Average	-0.2	4	↘
Resource-Allocation Efficiency	Average	0.1	6	↘
Geology	Weak	-1.1	11	→
Acts of Nature	Strong	1.5	1	

↗ **Getting better** ↘ **Getting worse** → **Flat**

very low (short rates at -0.1 percent), and the country is already printing money to monetize debt.

Internal disorder is a low risk. Wealth, income, and values gaps are narrow. Regarding inequality, the top 1 percent and top 10 percent in Japan capture 12 percent and 43 percent of income (respectively the sixth and third highest shares across major countries). Our internal conflict gauge is low. This gauge measures actual conflict events (e.g., protests), political conflict (e.g., partisanship), and general discontent (based on surveys).

On the eight key measures of power, Japan looks somewhat strong in aggregate. It has no particularly prominent strengths or weaknesses that I will call out.

THE POWERS AND PROSPECTS OF INDIA

This is our computer-generated reading for India as of August 2021.

Based on the latest readings of key indicators, **India appears to be a modest power (No. 6 among major countries today) in gradual ascent. As shown in the table, the key strengths of India are its strong economic and financial position and its cost-competitive labor (on a quality-adjusted basis). Its weaknesses are its large domestic conflicts, its weak relative position in education, its bad reading on innovation and technology, its corruption and inconsistent rule of law, and its lack of reserve currency status.** The eight major measures of power are somewhat strong today and are, in aggregate, trending upward. In particular, India's relative military strength, its innovation and technology, and its importance to global trade are increasing.

The table shows our aggregate country power gauge and the major drivers, as well as the rank of each measure of power across 11 major countries today and the trajectory over the past 20 years.

To understand a country, we start by looking at **the big cycles**, as well as **measures of power** that both reflect and drive the rise and fall of a country. While we refer to these factors individually, they are not separate; they interact with and reinforce one another to move a country along its cycle.

For India, **the big cycles look mixed**.

India is in a highly favorable position in its economic and financial cycles, with a moderately low debt burden and high expected real growth over the next 10 years (6.3 percent per year). India has slightly more foreign debts than foreign assets (net IIP is -12 percent of GDP). Non-financial debt levels are low (125 percent of GDP), though government debt levels are typical for major countries today (75 percent

INDIA—KEY DRIVERS OF OUR COUNTRY POWER SCORE

Overall Empire Score (0–1)	**Level: 0.27**		**Rank:** 6	↗
The Big Cycles	**Level**	**Z-Score**	**Rank**	**Trajectory**
Economic/Financial Position	Highly Favorable	0.8	1	↘
Debt Burden	Moderately Low Debt	0.1	5	↗
Expected Growth	6.3%	1.1	1	↘
Internal Order	High Risk	-1.8	10	→
Wealth/Opportunity/Values Gap	Large	-1.8	10	→
Internal Conflict	Very Low			
External Order				
Eight Key Measures of Power				
Cost Competitiveness	Very Strong	2.4	1	↗
Military Strength	Average	0.2	5	↗
Economic Output	Average	-0.2	5	→
Reserve Currency Status	Weak	-0.8	6	
Trade	Weak	-0.8	9	↗
Markets & Financial Center	Weak	-0.8	10	→
Innovation & Technology	Weak	-1.2	11	↗
Education	Weak	-1.2	11	→
Additional Measures of Power				
Character/Determination/Civility	Strong	1.3	2	→
Geology	Average	0.3	4	→
Resource-Allocation Efficiency	Average	0.2	5	
Infrastructure & Investment	Average	-0.3	6	↗
Governance/Rule of Law	Weak	-1.1	10	↗
Acts of Nature	Very Weak	-2.4	11	

↗ **Getting better** ↘ **Getting worse** → **Flat**

of GDP). The bulk of these debts (91 percent) are in its own currency, which mitigates its debt risks. The ability to use interest rate cuts to stimulate the economy is modest (short rates at 3.4 percent).

Internal disorder is a high risk. Wealth, income, and values gaps are large. Regarding inequality, the top 1 percent and top 10 percent in India capture 21 percent and 56 percent of income (both the highest shares across major countries). However, a wide wealth gap is less concerning in a fast growing country like India because the fast growth can create rising prosperity for all.

Looking in more detail at the eight key measures of power, India has the cheapest labor among major countries. Adjusted for worker quality, labor is significantly cheaper than the global average.

We net this against its weak relative position in education, its bad reading on innovation and technology, and its lack of reserve currency status. On years of education, India is bad—students have on average 5.8 years of education versus 11.5 in the average major country. PISA scores, which measure the proficiency of 15-year-old students across countries, are bad—336 versus 483 in the average major country. With innovation and technology, a small share (less than 1 percent) of global patent applications, a small share (3 percent) of global R&D spending, and a moderate share (3 percent) of global researchers are in India.

THE POWERS AND PROSPECTS OF THE UNITED KINGDOM

This is our computer-generated reading for the United Kingdom as of August 2021.

Based on the latest readings of key indicators, **the United Kingdom appears to be a modest power (in the bottom half of major countries today) on a flat trajectory. As shown in the table, the key strength of the United Kingdom is its strong rule of law/low corruption. Its weaknesses are its unfavorable economic/financial position and its relative lack of natural resources.** The eight major measures of power are somewhat weak today and are, in aggregate, moving sideways.

The table shows our aggregate country power gauge and the major drivers, as well as the rank of each measure of power across 11 major countries today and the trajectory over the past 20 years.

To understand a country, we start by looking at **the big cycles**, as well as **measures of power** that both reflect and drive the rise and fall of a country. While we refer to these factors individually, they are not separate; they interact with and reinforce one another to move a country along its cycle.

For the United Kingdom, **the big cycles look mostly unfavorable**.

The UK is in an unfavorable position in its economic and financial cycles, with a high debt burden and relatively low expected real growth over the next 10 years (0.9 percent per year). The UK has modestly more foreign debts than foreign assets (net IIP is -28 percent of GDP). Non-financial debt levels are high (260 percent of GDP), though government debt levels are typical for major countries today (106 percent of GDP). The bulk of these debts (90 percent) are in its own currency, which mitigates its debt risks. The ability to use interest

UNITED KINGDOM—KEY DRIVERS OF OUR COUNTRY POWER SCORE

Overall Empire Score (0–1)	Level: 0.27		Rank: 7	→
The Big Cycles	**Level**	**Z-Score**	**Rank**	**Trajectory**
Economic/Financial Position	Unfavorable	-1.7	9	↘
Debt Burden	High Debt	-1.6	9	↘
Expected Growth	0.9%	-0.8	6	↘
Internal Order	Moderate Risk	-0.2	8	↘
Wealth/Opportunity/Values Gap	Relatively Large	-0.2	7	↘
Internal Conflict	Average	-0.3	7	↘
External Order				
Eight Key Measures of Power				
Reserve Currency Status	Weak	-0.6	4	→
Markets & Financial Center	Average	0.0	5	↘
Cost Competitiveness	Average	-0.3	5	→
Education	Average	-0.2	6	↘
Economic Output	Average	-0.3	6	→
Innovation & Technology	Average	-0.3	7	→
Trade	Weak	-0.6	7	→
Military Strength	Average	-0.3	8	→
Additional Measures of Power				
Governance/Rule of Law	Strong	1.2	1	→
Resource-Allocation Efficiency	Average	0.3	4	→
Character/Determination/Civility	Average	-0.4	7	↘
Infrastructure & Investment	Weak	-0.6	10	↘
Geology	Weak	-0.9	10	→
Acts of Nature	Average	0.4	4	

↗ **Getting better** ↘ **Getting worse** → **Flat**

rate cuts to stimulate the economy is low (short rates at 0.1 percent), and the country is already printing money to monetize debt.

Internal disorder is a moderate risk. Wealth, income, and values gaps are relatively large. Regarding inequality, the top 1 percent and top 10 percent in the United Kingdom capture 13 percent and 36 percent of income (respectively the fifth and sixth highest shares across major countries). Our internal conflict gauge is average. This gauge measures actual conflict events (e.g., protests), political conflict (e.g., partisanship), and general discontent (based on surveys).

On the eight key measures of power, the United Kingdom looks somewhat weak in aggregate. It has no particularly prominent strengths or weaknesses that I will call out.

THE POWERS AND PROSPECTS OF FRANCE

This is our computer-generated reading for France as of August 2021.

Based on the latest readings of key indicators, **France appears to be a modest power (in the bottom half of major countries today) on a flat trajectory. As shown in the table, the key weaknesses of France that put it in this position are its unfavorable economic/financial position, its people's lower-than-average work ethic and low self-sufficiency, and its relatively poor allocation of labor and capital.** The eight major measures of power are somewhat weak today and are, in aggregate, moving sideways.

The table shows our aggregate country power gauge and the major drivers, as well as the rank of each measure of power across 11 major countries today and the trajectory over the past 20 years.

To understand a country, we start by looking at **the big cycles**, as well as **measures of power** that both reflect and drive the rise and fall of a country. While we refer to these factors individually, they are not separate; they interact with and reinforce one another to move a country along its cycle.

For France, **the big cycles look mostly unfavorable**.

France is in an unfavorable position in its economic and financial cycles, with a moderately high debt burden and relatively low expected real growth over the next 10 years (0.4 percent per year). France has slightly more foreign debts than foreign assets (net IIP is -25 percent of GDP). Non-financial debt levels are high (268 percent of GDP), though government debt levels are typical for major countries today (105 percent of GDP). France's debts are largely in euros, which increases France's debt risks, since this is not a currency that France directly controls. The ability to use interest rate cuts to stimulate the

FRANCE—KEY DRIVERS OF OUR COUNTRY POWER SCORE

Overall Empire Score (0–1) **Level: 0.25** **Rank:** 8 →

The Big Cycles	**Level**	**Z-Score**	**Rank**	**Trajectory**
Economic/Financial Position	Unfavorable	-1.2	8	↘
Debt Burden	Moderately High Debt	-0.8	8	↘
Expected Growth	0.4%	-0.9	7	→
Internal Order	Low Risk	**0.5**	**4**	→
Wealth/Opportunity/Values Gap	Narrow	1.1	1	↗
Internal Conflict	Average	**-0.1**	6	→
External Order				
Eight Key Measures of Power				
Trade	Average	**-0.5**	6	→
Military Strength	Average	**-0.3**	7	→
Markets & Financial Center	Average	**-0.3**	7	→
Education	Average	**-0.5**	7	→
Innovation & Technology	Average	**-0.5**	8	↘
Economic Output	Weak	**-0.5**	9	↘
Cost Competitiveness	Weak	-0.6	9	→
Reserve Currency Status				
Additional Measures of Power				
Infrastructure & Investment	Average	**-0.2**	**5**	↗
Governance/Rule of Law	Average	**0.3**	6	→
Geology	Average	**-0.5**	7	→
Resource-Allocation Efficiency	Weak	-1.3	10	↘
Character/Determination/Civility	Weak	-1.5	11	→
Acts of Nature	Average	**0.0**	6	

↗ **Getting better** ↘ **Getting worse** → **Flat**

economy is low for the Eurozone (short rates are at -0.5 percent), and Europe is already printing money to monetize debt.

Internal disorder is a low risk. Wealth, income, and values gaps are narrow. Regarding inequality, the top 1 percent and top 10 percent in France capture 10 percent and 32 percent of income (both the ninth highest shares across major countries). Our internal conflict gauge is average. This gauge measures actual conflict events (e.g., protests), political conflict (e.g., partisanship), and general discontent (based on surveys).

On the eight key measures of power, France looks somewhat weak in aggregate. It has no particularly prominent strengths or weaknesses that I will call out.

THE POWERS AND PROSPECTS OF THE NETHERLANDS

This is our computer-generated reading for the Netherlands as of August 2021.

Based on the latest readings of key indicators, **the Netherlands appears to be a modest power (in the bottom half of major countries today) on a flat trajectory. As shown in the table, the key strengths of the Netherlands are its high internal order and its strong rule of law/low corruption. Its weaknesses are its relatively weak military and its relatively expensive labor (on a quality-adjusted basis).** The eight major measures of power are somewhat weak today and are, in aggregate, moving sideways.

The table shows our aggregate country power gauge and the major drivers, as well as the rank of each measure of power across 11 major countries today and the trajectory over the past 20 years.

To understand a country, we start by looking at **the big cycles**, as well as **measures of power** that both reflect and drive the rise and fall of a country. While we refer to these factors individually, they are not separate; they interact with and reinforce one another to move a country along its cycle.

For the Netherlands, **the big cycles look somewhat favorable.**

The Netherlands is in a somewhat favorable position in its economic and financial cycles, with a low debt burden but relatively low expected real growth over the next 10 years (1 percent per year). The Netherlands has significantly more foreign assets than foreign debts (net IIP is 90 percent of GDP). Non-financial debt levels are high (286 percent of GDP), though government debt levels are low (53 percent of GDP). The Netherlands' debts are largely in euros, which increases the Netherlands' debt risks, since this is not a currency that

NETHERLANDS—KEY DRIVERS OF OUR COUNTRY POWER SCORE

Overall Empire Score (0–1) **Level: 0.25** **Rank:** 9 →

The Big Cycles	Level	Z-Score	Rank	Trajectory
Economic/Financial Position	Somewhat Favorable	0.0	5	
Debt Burden	Low Debt	0.8	3	↗
Expected Growth	1.0%	-0.8	5	
Internal Order	Low Risk	0.9	2	→
Wealth/Opportunity/Values Gap	Narrow	0.6	4	↘
Internal Conflict	Low	1.2	1	↗
External Order				
Eight Key Measures of Power				
Innovation & Technology	Average	-0.3	6	→
Economic Output	Average	-0.3	8	→
Markets & Financial Center	Weak	-0.5	8	→
Trade	Weak	-0.6	8	→
Education	Weak	-0.7	9	→
Cost Competitiveness	Weak	-0.8	11	→
Military Strength	Very Weak	-1.9	11	↘
Reserve Currency Status				
Additional Measures of Power				
Governance/Rule of Law	Strong	1.0	2	→
Character/Determination/Civility	Average	-0.3	6	↗
Geology	Average	-0.5	6	→
Resource-Allocation Efficiency	Average	-0.1	8	↗
Infrastructure & Investment	Average	-0.4	8	→
Acts of Nature	Average	0.5	3	

↗ **Getting better** ↘ **Getting worse** → **Flat**

the Netherlands directly controls. The ability to use interest rate cuts to stimulate the economy is low for the Eurozone (short rates are at -0.5 percent), and Europe is already printing money to monetize debt.

Internal disorder is a low risk. Wealth, income, and values gaps are narrow. Regarding inequality, the top 1 percent and top 10 percent in the Netherlands capture 7 percent and 29 percent of income (both the 10th highest shares across major countries). Our internal conflict gauge is low. This gauge measures actual conflict events (e.g., protests), political conflict (e.g., partisanship), and general discontent (based on surveys).

Looking in more detail at the eight key measures of power, we would call out its relatively weak military and its relatively expensive labor (on a quality-adjusted basis). A small share of global military spending (less than 1 percent) is by the Netherlands, and it has a small share of the world's military personnel (less than 1 percent). With labor cost, once we adjust for worker quality, labor is somewhat more expensive than the global average.

THE POWERS AND PROSPECTS OF RUSSIA

This is our computer-generated reading for Russia as of August 2021.

Based on the latest readings of key indicators, **Russia appears to be a modest power (in the bottom half of major countries today) on a flat trajectory. As shown in the table, the key strengths of Russia are its strong economic and financial position, its wealth of natural resources, and its relatively strong military. Its weaknesses are its relatively small economy, its corruption and inconsistent rule of law, and its relative unimportance as a global financial center.** The eight major measures of power are somewhat weak today and are, in aggregate, moving sideways.

The table shows our aggregate country power gauge and the major drivers, as well as the rank of each measure of power across 11 major countries today and the trajectory over the past 20 years.

To understand a country, we start by looking at **the big cycles**, as well as **measures of power** that both reflect and drive the rise and fall of a country. While we refer to these factors individually, they are not separate; they interact with and reinforce one another to move a country along its cycle.

For Russia, **the big cycles look somewhat favorable.**

Russia is in a somewhat favorable position in its economic and financial cycles, with a low debt burden and modest expected real growth over the next 10 years (2.5 percent per year). Russia has modestly more foreign assets than foreign debts (net IIP is 33 percent of GDP). Non-financial debt levels are low (99 percent of GDP), as are government debt levels (14 percent of GDP). A significant share of Russia's debt (25 percent) is denominated in foreign currencies, which

RUSSIA—KEY DRIVERS OF OUR COUNTRY POWER SCORE

Overall Empire Score (0–1) **Level: 0.23** **Rank:** 10 →

The Big Cycles	**Level**	**Z-Score**	**Rank**	**Trajectory**
Economic/Financial Position	Somewhat Favorable	**0.5**	2	
Debt Burden	Low Debt	1.0	2	↗
Expected Growth	2.5%	**-0.2**	3	
Internal Order	Moderate Risk	**-0.5**	9	↗
Wealth/Opportunity/Values Gap				
Internal Conflict	Average	**-0.5**	9	↗
External Order				
Eight Key Measures of Power				
Cost Competitiveness	Strong	0.7	**3**	
Military Strength	Average	**0.4**	**3**	→
Reserve Currency Status	Weak	-0.8	6	
Education	Weak	**-0.5**	8	→
Innovation & Technology	Weak	-0.7	9	→
Trade	Weak	-0.9	10	→
Markets & Financial Center	Weak	-1.1	11	→
Economic Output	Weak	-1.4	11	→
Additional Measures of Power				
Geology	Very Strong	1.9	1	→
Resource-Allocation Efficiency	Strong	1.3	1	
Character/Determination/Civility	Average	**0.1**	**5**	
Infrastructure & Investment	Weak	-1.0	11	↘
Governance/Rule of Law	Very Weak	-1.9	11	→
Acts of Nature	Average	**-0.1**	7	

↗ **Getting better** ↘ **Getting worse** → **Flat**

increases its debt risks. The ability to use interest rate cuts to stimulate the economy is high (short rates at 6.6 percent).

Internal disorder is a moderate risk. Our internal conflict gauge is average. This gauge measures actual conflict events (e.g., protests), political conflict (e.g., partisanship), and general discontent (based on surveys).

Looking in more detail at the eight key measures of power, Russia has a relatively strong military. A moderate share of global military spending (7 percent) is by Russia, and it has a moderately large share of the world's military personnel (13 percent).

We net this against its relatively small economy and its relative unimportance as a global financial center. Russia's equity markets are a small share of the world total (less than 1 percent of total market cap and less than 1 percent of volume).

THE POWERS AND PROSPECTS OF SPAIN

This is our computer-generated reading for Spain as of August 2021.

Based on the latest readings of key indicators, **Spain appears to be a modest power (in the bottom half of major countries today) on a flat trajectory. As shown in the table, the key weaknesses of Spain that put it in this position are its unfavorable economic/financial position, its relatively poor allocation of labor and capital, its relative unimportance to global trade, and its bad reading on innovation and technology.** The eight major measures of power are somewhat weak today and are, in aggregate, moving sideways.

The table shows our aggregate country power gauge and the major drivers, as well as the rank of each measure of power across 11 major countries today and the trajectory over the past 20 years.

To understand a country, we start by looking at **the big cycles**, as well as **measures of power** that both reflect and drive the rise and fall of a country. While we refer to these factors individually, they are not separate; they interact with and reinforce one another to move a country along its cycle.

For Spain, **the big cycles look mostly unfavorable**.

Spain is in an unfavorable position in its economic and financial cycles, with a high debt burden and very low expected real growth over the next 10 years (0 percent per year). Spain has significantly more foreign debts than foreign assets (net IIP is -73 percent of GDP). Non-financial debt levels are high (249 percent of GDP), as are government debt levels (114 percent of GDP). Spain's debts are largely in euros, which increases Spain's debt risks, since this is not a currency that Spain directly controls. The ability to use interest rate cuts to

SPAIN—KEY DRIVERS OF OUR COUNTRY POWER SCORE

Overall Empire Score (0–1) **Level: 0.20** **Rank:** 11 →

The Big Cycles	Level	Z-Score	Rank	Trajectory
Economic/Financial Position	Unfavorable	-1.9	11	↘
Debt Burden	High Debt	-1.7	10	↘
Expected Growth	0.0%	-1.1	10	↘
Internal Order	Moderate Risk	**0.0**	6	→
Wealth/Opportunity/Values Gap	Typical	**0.4**	**5**	↗
Internal Conflict	Average	**-0.4**	8	↘
External Order				
Eight Key Measures of Power				
Cost Competitiveness	Weak	-0.6	7	→
Markets & Financial Center	Weak	-0.6	9	→
Military Strength	Weak	-0.8	10	→
Economic Output	Weak	-0.9	10	↘
Education	Weak	-0.9	10	→
Innovation & Technology	Weak	-1.0	10	↘
Trade	Weak	-0.9	11	→
Reserve Currency Status				
Additional Measures of Power				
Geology	Weak	-0.6	8	→
Infrastructure & Investment	Weak	-0.6	9	↘
Governance/Rule of Law	Weak	-0.7	9	↘
Character/Determination/Civility	Weak	-1.0	9	→
Resource-Allocation Efficiency	Weak	-1.6	11	↘
Acts of Nature	Weak	-0.7	10	

↗ **Getting better** ↘ **Getting worse** → **Flat**

stimulate the economy is low for the Eurozone (short rates are at -0.5 percent), and Europe is already printing money to monetize debt.

Internal disorder is a moderate risk. Wealth, income, and values gaps are typical. Regarding inequality, the top 1 percent and top 10 percent in Spain capture 12 percent and 34 percent of income (respectively the seventh and eighth highest shares across major countries). Our internal conflict gauge is average. This gauge measures actual conflict events (e.g., protests), political conflict (e.g., partisanship), and general discontent (based on surveys).

Looking in more detail at the eight key measures of power, we would call out its relative unimportance to global trade and its bad reading on innovation and technology. Spain accounts for just 2 percent of global exports. With innovation and technology, small shares of global patent applications (less than 1 percent), global R&D spending (1 percent), and global researchers (1 percent) are in Spain.

GLOSSARY OF TERMS

Countries

ARG	Argentina
BEL	Belgium
BRZ	Brazil
CAN	Canada
CHE	Switzerland
CHI	Chile
CHN	China
COL	Colombia
CZK	Czech Republic
DEU	Germany
ESP	Spain
EUR	Euroland
FRA	France
GBR (or UK)	United Kingdom
GRC	Greece
HUN	Hungary
IDR	Indonesia
IND	India
ITA	Italy
JPN	Japan
MEX	Mexico
NLD	Netherlands
NOR	Norway
PLD	Poland
PRT	Portugal
RUS	Russia
SAF	South Africa
SGP	Singapore
SWE	Sweden
TLD	Thailand
TUR	Turkey
USA (or US)	United States
WLD	World

Terms

Adj	Adjusted
Ann	Annualized
Avg	Average
Bln	Billion
CB	Central bank
Chg	Change
Corp	Corporate
CPI	Consumer price index
Dutch EIC	Dutch East India Company
Est	Estimate
FX (or Spot FX)	Currency exchange rate
GDP	Gross domestic product
Govt	Government
Intl	International
Inv	Inverted
Log	Natural log
MA	Moving average
Mln	Million
Oz	Ounces
Pop	Population
PPM	Parts per million
PPP	Purchasing power parity
RGDP	Real (inflation-adjusted) gross domestic product
TWI	Trade-weighted index
Y (or Yr)	Year
Y/Y	Year-over-year change
$	US dollars
£	British pounds
12mma	12-month moving average
60/40	Refers to a portfolio of 60 percent equities and 40 percent bonds
6mma	6-month moving average

Currencies

CNY	Chinese yuan
GBP	British pound sterling
Guilder	Dutch currency
Maravedi Coin	Spanish coin of 12th–19th centuries
USD	US dollar

For definitions of commonly used economic terms, please see economicprinciples.org

ABOUT THE AUTHOR

Ray Dalio has been a global macro investor for nearly 50 years. He is the founder and co-CIO of Bridgewater Associates, an industry-leading institutional investment firm that is the largest hedge fund in the world.

Dalio grew up a very ordinary middle-class kid on Long Island, started investing when he was 12 years old, created Bridgewater out of his two-bedroom apartment when he was 26, and grew it into what *Fortune* assessed to be the fifth most important private company in the US. In the process, he became an advisor to top policy makers, which led *TIME* to name him one of the "100 Most Influential People in the World." *CIO* and *Wired* have called him "the Steve Jobs of investing" for his uniquely inventive and industry-changing way of thinking. He has also been named by *Forbes* as one of the 50 most generous philanthropists in the US.

In 2017, he decided to pass along the principles behind his success in a series of books and animated videos. His book *Principles: Life and Work* was a No. 1 *New York Times* Best Seller and No. 1 Amazon business book of the year, has sold more than 3 million copies worldwide, and has been translated into over 30 languages. His 30-minute animated YouTube videos "How the Economic Machine Works" and "Principles for Success" have together been watched more than 100 million times, and his book *Principles for Navigating Big Debt Crise*s was well-received by economists, policy makers, and investors.

In this new book, *Principles for Dealing with the Changing World Order*, Dalio applies his unique way of seeing the world to studying the rises and falls of great reserve currency empires. His hope is that the model shared in these pages will help readers prepare for the changing times ahead.